RUNNING CRITICAL

RUNNING CRITICAL

The Silent War, Rickover, and General Dynamics

PATRICK TYLER

Harper & Row, Publishers, New York
Cambridge, Philadelphia, San Francisco, Washington
London, Mexico City, São Paulo, Singapore, Sydney

RUNNING CRITICAL. Copyright © 1986 by Patrick Tyler. All rights reserved. Printed in the United States of America. No part of this book may be used or reproduced in any manner whatsoever without written permission except in the case of brief quotations embodied in critical articles and reviews. For information address Harper & Row, Publishers, Inc., 10 East 53rd Street, New York, N.Y. 10022. Published simultaneously in Canada by Fitzhenry & Whiteside Limited, Toronto.

FIRST EDITION

Designer: C. Linda Dingler
Copy editor: Ann Adelman
Index by Auralie Logan
Photo section researched, edited, and designed by Vincent Virga

Library of Congress Cataloging-in-Publication Data

Tyler, Patrick.
  Running critical.

  "Perennial Library."

  Includes index.
    1. War—Economic aspects—United States.   2. Rickover, Hyman George.
3. General Dynamics Corporation.
I. Title.
HC110.D4T95   1987   338.7'6234'0973   86-45365
ISBN 0-06-091441-6

87 88 89 90 91 MPC 10 9 8 7 6 5 4 3 2 1

For Linda, Silas, and Landry
. . . and to the memory of Eddie Paul Summers

CONTENTS

A section of photographs follows page 182

RUNNING CRITICAL

PROLOGUE

America has always depended on its navy to project its power around the globe. In modern times that power has been vested in a steel armada known as the aircraft carrier battle group.

This is the story of how the American armada has become increasingly vulnerable to the submarine forces of the Soviet Union, and how the United States responded to this critical vulnerability by launching a massive construction program to build a fleet of sophisticated—and flawed—nuclear attack submarines to defend it.

The new U.S. submarine fleet will stand until the end of the century as a deep-ocean garrison, a first line of defense against a larger and more threatening Soviet navy. The story of its creation is a story of ambition, commercial greed, and the exercise of unmoderated power in the peacetime system of defense procurement. The impact of these forces collapsed the nation's shipbuilding program into an industrial quagmire. The devastation toppled a corporate dynasty inside the country's largest defense contracting firm and shattered the reputations of men who had stood at the top of the U.S. defense establishment.

I met Admiral Hyman G. Rickover for the first time in January 1984, shortly after I had reported for *The Washington Post* that P. Takis Veliotis, the indicted former executive vice president and board member of General Dynamics Corporation, had surfaced in Athens, Greece, and was negotiating to become a witness for the Justice Department in the largest criminal investigation directed against a major U.S. defense contractor in recent history. Rickover had been in retirement for more than two years, but he still was running his office in the old Washington Navy Yard on the Potomac River waterfront as com-

1

mand central for his crusade against the cost-overrun claim settlements six years earlier. Under those settlements, the U.S. Treasury
had paid more than $1 billion to bail out the three largest private
shipyards in the United States. In those yards, the navy each year had
been spending an enormous chunk of the defense budget to procure
the fleet of aircraft carriers, cruisers, destroyers, and missile and attack submarines to protect American interests around the world.

The austerity of Rickover's surroundings, the cinder-block
walls, the paint-chipped rocker and its frazzled green cushion, the
navy-issue metal desk, was striking, and tended to focus all the attention on Rickover's small frame—and on the Rickover personality,
which was still larger than life in his eighty-fourth year. The visitor's
chair was placed in an unusual position, almost all the way around
behind the desk so he or she sat with a full view of the admiral. The
spatial relationship put the visitor in total engagement with the
schoolteacher, the term that best describes Rickover's relationship
with the world. He had a truly indomitable intellect; he had read and
written about virtually every subject, and his mastery of history and
philosophy seemed beyond reason for a government technocrat
whose specialty in propulsion engineering would have been more than
enough to consume the interest of most men. As I sat in the visitor's
chair that day, however, the legacy that Rickover appeared most concerned about was not the nuclear submarine fleet he had procured for
the United States, but rather the forty or so black notebooks in the
bookcase facing his desk. In them were Rickover's writings on what
he said were the one hundred topics most important to human knowledge. In two hours, he twice stopped the interview and sent me to
those shelves to browse through his wisdom.

I was there because Rickover had summoned me, having seen
my article in *The Washington Post* about the emergence of Veliotis as
a potential witness against his former employer, General Dynamics.
Veliotis had been Rickover's nemesis. They had tried to destroy one
another in the four years that Veliotis had run General Dynamics'
Electric Boat Division, builder of the first Trident ballistic missile submarine and the lion's share of 688-class fast-attack submarines that
serve as the U.S. Navy's vanguard strike force against the larger Soviet
navy.

Some said Veliotis had defeated Rickover; yet the admiral was
more than enthusiastic at the prospect that testimony from his old
enemy might vindicate Rickover's judgment that the cost-overrun
claims filed by General Dynamics during the 1970s had been exagger-
ated and fraudulent. In the privacy of his office, Rickover egged me on
to dig in to the overrun claims. It was the worst raid on the Treasury

he had ever seen, he said. The biggest ripoff in history. And a young man could make a name for himself by exposing it, but it would take some time and a lot of hard work and Rickover said he would help.

I remember my negative reaction to his words, his cynical view that all journalistic motives were selfish, somehow in contrast to Rickover's own motives. I was also skeptical that the story could be found in the massive, stultifying, and turgid record that had been laid down—with Rickover's help—in Congress over the years about all aspects of naval shipbuilding and the cost-overrun claims that were settled during the Carter administration. But Rickover still pushed me to take his advice and to model my efforts on the principles he had established for all of the young men who had followed him over the years—unselfish principles, he said, formulated by a Polish immigrant who had come to this country to work hard and seize opportunity and who had had the good fortune to become the father of the nuclear navy. He was an old man now and all he thought about was repaying this land of the free. I ought to take his advice, he said. "Don't I have a reputation for integrity in this city?" he asked. "Absolutely, Admiral," I replied.

The only pictures on the wall the day of my first visit were two framed photographs of former Navy Secretary Edward Hidalgo and his successor, John F. Lehman, Jr. Their presence seemed strange. It was Hidalgo, after all, who had steamrolled the cost-overrun settlements through the navy bureaucracy. And Lehman had succeeded in retiring Rickover after years of unsuccessful attempts by previous navy secretaries going all the way back to the Johnson administration. The photos were hung behind Rickover, out of his field of vision; without turning, he directed my attention to them over his shoulder.

"You might ask me why they're up there," the schoolteacher prompted.

"Why?" I asked.

"Two biggest goddamned fools who ever ran the navy," Rickover said with sudden gusto. "Now, you can't use that, but now at least you know why they're up there."

I noticed that Rickover had added a portrait of Benedict Arnold above the photos of the two Navy secretaries when I returned to his office later in the year.

That interview was my most difficult encounter with Rickover. I was there to confront him with evidence that he had accepted gifts from shipyard executives for a number of years. After my article about the gifts appeared on the front page of the *Post*, I was not sure whether I had made a mistake. It was Rickover's age, the austerity around him, his Socratic reflection on the large issues affecting the American democracy and its governance that made the reportorial task about the gifts appear, well, unseemly. Three months earlier, Veliotis had given me the thin file he had kept on one of the most blatant gift-giving episodes between a contractor and a U.S. military officer: another General Dynamics executive vice president, Gorden MacDonald, then general manager of Electric Boat, had given Rickover $1,100 worth of diamond and jade jewelry for Mrs. Rickover. The gifts had been disguised on Electric Boat's books as retirement watches and entertainment expenses. It was not clear to me at the time whether Veliotis was trying to settle an old score with Rickover, or whether he was simply trying to demonstrate to me that his former colleagues at General Dynamics were not the men of lofty business principles they claimed to be.

At any rate, I had not wanted to write about the gifts until after I had written about the more substantive allegations involving General Dynamics and about the cost-overrun claims that had sapped the taxpayers for hundreds of millions of dollars. By comparison, the jewelry seemed trivial, and I did not think it was fair to focus the issue on Rickover before focusing the issue on the claims.

My intentions were defeated by competitive realities when a colleague at *The Wall Street Journal*, Ed Pound, got onto the trail of the gifts from other sources. On July 16, 1984, the day before I left for Athens for my third series of interviews with Veliotis, I took a taxi to the Navy Yard in Southeast Washington and showed Rickover what was in the file. I dreaded the encounter. I did not want it on my tombstone that I was the heartless reporter who killed Rickover by exposing the fact that he took some baubles as an old man.

"Admiral, you've got to tell me what this is all about," I said, expecting that he might fall from his rocker, stricken by the shock of prospective disclosure.

I was surprised when Rickover looked me straight in the eye and told me he took gifts from the shipbuilders a number of times over the years. "Trinkets," he called them. He said he didn't remember the ones Veliotis had so carefully documented. Then in his schoolteacher way, he asked: "Did anyone ever suggest that I stopped taking them [the defense contractors] on? Did anyone ever suggest that I did not try to get the best deal I could for the government? What did they hope to gain by giving me the gifts?"

"They thought you could hurt them and maybe they thought you would go easier on them," I said.

"Well, I could hurt them. But did I ever stop taking them on? That's the question you ought to be asking."

"No, Admiral," I replied.

After the fifth or sixth time he had made the point that he had never stopped taking the shipbuilders on for the alleged fraud in their cost-overrun claims, I summoned the courage to say, "With all due respect, Admiral, that isn't the point."

"I know it isn't," he said in an instant, and for a moment I thought he was repentant for the sake of the tens of thousands of young men and women whose minds were shaped and whose commitment to public service and uncompromising integrity sprang from the example and high standards set by Hyman G. Rickover. But the instant passed and he was off again on the shipbuilders.

My worst fear about my disclosure of the gifts was borne out by the vigor with which Navy Secretary Lehman tallied up everything that could arguably have been classified as a gift during Rickover's last two decades in office. In the final detailed inventory that Lehman released to the press with undisguised relish, the secretary included among Rickover's transgressions the fact that he had asked Electric Boat to make up small wooden desk plaques engraved with a quotation that many Americans had come to admire as saying something unique about the American spirit. I remember seeing one of those desktop plaques on television as a boy. It sat on the desk of John F. Kennedy in the Oval Office and reminded everyone who came there that no matter how powerful we become, we are fragile beings whose only hope of survival is perseverance against the obstacles fate throws against us.

The inscription read: "O, God, Thy sea is so great and my Boat is so small."

Rickover had passed along this "gift" from Electric Boat to the young President who accelerated America's first seagoing nuclear deterrent, the Polaris ballistic missile submarine.

Lehman, whose gift to the shipbuilders was the most profitable contracts in navy shipbuilding history during the Reagan administration, and who showed a conspicuous disinterest in new evidence suggesting that the Treasury had been raided in the 1978 claims settlements, should have disqualified himself from sitting in judgment of Rickover.

Despite the impact my disclosure of the gifts had on Rickover's reputation in his last years, Rickover's former deputies were among the most important sources of historical material for this book. Several of them devoted an enormous amount of time helping me to reconstruct the history and engaging all the tough questions about

Rickover's strategies and tactics in the navy bureaucracy and about his personal quirks and failings. They never stopped believing in the visionary to whom they had devoted much of their lives, and I am extremely grateful to them.

I spoke only briefly to Takis Veliotis on January 13, 1984, after dialing Information in Athens, Greece, and leaving a message with his cousin of the same name. He told me through his lawyer in New York, a former federal prosecutor named John H. Gross, that General Dynamics should not have received one penny from the claims settlement, whose total benefits had amounted to roughly $1 billion for the company.

After writing the article about Veliotis's emergence in a new Justice Department investigation, however, I walked away from the story. I didn't think Rickover could really help me get at the core of what had transpired. After all, he had been on the navy's side of the dispute, and what interested me as much were the internal strategies and personalities at General Dynamics. When I telephoned Rickover to let him know that I was not going to pursue the story further, he just scoffed. I was sure that he had put down the phone and announced to whoever was sitting in his office that I was "no good." I made my exit nonetheless.

Then, in mid-March, a congressional investigator I have known for some time telephoned me and asked how he could reach Veliotis in Greece.

"Why don't you try Information, that's how I found him," I replied.

The investigator called back a few days later to tell me he had spoken to Veliotis, who had said that he was going to turn over to the Justice Department tape recordings, documents, and other information to support his allegation that General Dynamics' cost-overrun claims were false.

That piece of intelligence changed everything for me. The prospect that a senior executive of the largest U.S. defense contractor had carried away real documentary evidence and was prepared to break ranks with the closed fraternity at the top of the defense establishment was historically compelling. No modern study of the defense industry had penetrated the corporate veil of a major contractor in a way that gave the public a true insight into the motivations, strategies, and tactics that pervade the relationship between the companies and their most important customer. Here was a man who said he possessed a record of those strategies and—for whatever reasons—appeared to be on the verge of sharing his inside knowledge with the Justice Department, with Congress, and—I hoped—with me. From what I knew at that point, I was convinced that, taking Veliotis's record as a starting point, I could use it as leverage to get my foot in the door with the men who presided over one of the most controversial defense procurements in recent history. Armed with the power of this information, I thought it possible to make sense out of what had gone wrong beginning in the late 1960s, when the United States marshaled its powerful shipbuilding industry to match the immense buildup in submarine forces by the Soviet Union.

My odyssey began the next day when I left for Greece, having asked the *Post*'s executive editor, Benjamin C. Bradlee, to underwrite my trip on faith. From my hotel room at the Grande Bretagne in the center of Athens, I telephoned Veliotis and told him I would like to meet with him. He was apologetic. He said I had traveled a long way for nothing because he could not talk with me due to his pending arrangements with the Justice Department. It took thirty minutes of talking to convince him to meet me for coffee in the lobby of the hotel. I listened to his description of the agreement he was discussing with the Justice Department. He sprinkled this conversation and subsequent ones with vignettes about his inside knowledge of General Dynamics. Those initial discussions spanned three days and resulted in an agreement under which Veliotis said he would devote several weeks of his time to giving me a detailed account of his years at General Dynamics and turning over a copy of all of his tapes and documents for my use in a series of articles or a book-length history. This arrangement was confidential. I agreed to his restriction that I would treat our interviews as off the record until such time as it became clear to him that Justice was not going to pursue the case or, if a new investigation were opened, until publication would not jeopardize the case.

That was our initial agreement. But within a few weeks it was also clear to me that Veliotis had a competing and, at times, more compelling interest in fostering occasional newspaper and magazine stories about his allegations to keep the pressure on the Justice Department to move forward with a new investigation, with him as chief witness. Veliotis never asked me or the *Post* to publish anything about the case, and the only commitment I made to him was the commitment of time to tell the entire story. There was one other commitment, which I will explain momentarily.

At all times, Veliotis encouraged me to seek different perspectives—from David Lewis and others at General Dynamics. From the outset he said, "You will write the story the way you see it, and maybe

I will be disappointed, but I have been disappointed before." That is not to say that he was not a forceful advocate for his own view of the history.

My interviews with Veliotis began in April 1984, but were cut off at the end of May after Veliotis said he had received a telephone call from an unidentified man who threatened to harm Veliotis's college-age children if Veliotis did not shut up. The caller showed he meant business, Veliotis later related, by reciting the private street addresses of Joanna and Ted Veliotis in Florida and Switzerland, where they were attending their respective engineering schools.

The threats sent Veliotis into a month of isolation in which he cut off all contact with the Justice Department and with me. When he surfaced again in mid-July, he told me that he would cooperate with my research with on-the-record and unrestricted interviews, and he would turn over all of his material on one condition: that if any "accident" befell either of his children, *The Washington Post* would investigate to determine whether there had been foul play. I made the pledge. No accidents occurred.

During the last week in July, I went to Athens again, this time carrying sixty pounds of internal General Dynamics and Electric Boat documents that had never been made public. They were among forty boxes of documents that had been subpoenaed by the Securities and Exchange Commission in 1980, but had languished in the files of the agency, and they were made available to me through a confidential channel. As the only journalist with exclusive access to these documents, I was able to reconstruct an internal record of General Dynamics that was crucial to understanding how its managers had prepared for and then lost control of one of the largest submarine construction programs in history: the *SSN 688*-class fast-attack fleet that was designed to match the high-speed submarine fleet already deployed by the Soviet Union.

For seven days, working in a small office near the port of Piraeus adjoining Athens, Veliotis went through this chronological record of the *688* program and explained to me the fundamentals of ship construction, cost estimating, and scheduling. It was an insider's course on General Dynamics' operations that was invaluable to me in pursuing other facets of my research. At the end of the July session, Veliotis gave me four cassette tapes which contained about a dozen telephone conversations he had taped while he was running Electric Boat between 1977 and 1982.

This batch of tapes included a long conversation between Veliotis and Chairman David Lewis in which Lewis was actively urging Veliotis to refrain from firing one of his deputies because it might lead to the exposure of cost overruns on the nuclear submarines and force the company to record another loss on the ships.

When I returned to the United States with the tapes, my friend and colleague at the *Post*, Bob Woodward, took an interest in the story and was instrumental in arranging the initial interviews with David Lewis and former navy secretaries W. Graham Claytor, Jr., and Edward Hidalgo. Without those tapes, I am certain that General Dynamics would never have agreed to devote the time and energy of its officers to attempt to refute the damaging information that Veliotis had carried away with him.

The first interview with David Lewis began at eight in the morning on August 2, 1984, and ended at six o'clock in the evening. Lewis met with me and Bob Woodward in the conference room off his office on the twenty-third floor of Pierre Leclede Center outside St. Louis. He was flanked by his public relations man, Fred J. Bettinger; his general counsel, Robert H. Duesenberg; and an outside lawyer, Thomas G. Edwards, a former prosecutor who handled the company's dealings with the Justice Department and the federal grand jury.

Lewis was extremely warm and gracious, but also wounded, he said, over the circumstances in which a once trusted executive had turned against the company. "I was the supreme sucker," Lewis announced. He had backed Veliotis to the end, he said. The end for Lewis had been the day a federal prosecutor showed company officials the Swiss bank records proving that Veliotis had accepted more than $1 million in kickbacks from a subcontractor on ship construction. Lewis was adamant that the press—myself, Woodward, and anyone who visited Veliotis's doorstep—was being duped by a vindictive man who was trying to extort money from General Dynamics by the threat of embarrassing disclosures.

It was an understandable criticism. It was conceivable that a former executive could contrive evidence and by selective disclosure inflict severe damage on a corporation as part of some extortion scheme. But I told David Lewis that such a scheme would not hold up against a sustained inquiry, and I pledged to him that I would take the time to talk to everyone who was involved and to find out the truth. Lewis agreed that was the only way.

Lewis appeared very anxious to go through the entire history, patiently listening to all of the questions, occasionally cutting off his lawyers who were prone to jump in and recite their intricate legal explanations of why it was impossible to find criminal intent in the process by which defense contractors file cost-overrun claims against the government. Lewis was open, complimentary of Veliotis's capabilities as a shipbuilding engineer and waterfront manager. He conceded that Veliotis was truthful in much of the history he had reconstructed for me during the interviews in Athens. And Lewis was respectful of the Rickover legend, and would say nothing derogatory while we were on the record about the aged admiral who had crusaded so vigorously against the company. The gifts, he said, were a mistake; but Rickover, he asserted, had asked for them. After Lewis had listened to virtually all of Veliotis's allegations about what Veliotis had discovered when he took over Electric Boat in 1977, Lewis conferred this judgment: "His statements are true, but his conclusion—that it was fraud—is false."

To me, the question of whether the cost-overrun claims filed by the company were fraudulent by legal definition was neither as interesting nor as important as the basic attitudes inside General Dynamics, the company that has been the largest single supplier of weapons to the U.S. military in the last decade. What did the directors really talk about in the privacy of their boardroom? Did they talk about their contribution to the nation's defense as diligently as they talked about their contribution to their shareholders? Did they talk about their obligation to give the Pentagon the most efficient weapons systems at the best price? Were they as concerned about keeping pace with Soviet advancements as the military men who placed the orders for billion-dollar weapons systems? I was sure that there were lessons to be learned about the impact of personalities on defense programs and about the financial pressures imposed by Wall Street on those large corporations that build the weapons for our common defense.

After the initial interviews with Rickover, Veliotis, and Lewis, I concluded that it was possible to reconstruct an untold history of Rickover's nuclear navy: its initial struggle within the Defense Department to meet the Soviet submarine threat, and its larger struggle with General Dynamics and the other shipbuilders to build the extraordinary fleet of submersible war machines that each day engages in silent warfare against the Soviet Union. I decided to focus the narrative on the three men who had the greatest impact on this multi-year, multi-billion-dollar procurement: Rickover, Lewis, and Veliotis.

I conducted some two hundred interviews for the book, seeing some of the sources as many as five or six times. Halfway through my research I discovered that, to understand what had gone wrong in the submarine program, I had to go back to the battle that was fought in the late 1960s between Rickover and the Department of Defense over how to respond to the Soviet submarine threat. It was there, in that formative struggle, that I found the most alarming evidence that this vital defense procurement—an entire fleet of fast-attack submarines—had sprung from an ad hoc process among men and institutions whose basic mistrust and enmity for one another compromised what Americans would expect to be a rational scheme for designing and building our most important weapons systems. In peacetime, the consequences of this ad hoc process remain undisciplined and untested by the searing realities of the battlefield. The purpose of this book was to bring this process to life through the eyes of its key participants, who by their own actions and statements call into question the fundamental integrity of the system that provides our national defense.

The interviews were conducted in late 1984 and the first half of 1985. I am very grateful to those who sat for six- and eight-hour sessions, many of them more than once. Nearly all of the interviewing was done on the record except where there was a compelling reason to accept more restrictive ground rules. I have provided some notes in the text where the conflicts of fact are significant enough to warrant the reader's attention.

When I returned to David Lewis in August 1985, after he had announced his retirement, after he had been pummeled in Congress, accused of lying, accused of cheating the government, after triple bypass surgery had sapped his stamina, I found him combative, unrepentant, though he had publicly acknowledged his own miscalculations and had taken responsibility for many questionable billing practices on the defense contracts he had overseen during his fifteen years as the company's chief executive.

He had been at the pinnacle of his corporate career when we first met, the recipient of virtually all the honors that can be bestowed upon a man who rises to the top of the defense establishment. His rise in the aerospace industry had begun at McDonnell Douglas Corporation, where he had been on the team that developed the F-4 Phantom series of attack bombers, the workhorse of the Vietnam War. And at General Dynamics, he had personally directed the development of the F-16 Falcon, which was becoming one of the most successful aircraft procurements in aviation history. His self-image had been that of a benevolent dictator, loved by thousands of General Dynamics engineers and tradesmen who worked at the company's divisions from coast to coast. But in his own mind, all of his achievements were being robbed by the miscalculations he had made on the submarine program at Electric Boat and by the haunting allegations of Rickover and Veliotis.

What hurt him most of all were the charges that struck at his personal integrity, because David Lewis, the Southern-born patriot and businessman, believed he had always adhered to the conventions of a gentleman. The only truth for him was that he was an honorable man who had gotten "all screwed up" by a series of misjudgments: the submarines, Rickover, and most of all, Veliotis.

He told me over the telephone before our last meeting that he did not want to do the interview. He had to consider that he might be indicted, just as former Deputy Defense Secretary Paul Thayer had been for stock trading violations, just as General Electric officials had been for alleged contracting fraud. Something had gone wrong with the relationship between defense contractors and their customer, and David Lewis was feeling very much a victim of the system—the system being the press, congressional investigators, and the atmosphere of innuendo and unproved allegation that can conspire to drive a man from power before he is charged with any crime. He lumped me into that "system," saying I had buried his side of the story in one of the newspaper articles I had written about Veliotis's tapes.

Then he asked me whether there would be a newspaper story based on our final interview. I said I was not planning one; my purpose was to address the questions raised by a year of research.

"Good," he said. "I've had enough."

Lewis did the interview and he was a forceful advocate—just as Veliotis had been, just as Rickover had been—for his version of history. I finished what I considered to be a final draft of the manuscript at the end of 1985, and offered each of the main characters an opportunity to read those portions that dealt with him and his interaction with the other two characters. In the case of Rickover, who was by then recovering from a stroke, the offer was made to one of his close associates. I made these offers for two reasons: first, as a final method of fact checking; but more important, to keep faith with the men who had devoted a great deal of time to confronting the issues raised in the book about their performance in this vital national defense program. These readings did not spring from any prior agreement, but were done as a private courtesy at the end of the project and not as an attempt to elicit a seal of approval. In fact, in some cases the readings produced very negative reactions to portions of the manuscript. I took these reactions and their underlying arguments into consideration in making some final adjustments. In each case, the changes have improved the work, though in some instances they have not satisfied the objections raised by the principals. I am still grateful that they were willing to go through the process.

Now, having sorted through all three versions of the history as told by the main characters, and having cross-checked them with dozens of other important players and sources, including a documentary record of great volume and detail, the following story—much of which has not appeared publicly before—is the most careful reconstruction I believe possible.

—P.T.
Washington, D.C.
March 1986

I

THE
SILENT
WAR

Wednesday, January 3, 1968

The fishing trawler slowed just outside territorial waters off San Francisco. Abovedecks, she was a Medusa's tangle of wire antennae and chrome filaments glinting with flashes of the Pacific sunrise. Her diesel rumbled monotonously below and its hazy exhaust carried a sour whiff of bowel into the chilled salt air. The hungry cloud of gulls swirling above the occasional inbound tuna boat did not linger near her transom, which bore only the faded stencil of the USSR. She offered them no breakfast—her bilge and scuppers were barren—her only interest the electronic harvest for which she had been converted.

Naval intelligence had forewarned the aircraft carrier U.S.S. *Enterprise* of her presence. Throughout the Vietnam War, Soviet spy ships had maintained a constant and silent vigil along the California coastline. The trawler's antennae gave her away. She was packed with radio equipment and Soviet technicians working in shifts to scan frequencies on the high and low ends of the spectrum, searching for U.S. military communications.

From the bridge above the four-acre flight deck of *Enterprise*, Captain Kent Lee could detect the bulky profile of the Russian trawler through the seaward portals. The captain of the Soviet vessel undoubtedly had known *Enterprise* was coming out from her base at the Alameda pier, if for no other reason than the carrier's departure was a news event covered by local radio and television stations in the San Francisco Bay area.

But unknown to the Russian, U.S. intelligence technicians had focused their high-frequency radio antennae on the trawler's encoded transmissions. Navy analysts and signal specialists from the supersecret U.S. National Security Agency (NSA) were conducting an electronic counter-spy operation to penetrate the trawler's mission. As

17

Enterprise approached, the trawler's transmitter sent bursts of coded signals into the atmosphere. At the speed of light, the radio-wave energy arched northward.

Naval intelligence analysts had a good idea where the response to the trawler's signal would come from because they also had been monitoring a Soviet nuclear attack submarine now more than one thousand miles north of *Enterprise*. The Russian attack boat had crossed the Bering Sea the day before, working her way down the Aleutian Islands, which form the Northern Pacific's rocky necklace from Alaska to Kamchatka. Soviet attack subs had been operating in tandem with the trawlers to spy on U.S. military movements in the Eastern Pacific.

The coded Soviet messages were useless by themselves to naval intelligence. It would take weeks of analysis by NSA code breakers and dozens of hours running decryption programs on NSA super computers at Fort Meade, Maryland, to penetrate the Soviet algorithm, the random mathematical splay of numbers and letters used to scramble the message. But where the computer age had wrapped military signals in virtually impenetrable encryption puzzles, U.S. intelligence had shifted the bulk of its tactical energy to "traffic analysis"—the art of studying the pattern of military communications and applying the deductive reasoning of a detective to make educated guesses about what the other side was up to. In this case, the Soviet nuclear submarine had poked her high-frequency antennae above the waves just as the trawler began transmitting. When the trawler's radio went silent, the submarine let out a short burst of her own coded signals. An acknowledgment, the U.S. analysts deduced.

Suddenly, the submarine turned south, toward *Enterprise*. Her twin-reactor propulsion plant surged to higher power and U.S. technicians, listening with the aid of sensitive hydrophones bedded on the ocean floor, heard the submarine's propellers increase in speed. The intelligence analysts quickly reached their conclusion: the trawler had dispatched the Soviet attack submarine to conduct war maneuvers against the aircraft carrier and its battle group. The report was relayed as a top-secret tactical intelligence message to the U.S. Navy operations center at Pearl Harbor, headquarters for the commander-in-chief of the Pacific Fleet, CINCPACFLT. A duplicate message spewed out of the cryptographic equipment in the code room of *Enterprise*.

The Russian skipper had been given the honor of hunting America's most prestigious naval target.

A new day had begun in the silent war between the United States and the Soviet Union. Unlike the Vietnam War, there was no daily carnage, no body bags, nor even any casualties. It was a war not

covered by the news media, blacked out as it was by layers of classification, but it was a war, a secret war, nonetheless. Its consequences
were directly related to superpower strategies in the post–World War
II era where both sides stood ready for any global conflict that might
arise from the unforeseen event, the flashpoint in the Third World or
in Europe that would throw the military might, East and West, into
the vortex. Nowhere in the peacetime world did the armies of the
Soviet Union and the United States actively engage each other's
forces, but it happened every day under the ocean, where nuclear
submarines stalked in each other's wakes and shadowed each other's
surface fleets, feeding sonar data into fire-control computers that
spewed out angles, depths, and running times for imaginary torpedoes. Their commanders did everything but push the button, and they
planned for the day when everything would be real. Military advantage would be measured in seconds, speed, running times. Readiness,
the ability to respond, would be crucial determinants of the outcome.

Nuclear power had been the breakthrough technology that had
given the superpowers penultimate platforms for their weapons: ships
that could travel invisibly and indefinitely below the surface of the
ocean, carrying spy equipment and a lethal arsenal of torpedoes,
depth bombs, mines, and anti-ship missiles, some of them tipped with
nuclear weapons. The officers were sub drivers and theirs was the
silent service in the navy, its operations cloaked in secrecy because
they hunted and "killed" in the last frontier on earth, where the element of surprise worked, where stealth could be achieved, and where
the weapons of mass destruction could be hidden without fear of
detection.

Nuclear-powered attack submarines were the vanguard of
striking power in both the American and Soviet navies. They constituted a full third of the combatant U.S. fleet and their wartime missions included racing into enemy waters to sink, mine, and bottle up
the enemy's fleet, to claim the ocean basins for the carrier groups, to
clear them of warships and, along the way, to sink the opposing submarine forces. For the sub drivers, war was never farther away than
the final command to fire.

U.S. submarines regularly slipped into the Arctic seas off the
Soviet Union's northern coast to penetrate Soviet naval maneuvers, to
practice laying mines off navy bases, to monitor military communications, to gather coded messages on reels of tape, and to scoop up
emissions from air-defense radars so American bomber crews could
study how to jam them if the day ever came when they needed to get
through.

The Soviets had developed their own counterstrategies: one of them was to destroy the American armada of aircraft carriers such as *Enterprise*. The carriers were the biggest naval threat to the Soviets because they projected American power. They could burst into the Mediterranean and establish sea and air control with their squadrons of fighters and bombers. They could put up a bubble of protection over the Middle Eastern oil fields during a crisis, or establish theater control over the North Atlantic to ensure the safe passage of troop and equipment convoys to a European land war. Thus the order to intercept *Enterprise* had been a call to glory for the Russian submarine commander, who had quickly retracted his antenna mast and slipped deeper into the Pacific while his navigator plotted the vector he would take down the latitudes to bring the two ships together. He had reason to believe the element of surprise was in his favor. His combat crew looked forward to plotting torpedo solutions into the honeycombed hull armor of the unsuspecting *Enterprise*, whose escorts would not be looking for a Russian submarine in the friendly stretch of water between California and Hawaii. But they were wrong.

One of the first persons in Washington to hear about the Russian submarine dispatched to intercept *Enterprise* was Vice Admiral Hyman G. Rickover, who at sixty-eight was reaching the zenith of his power over the nuclear navy. It was the navy within the navy that Rickover had nurtured and fought for like no other naval officer in the fifteen years since the first nuclear-powered submarine, U.S.S. *Nautilus*, had gone triumphantly to sea, making steam for her turbines from the heat of neutron collisions in an atomic reactor.

On paper, Rickover's principality was the Naval Reactors Branch in the Naval Ship Systems Command, formerly the Bureau of Ships. Its offices were housed in one of the nondescript wooden annex buildings that had lined Constitution Avenue between the Lincoln Memorial and the Washington Monument since World War II. Nominally, Naval Reactors was outside the circuit of day-to-day fleet supervision, and under any other officer might have been relegated to the obscurity of the navy's propulsion engineering departments. But under Rickover, the influence of the Naval Reactors Branch extended into almost every facet of nuclear ship construction and operation. The reason was the man, the father of the nuclear navy, who had given the United States the revolutionary propulsion technology that transformed the nature of warfare in the ocean. Rickover claimed progenitor rights and at all times exercised them robustly, voraciously, ever expanding his claim, never contracting.

He had seen the potential for nuclear-propelled ships after the

Manhattan Project demonstrated the power of fissioning atoms with the Hiroshima and Nagasaki bombs. Ships were powered by hot water boilers that made steam. In the old days, they heated the water by burning coal, then petroleum. Rickover had asked: Why not by controlled nuclear fission? He had used clear thinking and compelling logic to make the case for nuclear power. He had pushed when the rigid structure of admirals in the Bureau of Ships had wanted to go slow and Rickover had overwhelmed them.

When the navy failed to provide adequate support, Rickover sold nuclear power in the Congress, where he built the strongest personal following of any modern military officer. Congress, not the navy—he liked to remind doubters—funded the first naval nuclear reactors for *Nautilus* and *Seawolf*. Rickover's patrons included the ranking members of the Armed Services committees and the powerful Joint Committee on Atomic Energy, men at the core of the defense establishment in Washington. They controlled the defense budget as much as any President and they believed Rickover was the smartest engineer and the wisest naval strategist of the modern era.

Rickover was as old as the century and he had survived two attempts, by Defense Secretary Robert S. McNamara and his Navy Secretary Paul H. Nitze, to retire him. Any secretary who wanted to fire Rickover found himself—as McNamara and Nitze had—facing monolithic opposition in the key committees that controlled the defense budget. No one could fire Rickover. With bureaucratic shrewdness, he had seized dual roles as the civilian manager for the naval nuclear propulsion division of the Atomic Energy Commission (AEC) and as the navy's manager for applying nuclear propulsion to ships. He had two suits (one civilian and one military), two hats, two budgets, and virtually no accountability to the navy hierarchy. To prod the navy, he wrote letters on the stationery of the AEC. To prod the AEC, he invoked the authority of the navy.

He shamelessly flattered his supporters and cajoled his adversaries. In public, he talked humbly about his achievements, his simple approach to life: hard work, service, and excellence. But there was a dark side to Rickover's personality and those who worked closest to him knew the deep suspicions he harbored about his "enemies," and the scorching mean streak that flared unpredictably. At his worst, he could be as mean as a wasp, petty and vindictive to those who opposed him, but also to those who unwittingly stepped in his path. You were either for Rickover or you were against him, and if you were against him, you were no good. If he could hurt you, he would go out of his way to get the satisfaction.

Rickover did business by yelling at people and when Rickover was yelling, his voice seemed to boom beyond the limit of his elfin frame. He was rarely angry when he yelled, but really, Rickover always was angry. If he thought something was wrong in the navy, Rickover yelled until it was fixed. If it was not fixed to his liking, he had shown the capacity to continue yelling about it for years on end. That was Rickover. He could be in the middle of a perfectly calm conversation and then go off like an air-raid siren, the tone and decibel level rising gradually, as if operated by a hand crank.

"Goddammit, don't give me that crap! Don't you think I know something about nuclear submarines? I AM RESPONSIBLE FOR THIS PROGRAM AND YOU OUGHT TO LISTEN TO WHAT I'M TELLING YOU!" he would say to anyone he thought was opposing him. It didn't matter if the opposition outranked him, or wanted afterwards to fire him. No one could fire Rickover.

Each year, Rickover had found more and more things wrong, not just with the navy, but with the world at large, with the American educational system, with the management of the U.S. industrial base, with the proliferation of lawyers in government contracting, with labor unions, and with television. Rickover believed that he put his judgment, intellect, and integrity on the line every day. So should everyone else. So he made it a habit of holding his fellow man responsible. If he didn't like an article in his morning newspaper, he would call the author and tell him the article was "CRAP!" That was Rickover.

He also understood that to win in the maddeningly large Pentagon bureaucracy, a player needed a variety of tools: stealth, cunning, good intelligence, political muscle and, on some days, just a bully's club to make mush out of the opposition. He had used them all to seize nuclear power for the navy. He had threatened to shut down private laboratories unless their management dedicated them to Rickover's programs, and he had steered a steady stream of business to contractors and shipyards willing to meet the demanding technical requirements for nuclear construction work, always trying to create two suppliers for every component so he could play one off against the other and get the best price.

As he had gotten older, his hair had gone totally gray and he looked physically decrepit, slight at ninety-nine pounds. His shoulders stooped and his skinny neck appeared incapable of holding his head erect. At five foot five, he looked up to most people. His clothes, both his navy uniform and his dark civilian suits, appeared intentionally baggy, oversized. But it was part of the Rickover disguise. The diminutive-looking Polish immigrant, the bookish introvert from the Class of 1922 at the U.S. Naval Academy, was outwardly frail, even feeble. Yet he had strength and self-discipline of truly historic proportions, and he had instilled those attributes into a large and highly motivated staff over the years.

He personally interviewed the thousands of naval officers who sought commands on nuclear-powered submarines and surface ships, and to survive the fiery Rickover indoctrination was a rite of passage that carried with it the responsibility to promote the Rickover cause and to protect the interests of the nuclear navy. Young men were drawn to him because he pulled from them their own capacity for excellence and instilled in them his own standards of logic, hard work, and uncompromising perfection. Rickover gave them power and responsibility and demanded from them total loyalty. These men, some of whom stepped off the navy's career ladder to stay in the Naval Reactors Branch, followed Rickover because they considered him a visionary.

By 1968, Rickover had tapped the navy's and the Central Intelligence Agency's top-secret channels monitoring Soviet submarine activity from underwater sensors and orbiting spy satellites so he could keep abreast of any new development in the silent war that might affect his nuclear submarine program. As *Enterprise* had set sail for Hawaii, one of Rickover's senior deputies received a telephone call from naval intelligence reporting the apparent message traffic between the Soviet trawler and the *November*-class submarine in the Pacific. It looked like some war maneuvers were in the making. The aide brought the news to Rickover, who instantly recognized the potential in the intelligence report and mobilized his staff, yelling instructions from his sparsely furnished office that they should seize the moment created by the Russian's silent gambit.

Since early in the decade, Rickover had begun to fear that the United States would lose its edge in the silent war against the Soviets, who were building nuclear submarines in unprecedented numbers at industrial facilities that dwarfed the U.S. shipbuilding base. The Russians also were innovating, experimenting with new designs; and, more alarmingly, their submarine program had the highest national priority.

From the intelligence, Rickover believed the Soviet submarine navy was going all out for speed to catch the American aircraft carriers, which were built to go fast to make wind across their decks for launching aircraft. The carriers' massive power plants gave them a high-speed advantage on the oceans and, historically, the only hope a submariner had of catching an aircraft carrier was by stealth, laying silent and submerged in the current, hoping one of the flat tops would slide unknowingly into the cross hairs of his periscope.

The submarines of World War II had run mostly on the surface, dipping below the waves on battery power for only short periods of time. Catching an American aircraft carrier meant doubling the eighteen-knot speeds of World War II submarines. The power demands for pushing tons of steel through the dead weight of the ocean at high speed were enormous, but nuclear propulsion made it possible. There were formidable engineering and design problems to solve. High-speed submarines would require the development of compact, high-energy nuclear reactors, and neither the United States nor the Soviet Union, according to all intelligence, had deployed high-speed submarines in the first decade of nuclear power.

But Rickover had seen it coming. He had been trying since 1964 to convince his superiors in the navy that the Soviets would soon develop high-speed submarines and that would change the equation in the next war. If the United States could not protect its carrier-based battle groups, there was no hope of stopping the worldwide Soviet fleet. On his own authority, Rickover had secretly begun work at General Electric's atomic power laboratory in Schenectady, New York, adapting a large surface ship reactor and propulsion plant for submarine use. By 1966, Rickover proposed building a single "fast escort" submarine to demonstrate the performance of his power plant, but Chief of Naval Operations (CNO) David L. McDonald killed the proposal.

Rickover's "fast escort" idea had rankled some of the admirals of the surface fleet, who jealously guarded their own mission of protecting the aircraft carrier task force with cruisers, destroyers, and anti-submarine aircraft. The interest-group politics within the navy had blocked Rickover's progress, but it was only temporary.

With the appointment of Thomas H. Moorer as CNO in the summer of 1967, U.S. intelligence reports increasingly showed that the Soviets had mounted a major industrial effort to build large numbers of sleek, high-speed nuclear submarines. Rickover went to Moorer seeking support to build a single fast-prototype sub. Moorer, who had served as the commander of the Atlantic and the Pacific fleets and who had chased German U-boats during World War II, was inclined to accept Rickover's view of the Soviet threat. Moorer also was a good politician and he wanted to reap the benefits from Rickover's influence in Congress. That was good for the navy. He counseled Rickover to drop the "fast escort" label to make his proposal less threatening to the admirals of the surface navy and, in late 1967, Moorer ordered the navy's senior staff to get behind the "High Speed Nuclear Attack Submarine." The compromise title was classified to keep the Russians from discovering the U.S. Navy's plan to match them in the silent war. Moorer and Rickover had thus begun their drive to sell the proposal in the Defense Department. Their largest remaining obstacle was the Office of the Secretary of Defense.

During his long tenure at the Pentagon, Robert McNamara had delegated great authority over weapons procurement to a group of "systems analysts." In the final months of 1967 they had refused to include funding for the navy's high-speed submarine prototype in the defense budget, arguing that high speed was not important to submarine warfare and that Soviet submarines were no match for the attack boats in the existing U.S. fleet. Rickover's prototype would cost twice as much as the current generation attack sub and McNamara's men had orders to cut defense spending. Soviet submarines were crude, noisy, vulnerable, they argued, and roughly comparable in speed to U.S. submarines.

Rickover knew better. Some conspicuous intelligence reports indicated the Soviets had deployed the first of a new class of high-speed submarines, the *Victor* class, in late 1967. Proof existed in one report from a U.S. carrier task force steaming in the Atlantic, which had been shocked by the sudden appearance of the conning tower of a *Victor*-class submarine. The Russian had popped up to thumb his nose at the Americans and to demonstrate a Soviet capability to penetrate the carrier battle group. It was a secret and unreported victory for the Soviet Union and an embarrassing and ominous moment for the U.S. Navy. Intelligence analysts had concluded that the interloping *Victor* had run at a very high submerged speed to overtake the task force.

Still, the CIA and the Office of Naval Intelligence had not been able to agree on the reliability of the information about Soviet submarine speeds, so they were presented in ranges. The *November* class, the oldest and the slowest boat in the Soviet fleet, had a speed rating of twenty-five to twenty-seven knots. But to Rickover's outrage, McNamara's deputies used the low figure to bolster their claim that there was little or no difference between the top speeds of Soviet and American submarines. Rickover wanted to expose the estimates as too conservative. If even the old Russian submarines were as fast as he suspected, the Defense Department would have to face up to the fact that its carrier forces were at greater risk. It would also have to face up to the fact that the U.S. submarine fleet was at a disadvantage in any hostile engagement, and that if they could not outmaneuver and outrun the weapons fired by Soviet submarines, the carriers would be lost.

By early 1968, Rickover was searching for dramatic evidence to make the case for an American high-speed sub. He found the opportunity in the telephone call from naval intelligence. It came from Captain James F. Bradley, director of undersea warfare in the intelligence directorate, which had been following the propeller noises of the *November*-class submarine since it had crossed the Bering Sea. The sub's location was continuously relayed to the Pacific Fleet Command at Pearl Harbor and to the National Military Command Center—the war room—beneath the Pentagon. Bradley and a staff of analysts worked behind triple-security doors on the fifth deck of the Pentagon in the navy's special operations center for intelligence. For months, they had been working closely with Rickover's staff in an effort to develop better information on the top speeds of Soviet subs. When the *Enterprise* report had come in, Bradley immediately notified Rickover's aides that U.S. sensors could track the *November*-class boat without the Russians knowing.

Rickover was elated. He posed the question to his key aides: The Russians, he said, believed their submarine movements were undetected. They were going to stalk *Enterprise* in a silent hunt-and-kill exercise. What if the U.S. Navy staged a race between *Enterprise* and the unsuspecting captain of the Russian attack sub? It was an opportunity to see exactly how fast Russian nuclear submarines could go. Naval intelligence could use its "ears" in the water to record the event with unquestioned precision. No one would be able to argue with that kind of intelligence.

Rickover believed the navy had to move quickly. There was only one man who could put the operation into motion overnight—the CNO.

The Pacific Fleet was sending Kent Lee regular reports on the progress of the Russian submarine. Three SOSUS stations along the West Coast were triangulating its position.

SOSUS was an acronym for Sound Surveillance System, a highly classified underwater network first installed by cable-laying ships during the 1950s. In the new age of nuclear propulsion, both the United States and the Soviet Union had studded the ocean bottom with networks of sensors and hydrophones in a technological race to render the oceans transparent, to "bug" the seaways and gain advantage in the silent war. Both sides had achieved some success, but the ocean remained a difficult medium to conquer. The race had become all the more urgent because the detection of the first Soviet ballistic missile submarines carrying nuclear warheads off the U.S. coast had become an important intelligence requirement for U.S. war planners.

SOSUS was a key instrument in the navy's anti-submarine detection arsenal, an early warning system against the approach of Soviet propellers. A Russian missile submarine could not leave its base on the Barents Sea or the Sea of Okhotsk to run the narrow straits to deep water without being detected by the SOSUS grid. The first missile subs that ventured to the edge of the North American continental shelf were tracked along every mile of their patrol, their movements fed to the Atlantic Fleet Command in Norfolk, Virginia, and to the war room at the Pentagon, where their locations were displayed electronically on wall-sized maps of the world.

Continuous, or "real time," tracking had become critical because those Russian warheads could reach Boston, New York, or Washington in ten minutes or less. In the first minutes of all-out war, it was crucial to take them out quickly. They would disappear in the blinding vaporization of nuclear depth charges lobbed from over the horizon by U.S. missile boosters.

The ocean-bed hydrophones were placed along the East and West coasts, near the Panama Canal, and along the seaways to and from the Soviet land mass, off the Aleutian Islands in the northwest and off Iceland in the northeast. Thousands of naval personnel manned the SOSUS stations, sitting in concrete block rooms for eight hours a watch listening with sensitive headsets to amplified noises from the seabed. Computers helped to eliminate ambient ocean noise, the din created by the sea itself—by wind across the waves and the cascading sound of a billion whitecaps. It was the noise of a seashell pressed to the ear and with computers, technicians could eliminate it so they could concentrate on the swishes, the whooshes, the whrrrs, the thrrrmmms, and the whine of propellers in the distance. Sounds faded in and out like short-wave radio signals because the ocean was a fluid medium, its temperature layers and columns of salinity deforming the sound waves moving out from their source like ripples on a pond.

Though the existence of SOSUS no longer was secret by 1968, most everything about the underwater network was classified, especially the location, sensitivity, and range of the hydrophones on the ocean floor. The SOSUS control center near San Francisco processed the sounds from thousands of miles of SOSUS tentacles from the Bering Strait to the Baja Peninsula, and the technicians there were intimately familiar with the Soviet *November*-class submarine headed for *Enterprise*. The *November*s* had been coming down from their northern bases for ten years, beginning soon after the first ships were completed at the massive shipyard at Severodvinsk on the White Sea, where tens of thousands of Russian workers manned frozen hulls year round.

For SOSUS operators, the broad distinctions between U.S. and Soviet submarines were easy. The Soviets built twin-reactor, twin-propeller submarines, while the U.S. fleet operated on a single-reactor, single-propeller design. The Soviets had hoped for greater reliability from the twin-reactor design, U.S. intelligence officials believed. If one plant shut down, the ship still had power. The U.S. Navy had built one twin-reactor submarine in the late 1950s, U.S.S. *Triton*, but the designers found that Rickover's reactors were so reliable the submarines could safely run on one.

A single large propeller also gave American submarines a greater advantage in silent running because it created a smooth and relatively undisturbed wake. Twin propellers were smaller and their wakes collided in a maelstrom of noise that could easily be detected. A tiny flaw in one of those propeller blades could result in a "singing" propeller, a high-octave screecher that could be heard on underwater microphones hundreds of miles away. So in their quest for reliability, the Soviets had built an entire fleet of noisy, twin-propeller submarines, giving the United States an early and clear advantage in the silent war. The Soviets also made no attempt to dampen the machinery noise of their nuclear submarines. The steam turbines, pumps, and motors that constituted the power plant were bolted directly to steel foundations and welded to the hull. All of the vibration and noise was transmitted directly to the ocean. Any difference between one *November*-class submarine and the other ships of the same class was catalogued, and this allowed U.S. intelligence to distinguish between them in the future.

Every year, more of the ocean floor was becoming wired for sound, which was fortunate for *Enterprise* because she depended heavily on the navy's anti-submarine warfare systems. *Enterprise* had no anti-submarine capability whatsoever. She had no sub-hunting airplanes or helicopters, no sonar systems to ping the ocean around her,

---

*The *November*-class designation was assigned by U.S. intelligence. It was the "N" class, but in military jargon, "N" was *November* just as "A," "B," and "C" were *Alpha, Bravo,* and *Charlie*. The Russian designation was *Leninsky Komsomol*, the name of the first ship and also the name of the Communist Party youth organization—a kind of Boy Scouts—honoring party founder Vladimir I. Lenin. The *November*s appeared so close in time to the deployment of the *Hotel* and *Echo* classes of Soviet nuclear submarines that U.S. intelligence analysts dubbed the first three classes the HENs.

no depth charges, no torpedoes. She was a vulnerable and high-value target, and she had to depend on other elements in the navy for protection against submarine attack. That mission fell to land-based sub-hunting planes and to *Enterprise*'s escorts, U.S.S. *Truxtun* and U.S.S. *Halsey*, both of which carried large scanning sonar domes in their bows. Their weapons included surface-launched torpedoes and depth charges—those trash cans filled with TNT catapulted off their fantails and left to sink to predetermined depths, where they were detonated in hopes that the stress from the concussion would crush an enemy submarine's hull or force the intruder to the surface. The sub-hunting airplanes were Lockheed Orions, long-range turboprops whose crews covered vast expanses of ocean from land bases. They sniffed out submarines by dropping small and expendable "sonobuoys" into the depths. The high-tech buoys sent back ocean noises to airborne technicians by radio signal. Once the target was located, the Orion crew could drop one or more Mark 46 torpedoes programmed to spiral down for the kill.

Aboard *Enterprise*, Lee spent his time between the bridge and his sea cabin, the little apartment just aft of the bridge that allowed him to live, sleep, and eat close to his work. When the message had come in from Pacific Fleet about the *November*'s mission, Lee calculated that the Russian would probably intercept *Enterprise* about one third of the way between San Francisco and Hawaii. Lee was a little irritated. With a full combat air wing aboard, enough ordnance and fuel to blow up half a continent, he was responsible for getting *Enterprise* to war duty in the Tonkin Gulf. He did not need the aggravation of the silent threat from a Soviet attack submarine.

He took a deep breath. Through the bridge portals, he could see the ocean swells rolling slowly from the north. The Soviet submarine, hundreds of miles away, had turned south on her intercept course. Lee knew that by Thursday he would have a Russian attack-boat skipper to contend with.

Thursday, January 4, 1968

Tom Moorer was in his office on the outer ring of the Pentagon early. Since taking over as Chief of Naval Operations, the moon-faced Alabaman arrived at his desk at seven o'clock every morning seven days a week so he could read the overnight messages from the fleet commanders before his first briefing. The message traffic about U.S.S. *Enterprise* had moved late the previous day because of the time difference, but Moorer had heard plenty about the Soviet submarine before he retired for the night. Naval intelligence had bumped the report up the chain of command, and later, Rickover had telephoned to urge that the navy seize the opportunity presenting itself in the Pacific.

Moorer was among the most shrewd and conservative CNOs of the postwar era, but his conservatism was wrapped in the affability of a drawling raconteur, whose schoolhouse manner was both a source for the iron discipline he imposed and also for the loyalty he built among his commanders.

As CNO, Moorer had given voice to the consensus military view that the rapidly expanding Soviet navy posed a threat to the security of the United States and its allies, and Moorer felt deep frustration over Robert McNamara's policies of restraint. McNamara had cut deeply into the navy's shipbuilding budget to help pay the $80 million-per-day cost of the war, and he had no friends in Moorer's navy. The U.S. fleet was facing "block obsolescence"—nearly half its ships were twenty years old, while the typical Soviet ship of the line was less than five years old. Moorer needed ships because the Soviet navy was deploying modern naval forces in every ocean. But McNamara was trying to keep big-ticket capital items out of the defense budget, and ships represented the biggest single chunk of defense procurement spending.

Moorer understood the glacial time frames of fleet construction, which was why he had been incensed when McNamara's Assistant Secretary of Defense for Systems Analysis, Dr. Alain Enthoven, decreed that the navy could only replace ships lost in battle in Vietnam. We weren't losing ships in Vietnam. That was not the problem, and McNamara knew it. The fleet—and the defense budget—was going to have to expand if the United States was to meet the threat of a large and modern Soviet navy in the 1970s.

When McNamara introduced systems analysis to the Pentagon, his goal had been to transplant the corporate planning regimen he had learned at the Ford Motor Company to weapons procurement. He had set out to bring more order to war planning, to defining the threat, to purchasing cost-effective weapons to meet the threat. But Moorer believed McNamara's system had degenerated into disingenuous, bureaucratic trickery to keep the pressure off the defense budget, whose resources were being mercilessly siphoned into Vietnam.

The systems analysts could defeat the need for any weapon by changing the war scenarios. The ninety-day war could be shrunk to the sixty-day war. The "kill ratios"—how many of their ships are sunk before we lose one of ours—could be enhanced through high-level numbers crunching. In late 1967, McNamara had submitted to President Johnson classified defense budget summaries recommending that nuclear submarine construction cease after the final two ships of the current *Sturgeon* class were built, thus leaving the navy a nuclear submarine fleet of sixty-eight ships. The number, lower than any fleet projection the navy deemed prudent, was justified by the assertion that the U.S. submarine fleet and its back-up forces could sink twenty-five Russian submarines for every American submarine lost during a war—a kill ratio of twenty-five to one. Never had the Pentagon been so wildly optimistic and without justification, in Moorer's view. The numbers were just crazy, and the arrogance of the underlying assumptions had dumbfounded senior navy officials.

U.S. war-fighting strategy since World War II was based in part on setting up "barriers" at chokepoints in the oceans through which the Russian navy had to pass to get to the deep-water basins of the Atlantic and Pacific. The most important of these chokepoints was in the North Atlantic between Greenland, Iceland, and the United Kingdom, the GIUK gap. Still, it was more than one thousand miles across, and would require a large number of submarines and anti-submarine surface ships and planes to stop the onrushing Soviet fleet.

It had long been apparent to Moorer that the Soviets were keenly aware of the bottlenecks through which their ships had to pass, and he had put the question to the war planners: What if the Soviet navy deployed early, before the outbreak of war? Would the systems analysts propose that the U.S. Navy attack Soviets ships running for deep water during a period of tension? Would we start the war ourselves at the first sign of Soviet naval deployments? Moorer had argued that there were too many surprises in the heat and confusion of war to base American strategy on the wild optimism of force superiority represented by a kill ratio of twenty-five to one.

Twice during this century the Russians had witnessed the United States projecting its power and supply lines across the Atlantic Ocean to win a major land war in Europe. The Soviets were good students of military history and their war planners understood this vital link.

In an age of nuclear submarines, defending those ocean supply lines was going to be much more difficult in the next war. Moorer was one of a relatively small group of military men who knew how close Hitler's U-boats had come to stopping the American resupply of Great Britain. For the first two years of the war, the Germans sunk American ships faster than the U.S. industrial base could replace them. It had taken until April 1943 for the lines to cross: the U.S. began building ships faster than the U-boats could sink them and Allied anti-submarine forces began sinking U-boats faster than the German industrial base could replace them. Without that change in statistics, the United States would not have been able to position the armies and supplies for the D-Day invasion a little more than a year later, in June 1944.

At the outset of any modern war, one sixth of the U.S. submarine fleet would be tied up in shipyards, out of service for overhaul, repair, or maintenance. Thus, McNamara's fleet of sixty-eight attack submarines would be reduced to fifty-six. It would take another two dozen U.S. attack boats to protect the six aircraft carrier battle groups that would be activated in the Atlantic and Mediterranean theaters, leaving thirty-two attack submarines to escort dozens of Atlantic convoys needed to resupply the European allies. With all of the U.S. subs so deployed, only a handful would remain to face dozens of Soviet nuclear submarines and surface ships streaming toward the American fleet in the open ocean.

McNamara's was not an honest analysis, Moorer believed. The navy needed a force level of at least one hundred nuclear attack submarines to perform the wartime mission; but McNamara had been holding firm. No one in the Pentagon had been more openly delighted than Moorer when McNamara announced he was stepping down by the end of February 1968. Moorer hoped the departure would end the era of systems analysis, the abused science.

Moorer respected the power of Soviet submarine forces and their threat to the American aircraft carriers. And so his alliance with Rickover was a joining of interests. The difference between sixty-eight nuclear submarines and one hundred nuclear submarines was more than $2 billion in additional funding at a time when the Defense Department was looking for $6 billion in cuts. For Moorer, that more than anything explained what the systems analysts really were up to. They insisted that any new ship the navy proposed be smaller, faster, and cheaper. Cost effectiveness was king, and McNamara's men had approached Rickover's proposal for a high-speed submarine with an attitude that it would never meet these requirements.

McNamara had cut the submarine from his budget recommendations to President Johnson and, in his final days, the Defense Secretary had turned loose his assistant secretaries for research and for systems analysis to begin an assault—by memoranda—on any future funding for the ship by arguing that it would cost twice as much as the current model. Since Soviet subs were judged to be inferior, a new U.S. attack just wasn't needed.

Moorer called these memoranda "snowflakes," because each was slightly different from the preceding one, and because they floated down to Moorer's office in great volume. He scoffed at the fuzzy thinking of the systems analysts in the folksy way he liked to dismiss misguided civilians. Moorer had pointed out to Assistant Secretary Enthoven that if the mayor of Washington, D.C., wanted to save money in the fire department, he certainly could sell all of the $100,000 fire trucks and purchase bright red Volkswagens equipped with fire extinguishers. The mayor would get a very cost-effective fire department, but, Moorer added, it would not be able to handle any emergency greater than a trash-can blaze.

Moorer believed the Pentagon had to be run like a money-losing charity because its mission was to protect the vital interests of the United States. If the civilian authorities wanted to skimp in providing for the nation's defense—as if the Pentagon had to show a profit—he would obey them because he believed in the Constitution, but he refused to swear allegiance to what he thought was bad defense policy in a dangerous world.

Through the final months of 1967 and into the new year, Moorer proselytized the civilians like a Baptist preacher, reciting parables and anecdotes with an Alabama drawl. One Sunday afternoon in the midst of the battle, Moorer had been dawdling over the sports page of *The Washington Post* when an analysis of an Arnold Palmer golf triumph caught his eye. He grabbed for a pad of paper and began writing. Palmer had won $70,000 in the tournament, roughly $1,000 per stroke during the final round of the match. The *Post*'s sports writer had dissected Palmer's winning game, noting that Palmer completed the final eighteen holes with only twenty-six putts. Of all the clubs in Palmer's golf bag, he had used his two iron and his four iron the fewest times during the round, hitting the two iron only once in a fairway shot and his four iron on three occasions during the day. Moorer smiled broadly as he scribbled the draft of his memo: "Dear Alain," it opened, and then informed the Assistant Defense Secretary that he was enclosing *The Washington Post*'s report of the tournament for Enthoven's consideration. From a systems analysis standpoint, Moorer said, Palmer had earned $26,000 from the use of his putter during the last round of the contest and had earned only $4,000 from the use of his two and four irons. If Palmer was interested in improving the cost effectiveness of his golfing arsenal, Moorer said, would Enthoven agree that Mr. Palmer should sell his two iron and his four iron and purchase two additional putters?

By eight o'clock, Moorer was ready for his morning briefing. He ambled from his office into the adjoining conference room, where his senior staff already had ringed the table. The tone was businesslike, but it carried the gravity of wartime and the tension that things were not going our way in Vietnam. The men in the room felt the frustration and there was little Moorer could do to change it. The situation reports on ship deployments and fleet exercises went quickly. Then came the report on *Enterprise*. Impatient at hearing what he already knew, Moorer asked whether naval intelligence was prepared to monitor the Soviet submarine without tipping off the Russians.

The briefer hesitated. Depending on weather and surface conditions, both of which affected the ambient noise in the ocean, the SOSUS listening network between California and Hawaii could provide one level of coverage. In addition, Lockheed Orions flying out of Moffett Field could add a second level of speed confirmation.

The operation was classified secret, as were all sensitive intelligence operations in the silent war. Moorer dictated a short message for the Pacific Fleet Command and for *Enterprise*. The carrier was instructed to maintain course and speed until apprised of the arrival of the *November*-class submarine in the area, at which time the carrier should increase speed and continue increasing speed until the submarine broke off the chase.

Moorer did not show it, but he was excited at the prospect of what he had set in motion. The intelligence operation was more than justified because of the need to refine U.S. understanding of Soviet nuclear submarine performance. But more immediately, the operation just might yield crucial and timely ammunition for the lobbying campaign that Rickover was mounting in Congress, whose spending decisions that spring would shape the navy—and its ability to engage the Soviet fleet—for the rest of the century.

"FROM CNO FOR CINCPACFLT INFO ENTERPRISE." Lee scanned the message and frowned. He was never going to get time for the man-overboard drills he wanted to run. The Soviet submarine was due to appear off *Enterprise*'s stern quarter in about eighteen hours. The Russian was making good speed. But if there was going to be a horse race, Lee did not think it would be much of a contest. *Enterprise*'s reactors were capable of delivering 280,000 horsepower to her four propeller shafts, and that was enough power to push the Empire State Building at freeway speeds. When the needle on the rpm indicator went all the way over, *Enterprise* would approach thirty-five knots and leave the fastest nuclear submarine miles back in her wake. It was just a matter of power and geometry.

A full load of supplies, jet fuel, and the air wing aboard would slow *Enterprise* down a bit, but not much. The hull inspection report showed the carrier's bottom was fairly clean, no barnacles or other marine growth to drag against the ocean surface, so Lee calculated that he would still get better than thirty knots. But *Enterprise* would never have to go to full power to lose the Soviet submarine. He had been briefed on Soviet submarines and he believed a *November*-class submarine had a top speed of about twenty-five knots. Still, Lee told his command staff that he wanted all eight of *Enterprise*'s reactors on line and available because the audience for this speed demonstration was the entire command staff back in Washington.

The trick would be not to make any move that indicated to the Russian skipper he had been detected. Lee folded the message. He looked out over the flight deck and felt a rush of adrenaline. His strategy would be simple. Take *Enterprise* up in speed in a way that looked perfectly normal to the Russian. Gradual increases, no sudden bursts that would telegraph to the Soviet skipper that his presence was known and that he was being challenged to a race. In Lee's experience, Soviet ships were very reluctant to demonstrate their full performance when U.S. naval forces were nearby. Both sides tried to save those capabilities as surprises in wartime. Opportunities to spy on Soviet ships, especially submarines, when they were running at battle-zone speeds were golden moments.

Like so many other things, the operation was being run out of Washington, and it would have been a little irritating to Lee to be merely a pawn on someone else's chessboard were it not for the competitive excitement he felt for the upcoming contest. He just wanted *Enterprise* to perform as perfectly as she could.

Robert McNamara was leaving the Pentagon, and a great deal of unfinished business, behind. But it was time to go. The last four years had not blotted out the highs of the first three, but they had depleted his spirit. The loss of Jack Kennedy—a president and friend—the miscalculations in Vietnam, the violent domestic opposition to "McNamara's war" had taken a heavy toll on the country and on McNamara personally. His slicked-back hair and rimless glasses symbolized to his critics the cold technocracy that had managed the war. It was an inhuman image, not at all like McNamara's image of himself.

The impressive buildup of the Soviet navy had concerned McNamara during his final days in office, but what had concerned him more was the response in the U.S. Navy, where the admirals used every new piece of intelligence to justify overreaching budget requests. What the admirals were ignoring, in McNamara's view, was the Soviet Union's historical evolution from a land power to a world power. That Russia had decided to acquire a modern navy was not cause to bankrupt the United States, he believed.

The Soviet Union had emerged from World War II as a formidable land power, but its navy consisted largely of coastal defense patrol craft, cruisers, and destroyers. In the late 1950s and early 1960s, the Russian leadership redirected major resources to build a bluewater navy that could support a more active Soviet foreign policy in distant parts of the world, such as Cuba, Africa, and the Middle East. The Soviets understood that they could not extend their influence to nonborder states unless they could support Soviet forces abroad with a naval umbrella and supply line. They had learned that lesson during the Cuban missile crisis of October 1962, when their ill-equipped warships were unable to challenge American seapower arrayed against them on the picket line set up by Kennedy and McNamara to stop the delivery of nuclear missiles to Fidel Castro. U.S.S. *Enterprise* had made her debut during the crisis, boiling through the Caribbean off Guantánamo, threatening to swat Castro with air strikes and providing air cover for an invasion plan that Castro and Soviet Premier Nikita Khrushchev would have been powerless to stop short of igniting a nuclear war.

An oceangoing navy was essential to a world power, and the Soviets had set out to build a modern fleet capable of challenging American naval superiority in any part of the world. McNamara believed this buildup required careful monitoring; but the U.S. response should be measured, aimed not at outbuilding the Soviets but at maintaining a qualitative edge using superior American technology to build cost-effective ships and weapons.

The principal obstacle to McNamara's policy for the past four years had been the little admiral who was in charge of naval nuclear propulsion. In Rickover, McNamara saw a threat to orderly defense policy that he had never envisioned when he came to the Pentagon. Dwight Eisenhower had warned of the creeping influence of what he called the military-industrial complex, a warning that would define the activism of a generation of reformers, but McNamara had disagreed with their view of the threat. In fact, he had once told Eisenhower as much. Enlightened management, he said, could discipline the military and its captive industry of defense contractors. McNamara had been confident that he could defeat waste and excess, and that cost-effective weapons procurement would free the budget for expanding social programs.

Yet after seven years of trying to bring order, McNamara realized that he had been wrong. He modified the definition of the menace Eisenhower had described to tailor it to Hyman G. Rickover—the "military-congressional complex," an axis of power that McNamara had never seen so skillfully constructed and manipulated by a single high-ranking military officer.

Fresh in McNamara's memory was his battle with Rickover over what kind of power plant to put in the aircraft carrier U.S.S. *John F. Kennedy*, a decision that would mean a cost difference of $200 million. McNamara wanted oil-fired propulsion because it would be ready sooner and cost less. Rickover was pushing nuclear power because it improved range and performance. McNamara not only questioned the higher cost of Rickover's propulsion system, but he and his chief of research and engineering, Harold Brown, believed that the eight-reactor design of *Enterprise* was inefficient. There was just too much piping and duplication of machinery with eight reactors.

Rickover had fought McNamara in congressional hearings. Putting only two reactors in an aircraft carrier could be a safety hazard, Rickover said. It was forcing reactor technology too quickly.

McNamara successfully defended his decision to put an oil-fired plant in U.S.S. *Kennedy*, but it had been a Pyhrric victory. Congress went along with McNamara's decision, but wrung a commitment from him that three future carriers would be nuclear-powered. After the congressional battle, McNamara discovered that Rickover had been feeding information and questions to congressional committee members, who were attacking McNamara's position. "I want to fire that son of a bitch," the Defense Secretary told his deputies. Hadn't Rickover broken the oath he took when he accepted his commission as a naval officer to obey the civilian authority of the executive branch? As an admiral in the navy he owed his loyalty to the Secretary of Defense, who represented the commander-in-chief.

After all of the acrimony over the carrier, McNamara had been surprised when Rickover had telephoned him for an appointment to come over and lobby for a high-speed submarine. McNamara seated the admiral and let him go on for nearly an hour, lecturing and making the case for more speed.

When Rickover was done, McNamara was brief. He said he agreed with Rickover that, as a general statement, speed was important to modern attack submarines. Rickover had been momentarily buoyed. But McNamara added that he was not inclined to include funding for such a ship in his last budget. Instead, he wanted his systems analysts and his research director to look into the whole question of submarine capabilities and advise him on the best course for future cost-effective alternatives.

McNamara had turned the knife skillfully, and Rickover left his office in a rage. "Doesn't he think I know something about nuclear submarines!" he shrieked when he got back to his office. Nothing offended Rickover more than the gratuitous questioning of his judgment about what kind of submarines the navy needed. He saw McNamara's decision to kill his high-speed submarine as a Parthian shot to settle all the old scores, and he was determined to defeat the lame-duck Defense Secretary.

"We've got to go to the Hill on this," Rickover told his senior staff. "He has left us no choice."

Friday morning, January 5, 1968

Enterprise was two days out of Alameda when the first sonar report on the *November* came into the combat information center. During the night watch a message from the Pacific Fleet had said the Russian sub would be coming in from northeast making high-speed propeller turns and running at one hundred fifty feet submerged. A sub-hunting Orion from Moffett Field had localized her position. The sonar operators on U.S.S. *Truxtun* and U.S.S. *Halsey* had waited anxiously, straining to hear the sub on their headsets. The Russian had begun a long sweeping turn to the southwest to fall in behind the carrier group when he finally came within range.

"Got him," snapped the *Truxtun* sonar operator. Word was flashed to *Enterprise*.

Lee was out of his sea cabin early that morning to prepare for the submarine's arrival. He wanted to make sure that everybody in the task force understood that the Russian was to be ignored. No course changes, no routine equipment tests of their active sonar search beams, because a single "ping" against the Russian's hull would signal him that he had been detected. Lee was glad the *November* had finally arrived and though he was anxious to get on with the operation, he admonished himself to be patient. Lee was acting out a scene in the silent war and it had to be done right. He thought about what was going on in the Russian sub. The Russian sonar man was listening to his headset and reporting to his captain each change in the bearing as they completed their turn toward the deep, pulsing Niagara of *Enterprise*'s four bronze propellers pushing back torrents of ocean. After matching course with the task force, the Russian throttled back his twin-reactor plant, reducing his propeller turns until he had matched the speed of the carrier group.

At sixteen knots, the bow sonars in *Truxtun* and *Halsey* would be sufficient to monitor the progress of the submarine for a time, but Lee knew that as *Enterprise* and her escorts started pushing up their propeller turns, the noise from their churning wakes and from the increased water flow over the sonar domes would set up an impenetrable cone of disturbed water astern. There could be a brass band underwater and they wouldn't hear it. After the initial speed increases, SOSUS and the Orions were going to have to take over.

Lee had decided not to make the first move to increase speed for a couple of hours. That would give the Russian time to adjust to cruising speed and convince himself that he had slipped into *Enterprise*'s wake undetected.

Lee wanted the Soviet skipper to get comfortable.

The dawn watch was still on the bridge when Lee told the officer of the deck to increase speed from sixteen to eighteen knots. The order was transmitted simultaneously to all four engine-room control stations, where four sets of reactor operators sat at their consoles. They opened valves sending more steam blasting against turbine blades, increasing the rotating energy delivered to the propellers.

The reactor control spaces in submarines and carriers alike were among the cleanest, most highly disciplined work areas in the world. The young reactor operators were cool professionals. They knew every valve, every pump, and every gauge in the propulsion system, and they understood reactor physics. Nuclear-powered warships had to be able to respond quickly to changing demands for speed and nuclear physics could accommodate those demands.

A naval reactor was a sealed steel vessel that contained uranium-235 fuel. Water circulated through the reactor under high pressure so it would not boil. Control rods inserted between the fuel rods prevented nuclear fission from occurring until it was time to bring the reactor on line. As the rods were slowly removed, the uranium-235 fuel elements bombarded each other with radioactive energy. It was the force of unstable atoms bursting apart and sending high-energy neutrons smashing into other uranium atoms until the release of neutrons from the bursting uranium atoms rose to a self-sustaining level. The water circulating through the reactor core served as the working fluid for the transfer of heat and its hydrogen atoms slowed down the high-energy neutrons created by fission. Billions of collisions occurred every second. Soon the reactor achieved a state of equilibrium, or criticality, the rhythm of energy release. Once the ship achieved this state, she was running critical.

The reactor operated as a closed loop of hot water that never left the reactor compartment. The hot pressurized water was pumped through heat exchangers, where a second loop of uncontaminated water circulated around its closed coils and flashed to steam to feed the turbines.

To increase speed, the engine room opened up the throttle

valves. The loss of steam into the turbines pulled more heat from the reactor, causing its temperature to drop slightly. Since cooler water was denser, its molecules packed more tightly together, the effect was to increase the collisions inside the reactor, making more neutrons available for fission. Thus, fission actually increased, pushing the reactor to a "supercritical" state, adding more heat to the pressurized water rushing out of the reactor to the heat exchangers.

The young reactor operators could recite the catechism of this "negative temperature coefficient" by heart and it allowed nuclear warships running critical to increase their speed without taking time to adjust the control rods in the reactors.

The Rickover system had taught the young reactor operators how to think and how to react; how to think before reacting. The safety of the ship and her crew depended on their instincts. Redundant safety systems had been designed into all naval reactors because nuclear power had brought a new set of dangers to the navy. The worst that could happen to a conventional oil-fired plant was a fire or a boiler explosion, and that could be a life-threatening event. But the nightmare that had always lingered in the background of nuclear technology was the catastrophic loss of coolant episode. Nuclear-powered warships had to meet the highest standards for protecting the health and safety of civilian populations while still in port and, during peacetime, they had to meet the same standard for protecting the crew. But their designers understood that they were war machines first and foremost, and so it was a given that a nuclear submarine might suffer a catastrophic episode in the heat of battle. But it was also a given that the danger to the crew from the highly radioactive heat machine in the reactor compartment should be less life-threatening than the blows delivered by enemy weapons.

A direct hit by a torpedo on a nuclear submarine running submerged might breach the reactor compartment, but the fatal consequences for the crew from the torpedo hit on the pressure hull of the ship would obliterate any concern about radioactive contamination. The highly toxic fuel might irradiate the ocean floor and its benthic life forms for thousands of years, but that was one of the acceptable trade-offs of war.

Most nuclear engineers believed a catastrophic accident was virtually impossible during peacetime operations. Safety systems were designed such that crew members could make mistakes and even fail to respond to serious reactor conditions, and still catastrophe could be averted. But the designers also knew that the crew's failure to respond to a sequence of three key events could lead to a loss of coolant. The reactors were designed with hairtrigger sensitivities to "scram," sending all control rods slamming back into the core to kill the fission reaction. The operators practiced manual "scram" procedures until they could do them in their sleep, or in the terror of battle. The reason was the risk—the random sequence of events that had never been predicted. It might occur from explosive shocks from enemy weapons, from a collision, or from metal fatigue. It didn't matter. It could happen. One of the reactor's main coolant lines would fail, and the hot pressurized water would burst through the breach. The dry reactor would automatically shut down, but the decay heat inside the vessel had to be carried away by the continuous circulation of water or it would quickly build to more than five thousand degrees, the kind of heat that melts anything.

Nuclear-powered vessels were equipped with emergency core coolant systems whose sensors monitored the temperature of the reactor. At the first sign of trouble, the emergency system flooded the reactor with additional water. But some of the emergency coolant water could flash to vapor, its molecules ripped apart in the white-hot environment. If unabated, a powerful explosive bubble of hydrogen gas could turn the steel reactor vessel—in a blinding millisecond—into a thousand lethal projectiles ripping through the ship and hull, spreading deadly radioactive contamination throughout the debris.

A second disaster possibility was a loss of coolant that could lead to a full core melt, sending a white-hot molten mass of fuel and radioactive slag to the bottom of the reactor vessel to melt through the steel containment. A shield tank filled with fission-stopping boron and water was the next line of defense, and the bulkheads of the reactor compartment were designed to withstand the pressure of the ocean so that if all else failed, the compartment could be vented to the sea, where the ocean would become the coolant of last resort for a runaway reactor. Over the years, detailed classified studies had assessed every event that could be imagined to improve these safety systems, and Lee understood what motivated Rickover in setting high standards for safety. As a practical matter, Rickover had grasped from the beginning that the first major accident aboard a nuclear-powered ship might be the last for the nuclear navy. So Lee, and the other officers who had passed through Rickover's domain, had embraced his creed.

It had taken a few minutes for the additional thrust from the propellers to increase *Enterprise*'s velocity through the water to eighteen knots, and soon after, the sonar operators heard a corresponding increase in the propeller turns of the Soviet sub. The first step had been easy.

On one level, Lee was just participating in an intelligence operation, a war game with a pair of propellers on someone's headset, but he sensed the consequences of the contest for the U.S. fleet. As captain of *Enterprise*, Lee was never very far from the acute and manic psychology of war. After all, that invisible and unknowable war machine seven miles behind and one hundred fifty feet down was full of hostile combatants; they were carrying live torpedoes, perhaps one or two of them nuclear-tipped. Despite her speed, mass, and aerial firepower, *Enterprise* made a good target. Her fantail was showing the Russian one hundred thirty-three feet of beam, and she was relatively naked without the anti-submarine weapons of her escorts and the land-based Orions.

In an instant, the silent war could be over and the real war begun. Lee would never know why, and by then it would not matter. The flash would come in code from the Pacific Fleet as an emergency action message. It would be Lee's job as tactical commander of the task force to order the sub's destruction. *Truxtun* and *Halsey* would quickly heel to lay down their pattern of depth charges and torpedoes, hoping to turn the *November*'s hull to wreckage before the Ukrainian torpedomen below loaded their fish and launched a cosmic farewell to the billion-dollar carrier and its air wing.

There was no time for philosophy in the prosecution of war. It was Lee's job to get up every morning and ask himself the question: What do I do if the war starts today and *Enterprise* is attacked? What evasion order would I give if the Russian got off a couple of fifty-five-knot torpedoes? There was no easy evasion, but in wartime the speed of *Enterprise* would be her most important asset, and the speed of American submarines to track and destroy the Russian intruder before it came over the horizon would be the first layer of *Enterprise*'s defenses. If the Russian broke through, and then survived the gauntlet of mines, depth charges, and air-dropped torpedoes thrown in his path by the Pacific Fleet, *Enterprise*, and all she represented for American security, would stand naked and vulnerable for the final conflict.

Within the hour, Lee read the new sonar report and realized the submarine skipper was hooked. Lee's tactic had paid off. The Russian was responding to routine increases in speed by his prey. He probably thought Lee was in a hurry to get to Pearl Harbor. The Russian could not surface and radio for new instructions without fear of detection by the carrier group, so he would follow *Enterprise* come hell or high water. If nothing else, the Soviet navy was disciplined, and Lee doubted that he would lose his shadow until he really started burning neutrons. If that was the case, then Lee was going to force the Russian to push to the outside of the envelope, the speed envelope.

Two hours later, Lee ordered eighty-five propeller turns and *Enterprise* pulled momentarily away from the Russian to level off at twenty-four knots. Lee believed he was within a knot or two of the Russian's maximum speed. The Russian was running blind now, the noise of the ocean rushing over the hull, the roar from his own turbines, coolant pumps, and gears making it impossible for his sonar operator to hear anything above the din. It was like driving a car with a steel windshield through a downpour. If there was anyone else on the highway, you wouldn't know it.

Lee wondered how long the Russian would run blind before cutting power to adjust his bearing on *Enterprise*'s stern. If he was suspicious—and Lee bet he was—he might think *Enterprise* was going to hit the brakes. He would make a fool of himself by running right under the task force like a blundering freight train. If he was smart, he was cutting power every hour or so just long enough to listen before he sprinted forward again.

One of the bridge officers handed Lee another sonar report. The submarine had matched the last speed increase. Lee was impressed and considered that the real value of this horse race might be in determining how long a *November* could sustain this kind of speed.

Either way, he felt the operation would be over by dinnertime.

Friday evening, January 5, 1968

Enterprise and her escorts barreled through the rolling swells at twenty-eight knots. The ship was operating perfectly under a starlit canopy, but Lee was restless.

"We're going to need one hundred twenty rpm before midnight," he told the reactor engineer. Lee had hoped to shake the Russian loose before the night was out so he could satisfy Washington and then return to the drills he wanted to run before *Enterprise* reached Yankee Station in the South China Sea, the small plot of ocean he would turn into an air base against the North Vietnamese. But the Soviet submarine had not broken off, and that was unsettling to Lee. For the last six hours, the Russian had matched every increase in *Enterprise*'s speed, showing no sign of strain, his twin screws singing in such a noisy chorus that the SOSUS stations on the West Coast were still picking them up.

Lee was sure that the brass in Washington by now all were sitting on the edge of their chairs because this Russian was breaking all speed records for the *November* class. He was still back there, like a dog snarling on your pants leg, and Lee was troubled because the Russian should have been losing ground by now. An element of uncertainty had been injected into the race. Was there something about this submarine that Washington was not telling Lee? He had never heard of a *November* demonstrating this kind of performance. They were old boats, inferior to American submarines. But at this speed, any top-of-the-line American submarine already would have fallen well behind.

Lee waited a little while longer. Then: "Go to one hundred twenty rpm." The watch rang up flank speed. Throttle valves slammed over in the engine room. After a few minutes, the carrier's speed stabilized at thirty-one knots, more than thirty-seven miles per hour. No submarine could go that fast. Not ours, not theirs. Lee was not going to leave the bridge until he was sure the *November* had disappeared over the horizon.

When the sonar report was finally handed out, Lee read it in disbelief. The Russian submarine had increased speed to thirty-one knots as if he had power to spare. This was astonishing. The Soviet Union's oldest attack submarine could keep pace with and menace an American aircraft carrier at speeds the CIA said the Russians could not go. It had taken ten years to discover the true speed of the *November*s. Worse, the oldest Russian submarines were faster than our newest ones. A lot faster!

The realization changed the whole tactical relationship between Lee and the Russian commander. One evasion option had disappeared. What would his order be now, tonight, if the war began? What would he do if those fifty-five-knot torpedoes came streaking across the space between them?

It had started out as a simple intelligence operation, but suddenly the consequences for *Enterprise* and all the floating fortresses in the American armada were shattering. A decade of crucial vulnerability had gone somehow undetected. In the peacetime years of warship design and construction, the navy and the defense industry had lost the discipline of war, which has its frightening and irreversible way of defining the survival requirements for any weapons system. The U.S. aircraft carriers' advantage against the Russian submarine fleet had foundered that January night in the dark Pacific near Hawaii. Someone would have to answer. Someone would have to explain.

Lee had been only one of the pawns on a billion-dollar chess board. Rickover and Moorer had set the moves, and their sobering vision of Soviet naval superiority would put the granite in their resolve to break the bureaucratic constraints against building a new fleet of high-speed nuclear attack submarines.

In the marble office building adjoining the United States Capitol, an air of urgency and expectation filled the hearing room. The classified report on the *Enterprise* incident had rocked the intelligence community. The CIA ordered a full-scale revision of speed estimates for all Soviet submarines. Overhead satellite coverage of Soviet shipbuilding was increased. The Office of Naval Intelligence set up a task group to improve undersea monitoring of Soviet sea trials and to attempt for the first time infiltrating covert agents into Soviet shipyards.

If the *November* class could go to thirty knots, how fast could the new *Victor*-class attack submarines go? What surprise was next? It almost was frightening to answer the question given the fact that U.S. nuclear attack boats could not come close to thirty knots. There was talk of a submarine gap becoming an issue in the presidential campaign, and it took fewer than three weeks for Moorer and Rickover to organize their congressional drive against the opposition in the executive branch.

Rickover's January 23, 1968, debut was scripted like a dramatic presentation and was set before his most friendly audience, the House Armed Services Committee, chaired by Representative L. Mendel Rivers, an eloquent pro-defense orator with silver hair and an alarming capacity for bourbon. The Charleston, South Carolina, Democrat was an unflinching supporter of the war in Vietnam and had seen the pressures mounting on the Johnson administration to cut spending. But Rivers was among the Southern Democratic chairmen in the congressional defense establishment who believed that the country could not afford to lose its military edge over the Soviet Union just because Vietnam had drained an increasing share of budget resources.

It was deep winter in Washington. The members of the committee had just returned from Christmas recess. After the last member entered the hearing room, the doors were sealed by a Capitol policeman. The assembly represented one half of the defense establishment in Congress. Rivers sat at the center of the dais and the ranking members arranged themselves in descending order of seniority, Democrats on his right hand, Republicans on his left. They included Melvin Price of Illinois, William Bates of Massachusetts, Chet Holifield of California, Charles Bennett of Florida, John Andersen of Illinois. Outside of Washington and their home districts, their names meant little to the average American, but in their hands was concentrated great power to shape U.S. defense forces: how many tanks for the army, ships for the navy, jets for the air force; which defense contractors would be favored, which bases opened or closed.

In the final days of McNamara's term, Rivers had not been hiding his contempt for the departing Defense Secretary and had complained to his colleagues that every time he attacked McNamara's budget recommendations, the next morning's newspaper carried another stinging report by syndicated columnists Drew Pearson and Jack Anderson, detailing Rivers's drinking habits and his junket-taking to lush vacation spots at taxpayer expense. The Defense Department provided airplanes for congressional travel, and Rivers knew someone in the Pentagon was leaking the salacious reports to the columnists. He held McNamara responsible and relished this counterassault.

Rivers looked down at the witness table and smiled at Rickover, who was flanked by his aides: William Wegner, deputy director of the Naval Reactors Branch, on his right, David T. Leighton on his left. They were the second generation of men to serve Rickover, and they brought separate strengths to his inner circle. Both were Naval Academy graduates who had resigned their commissions and foregone the traditional career path to selection as admiral in order to stay with Rickover in the Naval Reactors Branch.

Leighton was a broad-brow genius whose imagination and garrulous tongue never stopped working, and whose facile mind grasped the knottiest technical problem, turning it inside out and upside down before clicking off a range of possible solutions. Leighton became the most prolific draftsman for the book-length studies, reports, histories, and chronologies with which Rickover annually filled the Congressional Record to document the success of his programs and to debunk his critics.

Wegner was the owlish engineer whose political instincts and shrewd judgments on personnel made him Rickover's most effective deputy. He could interpret better than anyone Rickover's tempestuous style to the befuddled. More than one three-star admiral who had received an inexplicable telephone attack from Rickover had put down the telephone and yelled, "Get Wegner on the line and find out what the hell that was all about." Wegner had mothered a generation of Rickover favorites through the nuclear navy with an avuncular personal style, but he also was the voracious guardian of the Rickover legend. To those whom Rickover perceived as disloyal to the program or worse, incompetent, Wegner had become the cold instrument of the admiral's wrath.

In the months leading up to the *Enterprise* episode, Wegner had been given a sensitive mission by Rickover: to get inside the intelligence community and find out everything that was known about the Soviet nuclear submarine fleet. Wegner was shocked to find that the CIA did not share its satellite photography of the Soviet Union's sprawling shipbuilding complex with the Office of Naval Intelligence or with anyone else. By the same token, naval intelligence did not share its SOSUS data with the CIA. Each agency was jealously guarding its information, compartmentalizing facts and observations which, if shared, might shed light on a greater portion of the intelligence puzzle about Soviet submarines.

To get Wegner in, Rickover had made an issue out of the hoarding. He took Wegner to CIA headquarters and in a meeting with the Agency's director, Richard Helms, argued that the CIA was keeping the experts away from the raw intelligence and it was hurting the navy. Rickover's strategy worked. Helms granted a clearance for the outsider, and Wegner went to work. After all the trouble, Wegner was surprised to find poor quality and a lack of detail in the early photographs. The imposition of cloud cover or a roof over a construction hall was all that was needed to blind U.S. satellites to sensitive shipyard activities.

Still, the photos were intriguing. Wegner examined Russian submarine hull cylinders that had been captured on film while they were in transport, or being fitted together on exposed building ways.

CIA analysts working from the photographs had duplicated some Russian hull designs of new attack and missile submarines. It was clear from these models that the Russians were trying to solve the hydrodynamic limitations on the speed of submerged bodies—underwater friction that slowed ships down—just as U.S. Navy designers had done. The Soviets had studied the shape of whales, porpoises, and other aquatic forms to learn how to reduce drag under water.

Russian submarine models had been tested at the David W. Taylor model basin, a mile-long naval research complex that sits behind a ten-foot security fence on the banks of the Potomac River just outside Washington. From these tests, the CIA had made deductions about the weight of the submarines, the size and the power rating of their reactor plants, and therefore, the range of speeds they might achieve.

The airborne fleet of sub-hunting Orions had also gathered a wealth of data over the years. Virtually anytime a new Soviet submarine slipped out from its base on the Kola Peninsula for sea trials, some Western power was listening, logging its speed, analyzing its propeller noises, and sharing the information with others.

But if U.S. sensors tracked a Soviet sub at eighteen knots, there was no way to tell whether the Russian skipper was running at top speed. It was informed guesswork in the end.

Some of the satellite photographs had baffled intelligence analysts because they showed Russian hull cylinders made from—or coated with—an unidentified shiny material. The shiny metal had been spotted from outer space as the hull sections sat in temporary storage outside a construction hall in the central Soviet Union, where they would become a new class of attack submarine, smaller and sleeker than the *Novembers*—the *Alpha* class. The intelligence agencies were trying to gather more data on the *Alpha*, but the secrets of her construction and power plant would remain out of reach for nearly a decade.

Wegner had taken his findings to Rickover, who had looked at the data and applied simple deductive reasoning. The Russians were gearing their design efforts to achieve greater speed. After the *Enterprise* episode, there had been no need to delay any longer. Rickover had quickly arranged for a classified congressional briefing. Wegner and Leighton were dispatched to Capitol Hill to share with key staff members of the Armed Services committees the information that had been compartmentalized in the intelligence community.

Captain Bradley, from naval intelligence, served as the briefer. He had a deep baritone voice and a sense of dramatic timing, and Wegner had rehearsed him on the most effective presentation of view graphs, charts, and overhead photography from the CIA. Briefings by their nature were supposed to be neutral presentations of data and intelligence findings, but no policy-making effort, especially in Washington, was neutral. The mere selection of material and omission of other material required making judgments about what was important and what was not.

The lights dimmed in the hearing room.

"We have been asked to discuss the Soviet submarine threat," Bradley opened. The first transparency had not surrendered the detail of the original satellite photograph from which it was made. It showed the shipbuilding complex at Severodvinsk, three hundred miles from the Finnish border above the Arctic Circle. There was little he had to say to make the point. On top of the photo, Bradley overlaid a diagram of the Newport News Shipbuilding and Dry Dock Company, the largest American shipyard. It barely filled a quarter of the screen. Then he overlaid diagrams of all other U.S. shipyards. All could be placed within the boundaries of Severodvinsk. And it was just one of five large Soviet shipyards!

In one corner of Severodvinsk, the Soviets had been working on an unidentified class of nuclear submarines in a construction hall so large that it could accommodate within its walls the entire Electric Boat shipyard at Groton, Connecticut.*

---

*This construction hall produced the *Yankee*-class ballistic missile submarine, which first appeared later in 1968. The *Yankee* class carried the first long-range nuclear missile to sea for the Soviet Union to hit targets east of the Mississippi in the United States.

Five hundred miles inland from Severodvinsk, the Soviets were building submarines on floating barges at Gorky, then towing them upon completion to the colder clime of the northern sub bases. If the large construction hall at Gorky had been erected in Washington, D.C., Bradley said, it would cover all three branches of the U.S. government in Washington, D.C. In this and other facilities, he said, the Soviets were gearing up to produce twenty nuclear submarines per year— double the capacity of all U.S. shipyards. If the Soviets went to around-the-clock shifts, they could push their output even higher.

The news was alarming. The United States was spending about $80 million that year to build one *Sturgeon*-class nuclear submarine. McNamara had included two *Sturgeon*s in his last budget, at a cost of $160 million. But the Soviets were going to spend $1.6 billion for nuclear submarines in a single year, $8 billion over five years. They were outspending the United States ten to one!

Rickover searched the faces of the congressmen and saw the impact of Bradley's words as the navy captain raced through the numbers. While the Soviets had only sixty-five nuclear attack submarines to a U.S. total of seventy-four, the burgeoning output of their shipyards would overcome the difference by 1970. If the Soviets built at a rate of ten submarines per year, half their capacity, their fleet would grow to double the size of the U.S. submarine fleet by the mid- to late 1970s.

The Soviet central government had placed submarine construction at the highest level of national priority, meaning the shipyards had first call on steel plate coming out of the mills and forgings coming out of the foundries. If there was any doubt about Soviet intentions, Bradley said, one had only to read the speeches of the Soviet naval commander, Admiral Sergei Gorshkov, who had boasted that the United States had made a strategic miscalculation in relying on large and increasingly vulnerable aircraft carriers to project power in the world. The U.S. strategy would fail in wartime, Gorshkov alleged, because "the combat potential . . . of nuclear-powered aircraft carriers is inferior to the strike potentials of submarine and air forces."

Bradley built to the climax of the briefing. Earlier that month in the Pacific, he said, a Soviet attack sub had shattered all previous speed estimates for her class by pursuing the nuclear aircraft carrier *Enterprise* at a sustained speed of thirty-one knots between San Francisco and Pearl Harbor before the Russian boat broke off. The intelligence community for ten years had believed that first-generation Soviet nuclear submarines were not capable of carrier task force speeds, he said. But the community had been wrong.

This made the appearance of the *Victor*-class attack sub and the *Charlie*-class cruise missile boats all the more ominous, Bradley said. The United States had no cruise missile submarines and the *Charlie*'s mission appeared to be to strike at the task force from over the horizon. U.S. carrier forces clearly were sailing into a decade of greater jeopardy.

The room was hushed as Bradley ended the presentation. The congressmen seemed startled and perturbed. For years they had voted funds to build the most advanced nuclear submarine fleet in the world. Now they were being told it was inferior in perhaps the most important respect. But Rickover was very pleased with the briefing. Bradley had touched all the right chords, and those he had missed, Rickover had interjected. He gave the committee members a philosophical overview of the importance of what they were hearing. Rickover played the role of tutor to the men who believed in his judgment. After all, he had been right about nuclear power to begin with. Why would he steer them wrong now?

Rickover was trying only to steer them to the solution, his solution.

The impact of Bradley's briefing rolled thunderously through the back channels of the defense establishment in Washington. The *Enterprise* episode had caused telephones to start ringing all over the Pentagon. People were going to have to go up to the Hill and explain to some powerful congressmen why the hell Rickover was not getting what he wanted. Rickover attended each subsequent briefing in the House, Senate, and in the Joint Committee on Atomic Energy. He reminded the congressional leadership of Sputnik and warned them about the danger of complacency in national defense. He urged them to take the long view of history—to rise above the transitory political and budgetary pressures and look into the future through the dark portent of Soviet naval superiority.

His message came at a time of major reevaluation in the Johnson administration over the war in Vietnam. After four years of escalated American involvement, the resilience of the North Vietnamese and Viet Cong guerrillas appeared largely undaunted. During the Tet holidays, combined enemy forces had launched a massive offensive throughout the country, which, though it was repelled, demonstrated to the American public and to Congress that the war was far from over.

Frustration in Washington, in the country, was intense. Even as Bradley was delivering the first briefing, a U.S. intelligence collection ship, U.S.S. *Pueblo*, was seized by North Korean patrol boats in the Sea of Japan. The aircraft carrier task force led by U.S.S. *Enterprise* was ordered to the area in a momentary standoff that could have led to war with North Korea. President Johnson was unwilling to rescue the ship and her eighty-two crew members forcibly. When a Russian naval flotilla entered the Sea of Japan during the crisis and, in a provocative gesture, steamed at full speed toward *Enterprise*, Captain Kent Lee found himself on the bridge radio-telephone speaking directly to President Johnson. "Turn around and get the hell out of there," Johnson had ordered. Lee turned *Enterprise* around and retreated before the Russians.

The Johnson administration was at the eye of the storm, but its winds also swept through a troubled Congress. Rickover's message offered the congressional leadership a chance to do something that seemed positive and urgent for a more stable future, and he told them they could do it for a negligible amount of money—just enough to build the first high-speed power plant, its reactor, turbines, and gear train for installation in a prototype submarine. That was the big deceit, and everybody in the defense establishment knew it.

Rickover had no intention of selling a single submarine, but he had framed the issue so that it looked like the high-speed prototype was the correct response to the massive Soviet naval buildup and, of course, a single attack boat was not. But saying so—and creating an impressive and alarming record in Congress about the Soviet threat—made McNamara's intransigence seem all the more unreasonable. The senators paid little attention to the question of what would follow the prototype because the question would have revealed the enormous scale of Rickover's agenda and its cost: billions of dollars to build a fleet of high-speed submarines. And then someone might have asked: Is Rickover's high-speed submarine the best boat to build for the money, or are there alternatives that would increase the speed and performance of the U.S. fleet for less? But once the gate was opened, those questions would be lost in an insidious cycle of defense procurement where small-scale requests established a foothold in the defense budget one year only to balloon beyond all proportion in following years. By the time the public learned the true cost, the weapon system had gained unstoppable momentum and coalition support from political constituencies, contractors, and jobs in home districts. The alternatives would be forgotten.

Oversight of the Pentagon's strategic planning was not the long suit of the Congress, and Rickover's push for the high-speed submarine proved it. John Stennis and Mendel Rivers spent little time on questions about the future. They had staff for that, but the congressional staffs on the Armed Services committees were largely extensions of the military services and defense contractors they oversaw. No one was asking the questions. At a time of disarray in the Johnson administration, the entrenched power of Congress over the federal budget had given Rickover and his allies unique opportunity to seize the moment.

On February 8, 1968, the Joint Committee on Atomic Energy issued a statement expressing its concern over the "rapidly increasing Soviet submarine threat." Then the committee issued a threat of its own: If the Defense Department did not request funding for Rickover's single high-speed submarine, the Joint Committee would consider putting the money in the AEC's budget in the same way it had provided funds for the first naval nuclear reactors a decade earlier. The glove had been thrown down. Rickover would not let up. Yet there was still much opposition to be overcome—in the Defense Department, in the Congress, and, Rickover knew by instinct, in the navy itself.

Captain Donald H. Kern walked briskly along the mostly deserted Pentagon corridor. In his head he carried the concept for the navy's next generation nuclear attack submarine, and by Washington's Birthday 1968 he had begun to feel that he was stepping off a curb into Rickover's path. Government offices were closed for the holiday, but down the hall, behind the door where Kern was headed, Rickover's opposition had not taken time to rest.

Kern, an MIT-trained naval architect and marine engineer, was chief of the navy's submarine desk, which supervised all new submarine design. He had been summoned by a telephone call from the Pentagon's director of ocean warfare, and Kern was apprehensive. He had enough problems with Rickover without getting sandwiched between the old man and the civilians in the Defense Department who were trying to kill Rickover's high-speed submarine. And the director of ocean warfare came as close as anyone to openly despising Rickover, who had treated him like an idiot from the day McNamara had appointed him in 1966.

Though Kern had been fighting Rickover for control of nuclear submarine design, he supported the high-speed prototype. He was not sure the director of ocean warfare understood this and he suspected that the civilians wanted to use what Kern was working on—the Conform submarine—as a club against Rickover. Kern wanted to stay out of that trap. As long as Kern fought Rickover within navy channels, he was all right, but getting mixed up with the civilians could be viewed as treason by the navy brass. Yet there had been no reasonable way to duck the summons that brought Kern to the Pentagon that morning.

An athletic boatsman who missed few of the summer racing

seasons at Newport, Kern had supervised the navy's submarine design work for six years, one of a handful of highly specialized engineering duty officers who formed another of the navy's elite groups. For the past two years, Kern had been leading a research team set up to design a high-technology attack submarine: the Conform submarine. It would incorporate the ideal hull form, propulsion plant, and newest electronic features in a class of boats that would meet the Soviet submarine threat and serve the navy until the end of the century. The Conform submarine was a "concept formulation," the most important challenge of Kern's naval career, and he had Rickover's word in writing that he would support it.

It was an agreement known to no one outside the navy. In August 1967, Rickover had come to Kern and his boss, Rear Admiral Jamie Adair, seeking their assistance in selling the high-speed submarine. Kern was more than happy to give Rickover the submarine desk's support, but only in return for Rickover's pledge that he would leave the design of the next class of nuclear submarines to the submarine desk. Rickover agreed and had insisted that they put their highly unusual bargain in writing.*

But even with the agreement, Kern knew that his was a losing battle against Rickover's power. Nominally, the Naval Reactors Branch was only in charge of providing power plants. The submarine desk then took over, fitting Rickover's propulsion plant into the best hull package with the right mix of engine-room machinery, sonars, weapons, and fire-control computers. But Rickover was a master at grabbing control over more and more areas of the submarine, and Kern had only been successful in blocking him where there was support among the senior admirals of the shipbuilding command. But no one had the stomach anymore for taking on "City Hall," as Naval Reactors Branch sometimes was referred to.

Part of the reason was the loss of U.S.S. *Thresher,* a source of bitter residual tension between Rickover and the rest of the navy shipbuilding command. One hundred and twenty-seven men had died on April 10, 1963, when *Thresher* suddenly foundered during a deep dive. The navy board of inquiry had set the probable cause as a pipe joint failure in the engine room, which quickly flooded the after portion of the submarine and triggered the emergency shutdown of the reactor. Before *Thresher* could blow ballast and surface, she had been pulled

*On September 20, 1967, Kern, Adair, and Rickover met in Adair's office and each put his name to the pact, which said: "It was agreed that the fast submarine [as advocated by Rickover] would receive priority in new submarine design. It was further agreed that as soon as the fast submarine was authorized, Admiral Rickover would back to every possible extent the new attack submarine design as advocated by PMS-81 [the submarine desk under Kern]."

beyond her crush depth, her hull shattered by the grip of the Atlantic a hundred miles off Cape Cod.

Some of *Thresher's* designers at Portsmouth Naval Shipyard had suggested that *Thresher's* fatal leak might have sprung in the reactor compartment, where Rickover imposed the most stringent quality-control standards for piping materials and for welding. The debate had raged, but at the end of the inquiry, Rickover's record for safety was vindicated and *Thresher's* design team at Portsmouth carried the brunt of responsibility for the quality-control lapses that led to the tragic sequence of failures.

Rickover had used the *Thresher* judgment skillfully to expand his influence over the rest of the submarine, arguing that he was ahead of the navy in quality control. But Kern had challenged Rickover's claims. He had heard Rickover during the *Thresher* inquiry respond to a question on how many welds there were in a nuclear submarine. Kern knew there were more than eighty thousand, but Rickover had given an answer that was so low it was crazy. Rickover was not an expert outside the reactor compartment, and Kern had accused him of needlessly driving up the cost of new submarine construction by going far beyond the post-*Thresher* requirements for safe construction. Everybody had learned from *Thresher*, Kern believed, but Rickover had gone overboard. He was going to price nuclear submarines beyond the navy's ability to pay for them in adequate numbers.

That was why Kern believed it would be dangerous for the navy to let Rickover get control of the entire ship design. Rickover's focus had always been on improving the propulsion plant. He was not as qualified to oversee the emerging technologies outside the reactor compartment: sound quieting, sonar, weaponry, and fire-control computing. So Kern had fought him, and had given ground incrementally because Kern was no match for Rickover's power.

As Kern left the Pentagon corridor and crossed the threshold into the ocean warfare suite, he went over in his mind how he was going to handle its director. Kern had decided to urge the ocean warfare director to pacify Rickover. Build the high-speed prototype. That was the best way to keep Rickover from trying to gain control of a whole generation of new submarines, because, if that happened, Kern feared the navy would get stuck with a submarine fleet it did not want: one that might not go faster, one that might cost so much the navy could not afford to build it; in short, one that might fail to meet the Soviet threat. But the navy would be stuck with it for thirty years.

J. Kneel Nunan popped out of one of the doorways and greeted Kern. Nunan was one of those men who came to Washington but never seemed to understand how it worked, even with tutoring. When he telephoned people in the navy, he told them to go to a pay phone to call him back because he feared Rickover's omniscience. He instructed his secretary to type "Eyes Only" on his budget recommendations to keep Rickover from getting them and sounding alarms in Congress before they were acted upon. Yet Rickover's loyal network always seemed to turn them up, to Nunan's continuing exasperation.

Nunan worked for Dr. John Stewart Foster, Jr., the Under Secretary for Defense Research and Engineering, before whom all new weapons systems had to pass muster. Recruited by McNamara, Foster was the Pentagon's top scientist, a physicist by training who had spent most of his scientific career designing nuclear weapons.

Nunan was Foster's soldier against Rickover and had shown an appetite for taking on the old man and that was all right with Foster, who knew the strength of Rickover's congressional axis. Nunan had enlisted some powerful consultants to marshal arguments against the high-speed submarine, and they had criticized Rickover for not giving the navy all of the horsepower he could—given the weight and size of his propulsion plant. The "power density" of Rickover's reactors suffered in comparison to the power densities achieved by the Soviets.

The consultants had asked Rickover why he could not run his reactors at higher temperatures and pressures to get hotter, more efficient steam for the turbines. Why had he abandoned other promising reactor technologies, such as the sodium-cooled system first installed in *Seawolf*? There might have been more difficult safety problems to overcome, but there might also have been more horsepower generated from a smaller plant. After all, they were building war machines; greater risks were justified. But such talk enraged Rickover, who had made a religion out of reactor safety and reliability, and who told his designers to assume that one of their sons would serve aboard the ship they were building. If that led to overly conservative design, so be it. Where would the consultants be if there was a failure in the reactor compartment that killed young men? Rickover knew where they would be, in the lynch mob. As a practical matter, Rickover understood better than anyone after the loss of U.S.S. *Thresher* that peacetime accidents were just as threatening to the nuclear navy as wartime casualties. Safety was a political issue as much as anything.

Nunan had looked for ammunition among Rickover's primary defense contractors, Westinghouse and General Electric, but he had stretched what he learned, and that's why he was such a klutz in the defense bureaucracy. At one high-level Pentagon meeting early that February, Nunan claimed that some of the most knowledgeable industrialists in the country had told him that the weight of Rickover's propulsion plants could be cut in half at a cost of only $10 million. When Rickover heard it, he at first hooted and then telephoned Nunan demanding the names of the industrialists. Nunan refused, saying they feared Rickover reprisals. Rickover blanketed both companies with telephone calls until the officials came forward to say that Nunan had distorted the information they had provided him. Rickover accused Nunan of spreading disinformation and Nunan's credibility plummeted in Congress.

Nunan knew he was losing. He saw Kern as a potential ally and the Conform submarine as a foil against Rickover. With Kern seated in his office, Nunan quickly came to the point. "I want you to know that I am completely against this submarine. A submarine going thirty knots radiates a hell of a lot of noise in the ocean." Nunan was convinced that noise was the greatest enemy of submarines. He had canvassed some World War II submariners, who uniformly preferred stealth to speed in their boats. "In a war, it would never get to its station. It would be sunk. It's going to be like shooting fish in a barrel. I've told that to Rickover, but he is all over the Hill campaigning for this thing. Why do we need it?"

Kern believed he had to put everything in focus for the civilian, not just submarine technology and the need for speed, but he also needed to put Rickover in focus for Nunan.

The *Enterprise* episode, Kern said, had demonstrated something dramatic about the direction and advanced state of Soviet war planning. In any future war, U.S. submarines would be at a serious disadvantage if they could not match the performance of Russian attack boats.

Speed, stealth, and depth were the holy trinity of submarine capabilities. The history of how each capability had evolved in the U.S. Navy was arcane and largely secret. Kern was not sure himself whether Nunan, who had access to the information, actually understood it. Few people outside the nuclear submarine fraternity did. To the American public, indeed to the rest of the world, the nuclear navy, *Nautilus* and her progeny, were wondrous and mysterious achievements in the black arts that grew out of the Manhattan Project. How they performed and how they had developed was out of reach.

The genesis of the high-speed submarine had predated *Nautilus* by several years. A little-known experimental submarine, U.S.S. *Albacore*, had been designed and built in 1952 with a revolutionary hull shape, round and tapered like a porpoise, a single propeller for thrust. The hull design was referred to as a "body of revolution" because it was produced as if turned on a lathe. Any cross section of the hull was a circle and its steel skin was extremely smooth. The round design and bullet-nosed bow contrasted with the destroyer bows of World War II submarines, which were designed to cut through the waves on the surface.

Albacore's hull was packed full of batteries to generate enough power for the test. She slipped into the Atlantic from Portsmouth Naval Shipyard on the New Hampshire coast and hit twenty-nine knots during her high-speed run. Classified studies by *Albacore*'s design team concluded that submarines of the future built along *Albacore*'s lines and powered by nuclear reactors theoretically could achieve speeds approaching fifty knots. That was sixty miles per hour in highway speed! The military potential was staggering: a weapons platform capable of running submerged indefinitely at fast speeds. Such a weapon would have changed the course of World War II.

Albacore's impressive performance had made *Nautilus*'s demonstration of nuclear power all the more potent. *Nautilus* was not a fast submarine. Rickover had employed the conservatism of a pioneer in her design. He packaged his first low-powered reactor in the hull of a World War II–style submarine. *Nautilus* had not been intended as the ideal sub. The great achievement was the power plant.

The submarine prototypes built after *Albacore* and *Nautilus*, with few exceptions, were attempts to marry nuclear propulsion to an *Albacore* hull form. The first occurred in 1959 when U.S.S. *Skipjack* went to sea, a nuclear-powered porpoise. Rickover's new reactor was twice as powerful as *Nautilus*'s plant, but it was not powerful enough to push *Skipjack* at sixty miles an hour. That would take a long time and a lot more reactor development. During her sea trials, *Skipjack* had hit twenty-nine knots submerged, nearly thirty-five miles per hour. It was a great start.

Conquering noise was more subtle. Nuclear submarines were inherently noisy due to their high-speed turbines, pumps, and gears. The turbines screamed at as much as six thousand revolutions per minute, one hundred turns every second, a speed that was useless to a ship unless its power could be converted to the stronger and slower rotating speeds that get the best thrust from giant propellers. It was the same principle that made it impossible to pedal a ten-speed bike downhill in low gear. Thus, the turbines fed a series of "reduction" gears to reduce the rotation, but keep the power. The largest was the "bull" gear that nearly filled the diameter of the ship and turned at the speed of the propeller beyond the hull. It was a beautifully engineered system, but the noise of all those gears and turbines was the noise of an underwater locomotive.

There were a thousand things you had to do to kill noise. U.S.S. *Thresher* was the navy's first sound laboratory—as well as the first deep-diving submarine—when she went out for sea trials in 1961. Where *Skipjack*'s turbines and other machinery had been bolted or welded directly to the hull, *Thresher*'s turbines and giant reduction gears were "sound-mounted" on rubber-encased decks. Some machinery decks were suspended ingeniously so the vibrating equipment was totally isolated from the hull. The propeller shaft was fitted with a "resonance changer" that used a layer of pressurized oil in a specially designed bearing to block the incoming vibration from each propeller blade as it chopped through the ocean. Inside the ship, pipes were severed and short lengths of rubber hoses inserted to break "sound circuits" to the hull, and pipes that carried water under high pressure were wrapped in insulation.

Thresher was a triumph for the advocates of greater stealth and greater depth. Her hull steel and frames were fabricated from a "high-yield" steel alloy that could withstand ocean pressures of up to eighty thousand pounds per square inch. This steel was first introduced in *Skipjack*, but its thickness was increased to give *Thresher* a safe diving range to thirteen hundred feet and a crush depth of two thousand feet, nearly double the depth range of previous classes. Then she was lost. All submarine construction was halted during the inquiry; afterwards, the navy established more stringent welding standards for all pipe systems that were subjected to deep ocean pressures.

Research went forward and new classes evolved. *Thresher* was replaced by *Permit* and the *Permit* class gave way to the *Sturgeon* class. But as the navy added size and weight to the new classes— weight from thicker hull steel, sound-quieting material, larger sonars—the U.S. submarine fleet lost precious speed. The twenty-nine knots of *Skipjack* had dropped embarrassingly to twenty-five knots in *Sturgeon*. It seemed a narrow distinction to anyone outside the navy, but to a warship commander, each knot of speed gave him a crucial tactical advantage over his adversary. *Sturgeon* was forty feet longer and sixteen hundred tons heavier than *Skipjack*, yet both were propelled by the same Westinghouse S5W reactor. While the Soviets had been working on increasing the speeds of their nuclear submarines, the United States had been working inadvertently in the opposite direction.

It was time to reclaim speed, Kern explained to Nunan. The greatest advantage in a submarine dogfight wasn't silent running, it wasn't depth. It was speed—speed for sprinting toward the Russian wolf packs, for getting bearings and cross bearings for torpedo shots faster than the other guy, for outdistancing incoming torpedoes, and for getting the hell out of there when all the fish had been fired. After all, the best weapon against a submarine was another submarine.

Throughout history, speed had been crucial: "I wish to have no connection with any ship that does not sail fast for I intend to go in harms [*sic*] way," John Paul Jones had said.

Kern didn't think the powerful General Electric S6G reactor Rickover wanted was the best way to reclaim that speed, but he told Nunan that he was supporting Rickover's request for one ship.

Nunan was frowning. He was not convinced. He said he believed Rickover just liked to build big expensive drag racers and that he was a desk-bound admiral who didn't know what sub driving was all about. So that was that. Nunan had once considered throwing Rickover a bone, but that was no longer possible. Now Nunan was looking for an alternative.

Tell me about the Conform submarine, Nunan said.

Kern summarized the design work. He told Nunan that the Conform group was focusing most of its attention on an advanced attack submarine powered by a natural circulation reactor Rickover had developed with G.E. for the stealth submarine, U.S.S. *Narwhal*. It was a very exciting concept to Kern because such a submarine would be only slightly larger than the current classes, but she would develop a third more horsepower. She would be both quiet and capable of high-speed runs in the thirty-knot range.

Nunan for the first time was not drumming his fingers on the arm of his chair. He was jotting down some notes and asking more questions. This could be what the boss was looking for. Johnny Foster did not want to pay for two submarines—first Rickover's, and then a Conform submarine. If it was clear in advance that Rickover's high-speed drag racer was not the submarine of choice for the next class, Foster had told Nunan he did not want to waste the money. He wanted bolder submarine concepts and innovations, and Nunan believed Kern was much more innovative.

It was just before lunchtime on the holiday when Nunan got up and announced they were going in to see Foster.

"What the hell are we doing building two submarines?" Foster asked sharply as soon as Kern was seated. "We don't have that kind of money, we don't have the resources or the talent." If the navy wanted a new submarine, Foster said, it seemed to him that the navy could come up with a single optimum design. "We don't have the money to waste!" he repeated.

Alarmed at what he was hearing, Kern looked for an opening to respond. He was a little rattled. The navy, he said, traditionally had built prototypes before building new classes. *Albacore* and *Nautilus* were examples. They led to *Skipjack*. *Narwhal* was a prototype for the natural circulation reactor. The two-step process had proved itself the most efficient way to test each new combination of machinery. The prototypes were not experimental submarines, Kern added, but full combatants, so they were not a waste of money. *Nautilus* was still out there carrying a load of torpedoes.

But there was no time for prototypes, Foster cut him off. The Soviet buildup was real and the navy had to get moving to design a new class of submarines that would meet the threat. If the navy fiddled around with a Rickover prototype, a prototype that seemed flawed to Foster, it would delay design of a new class and the navy would not get high-technology submarines deployed before the end of the 1970s.

Kern took a deep breath for what he knew was his last try to get through to the impatient Foster. There was no penalty to the navy, he said, for going ahead on both fronts. A Conform design could be ready for construction beginning in 1971, contemporaneous to Rickover's prototype. And the bottom line was the Conform submarine would break thirty knots, just like Rickover's larger ship, but Conform would cost a lot less. But if Foster kept on insisting on building a new class without first building Rickover's high-speed prototype, Rickover would almost certainly try to take over the design of the new class— and Foster would get the submarine he did not want. If Foster was not careful, the navy was going to end up with an entire class of submarines based on a conservative Rickover design. The navy might end up spending twice as much money for a submarine of tremendous size and horsepower, but only marginally faster than the current class.

Foster could not seem to understand Kern's message, or else— Kern believed—he refused to understand it, perhaps thinking he could defeat Rickover in Congress. Kern silently wished him luck.

But Foster had done something shrewd, Kern realized. He had agreed there was a Soviet threat. He had agreed that speed was important, but at the same time he told the navy he would not go along with its plans. They were wasteful and the navy was not thinking big enough. He had embraced the goals of the navy on the one hand and on the other rejected its plan of action. Foster had few options. It was clear he felt he was unable to pay for two submarines before deciding which one was best. There was little ground to give in the defense budget. McNamara had laid down the law and would be gone in another week. Clark Clifford had been appointed to replace him, but Clifford was not going to walk in the door and take a swing at Rickover's jaw. Clifford, a brain truster who had been a power in Washington since he served under Harry Truman, was smarter than that.

Foster was in the kind of political bind that cried out for the only strategy that made any sense: stall.

After the meeting, as Kern retreated down the long empty Pentagon corridor, he knew that the civilians were going to pit the Conform submarine against Rickover's prototype. If that was the case, Kern knew he was dead.

"Fish oil?"

"Yes, Senator, fish oil," the Pentagon's chief scientist said, explaining why he had not yet approved funding for Rickover's high-speed submarine. Foster had been frenetically searching for the innovative ideas he could offer to Congress as proof that Rickover's boat was an Edsel in the defense budget, and he had seized upon the navy's classified fish oil project.

It was the search for the non-Newtonian fluid, something to make the apple fall faster to earth, and the fact that such a research project existed had been enough for Foster. Navy scientists studying the secretions of various species of fish had found that a thin coating of oil on the scales of some species enhanced their speed through the water by cutting down on the frictional drag across the surface of their bodies. The scientists had duplicated the secretions in chemistry labs and produced a synthetic long-chain molecule that was the chemical equivalent of fish oil.

The idea, Foster explained to the senators, was to store the fish oil in tanks aboard nuclear submarines and mechanically secrete it over the hull when a burst of speed was needed in battle. The experiments indicated that the present classes of nuclear submarines, if well greased by fish oil, might be able to approach thirty knots—until they ran out.

It had been a good sell, but the senators were not interested. What did Rickover think? they wanted to know.

"I have discussed this very, very briefly with Admiral Rickover," Foster replied. "It is my understanding that he feels that this is very much 'blue sky.' I must confess," he added too quickly, "I have not looked into the details of it, and am in the process of doing so."

The senators were on to the stall and they weren't going to stand for it from an administration whose defense policy was based on fish oil.

By the middle of March 1968, Senator John Stennis had begun a series of closed-door hearings to consider how Congress should respond to the Soviet submarine threat. Though the hearings feigned objectivity, their conclusion had been predetermined by the close working relationship between Stennis's staff and the staff of Rickover's Naval Reactors Branch. The lead-off witness on March 13 had been the baritone, Captain Bradley. He gave The Briefing, followed— actually interrupted—by Rickover, who seized every opportunity to instruct the members that a history lesson was in the making.

"The stories you always get in your Preparedness Committee are that we are the most powerful, most omniscient country on earth; that we do everything better than anyone else, that we can have Sputniks up first, that we are always going to be ahead of everyone. I think the lesson is that perhaps the bubble of optimism is bursting, and that you are getting much information that doesn't reflect actual conditions."

He talked about the U-boats during World War II, the fourteen million tons of shipping and the forty thousand men lost to Hitler's wolf packs. *"Unser Zukunft liegt unter dem Wasser,"* he quoted from the German military credo at the turn of the century—"Our future lies under the water." The danger was the same, if not worse, today.

"The concept of the high-speed attack submarine was thought up by me," Rickover told them. "But I have been stalemated for four years, first by the navy and now by the Department of Defense. When one goes through repeated instances of shortsightedness, sheer stupidity . . . he naturally wonders whether there is not something fundamentally wrong with the way DOD does its business."

He attacked Foster and Nunan for trying to reinvent the wheel in Rickover's reactor compartment by demanding more power. "I told Dr. Foster, that if he wanted to try out the laws of nature, he could jump off the top of the Pentagon; this would demonstrate whether the law of gravity still applies."

The first hearing, with no adversarial structure, had been like batting practice for Rickover. He railed against the McNamara era and the mandarin class of systems analysts under Dr. Enthoven and his crazy force-level study about how to defend the world with only sixty-eight submarines shooting Russians at a kill ratio of twenty-five to one.

"This is the sort of figure I would expect an academic [Enthoven had come from the Rand Corporation, a prominent defense-oriented think tank] strategist to come up with—a strategist whose field of effort is a sheet of government paper eight inches by ten and a half inches where the sea is always smooth, where there are no storms, where no one ever gets seasick, and where the only weapons you need are a divider, a ruler, a pencil and an eraser."

It had all built to Foster's appearance on the 19th. When he took his seat at the witness table at ten-fifteen in the morning, he came on fast, questioning the whole premise of high-speed submarines. "It is as if this is a competition between two manufacturers of [race cars]. The one with the [highest speed], assuming good [engine] reliability, will surely win. This is not the situation in the submarine, anti-submarine business . . . and I am not sure that we are taking even the right view of this enemy threat."

Senator Stuart Symington of Missouri, already showing irritability, interrupted him. "Do you base that concern on your knowledge of naval warfare, or on your knowledge of engineering?"

"On neither, Mr. Chairman."

"On what do you base it?"

"Just simply logic," Foster replied. We don't know enough, he continued, about whether Rickover's high-powered reactor would actually give the navy a high-speed submarine. The fundamental laws of physics in the ocean required enormous increases in power to get just a little more speed. Rickover's new reactor plant was nearly twice as large as the current one. One of Foster's big concerns was that Rickover could end up with a high-powered propulsion plant in a larger and heavier submarine that would be only a couple of knots faster at twice the cost.

"We have had a lot of testimony about this," Symington warned Foster.

"Yes, I understand."

"Is your apprehension about price the result of directives to the point where you don't want to spend the money?"

"It is not simply a matter of dollars," Foster said. "What I am saying is that [an additional] $80 million is a great deal of money to get the answer as to whether or not this boat is going to be faster."

Symington leaned forward, stern and impatient. "But Admiral Rickover wants it, doesn't he?" The rebuke in his voice filled the room.

"Yes, I understand he wants it."

"And he has some experience in the submarine field, hasn't he?"

"He certainly has, sir," answered Foster.

"Don't you think, if he wants it, and has had experience, and feels so strongly about it, as he has so expressed to this committee, that you are not risking too much of your engineering judgment by giving him one submarine to prove his point?"

Again, the issue had been hung in the illusionary frame, portraying the huge policy clash between Rickover and the Department of Defense as a fight for a single submarine. In fact, Rickover and most of the senators in that room understood that they were trying to establish a beachhead in the defense budget for a much larger submarine construction program.

Foster refused to be pinned down. He said he was awaiting the results of a number of studies that were under way, including the Conform study, and he hoped he could make a decision by July 1, when the Secretary of Defense made the final budget decisions for the fiscal year that would begin in the fall.

When he was done, Strom Thurmond's nasal South Carolina drawl was the first heard. "Dr. Foster . . . since I have been in the Senate, I have not come in contact with anyone who has impressed me as knowing more about what he is doing than Admiral Rickover."

Foster identified with Thurmond's praise, but Thurmond ignored him and kept going.

"He feels so keenly about this, Dr. Foster, that, frankly, it disturbs me. On several evenings following his testimony, my mind has reverted back to what he said that day. His demeanor, when he talked, flashed back in my mind as well. That rarely happens with people. I am very concerned about the submarine threat. He feels we should not hesitate, he has convinced me of that."

Foster said he was sorry the reservations he had just expressed had not impressed Thurmond.

"I am of the opinion," Thurmond continued, "that if we are going to stay ahead of the Soviets—whose every thought, every move, every action is to become superior to us and dominate the world—we should no longer quibble about a few million or a few hundred million dollars."

Foster knew that he could not argue with conviction so strong by men so mighty, men so willing to march over a cliff for Rickover. All Foster could do was filibuster, which he did for two more hours that day, and then for four more hours the following week. All he wanted was time: time to study the alternatives; time to put this momentous decision in perspective for a new Secretary of Defense; time to see whether there was a better way to spend the money; and time to wring a decision out of the shambles that was the Johnson administration.

But Rickover had mobilized the Congress and Foster was holding back a powerful tide. The only real question was: For how long?

They met in Barracks K, seven submarine commanders, most of whom owed their training and their commands to Rickover, and they had been given ninety days to design America's next nuclear attack submarine. Its hull number gave it a name: *SSN 688*. The only condition was that it carry the propulsion plant Rickover wanted.*

The idea of establishing a blue-ribbon commission, an ad hoc panel of experts to set the characteristics for Rickover's high-speed submarine, had emerged from Rickover's staff. Rickover quickly sold the idea to Moorer and Senator John Stennis, who formed a solid, military-congressional alliance to push the submarine through. The panel, they reasoned, was the needed response to the unrelenting scientific attack on Rickover's prototype. It would satisfy the political requirement that any major weapon have at least the appearance of consensus in the defense establishment to pick up the votes in Congress. Even Johnny Foster had said he would support setting up a panel of experts to address the scientific questions about the ideal new submarine.

But the panel Moorer and Rickover established was not what Foster had in mind, and when its work was completed, the civilians had been cleverly duped because the team gave only cursory consideration to the alternatives to Rickover's design. There was little time to do anything but validate the submarine Rickover knew he could get to sea faster than any other new sub. He knew there were design improvements in the Conform submarine that might be available in the same time frame, but Rickover was not willing to risk any of the delays that always come with new designs. He was fighting the calendar to capitalize on the political momentum he had going for him.

Moorer gave the panel the official imprimatur of the CNO, while Rickover kept a low profile by staying away. But he would be on the telephone every day giving advice to its members, who owed him their loyalty. For Rickover, the panel effectively supplanted the Conform study—without ever saying so and without disturbing its continued operation—and it would replace the independent-minded Kern with Rickover loyalists.

Moorer's deputy charged the panel members with justifying the "total employment" of a high-speed submarine in the U.S. fleet and demonstrating in as many ways as possible how vital high speed was to every aspect of a submarine's mission. The members, however, soon made the disturbing discovery that Johnny Foster had been right. Rickover's high-speed prototype was going to have trouble

---

*The members of this working group, led by Captain Joe Williams, Jr., who later became commander of submarine forces in the Atlantic, did not accept Rickover's guidance on all aspects of the high-speed prototype's design. The panel members were determined, with little support from Rickover, to improve quiet-running capabilities in any new sub for intelligence gathering and other missions. And they successfully fought Rickover to add a larger and heavier sonar system that would improve the ship's ability to detect hostile submarine forces.

breaking thirty knots—even with its increased horsepower—because it would have to be a much heavier submarine to accommodate the larger propulsion plant. The S6G reactor compartment weighed in at 1,050 tons compared to the 650-ton compartment in the current fleet. That was a lot of extra weight, and the ship was going to be sixty feet longer to balance out the weight in the engine room. The first big task of the panel was to look for excess baggage they could cut out of the ship to make her lighter. They considered taking out the auxiliary diesel and the extra air-conditioning unit Rickover had insisted on carrying over the years, but Rickover sent word that these back-up systems were not negotiable.

That left only one place where they could get the kind of weight reduction they needed: the hull itself.

And so a panel of seven submarine commanders made the fundamental and fateful compromise that would haunt the *688* class until the end of the century. They gave up what U.S. submarines had had since 1961—the ability to dive to thirteen hundred feet, the ability to run silent below the deep thermal cline where sonar beams could not penetrate and to head for the bottom to let the ocean absorb the impact of an enemy weapon.

By shaving the thickness of the hull, the panel members got most of the weight savings they were after, but they substantially narrowed the band of ocean in which the submarine could operate— to no deeper than nine hundred and fifty feet. It was less than three times the length of the submarine. Not a lot of ocean to work with, and in the holy trinity of speed, stealth, and depth, the submarine commanders had sacrificed one important attribute to acquire another.

At the time they made the decision, the panel members believed they were making a temporary trade-off on a single submarine. They also believed that after a very few years, at least by the mid-1970s, the navy would design a new class of attack boats with a new and stronger hull plating that would allow future ships to reclaim the depth they were sacrificing. They had no way of knowing these plans would fall apart.

Even the big compromise did not ensure that the submarine would exceed the thirty-knot barrier by a comfortable enough margin. Every additional knot of speed required a huge increase in power. The panel chopped down the size of the conning tower, or "sail," to further reduce drag through the water. The price they paid was the loss of one of the antennae masts carried by earlier classes. This made the *688* less capable of performing the wide range of intelligence-collection missions performed by the fleet.

Still, it was not enough. The computer simulations said the ship would barely break thirty knots, and to do so the hull would have to be perfectly smooth. So, as a final compromise, the panel removed all of the deck cleats used for docking lines and hid them in pockets recessed in the hull, making the 688s slightly more clumsy to handle in port. It was a final and minor concession, but indicative of the panel's desperation—Rickover's desperation—to guarantee that the *SSN 688* would convincingly pass the thirty-knot barrier.

When they were all done, the panel wrote up their findings in a two-volume report and the vice chairman was sent over to brief the Secretary of the Navy: "Mr. Secretary. The SSN 688 will meet the threat to the year 2000 with dramatically improved anti-submarine warfare capabilities over the 637 class and the restored speed advantage we have lost over the years. The SSN 688 will be able to achieve high speed and still have a substantial, knot-for-knot quieting advantage over the 637 class. In addition, our analysis shows the submarine will be capable of operating as an anti-submarine escort for high-value targets, such as the aircraft carrier task force, but not at the expense of its traditional anti-submarine warfare mission."

He did not mention depth.

And no one asked.

The final mugging of Johnny Foster occurred on June 21.

Going into Chet Holifield's hearing, Foster had tried about everything he could. The stall had bought some time, but not enough to get a full examination of submarine propulsion technology.

Holifield, the vice chairman of the Joint Committee on Atomic Energy, was one of Rickover's strongest supporters. He called the closed-door hearing to hammer away at Foster in the final days before the budget decisions were due from the Office of Secretary of Defense.

In his search for ammunition against Rickover, Foster had asked the staff director of the Atomic Energy Commission to review Rickover's reactor designs and determine whether less conservative designs might yield more power. But the AEC was home turf for Rickover. Its officials immediately informed Rickover what was going on and Rickover let his friends in Congress know that Foster was going behind his back. The AEC officials curtly told Foster they would conduct the study, but they wanted it understood at the outset that there were no reactor concepts on the horizon that would lead to significant reductions in the size and weight of the propulsion plant.

Holifield called Foster's tactics naive and wondered if during the days when Foster had run the Lawrence Livermore Laboratory, he would have appreciated one of his political opponents going to the staff of the lab to question Foster's judgment on nuclear weapons design. Holifield placed Foster and Rickover at the witness table together, and Rickover was at his most pugnacious in lashing Foster over his delaying tactics.

"I think the difficulty we are running into is that Dr. Foster wanted to have the perfect submarine, and the perfect submarine will come along about the same time the perfect woman comes along." In the clubby, male preserve of the closed Senate hearing, Rickover's remark brought laughter.

Foster protested that while he believed in the need for speed, he also wanted the navy to improve the "front end" systems of a new ship to make it superior against the Soviet threat.

Rickover accused him of trying to take over submarine design.

But Foster said it was his job to review new weapons. "What I have reviewed is a Soviet threat and a proposal by the navy. I have reviewed it as a proposal for a complete machine. I don't believe it is adequate. I believe the United States has the technology to make a submarine that is adequate to meet the threat." He added, almost gratuitously, that as soon as he got a few days' time, he would be able to complete his final review of the technology available for a new submarine.

"What is keeping you from having the time?" the committee's staff director asked.

Holifield answered for Foster. "It is the time he is having to spend coming up and talking to us. He explained it is taking him away from vital things which he is considering," he said, a little mockingly.

Rickover could not resist jumping in.

"Never since I have been in the navy has so much of my time and that of my senior people been taken up by useless things as it has been by these numerous studies that have come out so frequently from the Department of Defense. They keep us from doing our proper work. I am glad Dr. Foster begins to see what it means when somebody above him does the same to him once in a while."

Rickover suspected that Foster at the last minute was going to recommend that the navy build the Conform submarine powered by the natural circulation reactor. "I don't believe the issue has been made clear," Rickover said. "The navy has proposed a class of high-speed submarines to be driven by what I call the Rickover propulsion plant. The navy has backed this plant for the high-speed submarine. . . . Dr. Foster, however, is talking about possibly using the natural circulation reactor [and] making a number of studies about the rest of the propulsion plant [machinery]. . . . None of these studies is completed. . . . This is the issue and this must be made clear. He wants to delay making a choice of the type propulsion plant which will be used; the other choice cannot be available for some time. . . . He is not accepting the propulsion plant which is ready and which we know will work."

"That is simply false," Foster snapped.

But when he was asked whether he had accepted Rickover's high-powered reactor, Foster said, "No, I am not going to accept things piece by piece. I am not in the design business. I just want a vehicle that will go to sea and adequately demonstrate characteristics that are superior to the threat."

The members could not pin Foster down, but they had made it clear for the last time that the committee would authorize funds for Rickover's submarine whether or not Foster, Nitze, or Clifford asked for them.

Foster caved in a little more than a week later when the budget recommendations came down. In the end, it was a political decision. Stories were beginning to circulate in Washington about the ominous nature of the Soviet submarine threat. Congress was intent on funding *SSN 688* whether the Defense Department put the submarine in the budget or not. Why should Foster needlessly antagonize men who had the power to act without him? Without any leadership in the Pentagon, the White House, or in the navy to force Rickover to consider alternatives, Foster was powerless to stop the submarine's momentum.

The Conform submarine—and its promise—sank quickly, and no one added more water to the ship than Johnny Foster.

After the Secretary of Defense officially included *SSN 688* in the defense budget, the Deputy Secretary, Nitze, summoned Foster, Captain Kern, and the Navy Secretary to his office for a classified meeting aimed at stopping the *688* prototype from growing into a class of submarines.

The meeting was in part orchestrated by Admiral Elmo R. Zumwalt, Jr., the ambitious and increasingly powerful officer who was to become Rickover's last and greatest nemesis in the uniformed navy. In the McNamara era, Zumwalt had held the navy's Division of Systems Analysis.

Zumwalt came up through the nonnuclear side of the navy, a surface ship man who had shunned the nuclear navy because he loathed Rickover's style. The bad blood between them dated to May

1959, when Zumwalt had sought the command of one of the first nuclear-powered frigates and reported to the Naval Reactors Branch for his interview with Rickover.

"You are one of those wise, goddamned aides," Rickover had yelled at the young commander. "You've been working for your boss so long, you think you're wearing his stars. . . . You are so accustomed to seeing people come in and grovel at your boss's feet and kiss his tail that you think I'm going to do it to you." Rickover repeatedly sent Zumwalt out of the room when he did not like Zumwalt's answers and made him wait anxiously in a cell-like anteroom to be summoned back for more haranguing. After the ordeal, Rickover offered Zumwalt a command, but Zumwalt turned it down, preferring to return to the nonnuclear surface fleet, where he prospered.

Moorer knew the history and had wanted to avoid another collision between the two strong-willed men, so he had cut Zumwalt out of the circuit for reviewing the high-speed submarine project. Given half a chance, Zumwalt would have attacked it, Moorer believed Zumwalt was insulted by the end run. Before he left Washington for a new assignment in Vietnam, Zumwalt confided in Nitze that a Rickover steamroller was coming his way.

On Monday, August 19, all the players were in Nitze's office. Kern was the only person who wasn't an admiral or a presidential appointee, yet he found himself explaining the fundamentals of the Conform submarine to men who should have already understood them. Nitze asked dozens of questions. In response, Kern told the Deputy Secretary that the Conform boat would not trade away the navy's thirteen-hundred-foot diving capability in order to break thirty knots. It would also cost less than the *688*. The design team, Kern said, was going to give the Conform boat lighter gears and counter-rotating propellers—just like a torpedo's propellers—to get more speed out of a smaller package.* The Conform submarine, Kern believed, was going to be a technological masterwork.

It was as if Nitze was hearing about it for the first time. Kern wondered who the hell had been running the Pentagon for the past two years. The Conform group was more than one hundred-people strong. It was a budget item approved by the CNO and it had spent a hell of a lot of the navy's money getting preliminary designs done at the engineering department at Electric Boat.

"Is the study effort aimed toward the production of a class of submarines, beginning in 1971?" Nitze asked.

---

*The little experimental submarine USS Albacore had increased its initial top speed of 29 knots to 33 knots after being fitted with counter-rotating propellers.

"Yes, sir," Kern replied.

"Do I correctly understand that the navy's plan is to build one experimental prototype of the *688* and then build a class in 1971 drawing on the Conform study?"

Before Kern could answer, Foster interrupted. That was not the navy's plan, Foster said. Rather, the plan was to build a class of submarines based on the *SSN 688* design and continue production of a *688* class to the mid-seventies. Conform could perhaps contribute to the later design effort in the next decade. Foster always said he did not want two submarines. If the Congress was going to shove the *688* down his throat, there was nothing to do but dump the Conform design.

Kern just sat and watched. He was crestfallen, angry, and disgusted all at once. He had listened to Foster in total disbelief. Rickover had completely reneged on their agreement and Foster had suddenly bailed out on his commitment to building a superior high-technology submarine. The old man and his congressional cabal had won. Kern could not fight for Conform without attacking Rickover and the *688* in front of the civilian leadership of the Pentagon. To do that would have been the worst kind of treason against the navy. And so he sat in silent anguish as Nitze expressed bewilderment at Foster's statement. It was obvious the situation needed clarifying, Nitze said.

Without Foster's support, Nitze was not going to take on the Congress by himself. Nitze was a realist who knew that it was too late to break Rickover's momentum. There was one more meeting, but at the end of it Nitze had seemed at a loss for something to say and had gone off about how the navy needed to create a "critical mass" between the Defense Department and the shipbuilding industry for the construction effort ahead. Kern thought Nitze had gone over to the Land of Oz.

In the fall, Richard Nixon defeated the Democrats. Nixon was an old friend and admirer of Hyman Rickover; Rickover had accompanied Vice President Nixon to the Soviet Union during the 1950s as scientific adviser. He had played strongly to Nixon's political instincts during the trip—once pulling him away from a sickle-and-hammer backdrop during a photo session and another time urging him to stop his motorcade after one of the security cars struck a child on the streets of Moscow. Over the years the relationship had remained strong and, during the campaign, Rickover had made sure Nixon was briefed on the Soviet submarine threat—and Rickover's proposal to meet the threat.

By the middle of 1969, the Nixon administration had requested funding for twelve *688*-class submarines over the first three years of what it projected would be a long building program. Rickover had won beyond his wildest dreams.

In appreciation for the men who supported the *SSN 688* class in Congress, Rickover, at the suggestion of his aide, David Leighton, recommended to the navy that each ship of the new class be named for the American cities represented by Rickover's congressional patrons. "Fish don't vote," Leighton pointed out, and Rickover smiled. He began by honoring his friend from California, Chet Holifield, whose hearing in June had given the high-speed submarine its final boost.

The first ship of the *688* class would be christened U.S.S. *Los Angeles*.

Right after the election, the submarine desk in the navy's shipbuilding command was broken up and its functions dispersed among other sections. Never again would the sum of its parts challenge Rickover's control over nuclear submarine design. Kern, who had never worried about rank in his life, would never have to worry about it in the future after Rickover tagged him as the obstructionist who had tried to slow down the *688*s. Kern was transferred to Portsmouth Naval Shipyard. Three years later he retired, privately accusing Rickover of selling the navy an inferior class of submarines whose higher speed would be offset by the disadvantages of shallow running and whose hull was carrying around unnecessary weight to absorb shocks at thirteen hundred feet—a depth the ship would never see.

The defense contractors who participated in the preliminary design work on the Conform submarine had their funding cut off, and some time later, the thousands of pages of files, technical studies, and reports on the fast, deep-diving stealth submarine called Conform were burned.

II

COVER-UP

The noontime air was crisp on a spring day in 1971 when Hilliard W. Paige pushed through the turnstile into the wind tunnel that was Lexington Avenue. He would have to rush along the crowded midtown sidewalks to keep his lunch date at Rockefeller Plaza with the new chief executive of General Dynamics Corporation.

Paige, known to his friends as Hilly, was tall, thin, an avid skiier at fifty-one. He had boyish good looks, but had been spared handsomeness by an overall inquisitive bearing. He came from a New England engineering family. His father was a navy submarine designer who had gone on to become the chief engineer at the Electric Boat Company before dying suddenly of a heart attack in 1940. After engineering school, young Paige had gone straight into the General Electric Company, where he had risen to be one of four senior vice presidents under the chairman of the board.

As he walked, Paige eyed the narrow band of sky above him. It seemed farther away than usual and he frowned because the weather was one of the things you could never count on in Manhattan. The morning radio could herald clear skies throughout New England, but somehow, by the time you got into town, a gale was lashing the moving populace and the temperature seemed ten degrees colder than the season.

But Paige liked the lunchtime rhythm of the city. He liked the frenetic energy in the streets. The sun seldom reached the damp and tumultuous corridors between the high office towers, but there was light and sound in a million strains that gave the place intensity. It was the energy of commerce and money, and you could see it in the faces and stride of the managers and the executives who passed by.

Paige had flourished in the G.E. system. Considered effective and insightful, he had been running the company's aerospace and computer divisions, which contributed about $1.5 billion to G.E.'s annual sales. In the past year, however, Paige had lost contentment and felt he had been promoted beyond his usefulness in the upper reaches of the corporate ivory tower. He had arrived there at a time when chairman Fred J. Borch was about to retire and the politicking among the contenders for the throne was intense and uncomfortable for Paige. Beyond that, Paige was feeling the strong tug of his first-grade son, whom he felt he was losing to the demands of his schedule and to the long daily commute between Greenwich and Grand Central.

Paige set a brisk stride. His mind was not on his own company, but on the drama that had recently played out in the nearby corporate offices of General Dynamics, a drama that had thrust a strong and dynamic new leader to the top of the troubled corporation. Paige knew this man. He believed he knew him well—well enough, possibly, to throw in with him. He would see.

General Dynamics had been a company suffering from a fractious struggle over who would control it.

A group of investors headed by the aged Chicago financier Henry Crown had the previous year regained the upper hand in the boardroom. It had been a long fight back to power for Crown. In 1966, he had lost out in a dispute with management, and it had taken four years to reclaim what he told his friends was the "Crown Jewel" of his investment portfolio—the company he would remake as the giant of the defense industry, General Dynamics.

It was a hybrid corporation, as much a creature of the government as commercial enterprise. Its stock was traded on the New York Exchange and it answered to the investor community in every way except that it was within the cloistered sector of companies that depended almost exclusively on the U.S. Department of Defense as the primary market for its line of products. The government actually owned some of its production lines and leased them to General Dynamics under operating agreements to produce certain weapons. Under these arrangements, the company's only asset was the government contract itself and the workforce assembled to complete the task. That made General Dynamics a living appendage of the defense budget. Its corporate staff in New York was tiny, around two hundred fifty accounting and contract specialists. All of the action was at the division level, where plant managers had enjoyed long years of autonomy in dealing with military officials who planned and purchased weapons.

The men who built General Dynamics did not look at the world through the same lens as the rest of American industry. Market share and competition were irrelevant when it came to building critical military technologies. The customer was the Pentagon, an office building as large as any in the world, filled with men who served short terms at the top of the U.S. Army, Navy, Air Force, and Marine Corps. As a group, they tended to want new weapons by yesterday, and they paid for them with a check that was processed by a largely supportive Congress because, in the post–World War II era, the defense industry's fortune at any time was tied directly to the perception of an ever-increasing military threat posed by the Soviet Union.

On the whole, it was an ascending industry, its market forces also manipulable without the penalty of the anti-trust laws. The Darwinian currents that coldly strangled incompetence and inefficiency in an unending evolution on Wall Street could be restrained and channeled in the defense industry, especially where it was deemed to be in the national interest. Where there was competition, it was tempered by the Defense Department's vested interest in preserving and maintaining the industrial base for weapons manufacture. A contract lost to a competitor in one line of weapons could be offset by redirected contracts from another line. That was the difference between defense and the rest of the private sector.

General Dynamics from its inception had sought to dominate the defense sector and was slow to venture into the broader commercial market in any significant way. The corporation was born out of the Electric Boat Company, the submarine manufacturer at Groton, Connecticut, whose only customer was the navy. The parent conglomerate was conceived by industrialist John Jay Hopkins, who foresaw the postwar era as an era of armed peace in which defense industries would prosper. In the merger fever of the early fifties, Hopkins assembled a conglomerate that he hoped would become the General Motors of defense, and gave it a powerful, sweeping label for its line of weapons: General Dynamics. It was a name that conjured images of mammoth war machines rumbling across the plains and through the seas; of hot steel forgings and blast furnaces; of bomber squadrons eclipsing the sun; and of industrial armies riveting, hammering, and welding on assembly lines that stretched to the horizon.

Before cancer killed him in 1957, Hopkins had completed a string of acquisitions that endowed General Dynamics with aircraft and missile production facilities in Fort Worth, Pomona, and San Diego, as well as the submarine production yard at Groton. At the end of the decade, the company had orders for the B-58 bomber, the F-106 fighter, the Atlas-Centaur missile booster, and the lion's share of the navy's nuclear attack submarines and Polaris missile submarines. Thus Hopkins's early enterprise had quickly propelled General Dynamics to the top of the list as the nation's largest defense contractor.

It did not stay there long, however. After Hopkins died, the company outran the capabilities of its managers, some programs were canceled, and others ran into production problems that swallowed profits. The company fell behind its competitors in sales to the government. General Dynamics was in sore need of working capital when its board approached Henry Crown in 1959 to propose merging General Dynamics with the Crown family business, Material Service Corporation. Crown brought cash to the deal and took as payment for Material Service a large block of convertible preference stock that gave him four seats on General Dynamics' board of directors.

Soon after Crown stepped in, however, General Dynamics took one of the largest financial baths in history. It rolled out its line of Convair 880 and 990 jetliners only to find that its biggest customer, Trans World Airlines, was financially incapable of taking delivery. It was the largest program loss in the history of the aerospace industry, and before it was over, General Dynamics had written off $425 million. At that point, Crown could not afford to quit, and in the wake of the debacle, he put his personal fortune behind General Dynamics. He set up and chaired an executive committee of the board, and recruited a new management team headed by Roger Lewis, the executive vice president of Pan American World Airways. Together, they set about rebuilding the company.

Most people who knew Crown, and knew him well, called him "the colonel." He liked the military affectation that dated to his rank as a military procurement officer during World War II. By 1971, Crown was a spry septuagenarian, courtly, somewhat reclusive, who could be seen on most days leaning into the wind coming off Lake Michigan as he walked from the curb where his limousine dropped him to his office at the Mercantile Exchange Building on Chicago's Loop. The son of Jewish immigrants—a Lithuanian father and Latvian mother—Crown had made his first fortune putting together the largest concrete and building material concern in the world, Material Service Corporation, and his succeeding fortunes by investing the proceeds in other ventures. He founded the sand-and-gravel business in 1919; thereafter, he and "the family"—as he referred to the sons and relatives who accepted his patriarchy—acquired vast holdings in the coal reserves of southern Illinois and a portfolio of large stock holdings in TWA, Swift & Company, Esmark Incorporated, Chicago Rock

Island, and Pacific Railroad, and Hilton Hotels, whose owner, Conrad Hilton, was a longtime friend of the family. Crown traded real estate from the farmlands of the Midwest and Southwest to the canyons of New York, where he had bought and sold both the Empire State Building and the Waldorf-Astoria Hotel.

Though he was unique in his energy and achievement, he fit the profile of so many immigrant success stories in that he was intensely shy, showed discomfort at the ostentatious trappings of his wealth (he would not use the Rolls-Royce his wife, Gladys, had presented him one birthday), believed deeply in the importance of family, and surrendered to his workaholic tendencies even in old age. It had taken a lot of long days to salvage General Dynamics after the Convair loss. The company had gone to the brink of bankruptcy, its lenders so unnerved that they had attached accounts receivable as an added hedge against default.

Under Roger Lewis, General Dynamics showed a mixed performance. In 1964, Lewis convinced the board to purchase Bethlehem Steel's Quincy shipyard south of Boston for $5 million, but Crown had opposed the shipyard acquisition, arguing that the company still was too strapped for cash to finance further expansion. Nonetheless, Lewis asserted his independence and pushed the shipyard deal through the board. Within a year, the relationship between Henry Crown and General Dynamics deteriorated dramatically. Roger Lewis announced the company was going to repurchase the preference shares of the Crown group on the board using an obscure authority conferred by the corporation's by-laws.

Ostensibly, the repurchase plan would save the company higher dividend expenses, but to the financial community, it looked as if the management team feared Crown was going to convert his preference stock into a larger block of common shares to consolidate his control over the corporation. Roger Lewis's chief financial officer, John A. Sargent, masterminded the plan and pushed it despite Crown's assurances that he was not going to convert the preference shares even if it meant taking a multi-million-dollar tax penalty. But the board members, weighted by a majority of Lewis appointees, voted to repurchase the shares.

On March 16, 1966, the board met on the top floor of Rockefeller Plaza for the final vote to repurchase the remaining $49 million block of preferred shares. Crown looked into the faces of the directors and reassured them of his good intentions. He would not convert. The company could not afford doing what it proposed to do. But the directors voted with management and stripped Crown of his ownership leverage. Roger Lewis invited Crown to stay on the board, but he stood and left the meeting, refusing to participate where he was denied his investment. Most hurtfully, Crown was forced to walk away from the family business, Material Service, which had been merged with General Dynamics.

As the financial world was coming to understand four years later, Roger Lewis had made a big mistake by locking out Henry Crown, who liked to say that he had nurtured Material Service from infancy and raised its managers as part of the family. With Crown gone, General Dynamics began dismantling some of the old Crown interests, selling off some coal holdings to generate cash, and imposing stronger corporate control, causing some of the old Crown stalwarts to flee. Crown owned the Mercantile Exchange Building, where the company was headquartered, and kept his own office there even after he lost control. Family meant everything to Colonel Crown—and Material Service was family. What General Dynamics was doing to his family company was horrendous, Crown told his friends. Horrendous. It was one of his expressions.

Crown had been out of General Dynamics little more than a year when some of the institutional holders of the company's stock inquired whether he was interested in buying. The offering price was good, sometimes a couple of points below the market and, at first, Crown told his friends that he was buying only because it was a good investment. But the stock was in decline and no one else was buying. Crown continued picking up large and small blocks over the next two years while the stock remained in a down trend. Crown's intentions never seemed totally clear, but Roger Lewis had seen it coming, and the colonel had been less than subtle in sending his estranged chief executive messages: "Tell Roger I just bought another two hundred and fifty thousand shares of his stock," Crown announced one day to a Material Service executive sharing an elevator ride in the Mercantile Building.

Some said that Crown made up his mind to mount the final assault in 1969 after the untimely death of his eldest son, Robert, from a heart attack at the age of forty-nine. He may have been looking for a project to combat his grief, or the loss may have intensified the colonel's resolve to end General Dynamics' mistreatment of the family business. But later that year, Crown brought in an outside investor to bolster the family's purchasing power. The outsider was grocery magnate Nathan Cummings of Consolidated Foods, and over a luncheon in a Paris café, Crown and Cummings came to an agreement by which Cummings would contribute as much as $15 million in additional capital for a final series of joint stock purchases. On New Year's Eve 1969, exactly ten years after Crown had merged Material Service with General Dynamics, Crown telephoned Roger Lewis to inform him that the Crown group had acquired seventy thousand additional shares to put them over the 10 percent mark in ownership of the company's common stock. Lewis reacted politely, but every day brought him more evidence that the end was near.

Four months into the new year, the Crown group acquired about 18 percent of General Dynamics, the largest single ownership block, representing an investment of more than $60 million. Crown's position was enough to force Roger Lewis to come to terms. "We never have gone where we have not been cordially invited," Crown told an interviewer just before the annual meeting. Yet, "We know from Mr. Lewis's reports that the company hasn't done well. . . . I still think that with proper help, I hope he can do a reasonably good job."

Crown took the six seats on the board and worked quietly to consolidate his position. With less than a numerical majority, Crown did not want to force the issue of Lewis's job, which Lewis insisted on keeping, so the colonel's initial strategy had been to hire a president and chief operating officer to serve under Roger Lewis. "I don't know that I am particularly anxious for challenges," he told an interviewer. "I've had my share of challenges in my lifetime. I hope this develops not to be too much of a challenge."

It was around that time that Crown's headhunter came privately to Hilliard Paige and asked him if he was interested in the job. Paige inferred that after a decent interval the job would expand into the chairmanship, but the headhunter had not been explicit. Paige listened to the headhunter's pitch over lunch and decided immediately that he was not interested in an offer that was filled with so much uncertainty. If Paige were going to leave General Electric after thirty years, he wanted more security than the number two spot on a marked management team.

Later in the year, in October 1970, Paige had read that David S. Lewis, Jr., the president and heir apparent at McDonnell Douglas Corporation, had been lured away from the St. Louis aerospace firm to become the chairman and chief executive officer of General Dynamics.

Roger Lewis, who was no relation, was demoted to the number two position as president and vice chairman.

Paige had smiled when he read the announcement, realizing that his friend David Lewis had made a better deal, and that Crown must have wanted David Lewis badly enough to force the issue of control with the majority of directors. That did not surprise Paige, because David Lewis was one of the most successful aerospace executives in the country.

And so on that spring day in 1971, Hilliard Paige arrived at Rockefeller Plaza to talk to David Lewis about something Paige had never before seriously entertained—leaving General Electric after three decades. Paige was a team player, but over the previous months, the competition at G.E. among senior vice presidents to succeed chairman Fred Borch had grown so intense that it had obliterated any chance for a collegial atmosphere. Paige had gone to Borch and talked to him about his disappointment and about the rivalry. He confided that he did not see himself in Borch's chair. "All the better," Borch told him. That would make Paige the one member of senior management who was not constantly trying to undercut the others. But Paige had taken no encouragement from the assessment.

General Dynamics was an attractive company to Paige because most of its business was in basic engineering fields: aircraft, missile, nuclear submarine, and surface ship construction. Its problems required hands-on management. And Paige had always considered David Lewis to be one of the most charming and engaging personalities in the business world. He was highly intelligent and insightful, yet also warm and self-effacing: he had a way of disarming people with his Charleston manners. Paige and Lewis had come along similar career paths in the preceding ten years: Paige running General Electric's aerospace business and Lewis running the aircraft empire of James S. McDonnell. The two men had worked together on several joint ventures, and Paige had sold a lot of G.E. electronics to McDonnell Douglas for its lines of attack fighters and bombers.

David Lewis was waiting for Paige at the door to his office. They exchanged warm greetings. Lewis was of medium height, shorter than Paige, and combed his straight, graying hair neatly to the right. He had a set of eyes that made fond, brotherly contact, and his gracious South Carolina drawl set Paige immediately at ease.

As they settled down to lunch in the sumptuous executive suite, Lewis announced that Rockefeller Plaza was only temporary headquarters for General Dynamics. There was no reason for the company to be headquartered in New York. It had no operations there. It had as many employees in Texas and California as it did in New England, so he had decided to move everything out to St. Louis, which would be a more central location from which to run the company. Paige marveled at Lewis's ability to just pick up the company and move it. The corporate staff was not that large, about two hundred fifty people, but in effect it could look rather arrogant for a new chief executive to move the corporate headquarters halfway across the continent just so he did not have to sell his house or change country clubs. But David Lewis was on top of the world, and all Paige could think was more power to him.

The two men laughed and seemed to be enjoying each other's company. Paige was curious at how Henry Crown had convinced Lewis to leave McDonnell Douglas, where Lewis clearly had been tapped as the next chairman. Lewis leaned back into the plush upholstery and smiled. When Lewis was selling—and that's what he was doing at that moment—he liked to tell mocking stories about himself. And so he told Paige about the time that Eastern Airlines was threatening to sue McDonnell Douglas and Jim McDonnell had gathered his managers and lawyers in his office to plot strategy. McDonnell was a vigorous man who had passed his sixty-fifth birthday without even blinking and at seventy was still going strong. David Lewis was a fair-haired boy who had risen from aerodynamics engineer to be president of the company, but Mr. Mac didn't leave a lot of room for a president. He was all over everything. Lewis had started his work days at seven-thirty every morning so he could get something done before Mr. Mac came in at ten o'clock and pulled everybody into his orbit for the rest of the day, which lasted until seven or eight o'clock at night. That was Mr. Mac's constitution. McDonnell had told David Lewis that he would be the next chairman, but the date had never been set and it was always clear that McDonnell was going to be running the company as long as he felt good.

There they were in McDonnell's office, Lewis related, and someone started talking about Eastern's lawyer in Miami and whether he meant business with the lawsuit, when McDonnell announced that he was going to call "Uncle Fred" in Miami to get his opinion of Eastern's lawyer.

"Uncle Fred?" Lewis had asked with a sick feeling in his stomach.

It turned out that Uncle Fred was in his 101st year. Mr. Mac got his uncle on the speaker telephone and they had a good time visiting. Afterwards, Lewis couldn't even remember whether McDonnell had learned anything about Eastern's lawyer from Uncle Fred. All he could remember was that when Mr. Mac got off the phone, he said, "Good old Uncle Fred. He's still going strong. That's just like us McDonnells."

Lewis chuckled and smiled at Paige. "Mr. Mac said later that he figured it was at that moment I decided to leave the company." Paige laughed, feeling a kinship with Lewis over the shared confidence.

Soon after, Crown had offered Lewis the job as president of General Dynamics, but Lewis had said he was only interested in the chairmanship. Paige tried to calculate how many weeks after his own encounter with Crown's headhunter this Crown-Lewis meeting must have occurred; he decided not to mention anything about his own flirtation with Crown because it might sound competitive and that was the last thing Paige wanted to inject into the conversation. Crown had then gone to the closely divided board and convinced the members that David Lewis was the solution to their problems.

The problems—and the marvelous opportunities—were on Lewis's mind, he told Paige. There was a huge amount of Pentagon business coming down the pike and he had to get busy to position General Dynamics to capture a big share of it. He knew how to beat the competition because he had been the competition. McDonnell Douglas had been beating the socks off of its competitors for years because it had made a science out of developing advanced concepts for new air force fighters and bombers. Lewis had helped set up McDonnell's advanced design group in the early 1950s: out of that group came the F-4 Phantom series, the workhorse attack bomber of the Vietnam War and the most successful airplane procurement since World War II, with more than five thousand units sold.

In the navy, Lewis continued, Admiral Rickover had congressional support to build two large fleets of new submarines, an attack-boat fleet and a new generation of larger ballistic missile submarines. The potential to pull a big chunk of that business—billions of dollars of business—into Electric Boat was very real, and Lewis was sure that Admiral Rickover saw the experienced workforce at Electric Boat was an important element in the navy building program, even though other shipyards were in the competition.

Paige was fascinated to hear Lewis mention Electric Boat and Rickover. As a college student, Paige had spent his summers working at the Groton shipyard. He was a mechanics helper on the waterfront when they were building the diesel attack boats for the war, and one summer he cleaned out the blueprint room, which gave him a chance to rummage through the historical record of the underwater machines built there since the nineteenth century. After joining G.E., Paige's first assignment was to help Rickover's electrical engineers find a way to locate the new German mines that could be triggered by the propeller noises of Allied ships. It had been a high-pressure, urgent project, made all the more intense by Rickover's tempestuous style of dealing with defense contractors. Later, at the end of the war and in the aftermath of the Manhattan Project, Paige and two dozen G.E. engineers began work on a naval nuclear propulsion plant for Rickover. Then Paige had seen Rickover up close as a shrewd and pragmatic bureaucratic operator, who would fly in cases of hard liquor on the G.E. corporate plane so he could lubricate his navy bosses when they came down to inspect his reactor project at Oak Ridge, Tennessee.

General Electric, Paige believed, had found a successful formula for handling Rickover, whose goal was always to deal with the most senior man he could find in any contractor's organization. If the chairman of the board would return his call, then Rickover would only deal with the chairman. If not, he tried the next man down the line. G.E.'s top management had figured this out and had laid down the law with Rickover. He would have to deal with the general manager of G.E.'s nuclear laboratory. If he did not like the general manager, then he could suggest a candidate for the job who was satisfactory. But under no circumstances would he be allowed to undercut the general manager's authority.

The system had worked fine and Paige believed such a system was the only way you could deal with Rickover, because he bullied people if you let him.

Paige was therefore surprised to hear that David Lewis had walked right into Rickover's trap upon taking over General Dynamics. Lewis told it as another self-effacing story, his "baptism" at the hands of Rickover. When it was over, Paige realized he was too late to give Lewis some good advice, so he just kept it to himself.

Lewis had gone to Washington to introduce himself around the Pentagon as the new chairman of General Dynamics and to get acquainted with the staff of General Dynamics' lobbying office. Lewis always had supported a strong Washington presence and understood that the Washington office was as important as any other part of the organization. That's where most of the intelligence came from on new contracts, on congressional authorizations, and on Pentagon planning. Plenty of small favors could be done for congressmen and congressional staffers from the Washington office and a lot of goodwill sown with campaign contributions to the men who exert influence over the defense budget.

Lewis had been dealing with Pentagon officials for years, especially those who made the decisions to buy jet fighters and bombers for the air force and navy. But he had never done business with Rickover—and Rickover looked as if he would be General Dynamics' most important customer. Lewis chuckled as he recalled how he had telephoned Rickover's secretary.

"I'm going to be in Washington and I'd like to come by and meet Admiral Rickover," Lewis had said to the woman.

With a quavering voice, Rickover's secretary replied, "Oh, I don't make appointments for Admiral Rickover, but call me back tomorrow and I'll let you know."

Lewis had called the next day, but the secretary was even less encouraging. "Well, he's very busy, so when you get to town, call and we'll see if we can work you in."

When Lewis had arrived on the shuttle flight to Washington National Airport, he went straight to a pay telephone and dialed Rickover's number.

"Oh," the secretary said. "Mr. Lewis, yes. Well, I'll have to see if Admiral Rickover can see you."

The next voice that came on the line was Rickover's. "What the hell do you want?"

"Admiral Rickover?" Lewis said meekly into the receiver and then introduced himself. But suddenly, he went silent and an expression of shock and amazement covered his face. He had barely gotten the words "General Dynamics" out of his mouth when Rickover had shouted into the telephone: "BLOOD SUCKERS ON THE FACE OF HUMANITY!"

It had just gotten worse after that.

"I'll be goddamned," Rickover stormed. "This is just what I would expect from General Dynamics. Here you are in Washington. Your company doesn't know what it's doing. It cheats the government. It can't run a shipyard. It's full of loafers and idlers and here is the new chief executive officer and what is he doing? Is he trying to clean up the company? Is he trying to stop his people from screwing up? No, he is glad-handing around Washington like a politician."

Rickover then delivered his final message, never pausing long enough for Lewis to speak. Lewis just sat there dumbfounded, his stomach churning.

"Well, I'll tell you something, Mr. Lewis. I've got no time for you. I've got plenty of important things to do and when I need you for something, I'll call you." With that, Rickover hung up.

From that point on, if Rickover could not get immediate satisfaction from the general manager of Electric Boat, he went straight to Lewis and refused to deal with anyone lower.

Lewis had clearly enjoyed telling the story and Paige laughed good-naturedly. It would have been impolitic for him to say what he was thinking, which was that David Lewis had made a serious mistake by giving Rickover access to the top of the company. He would never get the monkey off his back now. Rickover would drag him into every minor dispute between the Naval Reactors Branch and the management of Electric Boat.

Beyond Lewis's initial missteps with Rickover, Paige was impressed by the new chairman's grasp of the problems at General Dynamics. The biggest problem was the Quincy shipyard. Having been purchased over Henry Crown's objection, the yard had turned into a disaster area of cost overruns on contracts for navy surface ships and commercial freight vessels. David Lewis had come in the door only to face write-offs at the yard totaling $250 million in 1970. He told Paige that if he didn't find a profitable program for Quincy, and fast, he was going to have to shut the place down because it was the hole in the bottom of the bucket for General Dynamics.

Lewis wound his way around to his closing. He needed a strong and able president to split up the work of whipping the divisions into shape. He especially wanted someone qualified to tackle the marine divisions, Quincy and Electric Boat, because Lewis said he was short on experience in marine manufacturing.

Paige thought it had been a great set-up for the charming punchline that followed: "Jesus, Hilly, if you've got time for these fancy New York lunches, why don't you come into the company as my president and help me out? I'm just about snowed under."

David Lewis was a great salesman. He had just sold Paige, and the crazy thing was that Paige was so attracted to the warm and collegial vision Lewis painted of the management organization he was going to build that Paige did not even bother to find out what it was like to work for Lewis. Besides, the terms that Lewis offered were so good that it didn't really matter. There was more money than he was making at G.E. and an option on seventy-five thousand shares of stock. Lewis set up an eight-year contract with a two-year "window" through which either party could escape. If it didn't work out, the escape clause gave Paige a $500,000 lump-sum payment and a $10,000-a-year retirement annuity. It seemed worth the risk of walking away from thirty years at General Electric. Paige still was not too upset when, after spending a week's time as the new president of General Dynamics, he realized he had made a horrible mistake.

On most mornings of the year it was cold, sometimes bitter cold, when the siren went off at the end of Eastern Point Road to announce the beginning of the first shift at The Boat. It echoed all up and down the last slow run of the Thames River, which drained the rocky woodlands of southeastern Connecticut into Long Island Sound. It was the daily alarm clock for commuters and merchants in the seaside towns of Mystic, New London, Groton, and Stonington, and for the sailors upriver at the nuclear submarine base.

For three quarters of a century, the Electric Boat Company had summoned thousands of New England blue-collar tradesmen to the shipyard. They scuffed through the gates with their lunch pails and hardhats, and streamed down the asphalt trails and roads to the building ways where the cigar-shaped steel hulls awaited them like cold beached whales at the water's edge.

The shipyard came to life in stages: first the big overhead machines that could hoist fifty tons of steel, then the welding machines, the diesel lifts, and the clanking chorus of lathes and drill presses in the machine shop. The noise built slowly over an hour's time until it reached a deafening cacophony. Trucks carrying shards of metal rumbled down the hill past jostling work gangs to deliver their loads from the warehouses. Crane operators fired diesel engines and pneumatic hammers set up a staccato pounding in the air. The high, irregular whine of grinders ricocheted off corrugated tin sheds and brick walls, and the shrill beeps from forklifts in reverse echoed over the din.

You could distinguish the workers by the color of their hardhats: blue for welders, orange for grinders, light green for machinists, dark green for riggers, brown for testers, yellow for radiation monitors, and white for the bosses.

The welders and grinders wore heavy leather jackets, like fighter pilots, to protect them from burns because burns were an everyday occurrence and the company paid scar bonuses for the bad ones. It took years to master the most sophisticated welding techniques. And only the best welders could perform the X-ray welding on the pressure hull, where the seam had to be perfect because a mistake could let the ocean in and kill a hundred men.

They checked out their equipment and mustered in groups to pick up their work chits for the shift. It took a half hour for a welder to collect everything he needed—helmet, tools, and enough preheated and vacuum-sealed welding rod to last him the morning—before making the long trip up the wooden stairway erected on the side of the hull leading to the deck hatch. Only one hatch was open because the other was needed to feed the thick electrical cables for the welding machines and the air hoses for ventilation.

Climbing into a nuclear submarine under construction was like descending into a dark desert mine, an intricate steel honeycomb with layered decks and cramped, mazelike passageways. The heat was the first thing that hit you. The unlit cylinder was more than thirty feet from top to bottom, but there was no feeling of space because the volume was filled up with pipes, decks, and machinery. What space was left was choked with men and their cables and their shrieking power tools. The noise, which had nowhere to go, was ear-splitting. Sometimes the smoke and dust in the steel cave were so thick you couldn't see, and men ten feet away disappeared in the dirty cloud where the vapors were acrid, and your eyes never stopped watering. Every morning you had to wake up and pry your eyelids apart from the crust and you knew it was going to make you blind someday.

The welders were the cowboys who had the worst jobs in the yard: they assaulted joints and seams along the curved steel hull and the bent I-beams used as inside frames. They set foundations in the reactor compartment and engine room by welding steel boxes and studs on the concave bottom of the hull where the reactor was mounted like a big steel Buddha as the first step in linking the turbines, pumps, and other machinery in the propulsion chain. They welded up steel tanks to store fresh water for the crew, saltwater for ballast and—for emergency core coolant—borated water to kill stray neutrons coming through the reactor wall. Other tanks would hold hydraulic fluid for the diving plane controls and diesel fuel for the auxiliary engine that was stuffed down in the bilge to get the ship home if the reactor plant failed.

The arc welders and gougers gave the scene a thunderstorm effect as the lightning from their electric torches struck the steel, raining fire and molten slag down from scaffolding onto other men. Gravity took everything—slag, sparks, and falling tools—into the black abyss of the bilge. The heat rose and swirled by convection, and you never forgot that it was all around you. Every once in a while the wooden scaffolding caught fire and the fire crews whooshed in with extinguishers because there was no way to get everyone off the ship if a blaze got out of control.

When the air got too bad, men put on their respirators until the ventilation system caught up. It wasn't unusual for a welder to pass out after he had climbed into a hole where the steel was pre-heated to 140 degrees for a weld. It was the watch crew's job to drag him out and wrestle his dead weight up the ladder and down the stairs for the ambulance ride to the shipyard hospital. No day passed without its siren being heard.

The lighting was poor in the boats. Most of the men carried drop lights, like car mechanics, and hung the mesh-covered bulb near their work station. The arc welders, however, needed little light. Their work made a fire brighter than the sun. They selected a welding rod for a butt joint or a seam, dialed up the correct amperage, clipped on the ground cable and—with a quick downward jerk of the head— dropped the protective mask over their faces before they struck the arc. Through the dark-tinted slit in the mask, they guided their lightning bolt and watched the steel puddle beneath them like dark soup.

The watch crewman stood by in case of fire or heatstroke, and if he forgot to wear his own tinted safety glasses, he could wake up in the middle of the night with the searing pain of an invisible burn on the cornea of his eyes.

It was always the heat you remembered. It was suffocating in the tight spots—and most of them were—where the pre-heating cables were tack-welded onto the high yield steel and when you pulled off the asbestos mats, the heat just radiated in the dark and you were sweating a river and hoping not to pass out. Some welders learned to use mirrors in the tight spaces where it was impossible to get your arms or shoulders or both hands in position to strike the arc. It took at least a year's practice to get good with a mirror because left was right, and vice versa. If you were really good, you could stand almost on your head in a tank, using a three-foot extension on your welding rod and a mirror to make a molten seam on the backside of a stiffener. For the real cowboys, it had been hard when the era of quality control came along in the mid-sixties and inspectors began coming around to check the work. Once upon a time, in the days of *Nautilus* for instance, if a welder said the weld was good, that was enough. A good welder was his own quality control, and any suggestion to the contrary from some nosy inspector was likely to start a fist fight.

The tradesmen who worked on the ship were broken up into gangs, one each for the forward ballast tanks, torpedo room, command and control center, reactor compartment, and engine room. They worked until noon—or until the heat and claustrophobia got to them. About a half hour before the lunch whistle, they lined up near the hatch ladder to get back out into the light and fresh air for thirty minutes, at the end of which the whistle sounded again. Some men wolfed down sandwiches, others drank their lunch from the pints they bought at Rag's Liquorette. Some of the young workers smoked marijuana in the toilet sheds, where the graffiti was mostly downbeat:

> When I die I'll go to heaven
> 'Cuz I've spent my time in hell

The geography of The Boat had been cramped by nature, backed up against a bluff that overlooked the river, so the waterfront machine shops and building ways for the ships were jammed together on the narrow strip of shore that had been built up with concrete and expanded out over the water as time went by, until it had become a continuous series of parallel piers and drydocks that made the best use of precious space. An old ferry served as the cafeteria.

The South Yard was a collection of wetdocks where submarines were tied alongside after they were launched in a state of semi-completion so the ways could be cleared for the next hull. The last six months of finishing work inside the ship could be done by work gangs while the ship was afloat. Most of the overhaul work on submarines coming in from the fleet was also done in the South Yard. The drydocks were called graving docks. They could be sealed and the water pumped out by the dockmaster so that the entire ship was beached and work could be done on any part of the hull. The North Yard was the primary work area, where new construction ships were assembled. The hull sections were rocked into place on long, sloping building ways made of oaken timbers. The ways had to be as long as the ship, nearly four hundred feet. Section by section the hull cylinders were fitted together like links in a sausage, and the seams welded, until the whole thing took shape as a nuclear submarine perched up in the air in a building as big as a stadium. They looked like caged steel zeppelins—underwater *Hindenberg*s.

The bluff overlooking the yard was called the Hill. That was where the bosses worked in the red brick administration building. The men in the union halls liked to say that Electric Boat was divided into two parts, the waterfront and the Hill, and the twain never met. The class distinctions were sharp. The tradesmen who worked on the waterfront were the sons of immigrant laborers, Italians and Irishmen and Northern European stock, while the engineers and managers who came down from the Hill in white hats and stiff shirts were the sons of Yankee traders and merchants. They were graduated from Yale, MIT, and Brown, and they avoided the beerhalls along Thames Street in Groton where the welders gathered at the end of the day to drown the taste of burnt steel in their gullets.

The waterfront operated under a strict union caste. Welders welded, painters painted, and grinders ground. There were twenty different trades altogether and their contracts prohibited cross-over work. A painter waited for a laborer to move his ladder, or for a carpenter to add a board to his scaffold. The rules accounted for much of the labor trouble at The Boat because management slowly had woken up to the fact that, on any given day, thousands of tradesmen were standing idle for up to half of their shift waiting for some other tradesman to show up and perform his task in the proper sequence. The rules contributed to the low productivity and the high overhead that The Boat was famous—or infamous—for in the navy.

The only thing that cut across these barriers at Electric Boat was a strong workforce pride in being at the center of the nuclear navy. E.B. was the shipyard that had built *Nautilus* for Admiral Rickover after the naval shipyards had turned him away. When *Nautilus* went to sea, it was a great triumph for The Boat, and the shipyard had gone on to build *Seawolf, Skate,* and *Skipjack.* One of the *Skipjack*-class hulls—round like a porpoise—already had been fitted up on the building ways when the navy ordered Electric Boat to cut the ship in half and insert a new hull section filled with vertical missile tubes. That was how the first Polaris missile boat, U.S.S. *George Washington,* was rushed to sea as the first seaborne nuclear deterrent. In the crash program ordered by President Kennedy after the Cuban missile crisis, The Boat produced more Polaris submarines—seventeen—than any other shipyard.

The community of naval architects and marine engineers at The Boat had designed every class of nuclear submarine except the first deep-diving boats, U.S.S. *Thresher* and her successor, U.S.S. *Permit.* Presidents and senators and secretaries of defense had traveled to Groton for ship launchings. They congratulated the workforce for their achievement and exhorted them to even greater contributions to the national defense. The launchings were moments of great festivity. The working-class families gathered picnic-style out along the broad pier, which was dressed for the day in flags and bunting. The management class and the dignitaries sat inside the construction hall on folding chairs below the decorated bow of the submarine. From the christening platform, the guest of honor delivered the Speech and his wife usually exploded the champagne bottle.

None of the dignitaries actually saw the man who really launched the ship. He was invisible back behind the speaker's platform and the bow, way beyond the bunting and a big green curtain that hid the grimy trusswork that was holding everything in place. The method of launching ships had been the same for a thousand years. At The Boat, before the first cylinder was lifted into place on the long wooden cradle of the building ways, work gangs coated the timbers with a thick layer of blond axle grease, about five hundred gallons to cover the whole platform. Wedges were strategically placed near the stern of the ship to keep it from sliding off prematurely and the wedges were connected to a "trigger"—a three-foot lever the trigger-man pulled on launch day just at the moment the champagne bottle cracked. He was the one who really launched her. And dozens of grunts, who had spent the previous twenty-four hours swinging battering rams in rallies to snug up the boat on her cradle and loosen the wedges, gathered round to cheer his final act. Back there among the greasy timbers, under the shadow of the hull, the men cursed the long-winded speechmakers because the launch had to be timed perfectly to meet the tide. There was a tight "window," just a couple of minutes either side of slack high tide, and if the triggerman didn't hit it just right, he could send the ship into a moving current that would slam her against the pier. Worse, he could jam her stern into the muddy bottom of the river. The triggerman kept his eye on the yard superintendent, who stood in a telephone shed connected by a wire to the speaker's platform. Like a Hollywood director, he gave the triggerman the signal: a jab of the finger in the air the instant the christening bottle ruptured on the bow a football field away. The triggerman pulled with a two-fisted yank. The wedges hit the floor and the triggerman's heart pounded as he looked up to see if the black steel sky was going to move, and when it did the cheer burst out of him from the thrill of sending five thousand tons of steel sliding into the river on cue. Everyone who cheered did so as a deaf mute because a blanket of sound covered the waterfront as the ship's horn blared like an ocean liner's.

Countless submarines had taken the long slide into the river as the waving crowds roared and the ship's crew stood at attention on the fast-moving deck, saluting the dignitaries while skidding backward at thirty miles an hour. The rush of emotion was overpowering and you could feel the pride of ten thousand men as she slipped into the river, taking a piece of each of them with her. But the first time you saw it you also wanted to laugh because all those white-suited bowling pins were out there on deck trying not to fall over—one hand saluting, the other holding the hand rail as the river slammed on the brakes.

People said that because of the history, *Nautilus* and all, The Boat was really Admiral Rickover's private shipyard. In many respects it was. Rickover had gotten the shipyard into the nuclear business to begin with, and it had taken five years to train thousands of men in all of the things they needed to know to put nuclear reactors filled with radioactive material into ships, to crack them open every few years to refuel them, and then to dispose of all that contaminated waste without exceeding the government's standards for radiation exposure. With Rickover's help, Electric Boat had been better positioned than most of the navy yards to lead the way in the Polaris program, and then to cash in on the long run of nearly twenty attack submarines the navy ordered from E.B. during the 1960s. The yard received a steady stream of overhaul business as well—contracts that had proved to be its bread-and-butter profit makers. Institutionally, General Dynamics always had recognized Rickover as its patron saint and Rickover had been ceded great influence over how the shipyard was run—and even over who was running it. For a decade, General Dynamics had gone along with an informal practice of letting Rickover approve or veto senior management promotions and it was well known in the shipyard that to ascend in the organization meant playing to Rickover's people, which meant playing to Rickover's agenda, sometimes at the expense of Electric Boat. Rickover insisted on daily telephone calls from the general manager, and on weekly self-criticism in writing, a kind of technical Maoism with Rickover in charge of everything, knowing everyone's faults and keeping them on file just in case he needed the leverage to get some more work done in the nuclear construction program.

Joseph D. Pierce had been one of those managers who had played to Rickover and Rickover's people during his entire career and it was ironic that Joe Pierce would become a victim of Rickover's rage at Electric Boat. Pierce had been named general manager in 1967. He was a big, ham-handed engineer with a barrel chest and the gruff style of the waterfront, where he had spent most of his professional life with a set of blueprints under his arm crawling around the insides of nuclear submarines. Pierce had worked in Rickover's electrical section of the Bureau of Ships during World War II. He came up through the ranks of Electric Boat's nuclear construction organization and had really grown up in the shipyard, working side by side with the waterfront foremen on every nuclear ship since *Nautilus*. He was an intuitive manager. He knew every inch of the boats, and how to question a barely literate welder after the man had crawled out of a 140-degree compartment to complain that the spaces were too tight to get to an invisible joint under a deck. Pierce knew how to coach a rookie, and how to persuade him to crawl back into that dark oven with an extension rod and a mirror to find the joint and fix it.

For all of his savvy on the waterfront, Pierce was not very polished at corporate politics. He tried to give the corporate office the best information he could on schedules and profits, and then he tried to accommodate the goals, sometimes conflicting goals, of the corporate office and Rickover.

At the end of the decade there had been a lot of anxiety about where the business was going to come from in the seventies, and that's why the fight between Rickover and Robert McNamara over the high-speed submarine had been watched so closely by General Dynamics. Joe Pierce had hedged the company's bets by taking a contract from the navy's submarine desk to do the preliminary design work on the rival Conform submarine—the submarine that a lot of people in the navy believed was going to become the next fleet attack boat. But then Rickover had defeated both McNamara and the submarine desk, and the Conform design was killed.

In the midst of the battle, Rickover in April 1968 had punished Electric Boat and Pierce for their disloyalty by convincing the navy to send the design contract for the *688* high-speed prototype to Newport News Shipbuilding and Dry Dock Company and that was fine with E.B.'s management as long as the *688* was going to be a single submarine. But then the next year, after Richard Nixon gained the White House, the *688* design suddenly became a class of twelve submarines. That was when everybody realized the mistake, not a fatal mistake, but one of many contributors to the later catastrophe. Newport News had built a lot of nuclear submarines based on designs by the elite engineering group at Electric Boat, but Newport News had never in its history designed a new submarine from the ground up. Its designers were expert in aircraft carriers, cruisers, destroyers—even oil tankers—but submarine design was a different dimension of engineering and naval architecture. You don't take aircraft carriers a thousand feet under the ocean and drive them blind with only a sonar for eyes and ears.

From a financial standpoint, it was always better to get the design contract because along with it usually came the contract to build the first ship of the class under an arrangement whereby the navy reimbursed all costs of construction plus a negotiated profit. It was hard to lose money that way. The method was justified by all the uncertainties of first-of-a-kind warship construction. Technologies changed, plans changed, et cetera. When the bids had gone out and were awarded in 1971, Newport News, the giant competing shipyard at the mouth of the Chesapeake Bay, had won a total of five of the twelve ships, including the lead ship, U.S.S. *Los Angeles, SSN 688*. The remaining seven were awarded to Electric Boat, starting with U.S.S. *Philadelphia, SSN 690*.

Joe Pierce was tarred unfairly for losing the *688*-class design contract, and when David Lewis arrived as the new chairman of the board, Pierce had been trying to walk the tightrope between Rickover and the corporate office for three years. Lewis's arrival was the beginning of Pierce's worst nightmare. Lewis changed everything about the company's relationship with Rickover. He gave the old man a grip on top management Rickover had never before enjoyed. As a result, almost from Lewis's first day, Rickover was all over the new chief executive with complaints about Pierce: Pierce had no imagination; Pierce was doing nothing about the loafing in the shipyard; Pierce was promoting sharp accountants, lawyers, and contracts men to cheat the government with clever negotiating tactics and claims; Pierce was a sloppy manager who was not paying attention to radiation safety.

Lewis was inclined to accept many of these criticisms. After all, Rickover controlled a cornucopia of business for Electric Boat, and Lewis understood that his own success at General Dynamics was directly tied to how much business he could get in the door in the coming decade. Lewis wanted to appease Rickover, to give him what he asked for, and if he could not, to at least appear to bend over backwards for him. When Rickover's calls came into the chairman's office atop Rockefeller Plaza, Lewis gauged the seriousness of the complaint by the tone of the admiral's voice. If Rickover came on the line yelling, Lewis was out of his chair standing at attention behind his desk: "Yes, Admiral, what is it?" Lewis found Rickover's rampages distressing and intimidating and sometimes when he got off the telephone, he sank into his chair disgusted at what he had to put up with to keep peace with the old man.

Rickover always landed on new managers to establish his control, and he did that several times to David Lewis. You could see Rickover's style just in the way he ran a meeting. He would start off yelling about something insignificant just so everyone in the room was thrown off balance and then he would launch into his agenda so that he could frame the issues in the way that suited him the best. It was a marvelous thing to watch if you weren't at the end of his barrel.

In May 1971 Rickover landed on Lewis over what looked like an insignificant study Electric Boat had conducted—with Pierce's approval—for the Pentagon's Advanced Research Projects Agency (ARPA). The research agency wanted Electric Boat's engineers to look at submarine concepts the navy might use ten to fifteen years in the future. After a year, the engineers came up with a whole range of innovations, including a promising concept of heat conversion that would allow a large nuclear mother ship to ferry dozens of small, high-speed submarines—each about thirty-five-feet long—into forward areas to attack Russian ships. The little nonnuclear daughter ships would draw their steam power from a carbon block "heat sponge" that could be charged and recharged by the mother ship. The small attack subs could carry external weapons and could be mass-produced at a very low unit cost.

The study had a dual purpose. Its sponsors wanted to highlight the mounting evidence that Rickover was getting far less power out of his nuclear reactors than the Soviet navy was getting out of its submarine reactors. By 1971, naval intelligence had begun cataloguing the first disturbing comparisons between superpower submarine fleets. They showed that Soviet ballistic missile submarines of the *Yankee* class were getting three and a half times more power per pound out of their propulsion plants than Polaris missile submarines in the U.S. fleet.*

Electric Boat's top submarine designers believed the United States was falling behind in the race to improve nuclear propulsion. And, some of them also believed, Rickover was becoming the chief obstacle to the development of alternative reactor designs that would yield more power.

When the Electric Boat engineers completed their classified report, they briefed the Pentagon's director of ocean warfare. The director got very excited and set up a briefing for Johnny Foster, the Pentagon's top scientist who had fought Rickover over the *688* class. But before the briefing could be scheduled, Rickover had gotten wind of the report. He telephoned Joe Pierce and demanded that Pierce discredit Electric Boat's own report. Pierce said he couldn't do that, and Rickover yelled with his most abusive and threatening tone before hanging up. Rickover then telephoned Lewis and went wild. He demanded action. He wanted all of the reports gathered up and burned, destroyed. His tone conjured for Lewis the dire consequences of inaction.

Lewis jumped to his feet when the blast hit his ear. He knew little of the research project. There was no reason for him to have been involved in it. But he assured Rickover he would do something about it.

After he hung up, Lewis did not hesitate. He telephoned Pierce and he telephoned his Washington lobbyist and told them to kill the report. Somehow, General Dynamics' chief lobbyist got the briefing of Foster canceled. Then the Washington office discovered that the report already had been delivered to the Defense Department. General Dynamics' lobbyists were dispatched to the Pentagon, where they retrieved as many copies as they could from several Pentagon offices, including off the desk of the director of ocean warfare. General Dynamics officials then destroyed the copies. The government had paid $150,000 for the study, but it was denied the results because Rickover saw the subject matter as a threat to his program and David Lewis

---

*Rickover loyalists point out that intelligence information supports their contention that the Soviet navy historically has operated its submarines in a higher risk environment by carrying less shielding around the reactor compartment in order to save weight and gain power performance. The U.S. Navy has adhered to a much higher safety standard to prevent any radiation exposure to crewmen aboard its fleet nuclear submarines, even at the cost of power and speed. However, the poor showing of U.S. submarines in power-density comparisons with Soviet submarines cannot be fully explained by the relative weights of reactor sheilding, according to a number of experts in the field.

was only too willing to be his enforcer. Electric Boat's top engineer for advanced research, Jack Van Leonard, was called on the carpet for conducting the study. His career was finished, Joe Pierce made clear. Within a month, Leonard—one of the most experienced submarine designers in the country—resigned, bitter over what he considered the book-burning environment Rickover had imposed on naval research.

In the aftermath of Rickover's blow-up, Lewis gathered his top managers around him for a "Rickover Problem Meeting" and lectured them. Studies like the ARPA one were a threat to the *688* program and to all subsequent Rickover programs, he said. Electric Boat had no business going off into new fields that would antagonize the admiral. Lewis reminded them that Rickover could pull his programs out of Electric Boat and build all the submarines he needed at Newport News and at Litton's shipyard on the Gulf Coast of Mississippi. Electric Boat was not in a strong competitive position against the larger and more modern shipyards. Their overhead costs were lower, and therefore, Electric Boat had to play to its strengths—and the Rickover relationship was strength, Lewis said.

The meeting was a bellwether of the Lewis doctrine. The potential to win billions of dollars' worth of business with Rickover's help outweighed everything else. The policy of Electric Boat would be not only a continued alignment of the company's strategic interests with those of Rickover, but a strict avoidance of other natural business pursuits that were antithetical to Rickover's goals. From that day forward and for many years, Electric Boat's engineering organization would not stray into nuclear submarine research fields that did not have Rickover's approval.

Right after the explosion over the ARPA report, Lewis attended one of his first keel-laying ceremonies at Electric Boat for U.S.S. *Lipscomb*, a stealth submarine prototype that Rickover had also rammed through the navy in 1968.*

A keel laying for a submarine was not much of an event: a single hull cylinder was rocked onto the ways and the sponsor's initials were burned into the steel with a cutting torch. But the late Representative Glenard P. Lipscomb had been a powerful Rickover ally on the House Armed Services Committee, and many of his old friends had gathered to honor him, including Representative Gerald R. Ford and Secretary of Defense Melvin Laird.

---

*Lipscomb, whose turbines produced electricity to power a giant electric motor connected to the propeller shaft, turned out to be extremely quiet running, but was a technical disappointment because she did not use the thermal power of the reactor as efficiently as other boats. As a result, her speed performance was disappointing.

Lewis met Rickover for the first time shortly before the ceremony.

"Well, at last you got to meet me," Rickover greeted him.

Lewis was as gracious as he could be, but was horrified when Rickover then added, "I thought you might tell that story about our first conversation."

Lewis was embarrassed at the thought of recounting in public how Rickover had mauled him on his first trip to Washington as the new chairman of General Dynamics. Aghast and fumbling for words, all he could think to say was: "Admiral, this is much too solemn an occasion for that."

"Well, aren't we going to have a reception?" Rickover asked, his face showing he was enjoying Lewis's torment. "That might be a good time to tell it."

The idea of humiliating himself gnawed at Lewis throughout the keel-laying ceremony, and during the limousine ride from the shipyard to the reception hall Lewis confided in Pierce and asked his advice.

"Oh dear God," Pierce said, "don't do that. That will just be awful."

"Well, he wants me to tell it," Lewis said in exasperation.

"Don't do it," Pierce repeated. Rickover was blatantly trying to show his power over the new chairman of the board, and Lewis should take a stand. As the guests mingled on the elegant waterfront estate rented for the reception, Pierce reported that he had overheard Rickover bragging to Lipscomb's daughters: "That son of a bitch [Rickover] is telling those two girls about how he really runs all of the companies and all the people, and [how] Lewis dances to his tune and he—Rickover—is really running the show."

Lewis was so taken aback he was not sure what to do, but when the moment came, he could find no alternative. Rickover was getting too pushy. So David Lewis knocked back a vodka and tonic and during dinner he stood up in front of the assembled dignitaries and their wives and let everybody know how Rickover had left him in a heap on the floor during his first week on the job. Lewis made the story sound funny: the legendary admiral and all of that, but he also knew Rickover was rejoicing at the inflation of his image in the eyes of all those present.

When Rickover came to the podium, he did not say a thing about Lewis's tale. He said a few kind words about his late congressional admirer, then left the banquet so he could get back to work.

Lewis did not realize how much he was playing into Rickover's hands. Pierce's warnings had not done any good and Paige was no help. Lewis thought he could sell anybody, and he thought he was selling Rickover by aggrandizing the Rickover legend every chance he got. And Rickover was dangling all of that business before Lewis's eyes, like the biblical tempter who took the prophet to the mountain-top and offered him all that he could see if he would just swear eternal allegiance. Lewis smiled that brotherly smile and looked at Rickover like a loving son. He was all allegiance.

The scale of submarine construction had been so great during the past decade that there was little incentive for the shipyard to con-sider its position if Rickover and the nuclear navy suddenly disap-peared. But after the Six-Day War in the Middle East had closed the Suez Canal, the commercial tanker market boomed, and the oil com-panies were looking for larger and larger crude carriers to bring oil around the horn of Africa, as well as other energy-carrying ships to tap the new gas fields in Algeria, Indonesia, and Prudoe Bay.

Pierce had some of his own ideas about the future of Electric Boat, whose engineering department had come up with a design for a giant submarine tanker that could bring crude oil or super-cooled gas in liquid form from Alaska's North Slope on a route under the polar ice cap to the markets on the Eastern Seaboard. It was a novel idea and eminently possible from an engineering standpoint. But when Rickover found out that Electric Boat was even considering branching out into other lines of shipbuilding, a new storm erupted.

"Why does Joe Pierce keep doing this?" Rickover yelled into the telephone at Lewis. "Whose technology are you going to use in building those submarines?" Rickover's tone implied his proprietor-ship over the manufacturing technology that Electric Boat had devel-oped over the years. He said he did not want the highly trained nuclear construction workforce at Electric Boat diluted by commer-cial projects, and that was that. Rickover demanded that Lewis put a commitment in writing that all of Rickover's programs would con-tinue to be performed at Electric Boat facilities in the New London area. Lewis agreed and allowed Rickover to dictate the language that he wanted in the letter, including a statement that Lewis and the General Dynamics board of directors were standing ready with master plans "for the development of a substantially larger Electric Boat complex in the event such a facility is required" to meet the construc-tion demands of the nuclear navy. With the October 1971 letter, Rick-over had taken the first step in keeping Electric Boat an exclusive naval shipyard—and he did it with the implication that he would make it worth David Lewis's while.

Lewis marveled at the company's history with Rickover. He

learned from Pierce that while Rickover railed against the cheaters and bloodsuckers in Electric Boat's management, he for years had been accepting—sometimes requesting—special favors from the company. It was mostly little stuff, but if someone had put a spotlight on it, Rickover would have been embarrassed because it was hypocritical. To Lewis, the special favors and trinkets the company had been providing Rickover were all part of the bonding between the admiral and his most important shipyard. There was no reason to disturb the relationship and, in fact, plenty of reason to encourage it. The favors had been handled discreetly, usually by a staff aide to the general manager of Electric Boat. It had started out with the "rig-for-Rickover" list—all the comfort items that the admiral wanted aboard any nuclear submarine he was taking out for sea trials: a set of foul-weather gear with his name on it; thirty pounds of fresh fish for the galley; fresh fruit; hardback books from *The New York Times* bestseller list; chauffeured transportation from the Groton Airport; a fresh set of navy khakis waiting for him and dry cleaning for his dark civilian suit that he left ashore while he went to sea for two days.

They were the kind of things you would do for a flag rank admiral who was conducting a military inspection. It was not any different from the perks that were routinely afforded visiting dignitaries from Washington, including secretaries of the navy.

But with Rickover, the favors had gotten more extravagant from time to time. There was the $300 set of encyclopedias he once asked for; the large oak block for his son's art project; the custom-made mahogany boxes for Rickover's personal papers; the ladies' scarves at Christmastime for his secretaries in Washington and the gold-plated fruit knives that the shipyard had reproduced at a cost of thousands of dollars because it had been so difficult to find Asian water buffalo horns to match the handle of the original Rickover presented for duplication. Rickover had asked for engraved ladies' watches to give away at ship launchings, along with gold, silver, and crystal trinkets to commemorate the events. He gave much of the booty away to people he considered important to his programs: congressmen and their wives, staffers and other government officials—but the extras were always shipped to Rickover's office in Washington, where he kept them in a locked cabinet that looked like a treasure chest after a few years.

For the keel laying of U.S.S. *Lipscomb*, the shipyard ordered—among other things—one hundred glass paperweights from Tiffany's, all but a dozen of which were shipped to Rickover for his disposal. He once called the general manager's office at Electric Boat and asked for a dozen shower curtains like the one he had admired in a New Jersey hotel. On another occasion, he asked for some small Italian-made appliances, combination hotplates and "bain-maries." For a party he threw for his wife, Rickover asked Pierce to supply a half-dozen fifty-dollar bills encased in laminated plastic for party favors. It had taken the shipyard three days to get the lamination right.

Though the first twelve 688s had been funded by Congress, the future of the program was by no means assured, and a horrible thing had happened in Rickover's life the year before when President Nixon elevated Elmo R. Zumwalt, Jr., to be Chief of Naval Operations in June 1970. The moment he heard the news, Rickover knew that Zumwalt would be out to kill the 688 program if he could. The congressional commitment to continue building 688s remained largely undaunted. But having sold the Congress on the need to build a fleet of high-speed submarines to meet the Soviet threat, the real tension for Rickover was the constant fear that his shipyards could not handle the workload. The instant someone like Zumwalt smelled blood in the water, he would rush to the Secretary of Defense and argue that Rickover could not spend all of the money Congress had generously awarded him. The money would then disappear overnight into other navy programs. Zumwalt's programs.

Zumwalt had tried right off the bat to strike a deal with Rickover: he would support building five 688s a year, but after three years he wanted Rickover to accept a cutback to three subs a year. Zumwalt would by then need the money to rebuild the surface navy with a new and innovative mix of ships.*

But Rickover didn't really need Zumwalt's support to get the five ships a year. He already had a commitment from Congress, and Zumwalt wasn't likely to succeed against Rickover on Capitol Hill where more powerful men had failed. Still, it was prudent for Rickover to try to get along with the new CNO, though any agreement Rickover made with Zumwalt would have been based on Rickover's thinnest intention to honor it. He would never feel obliged to keep a

*Zumwalt maintains that Rickover accepted this deal and later reneged on it. Rickover's deputy, William Wegner, maintains that Zumwalt never broached such a deal in the June 2, 1970, meeting with Rickover cited in Zumwalt's biography, On Watch. Wegner maintains that Zumwalt's advance man for the meeting, Captain Charles F. Rauch, Jr., came to Wegner saying he wanted to lay the groundwork for a deal Zumwalt intended to propose in the meeting, but Wegner cut off the discussion by telling Rauch that Rickover did not do business through advance men. Zumwalt could raise any issue he wanted with Rickover when they met. Wegner said he attended the meeting between Zumwalt and Rickover, and the deal Zumwalt later described never came up. Zumwalt, however, maintains that Wegner did not attend the meeting at which the deal was made.

bargain with the man he suspected of constant treachery against the nuclear submarine program.

Zumwalt felt that he and Rickover were circling each other like two wary jungle cats. To Zumwalt, the *688* submarines were a misbegotten class: shallow-running, unstable in tight turns, vulnerable at high speed, and too costly for the marginal advance they had given the navy over the previous class. Zumwalt was much more interested in less expensive alternatives.

The navy always had operated on the assumption that the best way to kill a submarine was with another submarine. But Zumwalt had an innovative mind and he wanted to shake up traditional navy thinking. He enthusiastically supported new research and development efforts into anti-submarine weapons, knowing that advances in that field might reduce the need for new submarine construction. If the United States could develop new and cheaper technologies to detect and kill Soviet submarines, Zumwalt believed, the navy would need fewer submarines.

And so, after barely a year in office, Zumwalt made his biggest play against Rickover, and he did it in total secrecy. He initiated—without Rickover's knowledge—a crash top-secret research program to develop the ultimate anti-submarine weapon: a technology that would render the oceans transparent, a detection technology that would leave Soviet submarines so vulnerable to kills from torpedo-carrying aircraft that the United States would no longer need attack boats to combat the Soviet submarine fleet. The silent war in the oceans would have been won and the Soviets would not know it until it was too late. But it all depended on secrecy.*

Zumwalt veiled it among the navy's largest "black" research programs, and its funding was disguised in the defense budget because it was too sensitive to explain openly to Congress. Only the chairmen of the House and Senate Armed Services committees could be briefed on the general nature of the research. Progress was hidden from all but a select few with security clearances that were both TOP Secret and "compartmented" under the project's code name to further restrict access. The scientists involved worked for the naval research laboratory in Washington and for ARPA. Their specialties included electromagnetic physics and computer modeling.

The phenomena they studied were not secret, but the applica-

---

*Fifteen years later, the crash program has evolved into successor programs whose code names and technical descriptions are never mentioned in the open press. And, while the goal of transparent oceans remains elusive, the new programs still hold great promise.

tion to anti-submarine warfare was. For years, navy scientists had observed that submarines were the source of electromagnetic waves. Tons of rotating steel in the turbines, gears, and propeller shaft sent extremely weak low-frequency electromagnetic wave pulses into the surrounding ocean, where the wave energy was rapidly dissipated. A decade earlier, this phenomenon had been studied as a possible means of detecting submarines from ships and from other submarines, but it had been discarded because the electromagnetic waves were too weak to detect from any distance.

But as is often the case in the advance of science and technology, an old idea can provide a revolutionary solution. The advances of radar technology in the atmosphere gave navy scientists a new way to look at the electromagnetic waves created by submarines. What if those waves were strong enough to reach the surface of the ocean from a submarine running submerged?

The big breakthrough of 1971 occurred when navy scientists secretly demonstrated they could beam electromagnetic waves from a radar generator against the ocean surface, and—with the assistance of a powerful computer—isolate the escaping electromagnetic waves emanating from a submarine running submerged. The news was rushed to Zumwalt by his deputy for anti-submarine warfare, Vice Admiral Harold Shear, and Zumwalt was excited at the potential for such a detection system. Deployed on airplanes—or on satellites—it seemed possible that the United States could track all submarines in every ocean. In war, it would just be a matter of dropping torpedoes at the right coordinates beamed down from sentries in the sky.

It was the weapon against Rickover and the 688 program that Zumwalt had never expected, and he reacted by clamping a lid on it and pumping money in. Zumwalt excluded Rickover from the classification order because he suspected that the admiral would try to attack the sensitive research project in Congress and breach its security while attempting to discredit it. After all, Zumwalt had witnessed Rickover's skillful use in 1968 of the classified data on the Soviet submarine buildup to push for a high-speed submarine in Congress. Zumwalt wanted to protect this secret and nurture it until it bore fruit. As he waited, Zumwalt described the electromagnetic program to Secretary of Defense Melvin Laird as a breakthrough technology that would "solve the anti-submarine problem" before the end of the century.

Laird, a longtime Rickover loyalist, privately criticized Zumwalt's strategy. But all during the Zumwalt years, Rickover never discovered that his nemesis was secretly using the "black" research program against the 688s in the highest councils of the executive branch.

The deal between Rickover and General Dynamics was struck over a period of a month as Richard Nixon achieved a landslide re-election to the White House over his challenger, Democratic presidential nominee George McGovern.

Rickover had won a five-year funded program from Congress, with a goal of building a fleet of twenty-three 688s before the end the decade. In January 1972, Newport News rocked the first hull cylinder of U.S.S. *Los Angeles* into place, and nine months later, Electric Boat held its keel-laying ceremony for U.S.S. *Philadelphia*.

With contracts for the first twelve ships already awarded, Rickover was looking for shipyard facilities to build eleven more 688s, as well as the first Trident ballistic missile submarine, a ship that was going to be nearly three times the size of a 688, a massive war machine capable of throwing twenty-four multiple-warhead rockets six thousand miles from its hideout in the deep.

On October 30, 1972, Joe Pierce telephoned Lewis to tell him that Rickover, in a private conversation, had said he was prepared to give the company contracts for half of the Trident submarines the navy would order over the next decade and a set allocation of 688s. In return, the admiral wanted Electric Boat to drop its plans to expand the shipyard beyond what was absolutely necessary to accommodate Rickover's submarine business. He also wanted to pass on the company's detailed plans for new facilities—and to that end, he was sending the navy's Trident and 688 project managers to Groton the following week.

Lewis could not believe the kind of power Rickover wielded. Ship construction contracts traveled through the same bureaucratic maze as all other government contracts. Final decisions were made in a chain of command that included the Secretary of the Navy, his Assistant Secretary for Shipbuilding, the chief of naval material, and the commander of the Naval Ship Systems Command. There were mountains of regulations to ensure that the bidding for those contracts was competitive and negotiations conducted at arm's length. Yet Rickover was acting as if the contracts were his to give.

In twenty-five years of dealing with the Pentagon, Lewis had never met a single military officer who had such solid personal control over the procurement process. And, in truth, it was the power to make Lewis fantastically successful as the chairman of the company that would build Rickover's fleet and, by so doing, propel General Dynamics once again to the top of the defense industry.

Two days later, on Wednesday, November 1, Lewis laid out Rickover's offer to Henry Crown and the members of the executive committee of the board of directors. The directors were very excited about the prospects for fantastic earnings from such a large construction program. On Lewis's recommendation, they voted the authority to spend up to $130 million to modernize and expand Electric Boat. Lewis sent word to Rickover that the company was poised to perform, ready to accept the challenge of building Rickover's fleet.

On Saturday afternoon, November 11, Rickover telephoned Pierce and laid down the final conditions Electric Boat would have to meet before Rickover gave the company a fixed commitment. Pierce relayed the conversation to Hilliard Paige. Rickover did not want the company to expand onto a piece of property it had acquired at Waterford, across the river from the shipyard, because, as Paige summed it up in a memo to Lewis, "He sees the Waterford property as considerably larger than required for our 688 and Trident needs [and] he would like to keep us so size-limited that we could not take on any non-Rickover work." And if Electric Boat was going to build facilities to handle the giant Tridents, Rickover wanted the company to drop its plan to launch the 17,000-ton monsters using a hydraulic drydock that moved up and down on the strength of large electric motors. Rickover was conservative about machinery—it was always wearing out and breaking. The motors would break down and you only dropped a $400 million Trident submarine once. Try a nonmechanical drydock, Rickover suggested, using the lifting power of water to float and beach the Tridents.

Paige debriefed Pierce extensively on his conversation with Rickover, then took his notes straight in to Lewis. In return for General Dynamics' compliance with his terms, "Rickover would agree to see that we get: a) one half of the 688 class submarines, b) the Trident lead ship, and c) one half of the remaining Tridents."

It was potentially the biggest arms procurement deal ever made, and both Paige and Lewis realized the enormity of what Rickover controlled. Congress was talking about building at least sixteen Tridents and probably thirty-five or forty 688s over the long run. Rickover was talking about $10 billion worth of business! That frail and demanding old man had just taken them to the mountaintop in a very real sense and the kingdom he showed them was vast and bountiful. All David Lewis could think about was doing what was necessary to make it come to pass.

It was just a few months later—after his own employment contract had been extended for the full seven-year term—that David Lewis pulled the plug on Hilly Paige. He believed that Paige had not shown the dynamic leadership qualities necessary to fulfill the basic requirement that he could someday replace David Lewis as chief executive officer. There were other reasons both stated and unstated, and the two men were very polite to one another and stayed friendly for years afterwards. But the most significant conflict in their working relationship was that Lewis wanted Paige to jump into Electric Boat after completing the assignment at Quincy. But Paige had seen the horrible vise Lewis had created for anyone who was going to try to run Electric Boat. Rickover would be going over his head on every decision. And Paige judged that Lewis was not the kind of chief executive who was willing to take the flak to protect his field managers.

After eighteen months in the president's office, Paige was demoralized at General Dynamics and had resolved that he would leave the company at the end of his two-year escape period. But then Lewis walked into his office on February 14, 1973, and announced that "it is our present plan" to exercise the company's option to get out of the employment contract. Paige did not show any emotion. If anything, he was relieved. General Dynamics' corporate offices had become shark-infested waters for Paige. And David Lewis, the gracious Southerner who had sold Paige on leaving General Electric for the new frontier, had too often shown himself to be an insecure micro-manager who competed with his immediate subordinates and played a constant game of one-upmanship with others in the executive suite.

Paige himself was not blameless, and Lewis—during those early months when he was working to consolidate his control over the corporation—had been forced to make accommodations to influential board members and their frequent involvement in management decision making. Still, Lewis had painted for Paige a picture of a close working relationship, team work, and it had not worked out that way. Above all, Lewis did not have the personality for a close relationship with his number two man. He was self-possessed, irrepressibly competitive, and domineering in the way that men who are uneasy with trust smother their subordinates with control. Lewis, as chairman of the board, rewrote virtually every press release issued by the company. He rewrote his subordinates' letters, designed the cover of the annual report, selected the photographs of his division managers, and when the company purchased a new corporate jet, Lewis took most of the day off to design the executive seating in the cabin. He even picked out the fabric coverings for the bulkheads and seats.

He was driven by his own consuming desire to prove to himself and to the defense industry that he could raise General Dynamics from the ashes of the previous decade; that he could mold prosperity out of the chaos he had inherited. All those years he spent in Jim McDonnell's shadow, and all of the management strategies on which he had subordinated his own judgment to McDonnell, drove him toward a goal of establishing David Lewis as the singular and undisputed force behind the resurgence of General Dynamics. It was an imagery that Lewis cultivated. It was not to be shared, and over the years he proved that he could not, and would not, share it. General Dynamics had become his life, his family. In the largest sense he cast himself in the role of a benevolent and gentlemanly dictator, all-seeing, omniscient.

In public, and before the tens of thousands of employees, middle managers, and production supervisors, David Lewis set standards that called for integrity in dealing with the government, and he projected his own Southern-born code of honor into the ranks. But in the inner circle of top managers, Paige had found a different David Lewis: one who thought he was a better lawyer than the company's counsel, a better accountant that his chief financial officer, a better aircraft designer than his top engineers, and a better politician and salesman than anyone who dealt with the Pentagon. In many respects, Lewis proved that he was right. He was brilliant at many things, but his style had a punishing effect on his subordinate managers. It was crazy to have a CEO who did everything. Yet Lewis was in his office at seven every morning and he could go twelve straight hours tearing through every division, getting comptrollers and production managers on the speakerphone, going through everyone's budget, quarterly plans, expense accounts, you name it.

Most of all, Lewis's style left little room for a president. Paige had seen some conspicuous flaws—the handling of Rickover among them—and he had feared the tragic consequences of Lewis's miscalculations at Electric Boat, the division that was critical to the company's financial stability and to its strategic future.

Lewis was a great salesman because he was a great actor, and he knew high-performance jet aircraft as well as anyone because Mr. McDonnell had singled him out as a young man for the highest calling in that company and made him learn everything the hard way. He had even made Lewis take a 30 percent pay cut once to leave a management post and go on the company's design board, where the salaries were lower but where the best minds worked to give shape to advanced aerodynamic concepts. Lewis had been stewing about it for weeks when his wife, Dorothy, pointed out what Mr. Mac was doing: he was preparing Lewis for greatness, and if he did not make the sacrifice, he didn't have what it took. It had surprised David Lewis that he had been so caught up in the dust that he had not recognized McDonnell's intentions. His wife's intuition had made up his mind and Lewis's career soared thereafter.

At General Dynamics, however, David Lewis singled out no one
as his successor. When Paige had arrived at the company, he met the
affable Gorden MacDonald, the new chief financial officer, who
seemed at first like a pleasant fellow with a pencil-line mustache and
a touch of gravel in his voice. But within weeks, Paige discovered that
MacDonald spent much of his time pandering to those members of
the board who wanted to participate in management decisions or to
peer constantly over management's shoulder. MacDonald's obsequi-
ousness with the board had hampered the independence of both
Paige and Lewis. And Lewis, who had spent so many years in Mr.
Mac's shadow at McDonnell Douglas, resented the style of his chief
financial officer, in Paige's view, but could do little about it after Mac-
Donald had cemented his relationships on the board. It was clear that
MacDonald had seen his future in the company as the eyes and ears of
the major stockholders. At one management meeting, after a few
drinks, MacDonald showed his true colors to Paige by quipping to a
colleague, "Why would you want to buy me a drink? I'm just a spy for
Henry Crown."

The first time Paige's wife met MacDonald, she pulled her hus-
band aside and said, "That man is after your job." Paige reacted philosophically. He told his wife if that was the case, and General
Dynamics turned out to be a place where every manager wore a dorsal
fin, he would leave, because he had the option of taking the $500,000
lump sum and bowing out. It was perhaps a delusion of the inbred
society of engineers and managers at General Electric, but Paige could
not abide an environment where people like MacDonald constantly
denigrated other managers and aggrandized their own role in the corporation.

Neither did Paige like what he saw in the constellation of men
assembled to guide General Dynamics. You could not call General
Dynamics' board of directors a collection of cronies, because they
were each men of some standing, but the line-up did not have the
breadth that Paige had expected for a large defense contractor. Henry
Crown had impaneled a board that included his personal lawyer, his
personal tax adviser, his investment banking adviser, and the top executive of a company Crown controlled. Later, he added his son Lester. The most troublesome and meddlesome member of the Crown
group of directors was Nathan Cummings, the aged founder of Consolidated Foods, Inc., later renamed Sarah Lee Corporation. Paige had
been appalled at Cummings's comportment at board meetings, where
he peppered management with suggestions of how to hype up the
value of the company's stock. It had gotten so bad in one meeting that
the board secretary threatened: "You are either going to have to stop

these discussions or I am going to have to leave the room, because if I stay here and write this down, we are all going to go to jail."

Cummings also had proved himself a thorn in management's side between board meetings. He was prone to billing General Dynamics for his expensive vacations on the pretext that he was out trying to drum up business for them. These ventures invariably turned up no new business and Lewis had tried to discourage Cummings from promoting himself as a salesman for the corporation. The first such vacation was at the exclusive Swiss ski resort Gstaad, where Cummings ran into the top executive of a French aerospace firm and insisted that David Lewis and Colonel Crown fly over for a dinner party. The dinner led nowhere since the French firm manufactured a competitive line of jet fighters, the Mirage series, but Cummings sent in an expense account that covered his stay at Gstaad.

The second Cummings business trip was to Acapulco, where he met an Italian nobleman who claimed to be personal friends with the Shah of Iran and who said he could assist General Dynamics in selling aircraft and energy ships to the Iranian government. The next thing Lewis and Paige knew, the Italian was soliciting a position as the company's agent to the Shah—on commission, of course—and was dropping Nate Cummings's name in his correspondence. Lewis was irritated at Cummings's interference, and asked Paige to draft a letter turning down the offer. Paige drafted a polite rejection letter, but Lewis sent him back, saying, "It's not nasty enough. I want Nate to get the message to knock this crap off." Paige returned with a draft that was abrupt and insulting. This time, Lewis smiled and said, "That's just right. Now you sign it."

Paige was stunned. He thought he had been drafting the letter for Lewis's signature and the incident showed him a side of Lewis that confirmed his worst fears about the Byzantine environment Lewis would preside over in the corporate offices of General Dynamics. Paige could not imagine trying to run Electric Boat and fending off Rickover's constant assaults while David Lewis was "backing" him in such a manner.

Cummings let it be known that he was insulted by Paige's handling of the affair and Paige knew that if he stayed, he would be forced to live with Cummings's hostility in the boardroom and MacDonald would only be egging him on.

From a performance standpoint, however, no one, including Lewis, could have faulted Paige on his contribution during those eighteen months he had been on the job. Paige—under Lewis's direction—had recruited a strong new general manager, P. Takis Veliotis, for the

Quincy shipyard, and he had overseen the first round of negotiations to build a series of natural gas tankers at Quincy under contracts that promised to return the shipyard to profitability. Paige believed that Lewis just did not want a president. Something about having a president at his side fed Lewis's insecurity, and besides, with Henry Crown sitting as chairman of the executive committee of the board, Lewis did not have the independence of many chief executives. In most corporations the chairman of the company also chaired the executive committee. But Crown had exercised his right of ownership. He wanted management to report to him and to the directors he had chosen to help him guide the company. Some of the other directors resented the idea that Crown was running the company out of the executive committee, leaving the full board with little responsibility beyond rubber-stamping the committee's recommendations every month. The arrangement left David Lewis lacking control. He was not the chairman of the board and the chief executive officer in the same way many of his peers at the top of other large corporations were.

That was not to say that Henry Crown wanted to manage General Dynamics, but he believed that he was uniquely qualified as a lifelong successful industrialist to guide management. And because he had lost control of his investment once before, he did not intend to give management a stronger grip on the composition of the board of directors than he himself exerted.

Crown also chaired the compensation committee of the board, and he had promised to make David Lewis a millionaire through a package of stock options, bonuses, and a salary that made him among the highest-paid executives in the Fortune 500 companies. In return, Lewis deferred to Crown's control over Material Service, even though it was a wholly owned unit of General Dynamics. Crown wanted his son Lester to oversee Material Service with relative autonomy. That autonomy soon caused the corporation one of its largest and most embarrassing scandals of the decade when it was discovered in 1974 that Lester Crown and several subordinate managers had participated in a scheme to bribe Illinois state legislators to introduce a bill raising the weight limits on state roads used by Material Service's ready-mix concrete trucks. Though the bill failed, the bribes were still paid. Lester Crown's contribution to a war chest of bribe money collected throughout the Illinois concrete industry was $15,000 from personal funds. To recoup the bribe money, Lester Crown and some of his subordinates then falsified their expense accounts submitted to General Dynamics. Albert E. Jenner, Jr., the Crown family attorney and a member of General Dynamics' board of directors, negotiated an immunity agreement on behalf of Lester Crown whereby he agreed to incriminate his business colleagues in the concrete industry in return for immunity from prosecution.*

Without informing David Lewis until after it was completed, Jenner also negotiated the immunity agreement on behalf of General Dynamics. Though he was chief executive officer, Lewis never had the option of taking action against Lester Crown for his illegal conduct.

In essence, David Lewis had the title of chief executive officer, but he ran the company under a less-than-detached chairman and major stockholder. In those early days, it had taken no more than the Crown group's disinterest to kill one of Lewis's major initiatives: to purchase the fledgling Federal Express Corporation. Jenner and others had attacked the idea in the executive committee and Crown had asked why a $2 billion company had its entire corporate staff tied up trying to acquire a $20 million small fry. The Federal Express deal fell on its face. In most any other big company, Lewis would have been able to push it through on the strength of his own authority. Under Crown, Lewis operated like a bank president with a tight lending limit and in that environment, there was little room for a number two man, in Paige's view.

When Lewis confronted Paige about the decision to drop his contract in February 1973, he said that Paige had not shown the qualities of a strong president. Paige did not try to contest the assessment. It was pointless to say what he really thought: that no one could work under David Lewis as president. So Paige tried to make a compliment out of it: "Dave, I don't think you need a president. You are your own best president."

Months later, after Paige's final troubleshooting assignment, Lewis came by to say farewell. He acknowledged that things had not been all they could have been on the management team, and that he felt bad MacDonald had been so unpleasant to work with.

"I'm sorry this hasn't worked out, Hilly," Lewis said, "but if it's any comfort to you, you can be sure that guy will never sit in your office."

Over the years, Lewis kept that promise, and Paige was content to leave it at that.

---

*Lester Crown was named an unindicted co-conspirator when the indictments were handed up against the assemblymen in December 1974. Shortly thereafter, Lewis nominated Lester Crown to join General Dynamics' board of directors on the strength of Jenner's assurance that Crown's behavior in the bribery scheme had been a total aberration.

According to the incident report that circulated at high levels in General Dynamics during the opening months of 1973, it had happened this way:

A welder at Electric Boat, who was not identified, had been given a work authorization to report to one of the submarines in overhaul. The welder had checked out his equipment and donned his protective clothing and boots. He clipped a film badge that recorded "hits" of radioactive particles so the radiation office could keep track of his annual dose. Routinely, when the film was developed, any trace of radiation showed up as black specs on the clear negative—little high-energy particles that had penetrated the encased piece of film just as they penetrated the human body, destroying or damaging cells they passed through, sometimes triggering cancer.

The welder had followed all of the correct procedures. He had stopped at the entrance of the reactor compartment so the supervisor could log him in. He passed the bright yellow barriers and warning signs, then climbed around the pipes and tanks until he got to the valve listed on the work authorization. The valve was on the main coolant line of the reactor, which means it had been subjected for five years to four-hundred-degree water under two thousand pounds of pressure. Superheated water was highly corrosive, and even stainless steel suffered from brittleness and fatigue eventually. The valve was due for changing as part of the overhaul manifest.

For some reason, after the welder had fired up his grinding tool to cut into the valve, he stopped. Something was wrong. It may have been instinct, it may have been a trace of water near the valve, but for some reason, he left the compartment and told the supervisor he could not make the cut because he believed that the coolant line had not been drained of its contaminated reactor water.

It took some time for the ship's engineers to check the work authorization, but after they did, they reassured the welder that everything was all right. Go ahead and make the cut, they said.

But the welder had refused. They were going to have to prove to him that the coolant line was drained before he put a torch to that valve because life was too short for him to be messing around with a hot line.

The engineers got mad. They hadn't gone to engineering school to be pushed around by some welder who thought he knew better. They ordered him to make the cut, but the welder stood his ground. Tempers flared and the argument went on for some time before someone did a more thorough check.

It turned out the welder was right. The coolant line had not been drained. Had he used the searing power tool to slice through the six-inch stainless-steel pipe, he and everyone else in the reactor compartment would have gotten a radioactive shower at dosage levels sufficient to bar them from nuclear work for the rest of their lives. More frightening, the breach of the coolant line could have sent thousands of gallons of contaminated water into the drydock. Without a lightning-quick response from the dockmaster, there would have been a serious radiation spill into the Thames River. It would have been a disaster. State authorities and the Environmental Protection Agency would have descended on the yard and probably would have spent months testing fish and shellfish before certifying that the river and the near reaches of Long Island Sound were free of contamination.

Electric Boat was so choked with overhaul work and new construction on the 688s in the opening months of 1973 that Joe Pierce didn't have time to see what was happening—to the shipyard and to him. The attack submarines *Nautilus, Dace,* and *Whale* were in various states of overhaul in the South Yard, along with the Polaris missile boats *Lafayette, Hamilton,* and *Kamehameha.* Two more Polaris boats, *Bancroft* and *Carver,* were due in after they completed their final sixty-day patrols in the Norwegian Sea.

Overhauling nuclear submarines was a dangerous and potentially lethal business, but it also was one of the mainstays of Electric Boat's profitability. Every five years or so, the fuel elements inside the reactors were depleted, their uranium-235 degenerated into highly toxic waste by-products. The fuel elements had to be removed and replaced with new fuel elements. That meant men covered in white radiation suits had to enter the reactor compartment, break the seal on the reactor fuel ports, and gingerly slide the fuel elements into shielded steel casks for shipment to the navy's spent-fuel repository. There physicists tested and studied them, searching for ways to improve the efficiency of the neutron "burn" and to prolong the interval between refuelings.

The spent-fuel cores were highly radioactive, and the danger from an accidental spill during the vulnerable hours they were carefully pulled from the reactor and sealed in their casks had inspired layer upon layer of safety precautions. A ruptured fuel element could send radioactive particles into the air, where they might be inhaled or ingested by a worker. The decay products included such toxic metals as strontium-90 and plutonium. An inhaled particle of plutonium might lodge in the lung tissue and bombard the surrounding cells with radioactivity until the reproductive coding in one of the cells was so damaged that it began wild and uncontrolled reproduction, forming a cancer that soon would engulf the lung. Plutonium also was a bone seeker, working its way into the marrow like a bad worm, and increasing the incidence of leukemia among those exposed.

Radiation safety was a science that virtually did not exist before 1945, and Rickover had been its pioneer for the nuclear navy at a time when there had been no textbook to guide his inspection teams. It was written along the way, but it had gotten tougher and tougher over the years as the scientific community came to the conclusion that any exposure above natural levels of radiation increased the statistical chances of cancer among nuclear shipyard workers. Rickover had begun the latest radiation safety campaign at Electric Boat in the spring of 1972, when the full inspection team, led by his deputy, Bill Wegner, swept through the shipyard. The team set up a drill to simulate a major radiation accident—such as the sinking of a submarine at a pier while its fuel elements were exposed, or a plane crashing into radioactive fuel bundles in storage—and the waterfront managers flunked. They did just about everything wrong. The drills were not conducted because anyone expected a plane to crash into a submarine, but because strange things had been known to happen. In May 1969, the nuclear attack submarine U.S.S. *Guitarro* sunk while tied at her pier at the Mare Island Naval Shipyard because the crew in the forward part of the ship was not paying attention to what the crew in the after part was doing. She went down in thirty-five feet of water and the saltwater intrusion did $50 million damage. There had been no nuclear fuel aboard *Guitarro*, but it was not hard to imagine a radiation accident caused by a random event. With the yard full of submarines and dozens more coming down the pipeline, Rickover chose early 1973 to crack down on radiation safety.

He had just made an amazing commitment to Lewis to order billions of dollars in submarines from Electric Boat. At the same time he had begun to hound Joe Pierce about the idlers and loafers in the shipyard. Pierce thought it was just Rickover being Rickover. There was an enormous amount of work to be done to get ready for the *688*s and to get the overhauls completed, including Rickover's pet project, *Nautilus*, which was turning into a nightmare of cost overrun because the ship was in such bad shape after two decades of punishing patrols. The work crews had found pipes down in the bilges so corroded that you could almost poke a finger through them. *Nautilus* should have been retired right then, but Rickover was sentimental about his twenty-year-old prototype. He was determined to send her back to sea with a new set of fuel cores for a final tour.

Rickover had begun sending floor walkers through the shipyard to count the number of men standing idle at any given instant during the day. The body counts were then turned into statistics that Rick-over called up and yelled about to David Lewis. The admiral had put a particularly aggressive young man named Ed Siskin in charge of the Naval Reactors Branch office in the shipyard as his on-site represent-ative. People thought Siskin was out to prove himself in Rickover's organization. He was everywhere and played to Rickover's love of omniscience. Rickover liked to claim that he knew more about what was going on in the shipyard than the shipyard general manager. One day he called from Washington to tell Pierce, "There's a fire in your shipyard. Did you know that? You'd better do something about it!" and hung up.

Pierce was dumbfounded. When he checked, there was a small fire. How the hell did Rickover know?

Of course, Rickover had been on the telephone with one of his men at the shipyard when the young man looked out the window and said, "It looks like something's burning in the shipyard, Admiral." Rickover immediately yelled to his secretary to get Pierce on the other line. He did it for effect. Rickover loved to stay one up on his yard managers.

Rickover's spies—as some of E.B.'s managers referred to them—wrote weekly reports to the admiral documenting problems at the shipyard. Rickover required a similar "critical items" report every week from Pierce. That was on top of the daily telephone call that Pierce had to make to give the admiral a status report and to find out if there were any items on Rickover's daily agenda.

Rickover's complaints about loafing, poor productivity, and lapses in radiation safety had been building, but Pierce just attributed it to the workload. Lewis and the corporate staff were sending so many memos to Electric Boat, they were conducting so many studies and demanding so much information from the shipyard that Pierce complained he was spending all of his time dealing with St. Louis and not enough time managing the shipyard. One study said that Pierce ought to cut one hundred seventy management positions because his organization had grown too fat. At the same time, Rickover was de-manding more people in production management and radiation con-trol. Lewis was pushing Pierce to cut his overhead costs and meet his profit projections because the company was still flat on its ass. And it seemed like every time Rickover complained, Pierce got a call from David Lewis. It was incredible. Lewis called one morning to say that Rickover was mad about the lack of cleanliness at the shipyard—too much clutter in the roadways and scrap metal in the construction areas.

Was that an item that ought to be taken up with the chairman of the board? But Lewis wanted to know what Pierce was doing about it. Pierce pointed out that it was difficult to institute a new cleanliness program at no cost. It became apparent to Electric Boat's managers that Lewis intended to micro-manage Electric Boat and the days of Pierce's autonomy, especially when it came to dealing with Rickover, were over.

Lewis blistered Pierce for failing Rickover's radiation safety inspections. "We must clean up this situation once and for all," he warned in one memo. It was true that the waterfront tradesmen had gotten sloppy about radiation safety, but Pierce was regularly chewing out the foremen to get the message across that they had to do better. Pierce had worked around the danger all of his professional life and had participated in the first radiation safety programs Electric Boat set up for *Nautilus* and for her first refueling two years later. When the first Polaris boats had come in for overhaul all at once in 1965 and 1966, it looked for a while as if occupational exposure to radiation was going to go off the charts. People were worried that the nuclear industry would not be able to find any workers if they all got their maximum lifetime dosage in the space of a few years. Radiation safety had thus become more than a safety issue. Worker exposure was a threat to the program.

Pierce, too, had learned the lesson. For Rickover or Lewis to act as if Pierce didn't understand the importance of radiation safety was just silly, in Pierce's view. But the basic problem was that Lewis showed little confidence in Joe Pierce. There seemed to be no natural chemistry between them. Pierce was rough-cut and loud; Lewis subtle and introverted. Lewis was bringing a new style to General Dynamics. He believed the aerospace industry was the highest evolution of industrial management and when he looked out over the chaos of Electric Boat, Lewis could only think of how untidy the place was, how no one had tried to upgrade ship construction since the Stone Age. Lewis intended to bring a new order, and Pierce represented the old guard. So, really, Pierce's days had been numbered from the moment Lewis arrived, but nothing had been said because Lewis liked to keep his moves secret. He didn't want anyone to walk out on him until he replaced them.

Pierce had suggested the previous fall that he ought to have an employment contract for greater job security and that he wanted to stay on as general manager "to keep the admiral happy." Lewis had said Pierce could stay on, but in the meantime, Lewis began talking to one of his aerospace executives about taking over most of Pierce's production responsibilities. Lewis bided his time. Then he let Rickover do the dirty work for him, not realizing that by caving in again to Rickover's pressure, he was giving the admiral more and more control.

On January 23, 1973, Rickover telephoned Lewis to tell him a letter was being hand-delivered at that very moment to Pierce from the navy's supervisor of shipbuilding, who was housed across the street from the shipyard along with a staff of three hundred inspectors, government contract accountants, and auditors. Rickover was dramatic, omniscient. He quoted from the letter. It was a lengthy indictment of Pierce. "Our areas of concern include widespread labor idleness and loafing, early breaking for shift change and lunch periods and lack of standards for start and clean up." It complained of "no evidence of management attention" to the problems, and warned that the navy could withhold part of the company's profits under penalty clauses in the contracts.

The navy supervisor's survey was based on a sampling of more than sixteen hundred workers, Rickover said. The results showed that 59 percent of the workers were knocking off thirty minutes before lunch and 90 percent of them were knocking off twenty minutes before the end of the work day. That was a lot of time stolen from the government when you considered there were twelve thousand workers at Electric Boat.

Rickover used an ominous tone. "Nothing is being done!" he yelled at Lewis. "Pierce is not paying attention to me or to you. I have been calling over and over again. Listen, I will take formal action if something is not done and done soon. You know, Mr. Lewis, you should have made a survey of the shipyard yourself. You are irresponsible and completely delinquent. Pierce is unresponsive to suggestions. Pierce will not listen to me—all he is doing is kidding me and you."

Lewis tried to calm Rickover down. He was horrified at the accusations directed at him personally. He wondered what kind of formal action Rickover was contemplating. What did Rickover suggest?

The shipyard needed better organization and a stronger hand in management, Rickover lectured. Pierce was okay for contracts and engineering, those were lighter duties. But he was not good enough to run the shipyard. Lewis needed to get someone in there who was more production-oriented, an assistant general manager whose job it would be to run the shipyard.

Lewis pledged to take swift action and Rickover said he would be waiting. Within three days of the telephone call, Lewis stripped Joe Pierce of his authority over the waterfront at Electric Boat. Lewis flew to Groton with one of his aerospace executives in tow, sat down at the conference table in Joe Pierce's office and cleared his throat. He had made notes of what he planned to say on a legal pad. Lewis liked to make a script outline for any important meeting, then he could think about his lines in advance, part of the training from his amateur acting days in college that he had found a useful carryover into business. After all, acting was merely the selling of an image. It required discipline of facial expression, of tone, and the power of articulation. Lewis said from time to time that he had never stopped acting since college.

"As you know," he began, "Electric Boat has a great near-term future and many opportunities along with some difficulties and major problems that must be solved to realize those opportunities." E.B. had done a fine job in total, he said. He mentioned all of the new business, the backlog of orders for submarines that was expected to double by 1975. He went on with the good news for about five minutes. Pierce just listened and chain-smoked.

As Electric Boat started into its expansion program, Lewis continued, the shipyard was not in very good shape. Lewis was getting heavy pressure from the navy on radiation control, excess overhead costs, and unacceptably low productivity. Without question, the shipyard's relations with the navy were horrible, he said underlining the point, horrible. The critical tempo picked up as Lewis catalogued the lapses of the previous six months. Lewis kept Rickover's name out of it, but there was no question that it was Rickover's list of Pierce's sins.

"The only conclusion," Lewis then said, "is that you and your management team need some help, Joe. We have studied the situation at length and concluded that the best thing we can do is to provide you with a deputy general manager in charge of the yard, building, and overhauling the ships, while you have time for other things."

The attempt had been to soften the blow, but there were no "other things" in Pierce's universe. Lewis had just taken away 90 percent of what he spent his time on, the job he felt he knew better than anyone.

"We have looked for our most experienced and best man in the company," Lewis was saying, "and we have selected Merle Curtis, who is now general manager of San Diego Convair and we will name him deputy general manager of Electric Boat."

It must have seemed to Pierce like a colossal mistake for Lewis to reach for a manager from his own field of experience, aerospace manufacturing, where none of the same rules applied, and thrust him into the helter-skelter manufacturing environment of shipbuilding, where rules of thumb about schedule and cost were not related and economies of scale and manufacturing sequence so dissimilar as to be meaningless.

Curtis, an intense and humorless assembly-line manager and engineer, had no shipbuilding experience. He was an aircraft engineer. Aircraft were built in clean, climate-controlled rooms or halls where each step of the assembly could be closely controlled and monitored. Parts could be stamped out to fit every unit. Tools could be neatly laid out as in an operating room. Each unit weighed a few thousand pounds and was fitted together in a neat sequence over a period of weeks or months.

Ships, however, were built over years on a filthy waterfront where something unexpected happened every day to foul up the schedule and routine. It could be the weather or a delivery of steel, the wrong valve or pump. And chances were that the work gangs didn't work in the same place from one week to the next, so there was no dramatic "learning curve" like the kind you get in aircraft production, where the same man does the same thing every day. A shipyard was a construction site. You gave the men work chits for things you wanted done that day. A welder could be in the torpedo room one day, the engine room the next, and the reactor compartment the day after that. The plans were drawn as you went because the total design took so long you didn't have years to wait. Besides, while you were framing up the hull, you didn't need to know exactly where the towel racks were going to be installed when everything was nearly done.

Each ship was custom-built in some respect. Big plates of steel expanded or shrunk, and in the end, each one was slightly different in size and shape. The heat from welding, and rewelding, further changed the fit of the steel.

But David Lewis believed the men who came from the aerospace production lines were superior. The shipyards were way behind, and that was one of the things he intended to change at General Dynamics. He felt the hubris of the industry that had put a man on the moon and could design a flying machine to soar through the atmosphere at greater than Mach 2. To Lewis, ships were like big airplanes whose construction could be "unitized" and packaged in a high-tech environment.

Rickover's threat to take action against him was the incentive Lewis had needed to take the waterfront away from Joe Pierce. The arrival of Merle C. Curtis was intended to put the Lewis imprint on Electric Boat's management. In fact, Curtis had arrived just as all hell was about to break loose.

Rickover's chief radiation enforcer, Murray Miles, was based in Washington in the new naval shipbuilding complex that had been erected as a series of boxy office towers in Crystal City, Virginia, adjacent to the airport and a stone's throw from the Pentagon. Miles had the friendly, round face of a morning news show host, but his expression was more oriental: you never really knew what he was thinking or what he was going to tell the admiral after he quizzed you about radiation control in the shipyard.

Miles had been to Electric Boat three times between the spring of 1972 and early 1973 and things just hadn't gotten any better. People were not thinking about radiation—not even after Rickover's warnings. Yet Rickover's ultimate leverage over a shipyard was that he could shut it down for radiation control violations, and Miles was the man to whom Rickover looked for recommendations.

The authority was part of Rickover's mystique—it flowed out of the Atomic Energy Act to the Atomic Energy Commission and thence to Rickover. It was the authority to control uranium-235 and all of the related nuclear material fabricated in government laboratories for nuclear propulsion reactors. Rickover used his authority to grant an annual authorization letter to shipyards building his ships. The power to grant was also the power to remove.

Miles thought Electric Boat was headed for a major radiation accident. The place was a time bomb, where the tradesmen ignored the rules and the radiation monitors were poorly trained or incompetent. Most of the incidents were minor, but that's where the fuses were lit. The painting department, for example, had been found wiping up and painting over radioactive water drips in the reactor compartments of the ships in overhaul—this made the new paint radioactive. The proper procedure was to scrape the paint where the drips had settled and then paint over bare metal.

On one occasion, a worker had emerged from a contaminated reactor compartment with one of his protective boots missing. Another worker had carried his lunch pail into a restricted radiation zone. People just didn't have religion about radiation. It was an attitude. Nuclear submarines and nuclear shipyard had to operate radiation free. The navy could not ask crewmen to work in the cramped spaces of an attack boat wearing bulky suits to protect them from contamination that had been tracked through the entire ship. The crew needed a radiation-free environment for peacetime patrols and for wartime campaigns. That's why Rickover had insisted that the reactor shielding meet such rigid standards—so the rest of the boat would be like any other boat and all radiation was stopped by the reactor compartment bulkhead. In *Nautilus*, Rickover had designed the shielding to a standard ten times that set by the AEC because he had reason to believe the standards would get tougher and tougher as the years passed and they did. He was conservative, but in the case of radiation he was also pragmatic.

Radiation accidents and worker exposure could alarm the public about nuclear power. Accidents were not only a threat to safety, they were a threat to the viability of the program. Mothers would not send their sons into a navy where they suffered exposure, cancer, and the risk of genetic damage to their children and grandchildren from radioactivity.

Miles had taken a number of steps to send the message to Joe Pierce, but Pierce was under so much pressure from the corporate office to cut his overhead costs and increase productivity that he relegated radiation control to the back burner. Each time Miles sent a report to Rickover on radiation violations at Electric Boat, the admiral got mad as hell at the company and at Pierce, who was guilty of so many other violations in Rickover's book. The latest three-month authorization for Electric Boat was due to expire on the last day of February 1973. Less than a week before the deadline, Miles received a formal request from Paige for renewal, but the letter did not address the shortcomings at Electric Boat. Miles thought it was defensive, misleading. If you had religion, you were not defensive. You were analytical, self-critical, Maoist.

Miles showed the letter to Rickover and added his negative assessment. "These people just don't understand that they can be shut down for this crap!" Rickover fumed. "When is Pierce going to learn? I have given Lewis every opportunity, but he is not listening and he is leaving me no choice. I am going to shut down Electric Boat."

Lewis had belatedly asked Hilliard Paige to help handle the crisis during Paige's last weeks at the company. But when Paige took the telephone call from Murray Miles on Monday, February 26, he was shocked that the situation at Electric Boat already was so out of hand. Miles's tone on the phone was cold and clinical.

"After your first trip to Electric Boat, I was convinced you understood the problem," Miles opened, "yet now it appears that E.B. has won you over. But you are being led down the primrose path. Your letter claims that you have made significant progress. That really galls us. Three Rad-con monitors [radiation-control inspectors] have been contaminated in the last three weeks. This is a nightmare, it can't be ignored. The situation is incredible."

Paige said the company was mobilizing to deal with the problem, but Miles said it was too late.

"This morning I recommended to the admiral automatic revocation of the authorization. Admiral Rickover is in the sheer state of frustration. In practical terms, it would be pointless for you to submit another meaningless letter. There is no way to turn off the expiration date. You are marching toward a March 1 shutdown. You can't dig out in two hours, it would be a mistake to try."

Paige had gone straight into Lewis's office with the news and Lewis was numb at the prospect facing him. The company could not afford a shutdown. It would cost millions of dollars in lost time. The publicity would be horrible. What was Rickover doing? Why the hell had Pierce let things get so bad? Lewis telephoned Pierce to find out what Rickover's people in Groton were saying. Pierce said that it looked like Miles was running the show. Someone ought to call Miles and find out if it was worth going to Rickover to try to talk him out of it.

On Tuesday morning, February 27, Lewis put his notes in front of him and dialed Rickover's office. Lewis thought he had a slim chance of heading off the disaster, but it called for a good performance. When the admiral came on the line, Lewis said, "We understand from your man Miles that there has been some kind of holdup on renewing our authorization to perform nuclear work." Calling it a "holdup" was a nice way to soft-pedal what Rickover was going to do to the yard. Lewis said he wanted to personally assure the admiral that the company recognized there had been too many delays in taking action in the radiation safety area, but the admiral could be confident that he now had the company's full attention and the corporation would be doing a lot of things to correct the problem.

But Rickover erupted.

"I've given you every opportunity in the world, Mr. Lewis! I've had it! You are not listening to me and you leave me no choice. I am going to pull your authorization."

Lewis pleaded for patience. He had expected Rickover to take a hard line and his outline included several fallback arguments. He said the radiation monitoring staff at the shipyard was being reorganized and placed in the chain of command directly under the top waterfront manager so it would have maximum clout. But more importantly, Lewis said, he had just brought a new manager into the yard to improve productivity. He feared that Rickover's drastic crackdown would only hurt the new man's effort to improve productivity.

Lewis had shrewdly stressed the last argument, knowing that Rickover was equally inflamed and distressed about the poor productivity in the shipyard. But Rickover compartmentalized problems. He told Lewis that he would not short-circuit radiation safety to improve productivity. He didn't work that way. Productivity was a separate issue. He was going to shut Lewis down. He already had made up his mind.

The shock wave from Rickover's action did not hit the navy until the end of the week, when the fleet commanders started getting informal notice that the overhaul of their strategic missile submarines would be delayed because Rickover had shut down the largest submarine yard in the country on his own authority. The project officer for submarine overhauls on Rickover's staff, William Bass, went berserk when he heard what had happened. There were seven goddamned nuclear submarines at Electric Boat, Bass protested. Four of the seven were Polaris submarines, and he was responsible for getting them back out on patrol as quickly as possible to protect the security of the United States of America. The radiation-control violations could not be so bad as to require such drastic action. With a stroke of the pen, Rickover was going to throw half the navy into chaos for months. Nuclear missiles that were being overhauled would have to be parked somewhere because now their ships would not be ready on time. It was not easy to park a nuclear warhead. Bass loved Rickover, but sometimes you had to tell the old man that he was off his rocker; it was the job of his loyal staff to prevent him from doing something dumb, and that's why Bass was mad at Miles. He should have stopped Rickover from going overboard.

But Bass did not understand the dynamic that was at work. Rickover was not happy about how Electric Boat was being run. The idlers, the cheaters, the loafers, and the people with no imagination—like Pierce—were never going to be able to build all of the goddamned ships Rickover was getting authorized in Congress if they didn't shape up. Rickover had brought the house down on Lewis so he would understand.

The shutdown threw the entire shipyard into chaos. All work, not just nuclear work, ceased as thousands of tradesmen were ordered to take refresher courses in radiation safety. Rickover called Lewis on almost a daily basis: "I will take General Dynamics on! You are the worst managers in history and you, Mr. Lewis, are a complete failure!" It just made Lewis sick.

Pierce went down to the waterfront and gathered the trades together on every shift, threatening to fire any man who did not get religion. Training centers were set up around the yard. Some of the old-guard waterfront foremen—those believed to harbor casual attitudes about radiation safety—were fired or transferred. Lewis and Paige drafted a letter for Pierce's signature which placed the blame for "unsatisfactory radiological control" on "the failure of division management." Pierce had a choice. He could sign it, or quit. He signed.

Paige, who was more reflective in those final days, made the comment to someone that it looked like Rickover was out to get Joe Pierce. The comment was reported back to Rickover, who went off like a rocket again and blasted Lewis over the telephone for not taking the shutdown seriously.

On Monday night, March 19, Murray Miles was standing on the damp floor of the drydock in the South Yard. The scene was like a moonscape. A huge dark hull towered above the open concrete pit. Miles had flown up that morning from Washington on one of those boxy commuter airplanes that bounces along the air currents between National Airport and the little airstrip at Groton. A warrant officer had picked him up and he made the front gate just after the morning shift was getting into full swing. Miles had stopped by Pierce's office to outline the testing and inspection program for the next two days. Pierce was subdued and Miles thought he looked like hell. Miles had spent the entire day in the South Yard around the overhaul boats and had already called back to Washington once to report angrily that people in the shipyard were clamming up. Someone had told them to say as little as possible because it might mean their jobs. That was totally unacceptable if the shipyard was going to get reauthorized.

Miles set up the drill for that evening. Now, after sundown, he was standing in the chilly drydock thinking that things really had not gotten any better. The submarine that filled almost his entire field of vision was in the drydock for refueling. A manhole had been cut through the pressure hull near the bottom to provide easy access to the engine room and reactor compartment. A bright yellow plastic tent was erected around the entrance as a warning that it was a radiation area. Protective clothing was required. Miles watched as one of the radiation monitors emerged to commence the drill. He was carrying a plastic jug like those used to take samples of the contaminated reactor water to the radiation lab for analysis. Just as another worker approached, the monitor stumbled and spilled the contents of the jug all over himself. The jug dropped to the floor, its contents draining out into a large puddle.

Miles did not say a word. He was there to observe. He knew the drill by heart. The correct response called for stopping the spill by picking up the jug, throwing a pile of rags on the puddle to soak up the contaminated water, cordoning off the area, setting up an on-scene command, isolating the contaminated worker, and transporting him to the decontamination station for a shower and a scrub. Any worker who walked through the spill had to be monitored, dose levels recorded with hand instruments and logged. The movements of those workers contaminated had to be mapped and recorded. Someone had to keep records, and passers-by had to be dragooned into service if assistance was needed.

Most important, word had to get to management, and a perimeter of control as large as was necessary had to be drawn immediately to stop the contamination from being tracked through the shipyard.

But what happened that night was very different.

The first radiation monitor who arrived on the scene stepped in the puddle. He had a meter to measure radiation, but he did not use it. The second monitor who arrived also stepped in the puddle. Then he started surveying what had happened. It took twenty-five minutes for the monitors to notify the dockmaster to stop the pumps. If the spill had been larger, much of it would have been sucked into the sump that discharged into the river. No one threw any of the rags stacked nearby onto the puddle. The monitors set up a useless barrier parallel to the spill so anyone walking through the area would not be prevented from stepping in the puddle. The on-scene command was set up two hundred yards from the spill, making communications virtually impossible.

Miles was thinking about the Keystone Cops, but when he got back to his hotel room at the Ramada Inn that night, he was angry and frustrated. It was worse the next day. Miles tested a large number of radiation monitors and tradesmen, and a third of them flunked. One of the men who flunked was the supervisor of training for radiation control. It was incredible. That was the word Miles always used when things were bad.

Before he left the shipyard, Miles went to see Pierce and was nicer about it than he needed to be: "I'm not sure the down trend has stopped," he said.

The next day Lewis and Paige flew from St. Louis to Connecticut to meet personally with Rickover, who had come up to look the yard over after getting Miles's report. The General Dynamics executives knew they were in for a beating. Already Lewis had decided to ask for more time to prepare for another inspection. Rickover turned the visit into a particularly vicious attack on him. After reciting a long list of faults, he upbraided Lewis for putting Paige in charge of handling the crisis. How incredibly stupid to send an administrative man to solve a highly technical problem, Rickover said. Later he repeated the criticism more strongly, calling Lewis a "stupid bastard" for entrusting radiation safety to Paige, who didn't know the first thing about what he was doing. Lewis sat there and took it for a long time as Paige looked on, seeing how Lewis was restraining himself. Paige himself was not upset by Rickover's criticism. He knew him too well.

When it was all over and Rickover had left, Lewis turned on Paige and criticized him bitterly for not coming to his defense. "You knew some of that stuff he was saying was wrong and just plain bullshit," he said. "Why didn't you speak up?"

Paige didn't really give an answer. He could have said what he was thinking, that Lewis was paying the price for ceding so much control to Rickover, who took everything you gave him and then demanded more. Lewis had let Rickover push him around. He had catered to him to get one up in the competition for the new submarines, but he didn't understand that catering to Rickover did not win you contracts. Either he had decided to give them to you or he had not. He just wanted to maximize his production lines. Lewis's mistake had been in giving Rickover the opening, in letting him undercut Pierce without question or challenge. Rickover moved into any vacuum. And after he moved in, he pushed his power to the limit. But Paige just shrugged it off. He was anxious to leave.

It came as a surprise when on March 22, two days after Miles's inspection and one day after Rickover had cut Lewis to ribbons, he restored Electric Boat's authorization to handle radioactive material.

He had made his point, even though there was scant evidence that radiation safety had improved. Miles called Paige and told him to make sure that the radiation monitors who had failed their inspection and testing not be allowed to go immediately back to work. "It wouldn't do," Miles said, "to have it show up in the record that we tested these guys on Tuesday and we had them out refueling the 607 [U.S.S. *Dace*] the following Tuesday. The whole world would know there is no way we could have retrained them to that extent in that short a time." Miles suggested that the monitors who failed be demoted to "assistant monitors" and made to wear large red armbands until their retraining was completed.

The big concern for the navy and for Electric Boat was that eight nuclear submarines still were tied up in the shipyard and there was a strong sense of urgency both to complete their overhaul and get them back to sea. "You have three ships sitting there with just a little work required to get them out," Miles told Paige. "It would seem silly not to crank up those ships and get them out."

In the wake of the crisis, the shipyard was turned over to the aerospace engineer, Merle Curtis, who Lewis said was among the best and brightest in the company. If he didn't walk on water, it only came up to his ankles, one of Electric Boat's more cynical managers had quipped upon his arrival. Curtis would make the best of serving as Pierce's deputy, but it was clear to the shipyard's senior managers that the new number two man was reporting directly to Lewis, who was so traumatized by the Rad-con shutdown that he granted ever more influence to Rickover over the running of the shipyard. Faced with such a convincing demonstration of Rickover's power over General Dynamics' largest division, Lewis would never cross Rickover lightly or take him for granted.

That was exactly what Rickover wanted.

Before the year was out, the navy awarded all eleven 688-class submarines to Electric Boat, and the managers at the shipyard knew they were going to pay a high price for David Lewis's triumph because he had reduced the bid significantly to shut out Newport News and keep Rickover happy.

Some of the non-Rickover people in the navy said it looked like Lewis had "bought in" on the contract, meaning he deliberately underbid to get the business, figuring he could break even somehow or get his earnings by filing claims later on.* That was the thing about government contracts. The Pentagon had no means—and still does not today—of preventing a defense contractor from submitting an excessively low bid to win the award. It was one way to game the system because, if you were tough enough or crafty enough or, in some cases, dishonest enough, you could try to win later concessions through claims or contract adjustments by arguing that the government somehow was unfair, delinquent, or negligent.

In the private sector, such gamesmanship would most often result in immediate default and punitive actions against a supplier. But in the insular world of the defense industry, the Pentagon was hardpressed to take punitive action against the defense industrial base. Most military officials saw taking on a large defense contractor as a bad career move; others just did not have time because the average tour for senior military positions was two or three years. The system mitigated against the testing of big contractual disputes and the pressure was always there to settle. The contractors, of course, had figured this out.

---

*Lewis acknowledges that he reduced the bid significantly, but denies that he did so with the intent to file bogus claims later to make up for any losses. He maintains that he was optimistic E.B. under his guidance could achieve the productivity targets set by the bid. He believed that the shipyard had achieved such productivity levels during the sixties and could do so again, assisted by the new and better facilities that General Dynamics' board had agreed to fund.

When David Lewis arrived at General Dynamics, he faced $40 million in write-offs at the company's missile division in Pomona because, as he said himself publicly, the division had bought in on a big contract in a competitive fever. He told one interviewer later, "We're telling our competitors that we're bidding high so the word gets around and we don't get into these damn bidding wars. You can have the greatest controls in the world, but if you bid low, there's nothing you can do about it."

The statement was a clever ploy made at a time when Lewis had no intention of bidding high. Faced with the prospect of winning all of those submarines, David Lewis cut Electric Boat's bid with a competitive vengeance.

The navy solicited the bids for the next eleven 688s in January 1973. In the new aerospace lexicon of Lewis's management, the submarines in the second contract were dubbed "flight two." By March, Pierce had pared down as much as he could the shipyard's estimate of how many million man-hours it would take to build the submarines. Ship construction was estimated in man-hours. You broke up the ship into sections and calculated how many man-hours it would take to do all the welding and installation in that section. Then you applied the average labor rates to come up with a dollar estimate. It took somewhere between three and four million man-hours to build a nuclear attack submarine during the 1960s. But the 688s were more complex and carried about 40 percent more weight. Both Electric Boat and Newport News had been hungry for the business in 1971 when the first twelve were up for grabs. Both yards submitted lean bids—too lean, as they had been finding out during the first year of construction.

All the reports from the shipyard indicated that Electric Boat should submit a higher bid for the new submarines because it was going to take more man-hours to build them than anyone had bargained for. But in early 1973 Lewis was acting as if he didn't care. His attitude was making Pierce and the others nervous. Even as Paige was preparing to leave the company, he had avoided getting involved in the bid preparation for the flight two submarines because he believed Lewis had a number in mind and was going to bid low just to get the business, and Paige thought that was a mistake. The bid review was set for April 5 in St. Louis. Joe Pierce and his new production deputy were still inundated by the Rad-con crisis. In their place, they sent the division comptroller, Arthur M. Barton.

Art Barton was becoming a pivotal figure in Electric Boat's management. Pierce had given him the top financial job in the division in 1972, and some of Rickover's people had screamed because they considered Barton the prototype for a new generation of contractor accountants whose sharp pencil was always finding ways to gouge the government. Barton got his job, in fact, because he had the sharpest head for figures of anyone in division management and was trained as a lawyer as well. It was a combination of skills that made him indispensable in the complex and arcane negotiations Electric Boat carried on almost constantly with the navy. Barton was wiry, birdlike, and a little on the high-strung side. He could talk for hours in a negotiating session and could spin the most elliptical rationale his navy counterparts had ever heard to support requests for more money. These arguments often sounded so convincing the first time you heard them, you almost agreed the government should pay for whatever add-on Barton was after. It was only later that you realized he had been blowing smoke at you.

Barton had a fine mind, and he used it to advance himself in Electric Boat by coming up with money-saving and money-making strategies that pleased his bosses. That's what Barton liked to do most, keep his boss happy. And Pierce, ever the grizzled waterfront engineer who seemed a little at sea when it came to higher accounting, had made Barton a crucial member of his team.

By 1973, General Dynamics corporate headquarters was long gone from the windy reaches of Rockefeller Plaza. David Lewis now held court on the twenty-third floor of an office tower in Clayton, Missouri, a distant suburb of St. Louis. It was one of those buildings that used brown gravel imbedded in cement as a facade and one of the walls in Lewis's conference room was done in matching, interior gravel. The credenza along one wall displayed small plastic models of the jets, rockets, and ships General Dynamics had sold to the government over the years. An overhead projector sat at one end of the conference table so the division managers could show the viewgraphs charting their performance at the two-day quarterly management meetings Lewis ran.

On April 5, 1973, Barton was at the conference table early; that's when Lewis liked to start. It was Barton and the 688-program manager on one side of the table and Lewis—flanked by five members of the corporate staff—on the other. Barton never had a chance. But as he later explained to Pierce, he made a valiant effort to present the shipyard's case that it was bidding as low as it possibly could. He had prepared spread sheets and charts showing how the "returned costs" coming in from the shipyard were running well above all the projections on the first group of submarines. The startling truth was that the estimate of the man-hours required to build each of the 688-class submarines had grown by 360,000 man-hours per boat in a very short time—just nine months since the shipyard had been getting hands-on experience with U.S.S. *Philadelphia*. The trend lines all were terrifying.

Barton acknowledged that the shipyard managers planned to do a number of things to improve productivity. "However," he added, "from an estimating point of view, they have not happened yet. We have no evidence to indicate that they would be successful, and it does not seem prudent to task the bid" on the assumption that things would get dramatically better.

But Lewis just flattened Barton's arguments. The performance of the shipyard was very poor, he said, and there was a large margin, a very large margin for improvement. Lewis was bringing change to management. The corporate office was bearing down on the problems at the shipyard and performance undoubtedly would improve substantially—at least enough to absorb the additional man-hours that were coming in from the shipyard. By the end of the meeting, Lewis had reduced the shipyard's bid for the next eleven submarines by 300,000 man-hours per boat.

When Barton returned to Groton and told Pierce how much Lewis had reduced the bid, Pierce went into a rage because he had already cut 100,000 man-hours out of each boat before he sent the bid to St. Louis. He had tried to be a team player and to satisfy Lewis's competitive instinct, but this was crazy. Pierce protested, but Lewis was not listening because Pierce was persona non grata in the corporate office. Pierce was just going to have to live with the bid, Lewis said; he would have to perform to the standard that Lewis was setting for the shipyard.

Lewis had ignored the central fact that the *688* class could not be compared to the *Sturgeon* class, from which Lewis was drawing his productivity data. The *688*s were both larger and more complex. Even if the shipyard operated as efficiently as it had during the sixties, it could not build *688*-class submarines in the same relative time frames it had built the *Sturgeon*s.*

---

*Lewis appeared to ignore other important factors: Electric Boat could not build eighteen large attack submarines as well as the first Trident with the facilities that existed. That meant the massive construction program was going to disrupt the already cramped shipyard while it was trying to perform to superhuman expectations. Secondly, the workforce of the early seventies was not the workforce of the previous decade. Electric Boat had scaled back employment when the *Sturgeon*-class building program wound down. The overhaul business had kept a core workforce in place, but the building program ahead was going to require Electric Boat to go from twelve thousand workers to more than twenty-five thousand in a very few years. All of those learners and unskilled workers entering the shipyard were not going to enhance efficiency, they were going to erode it.

As it turned out, Lewis's bid reduction was unnecessary. The only other bidder, Newport News, effectively withdrew eight months before the award. Word reached Lewis during June—by way of Joe Pierce—that a General Dynamics manager had bumped into the president of Newport News at a shipbuilding conference. The Newport News president was fuming about Rickover and he said, very straightforwardly, that he was going to sit out the current round of 688 bidding. Lewis drew a big question mark in his notes when Pierce related this intelligence over the telephone, wondering whether the statement was candid or a clever competitive ploy. But all other signs were that the Newport News president was being truthful. The Virginia shipyard was in trouble on the first five 688s. Its president was not about to invite more trouble by locking himself into a tight production schedule he could not meet.

Lewis, however, was not paying attention to contract terms or tight schedules. Indeed, he seemed oblivious to how tight the contracts were becoming and how events in the world around him posed an additional threat to the economic well-being of Electric Boat. There was trouble building in the Middle East and shipbuilding was a highly energy-dependent industry. Where Newport News was demanding that an energy crisis be treated as an "act of God," releasing the shipyard from schedule and cost restrictions, General Dynamics ignored the threat. Lewis was following one course, Rickover's course, and Lewis thought he was getting business for the shipyard—filling up the bathtub, as one Electric Boat manager put it. Lewis was not listening to the professional shipbuilders in his organization who were waving red flags at him. He was imposing his own judgment—or suspending it—in an area where he had no experience.

On the same day Lewis got word that Newport News was pulling out of the competition, he also got a message from Rickover that Electric Boat had "a great opportunity" to do well in the bidding. Lewis understood what Rickover wanted and he was going to give it to him. Lewis was just not going to risk losing one of the navy's biggest orders for submarines and he had induced a competitive frenzy in the corporate office, where one manager reported the prevailing strategy as: "Going after all the business in sight on the theory that if the yard is full of 688s, Trident can go hang."

In early August, with the 688 bid still pending, fresh reports from the shipyard showed that the scope of the work on each submarine had been revised upwards again, this time by another 200,000 man-hours per boat, but Lewis refused to raise the bid to reflect the increase in work. The 688 bids went in as Lewis decreed. When the final award was made in November, Lewis had cut nearly 500,000 man-hours—about 12 percent—off the estimate of what it would take to construct each ship. In effect, what Lewis had done was reduce the bid on the second group of submarines to match what the company had bid on the first group—three years earlier.

Rickover was very pleased at how the bidding turned out. Lewis's low bid had disarmed the critics. Let Zumwalt look over Rickover's shoulder for the first sign of cost growth in the *688* program. Let Zumwalt tell the Secretary of Defense, the President, and the Congress that Rickover's already large and expensive attack submarine was going to get even more expensive. That wouldn't happen now, thanks to David Lewis.

Just to keep Zumwalt on the defensive, Rickover telephoned his nemesis on November 30 and accused him of trying to kill funding in Congress for the submarines that Rickover had worked so hard to get.

"There are a hell of a lot of rumors . . . that you want to kill four submarines," Rickover said. "My feeling is that you're against nuclear power—I have that feeling . . . but that's all right—you're CNO, you're boss, but I don't agree we ought to reduce [them]."

"That is not the way it works," Zumwalt replied just as testily. "My perception is I'm trying to get nuclear-propelled ships and non-nuclear-propelled ships and you're on the Hill killing my non-nuclear ships."

"No, I'm not," Rickover protested. "Something can be dispelled right at this moment instead of going on and on and on and on! . . . When we started, you used to come through me [to discuss submarine funding]—and then all of a sudden it changed. It doesn't do any good for the navy. . . ."

"We waste a hell of a lot of effort," Zumwalt agreed.

"I've got my people . . . doing nothing but this goddamned crap. . . . If issues were settled between us we could knock off all that and get to work. It takes up a lot of your time too. I'll make a deal with you—I'll help you lobby for your goddamned stuff too. Not against your stuff, [I'm] only against killing nuclear ships. [I am] no expert on other ships, I don't have time."

But the issues were not settled between them, and Rickover fed the opposition to Zumwalt's agenda in Congress while Zumwalt continued to argue in top-secret channels that the breakthrough anti-submarine system he had under development obviated the need to build five of Rickover's monsters every year. By 1973, Zumwalt already had converted the Deputy Defense Secretary to that notion, but Rickover was a formidable adversary and he was still winning.

David Lewis's reward for bidding right on the 688s was swift and immensely valuable to General Dynamics: Rickover coached Lewis on how to win the $300 million navy contract for the first Trident ballistic missile submarine. In their private telephone conversations during December 1973, Rickover specifically encouraged Lewis to accept Rickover's guidance as a means of overcoming General Dynamics' only potential competitor in the bidding, Newport News.

The telephone call was made on Monday, December 10. Rickover told Lewis that General Dynamics should withdraw its bid for the first Trident and resubmit it in a different format. Rickover urged that General Dynamics resubmit its bid as a "fixed-price" bid, but Lewis expressed concern about the uncertainties in predicting the cost of Trident. Rickover reassured him that the company could "restructure" the contract so it would cover all of the company's costs of construction. The new format would appear to be a better bargain for the government—but in name only, because it would be labeled a "fixed-price" contract, and that's what Rickover was after. The difference in Washington, and Rickover knew this better than anyone, was that the appearance of cost savings was just as important as the fact of cost savings. A fixed-price contract looked like a better deal to the Congress and to the taxpayers, even if it was just shrewd public relations packaging.

Rickover cajoled Lewis and assured him that General Dynamics would be hardpressed to overrun a fixed-price contract if the "fixed" price were set high enough. And then Rickover played on Lewis's competitive instincts: "You should be smart and protect your position to keep out Newport News," he said.

It was a startling statement for a government official to make. If Rickover's private words, as reflected in Lewis's notes of the conversation, had been reported on the front page of the newspapers, the Trident program would have been savaged by its critics and Rickover and Lewis would have been challenged for the appearance of impropriety on this vital defense contract. But the conversations remained secret, and David Lewis did not mention them later when other senior navy officials questioned his bidding strategy for Trident. Rickover told Lewis to move on the bid strategy "pretty damned quick." And so, within weeks of the conversation, General Dynamics withdrew its cost-plus-profit bid for the Trident and resubmitted a "fixed-price" bid just as Rickover suggested. The "ceiling" in the bid—the fixed point past which the government would stop paying—was higher than in any previous navy contract and was criticized throughout the Trident construction program as making a mockery of the fixed-price concept.

Rickover's motivation to coach Lewis obviously flowed from Rickover's drive to personally distribute the workload for the nuclear submarines he had won from Congress. It was part of the self-generated mystique that he was personally responsible for the nuclear submarine program—every aspect of it—and, as he had told Zumwalt, that he was just trying to do something for the United States because it had done so much for him, an immigrant kid from Poland who had become the father of the nuclear navy on his own initiative and hard work. He didn't have much time because he was an old man, so the navy would have to pardon him if he seemed to write his own rules.

But Rickover was not above the law. By dealing through back channels with David Lewis and other contractors, he instilled in them a notion that the established procedures for procurement could be circumvented by stealth and bullheadedness. Later, the contractors would adopt similar tactics in turning on Rickover and filing massive claims against the navy to recover their cost overruns on the 688s. Then Rickover would cry foul and crusade against the claims while preaching about the need to restore "contract sanctity."

But there would be a measure of hypocrisy in his indignation.

This made the greed of the contractors no less excusable since they continuously maintained the option—and often exercised it in the case of Newport News—to reject his "deals" along with his guidance and daily suggestions on how to run their shipyards. Lewis, however, was new to the game, and did not heed the many warnings from his own people that Rickover was no contractor's friend and concessions made in the bidding process were made for free. It was a one-way street.

By late 1973, Electric Boat was in the midst of what some believed was an institutional nervous breakdown, a kind of gridlock that swamped the yard managers with so many new problems every hour of every day that they lost track of them, so that the problems just kept compounding like interest on a bad loan.

Right smack in the middle of the North Yard, construction crews were trying to erect a massive building hall whose completion was essential if Electric Boat was going to be able to meet the deadly pace of three 688s per year plus one of the giant Tridents. Half the people were working on facilities and the other half were trying to work around them in the cramped confines of the yard. Submarine hulls seemed to be strewn randomly through the ramshackle buildings and temporary work sites.

Some of the yard managers wished that the *688* program could be halted for a year to let the engineers and operational managers regroup, catch their breath, and sort out the madness in the yard. But time was money, and the managers knew they were dreaming to think anyone would give them a little time for free. The navy—Rickover—would have gone crazy if someone suggested a year's grace period under the contract because someone would have to eat the cost of that time. Besides, he had been sending his senior aides to testify in Congress that Electric Boat could handle the fleet construction in the time frames set by the contracts.

So the schedule was the killer. Everybody's reputation was tied to it and the financial strength of General Dynamics depended on it. There was no time to stop and sort out the problems, to find the materials, to hire and train the welders, to change the manufacturing layouts and still keep the goddamned schedule. On any given day, it seemed like a third of the workers in the yard were standing around: a welder waiting for a bulkhead support that had to be retrieved from a distant warehouse; a machinist waiting for his next piece of work; a grinder waiting to grind the rough edges of a fresh weld; a foreman waiting for an inspector to check the welder's work; an inspector waiting to radiograph a weld to make sure there were no bubbles inside; a painter waiting for a laborer to set up his scaffolding; a shipfitter waiting for a planner to explain something in a drawing.

Everyone was waiting for someone else to finish or for material to arrive, but no one was making the system move forward fast enough to keep everybody in equilibrium. The clock was ticking. There weren't enough good people to do the work and consequently the rejection rate for welds rose to 30 percent, an unprecedented number. There was one thoughtful fellow in the planning department named Craig Haines who started writing memos trying to warn people about what was happening. The shipyard had stopped hiring in late 1972 during difficult labor negotiations and the waterfront was soon falling short of its goals for training new welders, who were essential to meet the schedule for framing up U.S.S. *Philadelphia* and the other five hulls that would become *688*-class submarines. As the yard got desperately short of good welders, the schedule starting slipping. Then the overhaul work hit the yard, and overhaul work was bread and butter to management, so Pierce started pulling the experienced welders off the *688* program and sending them down to the overhaul boats in the South Yard. Meanwhile all those green welders who stayed behind made a mess of the first 688s.

A lot of men who worked on U.S.S. *Philadelphia* later said that the ship was built twice because just about everything installed had to be ripped out at least once due to faulty workmanship, changed plans, or improper sequence.*

On top of everything, the 688s posed some learning problems that the shipyard had not faced in more than a decade. A good example was Rickover's new reactor compartment, the very heart of the ship, where everything had to be perfect. No one was allowed inside the reactor compartment of a nuclear submarine when it was running critical. All adjustments to the reactor were made remotely from control panels on the top deck of the engine room. The radiation inside the reactor vessel was so intense during fission that some of the energy passed right through the thick steel wall of the pressurized chamber. The escaping radiation included the highest energy by-products of nuclear fission: gamma rays, X-rays, and high-velocity neutrons. Thus the reactor compartment had to be a fortress to contain radiation to protect the crew.

The reactor sat on a heavy foundation in the dead center bottom of the hull. Thick bulkheads were erected ten feet forward of the reactor and ten feet aft. The bulkheads had to be strong enough to withstand the pressure of the ocean, because if anything ever happened inside the reactor that caused it to lose its coolant, automatic valves would open and the ocean flood in to stop the meltdown. The reactor vessel was sealed in a neutron shield tank, a large tank of water whose purpose was to stop high-velocity neutrons that penetrated the reactor wall.

Electric Boat had been building the same reactor compartment since *Skipjack*, and the same shield tank around the Westinghouse S5W reactor. Some of the old-timers at the shipyard felt they could build the Westinghouse compartment with their eyes closed. But the 688 class had an all-new reactor compartment to house the much larger S6G reactor from General Electric. The spaces were much tighter and the neutron shield tank was proving to be a devilish and

---

*One survey showed that 25 percent of the rework on the submarines during 1973 had been due to poor engineering or changes in plans coming from Newport News, the navy's design agent. But when Electric Boat conducted a major internal assessment of the waterfront a year later, the shipyard managers concluded, "Many allegations [have been made] that changes are a major cause of overrun, [but the] volume of contract changes has not been large [and] drawing changes [are] within bid expectations [and the] effect to date has been small. . . ."

painstaking installation. Getting those big chunks of metal into the reactor compartment was almost like building a ship inside a bottle. Once the pieces were in there, they had to be fitted together and welded to the supports and stiffeners that protected the integrity of the tank from the shocks of war.

One of the first things the shipyard discovered on *Philadelphia* was that if you didn't hoist the tank pieces into the compartment in the right sequence, you couldn't get other parts of the tank in at all. It was worse than painting yourself into a corner. Some of the welding problems seemed impossible at first. The space where the bottom of the tank fitted to the hull of the ship was barely big enough to squeeze in a man's head. Yet the steel in that hole had to be pre-heated and welded. It took a lot of time and a lot of welders working on short shifts to master the installation.

The steel used for the tank was the special hull steel that could withstand eighty thousand pounds of pressure per square inch, but the problem with the special steel was its propensity for delayed cracking if the slightest impurity got into the seam. The only way to make sure the weld was good was to let it stand for seven full days. Not much else got done while you were waiting because if you welded up more parts of the tank and then found a crack, the whole mess had to be ripped out and it took weeks to get back to square one.

Pierce understood what was happening in the shipyard, but he could not very well go to Lewis and say, "I told you so!" Lewis and the aerospace man he had sent to run the waterfront seemed helpless in the face of impending disaster. Electric Boat's managers did everything they could to turn around the 688 program during 1974, but events like the Arab oil embargo worked against them.

Electric Boat's chief procurement officer heralded the new year by warning, "The outlook is for runaway lead times" on all equipment and steel orders. "Prices are up, material shortages are up, and things look like they will be getting worse, leaving only one direction for price and deliveries to go—up," he concluded.

Shipbuilding was energy-intensive and the cost of energy was suddenly soaring. The price of coal used for steel production leaped 118 percent in three months. Fuel oil for industrial burners jumped from $30 a ton to $130 a ton. Deliveries stretched four to six months beyond contract deadlines.

Manpower problems were equally acute. Experienced structural welders were extremely scarce. In his weekly letters to Rickover, Pierce cited the lack of skilled welders over and over again until the 688-program manager pointed out to Pierce that Electric Boat would never sustain a claim for cost overruns if the company had admitted all along that it did not have enough men working on the ship. Then Pierce stopped reporting the welder shortage and diverted the most experienced tradesmen to the overhaul ships, which paid a better profit.

Everything had thus conspired against U.S.S. *Philadelphia*, and it was clear to everyone in the yard that she was far from ready when her launch date arrived in October 1974. But more fearsome to General Dynamics and to Rickover was the public relations disaster from delaying the launch of the first *688*-class submarine at Electric Boat. There would be questions in Congress and the stock analysts on Wall Street wouldn't like it. Delay was the wrong signal and could cause trouble for the program.

The solution was effective, if also inelegant and deceptive. The work gangs pulled the cables out of the ship and sealed the hull so she could slide down the ways into the river without sinking. After all the dignitaries and the reporters went home from the launching ceremony, Electric Boat tugs nudged the lifeless hull into a drydock and pumped out the water to beach her once again. Work resumed the following week. It would take three more years to complete U.S.S. *Philadelphia*.

The cover-up of what was happening at Electric Boat began toward the end of 1974.

The thoughtful memos about what was going wrong with the *688* program changed in tone, and some of the yard managers started to get panicky because they were the ones who were closest to the ships and they could see the disaster building.

The other person who could see it was Art Barton, the nervous comptroller, who faced the worst kind of dilemma for an ambitious organization man: he was the chief financial officer of the division, and therefore had a legal responsibility to keep his superiors informed about cost overruns in the shipyard. But his superiors desperately wanted to keep a lid on any bad news about the *688* program. That was why Barton had been told to shut up, first by Mel Curtis and later by Gorden MacDonald, the chief financial officer of the corporation.

Barton's original estimate that "losses on these two [*688*] contracts could exceed $100 million" was handed to his superiors in August 1974, along with his conclusion that the "current cost to complete forecasts" for the *688* program "appear to be inaccurate." Electric Boat had projected it would take 35,000 man-hours for every 1 percent of progress on the ships, but during 1974 this key indicator had steadily been running at more than 60,000 man-hours for each percent of progress. The yard was going to overrun by nearly 100 percent at that rate. It was difficult, some said impossible, to make up time on submarine construction once you got behind, because there were only so many men you can get on the ship at one time.

Barton said ruefully in a private note to a sympathetic colleague, "Any time men believe they can predict the future and then manipulate events to make their predictions come true, they are bound to make terrible mistakes."

Curtis got angry and told Barton to stop trying to estimate how many man-hours it was going to take to complete the ships. After all, the shipyard had not even completed the first ship; there was plenty of time to make up the lost schedule. Curtis said he would dictate the cost projections and Curtis's projection was the one in the contract with the navy, period. He would not tolerate any suggestion that the yard was going to overrun it. "We'll make it up," he said, and then he told Barton to keep his nose out of it.

It was the wrong thing to say to Barton. If management did not believe his estimates, that was one thing, but Barton said he was going to do his job. And so almost from the moment Lewis reduced the bid on the second *688* contract, Barton began keeping a diary of what he told his bosses and what his bosses said. It was one of those small, six-ring notebooks with a black cover and lined filler paper. He kept it in a desk drawer in his office on the first floor of the administration building, just down the hall from Joe Pierce and Mel Curtis. At the end of staff meetings, he returned to his office and closed the door so he could scribble his entries in private. He kept the diary with his cost reports and memos of meetings that he attended with Lewis. Barton did what his bosses told him to do and he remained an effective and loyal member of the management team. But if the day ever came, Barton would be able to prove that he had told them just how bad things were.

At the outset of 1974, Electric Boat's program manager for the *688*-class boats had said that "to meet the 1974 plan, we must reduce the projected manhour expenditures by approximately 4,500,000 manhours." That was a lot of man-hours to cut. It was in fact enough man-hours to build an entire nuclear submarine. It led Lewis to castigate the yard managers for spending too much time and money flying to Washington (a one-hour trip) to haggle with the navy. Lewis suggested cost-savings measures that trivialized the enormous problems: "Cut back on the number of people on distribution [lists] for memos,"

Lewis mandated. "Eliminate distribution of irrelevant memos and," he added, "print on both sides of the page."

The shipyard was going to hell and Lewis thought printing on both sides of the page was going to pull them out.

Before the end of the year, Lewis had asked Barton to prepare a full review of the cost projections on the *688* program. Barton flew to St. Louis and presented them on November 19, 1974. Lewis was genuinely shocked at the results: Electric Boat would overrun its $1.2 billion bid on eighteen attack submarines by about $800 million. Such a loss would be twice as big as the worst disaster in the company's history, the Convair debacle of 1960.

The devastating projection had been the last thing David Lewis wanted to hear, especially so close to the end of the financial reporting year. The securities laws required Lewis to report a loss as soon as he learned about it, and he understood the law and its purpose. Profits could be declared incrementally over the life of a construction program, but projected losses had to be taken all at once—as soon as they could be calculated. The requirement was conservative accounting, but it protected stockholders from managers who used tricks to push their losses out into the future and thereby forestall the day of reckoning.

But instead of recording a loss on the *688*s, Lewis insisted that he did not believe Barton's figures. As chairman of the company, he did not have to report something he did not believe. Lewis sent Barton back to Groton and announced that he would send a corporate audit team to the shipyard to review the *688* figures. Privately, Lewis was sick about what was happening and felt at a loss to control events in the shipyard. The confidence of his training in the high technology of aerospace production was failing him for the first time, and in a disastrous way. Quarter after quarter there was no improvement. The detailed reports Lewis monitored from the chairman's office showed no evidence that his management changes were having any effect. In his anguish, Lewis realized that he was facing the first loss that could be attributed to his management at General Dynamics. He was not about to take responsibility for it. And, if he could avoid it, he was not about to declare a loss because he believed that once you declared a loss, that money was gone forever, and Lewis hated the finality of the decision.

As far as Lewis was concerned, the navy was responsible for any overrun on the *688*s. Rickover had taken the *688* design contract away from Electric Boat and some of the early drawings had been late. Rickover had shut down the shipyard at untold expense over radiation safety violations and no one had foreseen the inflation touched off by the energy crisis and how it had ravaged the heavy industries that supported Electric Boat.

Lewis believed that Rickover would see the equity of coming to General Dynamics' rescue. After all, he had put himself under Rickover's guidance. Surely the admiral did not want Electric Boat to take a bath since the *688* program was so important.

He was right up to a point. Rickover did not want any publicity that Electric Boat was incurring large cost overruns. That would just feed the opposition and tarnish the Rickover legend. Rickover also believed the navy shared some of the responsibility for the overrun on the first seven submarines because Newport News, the design shipyard, had dropped so far behind schedule and some of the drawings had been late. Contrary to the intent of the contracts, Electric Boat was getting very little benefit from the lessons learned in the construction of the lead ship in the class—U.S.S. *Los Angeles*—at Newport News. It didn't seem fair and it wasn't.

Rickover recognized this, and he told the senior admirals of the shipbuilding command that if the navy owed Electric Boat some money, the navy ought to settle and settle fast, because the longer they waited, the more likely it was that Electric Boat would blame the navy for any additional overruns that were not the navy's fault.

On the night of December 2, the navy's deputy project officer for the *688* program flew to Groton and met privately with Pierce and his *688*-program manager. He proposed a settlement in which the navy would pay Electric Boat $100 million, no more. It was a hip-pocket estimate that was based as much on Electric Boat's reports to the navy as on any naval analysis of the government's responsibility for a portion of the overrun.

The deal showed the extent to which the relationship between the navy and one of its leading contractors had gone awry. The navy may have been motivated by the good intention of owning up for part of Electric Boat's overrun, but to offer $100 million to a defense contractor without any analysis, without any administrative review of the overrun, without demanding to know what Barton knew about the true size of the overrun, was an abuse of the navy's authority. It fed the notion that government contracts were fungible instruments, whose terms and conditions could be undermined out of public view and away from the scrutiny of Congress.

The charade of a negotiating session scripted in advance to support the conveyance of $100 million reflected a cynical regard for the arm's-length relationship the navy touted in its public dealings with the defense industry.

"Don't be greedy," the navy's project officer had cautioned. Pierce reported the conversation to Lewis the next day, noting he was not sure the project officer could "make this work; however, he has done well in the past."

The deal took a month to fall apart because in the end, Electric Boat went back to one of Rickover's negotiators and demanded greater and greater sums of money. Electric Boat's problem had grown bigger than $100 million—only David Lewis didn't want to tell anybody. Lewis's corporate team returned from Electric Boat and reported that Barton was right: the shipyard was facing a large overrun, not as large as Barton predicted, but in the neighborhood of $500 million. The team projected a loss on the first contract of $220 million and a loss on the second contract of $250 million.

Although Lewis had been told twice during the final quarter of the year with all the authority of his best financial analysts that Electric Boat was going to suffer a massive loss on the *688* program, he did not share this information with the navy, with the public, with Arthur Andersen & Company, the corporation's outside accounting firm, with the shareholders, nor even with Colonel Crown and the board of directors.* Such a loss would have devastated General Dynamics—and Lewis's reputation as its savior.

Instead, Lewis put a tight lid on the corporate team's report and revised the figures drastically downward to reflect a more optimistic future. By so doing he sought to escape from the painful misjudgments he and others at General Dynamics had made, while he prepared to execute a series of threatening strategies against the Pentagon to generate more cash under the contracts. Some of these strategies would strike at the core of national security concerns over the timely delivery of the attack submarines and ballistic missile Tridents—key elements in maintaining the balance of power in the silent war with the Soviet Union.

---

*At the December 1974 board meeting, Lewis told Crown and the other directors that, in the worst case, General Dynamics was facing a $100 million loss on the first seven ships, which would be partially offset by a $50 million profit on the second group of submarines and by a successful claim against the navy. Lewis maintains that at the time he did not believe the alarming estimates being generated by E.B.'s professional cost estimators and that at every stage of evaluation he believed that the company could recover any losses through productivity improvements coupled with navy contract concessions or by claims filed for what the company alleged were navy-caused delays and cost overruns flowing from design changes. Today, Lewis says he was "naive, maybe; stupid, maybe; wrong, maybe; but in our judgment at the time we believed honestly that the navy . . . had screwed this thing up . . . and that we were going to get all or essentially all of these overruns, which we clearly saw, covered through the claims process."

By the end of 1974, Electric Boat had suffered a cash drain of $90 million. What profits there were in other General Dynamics divisions were being sucked into the shipyard to cover the mounting overrun and to pay for the facilities expansion that was absolutely crucial to completing the ships. The secret knowledge that the corporation could lose $500 million or $800 million at the shipyard would have perhaps bankrupted General Dynamics had it been publicly disclosed. The corporation was bumping up against the limits of the bank lines of credit it maintained to finance its day-to-day operations. Negotiations were under way to raise and extend the lending limits. It was a crucial period for the company because General Dynamics, like most government contractors, financed its day-to-day operations with short-term borrowings and did not have access to long-term debt capital. The banks and the financial community believed that weapons could get canceled overnight by the whims of Congress. From a banker's perspective, the fortunes of defense firms rose and fell much more precariously than their more stable counterparts in the nondefense sector. As General Dynamics' treasurer pointed out in a letter to Pierce, "the banking community is extremely nervous as to the short term and the long term viability of companies which are heavily engaged in government business, particularly a company with a substantial stake in shipbuilding."

Had the banks known the frightening cost estimates in General Dynamics' shipbuilding program, the company's lines of credit might well have been frozen or called in, forcing General Dynamics into a crisis that only a government bailout or the protection of the bankruptcy statutes could have solved.

David Lewis thus adopted a strategy by which he "retargeted" the cost-overrun estimates to reflect much smaller loss figures than could be covered by a successful claim against the navy. These estimates reflected his optimism that a miracle would occur in the shipyard. By so doing, he avoided having to declare a loss under the accounting rules of the SEC. General Dynamics announced to its stockholders that it was carrying the 688 program on a "break even" basis—meaning the company would not record earnings or losses—until at least one of the submarines had been completed and provided a basis with which to make an accurate prediction about the future.

It was a strategy for keeping the burgeoning overrun off the books.

Filing a claim on the first seven submarines was tricky for Lewis since General Dynamics had not acknowledged publicly that

Electric Boat was facing an overrun. Lewis couldn't very well file a claim for hundreds of millions of dollars without raising a lot of suspicion in the boardroom and on Wall Street. So when the Electric Boat claims team in January 1975 came up with a $300–350 million loss projection on the first seven submarines and recommended a claim be filed in that amount, the corporate office balked and sent a directive to Groton to cut the amount of the claim.

The head of the claims team was an outside consultant who had worked at the shipyard for twelve years as a cost estimator and claims specialist. He worked for three months to refine his estimate of the overrun on the first seven ships and he was infuriated when the corporate office changed signals at the last minute. "I am sorry that I cannot provide my services in changing the claim estimate cost numbers from the $300 million-plus range to the $200 million-plus range directed by corporate management. To do so would involve a compromise of my professional ethics which I am not prepared to make," he said in his termination letter to Barton.

And so Barton completed the work. It was no coincidence that the amount of the claim was finally set at the precise amount that the corporate audit team fixed for the overrun in December: $220 million. But few people knew of the correlation between the figures because the audit team's report was locked away. As far as the board of directors knew, the overrun was $100 million on the first ships. That's what Lewis had told the board in December. Filing a claim for double that amount did not raise suspicions since it was common strategy in the defense industry to submit a claim for roughly double the amount a contractor hoped to recover.

The company did not even call it a claim. The "Request for Equitable Adjustment" was quietly filed in February 1975. Lewis just hoped that someone in the navy was going to come through with some money to keep Electric Boat from becoming the new hole in the bottom of the bucket.

He had told Colonel Crown that he would have the overrun problem solved by February 1975, but February came and went; month after month, Lewis put off telling the board about Barton's projections or those of the corporate team. Month after month the data coming out of the shipyard continued to show no improvement. Indeed, it showed further deterioration. Lewis put it off as long as he could. Finally, in June 1975, he updated the overrun estimate for the board. But he did not give the directors Barton's estimate, or the corporate team's estimate. Instead, Lewis gave the board members his own "retargeted" estimate, which was wildly more optimistic than those of the professional estimators at Electric Boat.

Still, the prospect of a $100 million loss shook the board. Crown, whose investment in the controlling block of stock was $62 million, was crestfallen. What had gone wrong? There was much recrimination in the long and extremely heated discussion that ensued.

The June 1975 board meeting was something of a watershed for Lewis and the board, because the new figures convinced the board that Lewis could not stand alone as the micro-manager for all of the divisions. He had to put someone over the marine divisions, someone who could get a grip on Electric Boat and Lewis knew he was going to have to make a concession to the board because his credibility was wounded by the surprise of the new loss projections. He had been very much on the spot at the meeting, but Lewis made a shrewd political move by recommending that Gorden MacDonald be given extended authority to supervise Electric Boat.

MacDonald, whose pandering to board members had made him a thorn in Lewis's side, had no shipbuilding experience whatsoever, which should have immediately disqualified him as a candidate to oversee the urgent problems at Electric Boat. But MacDonald wanted operating experience if he was ever going to become president of the corporation and take the seat Paige had left vacant. Further, it might well have suited Lewis to get MacDonald out of the corporate office, where MacDonald had been feeding the intrusions of those directors who wanted to look constantly over Lewis's shoulder. MacDonald had done a good sales job on the directors and a number of them believed he might be the solution to Electric Boat's needs. But Lewis could not have been blind to the likelihood that MacDonald would founder. It may have been what Lewis wanted—to take the glow off of the tough-manager image MacDonald had projected to the board of directors. And while MacDonald was out of town, Lewis could work on replacing him. If MacDonald fell on his face and had no corporate office job to come back to, maybe he would leave the company.

The day that MacDonald arrived at Electric Boat, the eleven thousand members of the metal trades unions walked out on strike. The next day, July 3, the cost-monitoring organization under Barton generated new figures, projecting an overrun on the combined submarine contracts of $940 million.

As one of his first acts as the new executive vice president over the marine division, Gorden MacDonald called Barton into the front office at Electric Boat and told him that his days as the top cost estimator of the division were over. He was to stay out of the process.

MacDonald was going to change the rules as to how the division developed its cost estimates. He asked the operational managers to give him a "best efforts" projection of how well they could perform in the best possible circumstances. To those optimistic estimates, MacDonald then applied productivity improvement rates that had never been achieved by the shipyard. The result, of course, was a projection that the shipyard would make a miraculous recovery. From that point on, MacDonald used his new standard of cost estimating in all briefings of the board of directors, of the outside accountants, the navy, and the Congress. Barton continued to keep some very private estimates based on "current performance," but he kept these in handwritten form, locked away with his diary. Barton's private estimates never varied much. From 1975 onward, they all were around $1 billion. But these estimates never reached the board of directors, the stockholders, the accountants, or the navy.

Barton's cynicism over what was happening flared occasionally and sometimes got him in trouble. In June 1976, he blurted out to one of the Arthur Andersen accountants that he didn't make projections of potential overruns anymore because the last time he had challenged the numbers he had been severely criticized and told in essence to keep his nose out of it. From Barton's account of what was going on at the shipyard, the alarmed and shaken Arthur Andersen man wrote a confidential memorandum to his files concluding that first Curtis, and now MacDonald, had been running the shipyard like dictators, covering up the truth about the overrun. "How can we rely on estimates of the division . . . if there is still someone forcing a number down the throat of the operations personnel?" the auditor asked.

General Dynamics avoided recording a loss between 1975 and 1977 by insisting that the overruns at Electric Boat were never greater than the amount of money that the company could recover from a successful claim against the navy, and from substantial improvements in productivity at the shipyard that management was sure could be achieved, all other evidence to the contrary.

During the final months of 1975, the men at the top of General Dynamics had papered over what was becoming the largest cost overrun of the decade. The cost-monitoring process at Electric Boat had been surgically removed by MacDonald and replaced with cost optimism. Shortly before year's end, David Lewis exercised his option to purchase, and then sell one hundred thousand shares of General Dynamics stock. The option was due to expire and Lewis decided to take out a short-term loan and make the purchase. He would not leave his investment in his own company, even though he was optimistic that he was going to turn around the submarine program. He sold the shares, repaid the loan, and took his $1.7 million profit.

MacDonald continued to assure the directors that he would bring success to the shipyard by imposing a "learning curve," under which men who performed complex tasks on a production line would become more efficient at their work over time. But MacDonald did not realize that Electric Boat was so out of control that a reverse learning curve had taken hold, and MacDonald was doing little to address the basic problems that were defeating improved efficiency:

—The shipyard was hiring thousands of new workers, but their inexperience was working against efficiency. Absenteeism and turn-over in the workforce were running at 30 and 40 percent.

—The massive facilities expansion program was disrupting the orderly construction of the ships. Seven different hull-erection plans had been used for the first seven submarines.

—Material shortages were rampant and the materials on hand were not controlled by an inventory system. As a result, the shipyard had hired hundreds of workers to search for materials in the network of Electric Boat warehouses around Groton. There was no system that concentrated on getting materials to the right place in the shipyard at the right time when work gangs were ready to install them.

It was the kind of strain that could nearly kill a man. It took Mel Curtis out of the line-up in May 1976 with a serious stroke. Mac-Donald named himself general manager and told Pierce he could stay on as an executive assistant, but Joe Pierce had too much pride for that and he finally walked out.

"You made out well!"

Lewis recognized the almost boyish tone of Rickover's voice. Today the tone was friendly. No air-raid siren to make his stomach churn.

"You took all the money the navy has," Rickover said.

In April 1976, they had finally reached a settlement on the $200 million claim on the first submarine contract. General Dynamics would get $97 million more for the seven ships, not quite half what the company had asked for.

The lesson from the long negotiation, Rickover added, was: "Put in honest-to-God claims and don't pad them. You got only what you deserved." But Lewis could not afford to agree with Rickover. The cash was sorely needed at General Dynamics, yet there was an imme-diate realization that it was not nearly enough to cover the still hidden and rapidly growing overrun. During the final weeks of negotiations in early 1976, Lewis had flown to Washington and offered to release the navy from claims on all eighteen submarines if the navy would increase its settlement offer to $150 million. If he just got enough cash to stop the hemorrhaging, he could worry about the rest of the overrun later.

It had been a tempting offer to some navy officials who liked the idea of foreclosing any future claims, but Lewis's suggestion amounted to selling protection to the government. It was too much like the neighborhood tough selling insurance to the merchants on Main Street who didn't want their windows broken. The navy's position was to acknowledge some responsibility for the overrun on the first seven submarines, but to disavow any liability for overruns on the eleven 688s awarded in late 1973. Lewis wasn't asking for that much money, but it was the principle: The navy did not owe General Dynamics a nickel for the "flight two" submarines because the company had had plenty of information and virtually all of the plans to make an intelligent and prudent bid. So the navy turned down Lewis's offer, saying the government could not pay protection money. Those same navy officials later regretted their decision. Later on, it added to Rickover's rage when Lewis pushed gamesmanship to the limit and piled on even larger claims.

In the fall, Democratic presidential contender Jimmy Carter defeated Gerald R. Ford and Washington entered the quadrennial phase of transition.*

Policy decisions were suspended as thousands of high-level jobs in the executive branch changed hands. The news media were preoccupied with the Georgians who swept into the city and prepared for power. The carpenters worked through the holidays building the bleachers on the East Front of the Capitol and along Pennsylvania Avenue for the inauguration.

At the navy complex in Crystal City, Rickover and his staff watched the change with great interest. They had been delighted

---

*Over a three-month period in 1976, President Gerald R. Ford's Deputy Secretary of Defense, William P. Clements, Jr., a Dallas businessman and later Republican governor of Texas, attempted to settle the problems of the shipbuilding industry in one large negotiation. For General Dynamics, Clements proposed to revise its inflation clause and pay the company an additional $170 million for the eighteen submarines under contract. Rickover attacked Clements's plan in Congress as "one of the biggest rip-offs in the history of the United States." The settlement fell apart when Newport News and Litton held out for more money. Clements was left to set up an independent Navy Claims Settlement Board to evaluate the merit of the still-mounting claims. He then walked away from the effort, saying to his staff: "We might as well just piss in the campfire and go home."

when Carter revealed during campaign interviews that his early aspirations for excellence had been kindled in Rickover's nuclear training program. Carter's campaign biography, *Why Not the Best?*, had borrowed its title from Rickover's admonition to Carter during his entry interview in the nuclear navy.

In truth, Rickover didn't really recall Carter's brief stint in the nuclear navy and during the presidential campaign Rickover took a very low profile due to his much closer historical working relationship with Ford, a former congressman from Michigan and a longtime supporter of Rickover's programs. Still, after the election, Rickover was happy to have a new admirer in the White House because Carter's appointees in the Defense Department would soon have to contend with the massive and unresolved shipbuilding claims and Rickover hoped to guide them.

While Rickover worked behind the scenes to tutor the new President, General Dynamics pressed its case on other newcomers in the administration. Before the inauguration, David Lewis met over dinner with Harold Brown and Charles W. Duncan, Jr., who had been designated by Carter to take the top two positions at the Pentagon. It was mostly a renewal of the old acquaintance between Lewis and Brown, who had been Secretary of the Air Force during the last three years of the Johnson administration when Lewis was selling McDonnell Douglas fighters to the service. But during the course of dinner, Lewis made a point of saying that he was sure Brown had heard about all the problems at Electric Boat. Lewis assured the new Secretary of Defense that the company was going to straighten out the problems and, to that end, Lewis explained that he had put a new man over the shipyard, Gorden MacDonald.

Lewis's advantage in the conversation was the advantage of longevity. He was selling to the new Defense Secretary, playing the actor and the role of the earnest board chairman working hard and unselfishly for the good of the country. Brown, who had been McNamara's top scientist (before Johnny Foster) and then Air Force Secretary before leaving the Pentagon for a long stint at Cal Tech, had been away from Washington and away from the naval shipbuilding program. Lewis had gotten to him early so Lewis could shape the issues, talk about how Rickover had squeezed down the bids on the 688s. It was the inherent advantage of the defense industry over the civilians and military leaders, who served for only short periods of time. The contractors controlled history in a very real sense, serving as the source of information for those who made policy. The defense industrialists and their broad Washington lobbying organizations were there to offer historical perspective during transitions in power. They gave it calmly, quietly, repeatedly, while everyone else was rushing to get out of town or into a new job.

To the Carter transition team, it looked as if Rickover had piled too many submarines on Electric Boat after awarding the design and prototype contract to Newport News. The problem was called "concurrency" by the new Pentagon managers. To deal with it, they felt they would have to move quickly before it brought the navy shipbuilding program to a standstill and embroiled government and industry in massive litigation.

But even as the Carter administration reached these early conclusions, no one conducted a basic analysis of the $2.7 billion in cost-overrun claims filed up to that date against the navy to determine who should pay. The notion that the claims must be settled to avoid what was described as monstrous litigation repeatedly supplanted the equally valid notion that the claims should have been litigated in full, or in part to restore public confidence in the contracting process.

Without an evaluation, Congress and the public were left with competing and unresolvable assertions by the shipbuilders and by navy officials that the other side was to blame. That the truth lay somewhere in the middle was painfully obvious, but throughout the controversy, the government officials charged with protecting the taxpayers' interest never discharged their obligation to find out where.

In December 1976, eight months after their first settlement, General Dynamics filed the largest cost-overrun claim in its history against the navy: $544 million. Both Rickover and David Lewis knew that the claim was a declaration of war, a slap in Rickover's face, an attack on his management of the navy's nuclear submarine program, and—worst of all—an attack on the Rickover legend.

All of the intelligence reaching Rickover had indicated that another claim was coming because the shipyard was falling further behind, but Rickover believed that the new claim would come in at about $350 million. When it turned out to be nearly $200 million higher, Rickover's shock and outrage were compounded. The admiral believed that whatever sins the navy committed it had paid for them with the settlement of the "flight one" claim—$97 million. That's all the bastards were getting; that's all they deserved.

The new claim asked the U.S. Treasury for half a billion dollars beyond the contract on eleven submarines for which Electric Boat had had the plans since 1973. Still, the new claim repeated the allegation of the first claim: the navy was late delivering design data. It alleged much of the data was "defective," without providing evidence to back this assertion, and it alleged that the navy had crushed productivity in the shipyard by issuing 27,000 drawing revisions during the first four years of construction. All of these things had so disrupted the shipyard, the claim alleged, that the navy bore full responsibility for Electric Boat's overruns on the eighteen ships.

Rickover and a solid line-up of admirals in the shipbuilding command were stunned that Lewis seemed to be desperately going for broke. The claim even charged the navy with responsibility for the five-month strike by eleven thousand Electric Boat workers, arguing that the ships could not have been delivered any earlier had there been no strike because the navy had so disrupted the shipyard with changes and revisions. The admirals were appalled that the shipyard had counted up the routine paperwork revisions and turned them into an onerous intrusion by the navy. Any marine engineer understood that counting up drawing revisions had little or nothing to do with cost overruns in the shipyard. Navy officials began to realize just how much Electric Boat had been hiding about the shipyard's problems and they wondered how the navy could be responsible for cost overruns on ships whose plans were issued in 1973—before the bids went in—and whose first keels were not even laid down until late 1976.

Lewis was trying to get the government to pick up the company's losses to save his own ass on Wall Street, Rickover believed.

"I'm going to take those bastards on!" he declared.

The speed fixes on *Soviet Alpha-2* were inconclusive, but nonetheless astounding to U.S. intelligence.

A Lockheed Orion flying out of Keflavik, Iceland, had picked her up on a sonobuoy track while the Russian sub was making high-speed turns in the Barents Sea. The Orion lost contact, but then a little while later, the U.S. reconnaissance plane picked up *Alpha-2* again. By doing a time-distance plot, the sub hunters had calculated that *Alpha-2* would have had to be going thirty-nine knots to get from the point at which they first observed her to the second contact point. Afterwards, the official CIA verdict was that the encounter with *Alpha-2* was inconclusive because the airplane had lost contact and this gave rise to skepticism about whether the speed observation was credible. Maybe there had been a second *Alpha* out there that day.

But by 1977 there was a growing body of intelligence from spy satellite photography, underwater sensors, and the first-ever infiltration of the massive Soviet shipbuilding complex that the Soviet Union had outdistanced the United States in key submarine propulsion and manufacturing technologies, thus further eroding the qualitative advantage the U.S. submarine fleet had enjoyed since the dawn of nuclear propulsion and the beginning of the silent war.

A week after the election of Jimmy Carter, the first *688*-class submarine, U.S.S. *Los Angeles,* was commissioned as a combatant attack submarine of the Atlantic Fleet. But it was a bittersweet debut for Rickover and the U.S. nuclear navy because *Alpha-2* already had slipped into Arctic waters for an impressive series of sea trials, demonstrating capabilities that the crew of *Los Angeles* could only dream of.

Alpha was the most formidable weapon to be developed in the silent war, and her existence and the evidence about her performance were kept as a closely held secret for years.

U.S. intelligence satellites since the late 1960s had watched the Soviet Union building *Alpha-1* and then *Alpha-2* at the Gorky shipworks three hundred miles northeast of Moscow, but it had taken a decade for the CIA and naval intelligence to solve *Alpha's* mysteries. Her shiny hull cylinders were the same ones pondered by U.S. intelligence analysts in 1968, when they were photographed by the first generation of spy satellites.

The *Alpha*s were about half the size of a *Los Angeles*–class submarine. *Alpha-1* was completed in 1970 and floated by river barge the five hundred miles between Gorky and the northern submarine bases around Murmansk. But *Alpha-1* had never entered the Soviet fleet. She had gone out for initial sea trials, then come quickly back to her base, where she was tied alongside. Technicians worked on the boat for some time and the CIA watched them from outer space. There were so many apparent technical problems that the Soviets eventually gave up on *Alpha-1* and later she was cut up and dumped in an estuary of the Volga River.

The sea trials of *Alpha-2* were first monitored in 1975 by the Norwegian navy, which operated an underwater hydrophone system off Norway's northeastern coast, giving its listeners a long, underwater earshot down the Soviet Kola Peninsula on the Barents Sea. It was the Soviet navy's backyard. Three submarine bases were bunched together within fifty miles of Murmansk. New submarines went out for trials in the icy waters that adjoined these bases, and Soviet attack boats conducted regular patrols to sniff out U.S. submarines on spy missions.

Alpha's shiny hull cylinders had stumped intelligence analysts, who at first had speculated that the Soviets were giving their ships an aluminum coating to protect them from magnetic mines in the shallow waters off the sub bases. But the mystery finally had been solved when an agent working for naval intelligence had gotten into Gorky wearing special shoes, and after leaving the shipyard, the soles of his shoes had offered up metal shavings that removed the final doubts. The Soviets had mastered titanium-welding technology for hull construction.

It sounded arcane, but the achievement was colossal: titanium was the strongest metal known to man, as well as anti-magnetic. It could not be welded in the earth's atmosphere. The presence of oxygen caused the welds to crack. The aircraft industry had successfully employed titanium in jet-fighter construction, but jet fighters were tiny, and it was relatively easy to design a welding machine that removed air from a small surface area. Ship construction, on the other hand, was done on a gargantuan scale, and that's why the titanium shavings from Gorky had made sense out of the other mysteries surrounding the huge construction hall where the *Alpha* hulls were assembled.

Intelligence analysts had puzzled about the large climate-control machines outside the hall. Now it made sense: the Soviets had pumped the air out of the building and filled it with an inert gas, probably argon, so the welders—wearing space suits for breathing and to protect them from heat—could enter and weld the titanium-hull cylinders in an artificial atmosphere. It was an enormous technological advance, representing an investment by the Soviets of billions of dollars in submarine construction.

Titanium-hull construction meant that *Alpha* was an extremely deep-diving submarine. As U.S.S. *Los Angeles* had gone to sea limited by her operating depth of nine hundred fifty feet, CIA gave *Alpha* a diving range to two thousand feet. There wasn't a torpedo in the American fleet that could hit an *Alpha* running at a depth of two thousand feet. The standard load for the U.S. fleet was still the Mark 37, the torpedo that submarine commanders thought was useless unless they were close enough to throw it at an enemy nuclear submarine. The new Mark 48 high-technology torpedo was in production, but even the Mark 48 would have to be modified to get down to two thousand feet. There would not be many Mark 48s in the fleet for a long time because each torpedo cost $2.5 million, and that was an expensive shot.

Solving the mysteries of *Alpha* had been given a high priority for another reason. The small, sleek submarine was the first Soviet nuclear submarine designed as a round "body of revolution" tapering to a single propeller. Clearly she was designed for high speed. Navy analysts looked at photographs of *Alpha* and worried that the Russians had come up with a way to package extremely high-powered reactors in a small hull. It was something the U.S. Navy had not been able to do and it was something on which almost no U.S. research was ongoing because Rickover had smashed the engineering groups in the navy and in private industry who showed any interest in pursuing alternative reactor concepts. But with the appearance of *Alpha*, the CIA would commission new studies, and those studies would conclude that *Alpha* got five times more power per pound out of her propulsion plant than the most efficient U.S. nuclear submarine. It was a serious indictment of Rickover's lock-step control over naval propulsion research and development.

The Soviet *Yankee*-class ballistic missile boats had shown a more than threefold advantage in power efficiency over U.S. missile boats. *Alpha* had a fivefold advantage in power density over the *688s*. That was a tremendous achievement. To some engineers it meant the Soviets had gone on to a new generation of nuclear power, one in which the reactors ran at extremely high temperatures and were cooled by liquid sodium or some other high-temperature coolant. The U.S. Navy had abandoned research on solving the technical and safety problems associated with sodium reactors after demonstrating with U.S.S. *Seawolf* in 1955 that a sodium-cooled reactor could be designed for a submarine. Having once turned his back on sodium-cooled reactors, Rickover subsequently refused to revisit the technology.

The Soviets had given *Alpha* a double titanium hull, which made the little ship even stronger. Some analysts speculated that if *Alpha* were hit by a U.S. torpedo, there was no assurance the explosion would penetrate the inner pressure hull that protected the crew.

From these analyses, *Alpha*'s mission in the Soviet navy emerged: she was a barrier breaker, a strike boat designed to race at incredibly high speeds through the ocean chokepoints that restricted the Soviet fleet and into the ocean basins to quickly challenge American seapower in wartime. With her titanium hull, *Alpha* would be immune to the magnetic mines that would be laid off Soviet naval bases in any war. With her double hull and diving range, she might survive depth charge and torpedo hits. And with her high speed—perhaps as high as fifty-five miles per hour—she could roar into the ocean firing missiles and torpedoes against her primary target: the American aircraft carrier battle groups. There wasn't an aircraft carrier built that *Alpha* could not overtake.

Alpha was the fulfillment of the dream that began with U.S.S. *Albacore* and *Nautilus*. She was the *Skipjack* of the Titanium Age, carrying a power source from the twenty-first century. And she belonged to the Russians.

Alpha was no match for the *688s* in quietness at cruising speed, but the *688s* could not compare with *Alpha* overall. Judged against the holy trinity of speed, stealth, and depth, *Alpha* was decidedly superior to any U.S. submarine.

The appearance of *Alpha-2* and the foundering of the *688* program in an industrial quagmire of cost overruns and manufacturing chaos had combined to defeat Rickover's last attempt to field an attack submarine that would maintain superiority over the Soviet fleet to the end of the century. All during Zumwalt's tour as CNO, Rickover pushed an even larger attack-and-cruise-missile submarine with a power plant twice as big as *688*'s, capable of running at a top speed of thirty-six knots. Zumwalt killed the proposal every time it came up, and Rickover did not try to force the issue on Capitol Hill because there effectively was no place to build such a submarine while the yards were tied up with *Trident* and the *688*s.

When James T. Holloway III succeeded Zumwalt in the summer of 1974, Rickover was delighted because Holloway, a naval aviator by background, also was nuclear-trained. Rickover had gone to Holloway early to request funding for a new type of submarine, one whose hull was constructed out of a new and stronger steel alloy that could take ocean pressures up to 130,000 pounds per square inch. Rickover was bitterly disappointed when Holloway turned him down.

There were too many problems with the submarine fleet already under construction, Holloway said. And with the cost overruns and claims, he could not justify the expense of a building a new class based on a new hull steel. For three straight years, Rickover returned to Holloway's office seeking funding for a new attack submarine with a stronger hull, and Holloway turned him down each time. Rickover never complained that the *688* class was becoming a large fleet of depth-limited attack submarines. He never indicated to Holloway that there was any dissatisfaction in the submarine fleet about the limitation, but there was. Rickover did not force the issue of reclaiming depth in Congress or in the navy bureaucracy because his position had been weakened by the mess in the *688* program. And besides, when Rickover had so forcefully sold the *688* class to begin with, his staff had persuaded the congressional funding committees to issue classified reports saying depth was not all that important—just speed and stealth. Then *Alpha* had gone to sea in her deep-diving titanium package. Rickover couldn't very well argue forcefully that he was trying to reclaim something he had characterized as unimportant.

It was during the first year of Holloway's tenure that Rickover learned of the secret anti-submarine research program Zumwalt had been using to try to kill funding for the *688*s.

A Rickover loyalist who had learned the details of the "black" program and who vigorously challenged Zumwalt's claim that such a system would render the oceans transparent violated the still-standing classification order and briefed Rickover's deputy. The "black" program was in trouble because the new technology was not panning out the way some of the scientists had expected. There was still great promise, and the research had yielded successor projects that were equally as promising, but it was becoming clear that the ocean was not going to be rendered transparent any time soon. In addition, naval intelligence had discovered that the Soviets had begun a program to quiet their submarines, making detection by SOSUS and other sonar systems more difficult. But none of these things tempered Rickover's rage when he discovered what he believed was Zumwalt's worst treachery.

No wonder Zumwalt had stopped consulting with Rickover about funding for submarines. No wonder senior officials in the Pentagon had lost some of their commitment to a large fleet of 688s.

Rickover went straight to Holloway and screamed about being kept out of the circle of navy officials cleared to know about the "black" program. That goddamned Zumwalt had really stuck it to him and he'd be damned if he'd let it pass. Rickover announced that he was going to go to the Congress and expose Zumwalt for the treacherous bastard that he was. Rickover said he was going to go to Senator Scoop Jackson and together they would blow Zumwalt's reputation out of the water.

Holloway was alarmed at Rickover's rage. At first the CNO did not think Rickover was serious. A U.S. senator could not be cleared to know about something that was as highly compartmented as the anti-submarine research project. But Rickover was serious. He couldn't care less about the classification order because he was certain that Zumwalt had been using it as a political instrument: to shield the new technology from rigorous challenge by submariners who knew there were no quick fixes in the ocean and to block Rickover from challenging Zumwalt's strategy in the classified councils in the navy and in the Congress. That was part of the treachery. Zumwalt had trumped up a highly speculative piece of scientific research, some electromagnetic phenomena observed in the environment, and on that thin basis he had tried to kill Rickover's nuclear submarine program. Well, Rickover said, he was going to have the last word.

The only thing that stopped Rickover from disclosing the secret research project in Congress was Holloway's warning that Rickover would be court-martialed and jailed for breaking the classification order, which Holloway had kept in place. No one could know, Holloway insisted. Even if Zumwalt had oversold the promise and the "breakthrough," no one could know because someday the progeny of that technology were going to give the United States a real and formidable advantage in the silent war. The first superpower to render the oceans transparent would be the nation that controlled the seas, rendering impotent the submerged weapons platforms of the other side. That was a secret worth keeping, he said.

In May 1977, Rickover offered to take the President of the United States out for a ride in U.S.S. *Los Angeles* and Carter had not been able to refuse the invitation from his old boss. The man who set up the presidential submarine cruise was Joe Williams, Jr., a vice admiral and commander for submarine forces in the Atlantic. Williams had been present at the creation of the 688 class and he had fought at Rickover's side against Zumwalt during the early seventies.

The U.S.S. *Los Angeles* steamed south for Cape Kennedy, where the crew picked up the President under tight security. Carter and his wife, Rosalynn, came aboard with Rickover. As *Los Angeles* slipped into the Atlantic, Rickover took the President to his part of the ship, the propulsion spaces, where he let the President operate the throttle that opened the steam valves to the turbines. In a private moment that day, Rickover told Carter he would have foregone the honor of being the father of the nuclear navy if it would have been possible to uninvent the terror of nuclear weapons. Carter never forgot those words. The President sat at the diving-plane controls and maneuvered the ship, but shortly after the nine-hour cruise began, he left Rickover and went forward with Joe Williams. The two men hit it off and spent hours crawling around the torpedo room, navigation, sonar and control spaces together. Williams and the President plotted torpedo solutions on the fire-control computers and the President marveled at the technology. These were the systems on the submarine where Rickover was not an expert; but to Williams, the lifelong sub driver, they were second nature.

For the balance of the day, Rickover stayed in the ship's small dining hall and played host to Rosalynn, who knew nothing of ships. But at the end of the day, after the President and his wife departed, Rickover exploded, accusing Williams of monopolizing the President's time. Rickover had missed a chance to talk about all the things on his agenda. Perhaps he had wanted to lobby Carter on how to handle the shipbuilding claims or what kind of submarines Rickover wanted for the future. But Williams had robbed Rickover of those golden moments with his presidential student. It didn't do any good for Williams to protest that he had only accommodated the President's curiosity.

Rickover was seventy-seven years old and after years of association with Williams, after all the battles they fought together for the *688*, he had just decided that Williams was no good. It was the bad side of Rickover taking over—the petty, vindictive side that had hardened in him. His twenty-year friendship with Williams ended that day.

The final days of Gorden MacDonald at Electric Boat were a kind of slow torture for the self-promotional executive who had sought operating experience that would propel him into the vacant president's office at General Dynamics.

Rickover had started pinging on Lewis even before Curtis's stroke. "We have to have action," the admiral had said. The shipyard was supposed to be producing three *688*s per year by 1977, but *Philadelphia* was still sitting in drydock and U.S.S. *Omaha* and U.S.S. *Groton* were far from ready for delivery. The first Trident submarine was slipping farther and farther behind schedule as well. Rickover's studies showed that the shipyard's output was running at about half of what was needed to meet the schedule and fulfill Electric Boat's obligations to the navy.

"How long can you keep the lid on the situation?" Rickover asked Lewis. "It's the worst it has ever been."

But Lewis took no action. If he removed MacDonald, who would replace him? If Lewis recruited someone from outside the company, would the outsider be willing to step into a program that was overrunning its budget to a much greater extent than the company had acknowledged? Would the outsider go along with the cover-up of the cost projections?

In truth, Lewis was unable to act until he could find the right person. In the meantime, MacDonald was proving that the superman image he had created for himself in the boardroom was wearing extremely thin.

At the end of 1976, General Dynamics' accountants for the first time qualified their certification of the company's financial statements, saying, "The financial results of the corporation's SSN 688 program are dependent upon recovery of a substantial portion of the $544 million of claims filed with the U.S. Navy and achievement of the productivity improvements included in the program cost estimates."

Normally, an accounting firm's certification was a Good Housekeeping seal of approval for any corporation that traded its stock. Therefore, any qualification of the statement was a giant red flag on

Wall Street that signified something terribly wrong. That was not the image David Lewis wanted to project about General Dynamics, but he had not been able to stop it after three years of deterioration. The only positive aspect of the qualification for Lewis was that it reflected poorly on MacDonald. Lewis was anxious to transfer responsibility for the failure. So he took the occasion to draft a harsh memorandum to MacDonald about his performance as general manager of the shipyard:

We have added a large number of new facilities and have also added a great many new people to the Electric Boat rolls in the past few months. The records show that the total output of the yard on the 688 contract has not increased at all, even though the number of people assigned to many of the ships have been increased by one hundred percent or more. The short visit we made to the yard on 26 January [1977] was very revealing and extremely painful.

. . . How in the world the yard management, from the first line to the operations manager, can watch their terrible situation evolve and develop without taking action is more than I will ever be able to understand. . . . I am deeply concerned about the future of Electric Boat. The warning bells are everywhere. We have seen our schedules slipping, our forecasted cost-to-complete increasing and we have been hit by several quality control problems almost simultaneously. We have to act and quickly!

But Lewis's memorandum never left draft form. Whether he showed it to MacDonald or not, the conversation between the two men at that stage was predictable. Lewis and MacDonald had gone down the road together. They had kept the "lid" on together. While MacDonald played up to Crown and to Cummings and to other board members, he still had toed the management line: The overrun was not that bad. It could be offset by claims and better productivity soon to come. So Lewis did not send the memo. MacDonald could have seen that he had failed. The board could have seen it as well. The memo, in the end, had not been necessary.

MacDonald probably was relieved when Rickover telephoned in May 1977 and asked that he and Lewis come down to Washington for the climactic meeting. Rickover was businesslike and straightforward. He just laid out the facts about the production rate at the yard. In the twelve months since MacDonald had been named general manager, he had increased the trade workers and support personnel in the shipyard by 30 percent, representing thousands of additional workers on the submarines. But even so, the output of the yard had only marginally increased and there had been no real improvement in the efficiency of the workforce. Absenteeism was running 50 percent on some days.

MacDonald just listened. Lewis took notes.

Rickover pointed out that MacDonald's failure was in not getting into the details of shipbuilding, and the reason was simple: he had no background in shipbuilding. He had not put adequate pressure on the manpower problems and was unable, because of his background, to evaluate those problems and then take strong action to solve them. MacDonald might be aware of his shortcomings, Rickover said, and he might be toughening up, but it was too late. The pressure MacDonald applied was too sporadic and he was away from the shipyard too much of the time handling the financial matters of the corporation.

The Naval Reactors staff had identified specific problems for MacDonald relating to the material shortages and schedule slippages, Rickover said, but there had been little improvement in those areas and the improvements were too slow to reach the goals that needed to be reached. MacDonald was totally honest and strong, Rickover said, and he had been responsive on narrow issues and on detail items that Rickover and his staff had raised. But it was inadequate. MacDonald didn't know shipbuilding, and therefore was not perceptive as to how to make day-by-day operations better. He was not able to make the departments work effectively together to support the waterfront. MacDonald's hallmark of management, Rickover said, was to solve problems by realigning the organization and shifting people around, and that would not do.

Rickover stressed that he would not publicly attack MacDonald, but there had to be a change.

It was the second time in four years that Rickover had told Lewis to get a new man to run the shipyard. Rickover was appalled that Lewis seemed to be paralyzed against action. Later in the summer of 1977, as MacDonald prepared to leave, Rickover grilled him over why General Dynamics had taken so long to face up to the problems. MacDonald used the occasion to give a self-serving account that made Lewis appear indecisive and weak and MacDonald appear like a troubleshooter who reported directly to the board of directors.

He told Rickover that the board, not Lewis, had sent him to the shipyard in July 1975 to investigate the problems there. After six months of study, MacDonald said he recommended that Pierce and Curtis be removed from their jobs.

Why? Rickover asked.

It was based on a number of observations, MacDonald said, but one example was that Pierce made all decisions by taking a vote of his senior staff and only exerted himself when there was a tie vote.

Why weren't they removed then? Rickover asked.

Because Lewis wanted more time to study the situation, Mac-Donald replied. MacDonald had made his investigation during the five-month strike and Lewis did not think it was valid. MacDonald said he returned with identical recommendations in February 1976, but Lewis deferred action. By April 1976, the board of directors was ready to give MacDonald the authority to act.

Why did the board give the authority to him and not to Lewis? asked Rickover.

Because, MacDonald said, he was the executive vice president for marine operations.

It wasn't an answer, and both men knew it.

Why did it take so long for St. Louis to recognize that there was a problem at Electric Boat? Rickover went on.

MacDonald had recognized the problem shortly after he came to the company, and had written a twelve-page memorandum to Lewis about the problems in the shipyard as early as late 1973. Mac-Donald said Lewis had just not seen the inadequacy of Pierce and Curtis. Curtis, he added, had been selected because he had done a good job building the DC-10 air frames at the Convair division in San Diego, but Curtis had not been suited for the much more complicated problems of submarine construction.

He said he had warned Lewis that Curtis had no initiative and would have to be pushed.

Rickover made MacDonald sign a memorandum summary of the account he gave. It was filed away as yet another piece of evidence that General Dynamics had poorly managed the shipyard.

MacDonald had been obliged to give evidence against Lewis—distorted as it was to reflect favorably on MacDonald—and he was most likely motivated by his intense desire to get out of Groton without being publicly attacked by Rickover for the conditions at the shipyard.

Rickover held this leverage over him like a club. Twice during the summer months, as MacDonald was preparing for the succession, he called in one of his aides, William Pedace, who handled special projects at the shipyard such as arrangements for Rickover at ship launchings, and instructed Pedace to purchase expensive pieces of jewelry for Rickover's wife.* Pedace carried out the orders and flew the jewelry to Washington, where he hand-delivered it to Rickover.

The first piece was a $695 pair of diamond earrings; the second,

---

*MacDonald has asserted that Rickover requested this jewelry, but there is no contemporaneous record of this request.

a $400 jade pendant. Pedace covered up the purchases with the jewelry salesman's help. The earrings were charged to the company as retirement watches, the pendant as petty cash for entertainment of division guests. MacDonald told him to keep everything about the gifts quiet.

They were farewell gifts from MacDonald. A little protection to get him out of town and to keep the hot blast of Rickover's criticism from scorching him.

It worked.

III

THE
TAKEOVER,
THE BAILOUT

Takis Veliotis had planned the October 24, 1977, takeover of Electric Boat like a military operation. It was going to be a long day, and he would have to be intensely alert to any threat to his plan—a management revolt, violence in the yard—because things could happen in the explosive circumstances he was about to ignite.

At 7:00 a.m. the line of cars, motors running, stood outside the Norwich, Connecticut, hotel as the Quincy Eight team prepared to sweep into the neighboring Groton shipyard to lay the groundwork for the industrial rescue. The Quincy Eight were the shock troops. They would establish control, making sure the offices had been emptied on the first floor of the administration building and that all of MacDonald's deadwood managers had been scattered upstairs. Then they would call the 8:00 a.m. meeting where Veliotis would prepare them for the painful cuts and hard work ahead.

The team members—all of them waterfront engineers or seasoned financial men—had each been recruited personally by Veliotis months in advance. They had not been allowed to tell anyone except their wives about their new assignments. Security was critical: if the unions or the politicians found out what Veliotis was planning, they would try to stop him.

The preparations had taken a total of five months and had been conducted in total secrecy at Quincy. Lewis had insisted that Electric Boat's financial records be reviewed in strictest confidence. There was only minimal contact with the corporate office in St. Louis and no contact with MacDonald, except to arrange some briefings on Electric Boat operations for the team members. Even that was done with a cover story. Veliotis's chief of security had boarded up the windows of the large conference room where records were shipped in from Electric Boat and the walls papered with organizational charts, schedules, and personnel lists. Veliotis insisted on secrecy and he had compartmentalized the planning. One member of the team studied personnel, others planned the changes on the waterfront, and each reported separately to Veliotis. He preferred it that way. Every manager was a spoke of the wheel; he was the hub. Only Veliotis knew everything.

The men at the core of the Quincy Eight believed they had enlisted in the command of General Dynamics' next chairman of the board. Veliotis had become the leader to whom they accorded a military-style loyalty; the struggles at Quincy—with the union, with the ships, with the customers—had seemed more like violent battles than business transactions. Shipyards were violent places anyway, dangerous places where men and machines assaulted tons of steel until it surrendered its shape. It took a strong man to run a shipyard. Veliotis had that toughness and it showed in his stern and confident bearing. If you were part of the team, he made you feel like you were his brother, his best friend, and partner all at once; unless you weren't following his orders, and then Veliotis could make you feel like you were dead and had never existed. The team accepted his leadership. Its members saw him as a polished immigrant; a godfather, not of the underworld, but a man who had hustled all his life and who had worked harder than most to get where he was. He seemed smarter, shrewder than the men at the top of General Dynamics, and he had the survival instincts of one who had seen family and country ravaged by civil war.

Almost overnight, because of what he had accomplished at the long-cursed Quincy shipyard, Takis Veliotis had become a crown prince in the corporation. He had saved one major division and was moving to the next. The board of directors and the corporate staff in St. Louis—those who knew what was going on—watched expectantly to see whether he could pull Electric Boat out of its long and chaotic slide. If he could, he would have achieved back-to-back miracles at the corporation's most troubled divisions.

He had come from the tough, competitive waterfront of the St. Lawrence River, whose sea lanes connected the inland markets of the Great Lakes region with the rest of the world. Hilliard Paige had found Veliotis in Quebec, running one of the largest and most efficient shipyards in Canada. In checking Veliotis out, Paige had discovered that he was not only an innovative engineer, but a highly motivated businessman. He had established a system of "bird dogs" among the radio operators of the St. Lawrence as a private intelligence network, which told him when any inbound freighter captain mentioned mechanical troubles. Veliotis could instantly be on the ship-to-shore radio offering the repair services of Davie Shipbuilding. Veliotis usually got the business—and he sent liquor aboard for the captain when the ship tied up. The bird dog got a commission.

That was business on the waterfront. In the final analysis, Veliotis's reputation as a smart, tough, and profit-oriented production man was the thing General Dynamics had been after.

In the four years since Veliotis had joined General Dynamics as general manager of the Quincy yard, he had built a reputation as the toughest waterfront production man in the company, maybe in the country. He had put Quincy back on the map by constructing the company's first liquefied natural gas tankers to haul supercooled gas from the fields of Algeria and Indonesia to Japan and the West.

There had been enormous obstacles to overcome: a corporate partner, Burmah Oil Tankers, Ltd., had filed for bankruptcy protection in the midst of the building program. Then Pittsburgh–Des Moines Steel Company, the company that was building twelve-story-high spherical tanks to sit inside the tanker hulls like giant eggs in a carton, could not perform. Other companies tried to move in on General Dynamics' business and Veliotis fought them off. Then the press had gone after the tankers on safety grounds. One documentary suggested the ships would be time bombs that could explode with the force of an atomic blast in populous harbor cities such as Boston.

But Veliotis had toughed out the program. The first ship was christened in May 1977, and the rest were on a tightly scheduled production line. He knocked down barriers that had defeated other managers. He had indefatigable self-confidence, an imperial will, and an instinct, almost paranoid at times, about where trouble was coming from next.

Some of General Dynamics' customers and partners had been bruised by Veliotis along the way. When Burmah went under, the Bank of England had guaranteed its performance, and so Veliotis had shouted at the Bank of England man: "You pay, mister!" He was volatile and kept his adversaries on the defensive. In negotiating sessions he was menacing because he was a big man and at six foot five he towered over most people and when he got angry, his chest swelled and he gestured and cursed in a way that filled the room and there sometimes was the hint of violence in his manner.

"I am not an easy person," he would say apologetically. But it never was an apology.

His style of management was effective against union bosses, demanding customers, and business competitors. It was a style that made David Lewis a little uncomfortable, but he had backed Veliotis, backed him to the hilt. A bond had developed between the two men over four years. "I will go through a brick wall for Dave Lewis," Velio-tis said to people, and that was the way he had felt during the difficult years at Quincy. But the two men were not close friends. The compact between them was like the compact between a general and his field commander. There was loyalty to the same cause, commonality of interest, even mutual admiration, but not friendship.

Veliotis had grown up around ships. He came from a good fam-ily that had acquired modest wealth. He was doted on by a strong mother, who schooled him in discipline and manners and took him to Sunday mass in the Greek Orthodox Church. Veliotis took naval train-ing in the Greek naval academy and an engineering degree from the national university in Athens.

For most of his life, Veliotis had gravitated to one kind of work-ing relationship. He had started his career working for his father in the family business, E. G. Veliotis Shipowners, in Piraeus. Veliotis's father died a few years after World War II and the shipping business was lost to the depression. During those last years in Greece, before he emigrated at the age of twenty-seven, Veliotis felt the desperation of business failure and the hopelessness of opportunity in his own coun-try, which had been torn and terrorized by the struggle against the Communists.

In search of a career, young Veliotis emigrated to Canada and went to work for an older man, T. Rodgie McClagen, the chairman of Davie Shipbuilding, Ltd., of Quebec. McClagen started Veliotis in the drafting room, and for over a decade nurtured the younger man's career, much as his own father had, until Veliotis was named pres-ident of the shipyard in 1962. Veliotis had built naval warships, tank-ers, and freighters for McClagen's customers, and the yard had prospered.

After joining General Dynamics, Veliotis quickly placed Lewis on the same kind of pedestal. He made it clear he worked for no one but Lewis and would answer to no one but Lewis. But it was not the same as working for McClagen. Veliotis and Lewis were too close in age, and dealing with Lewis on an emotional level was awkward. Lewis could be extremely warm and friendly, but he did not have many friends. He got up early, worked all day and then into the night, and he worked the telephone through the weekend, talking to division managers and his lobbyists in Washington. Much later, Lewis's wife, Dorothy, told Veliotis in a moment of levity that if Dave ever retired, he'd have nothing to do but become an alcoholic.

Veliotis had seen Lewis's flaws, but he had pushed them to the back of his mind because, overall, the relationship was strong. Yet they remained there, a mental log of what Veliotis considered character failings in Lewis which manifested themselves both in dealings with his subordinates and in business. The first one appeared the very day Veliotis reported to work at Quincy in January 1973. He discovered that Lewis had deliberately kept the preceding general manager in the dark about his firing.

So when Veliotis arrived at the shipyard, he and Paige were forced to confront the man Veliotis had come to replace. Veliotis introduced himself as the new general manager and told the bewildered man that there could not be two general managers—he would have to leave, right then. Paige later explained that Lewis had overruled a suggestion that the man be told he was being replaced. "Don't tell him anything," Lewis had said, concerned that he would be left in the lurch until Veliotis arrived.

That was one of the differences between them. Veliotis was capable of confronting a difficult person or problem straight on. Lewis preferred indirection, and had often sent MacDonald or someone else from the corporate office to tell a division manager that he was not performing to Lewis's expectation. So thoroughly did Lewis avoid direct human confrontation that he would generally settle a dispute whether or not the merit of the opposing claim had been established. When Pittsburgh–Des Moines appeared incapable of building the giant spherical tanks, Veliotis had recommended that General Dynamics take over the Charleston manufacturing facility. Lewis agreed, but he had wanted to part company gracefully with Pittsburgh–Des Moines. He recommended offering the steel company $25 million for the plant. Veliotis could not believe it; the plant could not have cost more than $8 million to build. He had protested: "We should not be paying them, Dave. They should be paying us." While Veliotis openly supported Lewis's position, privately he sent a messenger to plant questions with General Dynamics' board of directors. When the transaction was more closely examined, the board took the hard position Veliotis had avocated.

Later that year, 1973, Veliotis accompanied Lewis and another manager out for a night on the town on a stopover in Copenhagen while returning from Moscow. Veliotis was surprised the next morning when Lewis announced they could not charge the entertainment to their expense accounts and asked each of them to contribute to the cost of the evening. Lewis was the chairman of the board; he made a lot of money, yet here he was divvying up entertainment expenses like they were a bunch of insurance salesmen.

It was a matter of style to Veliotis. If you were the boss, you picked up the tab. It was a little thing, but it had stuck with Veliotis as revealing a weakness, some flaw in Lewis's character.

What Lewis admired in Veliotis was his keen engineering instinct. He truly was a talented shipbuilder, and Lewis felt he had been lucky to steal him from competing recruiters at Newport News. Veliotis had walked into the Quincy shipyard and after just a few days' study told the engineering department that its plan to build the natural gas tankers would not work. He showed them on paper how they could drop the first 850-ton sphere into the hull, and then the second, but they would never be able to lift the third into place with the crane they planned to use. He was right. One of the first things Lewis and the board authorized was a large Goliath crane that could handle the placement of all five spheres in each of the tankers.

The tanker project had been hit by one crisis after another, so Veliotis had gotten a lot of Lewis's attention in four years. Lewis had described Quincy as the hole in the bottom of the bucket; only a strong manager could save it. The tankers looked like a good deal because the construction costs were borne by the banks and subsidized by the U.S. Maritime Administration. It had been a gamble for Lewis and for Veliotis. When something goes wrong in ship construction, the sky can fall on you because ships are so capital-intensive. In Detroit, a foul-up in automobile production can force the write-off of a few units at a cost of several thousand dollars each. But a failure in ship construction can bankrupt a company. That's why the Pittsburgh–Des Moines failure posed such a threat.

Thus, when Veliotis became the first manager in more than a decade to turn a profit at Quincy, Lewis became his biggest champion, reminding anyone who needed reminding that he had had the wisdom to hire Veliotis. Veliotis was part of the new Lewis team. He ran a clean and neat shipyard, and Lewis liked cleanliness. So, in early 1977, Lewis believed that Veliotis was the only solution to the disaster at Electric Boat. Lewis made his appeal on the day the board of directors came to Quincy to tour the shipyard and to conduct their monthly business meeting. The day started off with a crisis over the barber who had not shown up at the Boston hotel to give Colonel Crown his morning shave. Crown apparently had long since forsaken the rigors of conducting his morning toilette without the assistance of a barber. When he traveled overnight away from his homes in Chicago and Palm Beach, he insisted on certain comforts: the barber was one, the king-sized bed was another. Fortunately for Veliotis, the Quincy shipyard had many friends among the Boston hotel proprietors and a second barber was quickly found.

Lewis saw Veliotis before the meeting to go over Veliotis's presentation to the board. But when the two men sat down in Veliotis's office, Lewis quickly dispatched with the script. He had never been one to confide about his problems at another division, but suddenly he was telling Veliotis about the desperate conditions at Electric Boat—and he blamed everything on Rickover and MacDonald.

MacDonald, he said, had pandered to Rickover just as MacDonald pandered to the directors. Ever since Paige had left the company, MacDonald had been after the president's job. Some of MacDonald's patrons on the board had urged him to get operating experience under his belt so he would be better qualified, but the shipyard was a tough place for on-the-job training.

Things had continued to deteriorate at an alarming rate. MacDonald couldn't handle the job, Lewis told Veliotis, and had been spending too much time at his condominium in the Bahamas. Things were out of control and it was time to get him out of there.

Lewis paused to give Veliotis an opportunity to ask for the Electric Boat assignment, but Veliotis was not going to surrender his advantage by doing so. Veliotis did not have to be at Groton to hear the horror stories about how late the submarines were and how seriously the yard was over budget. It was apparent at quarterly management meetings in St. Louis that all of the corporation's working capital and lines of credit were tied up supporting the debt load at Electric Boat. Lewis had no one else to turn to. So Veliotis feigned disinterest in career advancement and talked about retiring. He was sympathetic, he said, but what did Lewis expect him to do? He was completing the task Lewis had given him four years ago. He did not know what he would do afterwards. He was not inclined to take another tough assignment in General Dynamics. Besides, what reward could there be? Half of his salary went to taxes and, unless the company was willing to give him better stock options, there was very little General Dynamics could do to make Veliotis want the kind of long-term commitment Lewis was talking about. He had an offer to run a Greek shipping company, but he was not sure he wanted to continue working. The natural gas tanker program had been one long crisis. He was tired. His wife, Paulette, was complaining that he was tense all of the time and over-absorbed with work. So he was thinking about getting out at the age of fifty-one.

There was an additional consideration, which Veliotis could not confide to Lewis. By 1977, Veliotis had secretly accepted more than $700,000 into his Swiss bank account through a maze of intermediary companies that led back to a vice president of Frigitemp Corporation, the subcontractor that had done much of the insulation work on the spherical tanks at Quincy.*For Veliotis, it apparently had been too much money to walk away from, and the insulation work had been done reasonably well and on time. The kickbacks would not have made the difference between profit and loss on the tankers. The tankers were going to make money for General Dynamics.

Veliotis came from a background where kickbacks and commissions were part of the shipping industry, in his native Greece and throughout the shipping world he knew. It was a world in which the first loyalty was to bring the job in at a profit for the boss, and the second was to look out for yourself. If a man satisfied the first loyalty, he was a fool to forego the second. On the multi-million-dollar scale of expenditures in shipbuilding, commissions were a negligible part of the transaction, but in Veliotis's world they served the same purpose as the grease on the ways—they got the deal done, the ship to sea. That was the code of the international waterfront, and by all of the evidence that lay hidden in the private banking channels between Boston, Montreal, the Cayman Islands, and Switzerland, Veliotis had mastered its science.

The irony of Veliotis's becoming ensnared in the Frigitemp kickback scheme was that he had always demanded quality from subcontractors. As the kickback checks flowed into his Swiss bank account, he should have known that nothing stays secret forever. Exposure, though it might have seemed unlikely at the beginning, would mean certain ruination for the reputation he had invested decades building. And when it happened years later, the flaw in his judgment would appear with dreadful clarity: he had compounded his ambition with unthinking greed, not knowing how it would lead to his undoing in the end; not knowing how it would steal from him the opportunity to ascend to the top of the American defense establishment, and not knowing how much he would regret the criminal allegations that stick like a horrible tar to a man's reputation when the day of reckoning comes.

Lewis was speaking under pressure to offer some inducement that would persuade Veliotis to stay.

"Taki, you are the only person in the company who can save Electric Boat," he said now. The horrible problems at the yard were threatening to drag the entire corporation down the drain. Veliotis was extremely valuable to the corporation, Lewis emphasized, and he had the opportunity to save the entire company by taking on Electric

---

*Source: Frigitemp indictment filed with U.S. District Court for the Southern District of Manhattan, September 6, 1983.

Boat; to stop the hemorrhaging and to complete the attack submarine fleet and the first Trident for the navy.

Most important—and Veliotis ought to think long and hard about it, Lewis said—if Veliotis turned Electric Boat around, he would claim a major victory in the corporation just two years before Lewis's sixty-fifth birthday. Veliotis would be the leading contender to take on Lewis's job as chairman of the company, and he would have Lewis's and the board's support. If Veliotis needed any further assurance on that point, the board of directors would confirm it.*

Veliotis tried not to show his feelings. What he had thought an impossibility was suddenly happening. He was tantalized at the prospect of becoming the chairman of one of the most prestigious defense companies in America. He had sought to conquer the shipbuilding industry and considered himself the most qualified shipbuilding executive in North America. But in a single conversation, Lewis it seemed had offered him the chance to rule a kingdom much more vast and more powerful—an opportunity to sit at a much more exclusive table with men of great stature in the defense establishment, men like Jim McDonnell, David Packard, and Henry Crown.

It would all be new, challenging, and there was more. Veliotis would be the man who completed the newest and most formidable weapon in the American strategic arsenal, the first Trident ballistic missile submarine. He would preside over a proud moment in defense history. Veliotis had not become a U.S. citizen during the hectic years at Quincy because he had yet to complete the five-year mandatory residency requirement. He had not even been sure that he would stay in America. Up to this point, he had been a Greek boy who had made a name for himself in shipbuilding. Now he would have to think big, really big.

One of the first people Veliotis telephoned after the meeting was Hilliard Paige, the former company president, who had recruited Veliotis and who was now running a small satellite company in Washington, D.C. "Dave wants me to go down and run Electric Boat," Veliotis said. "Do you think I should do it?"

Veliotis knew Paige's views on the impossible situation Lewis had created for anyone trying to run E.B. As long as Rickover had direct access to Lewis, any general manager of the division was at his peril in bucking the admiral.

---

*Lewis denies making any commitment to Veliotis about the chairmanship of the company. At the time, however, Veliotis acted as if he had such a commitment, and thereafter confided in at least three of his senior managers that Lewis had promised him the chairmanship if he saved Electric Boat.

"The question is how are you going to get along with Rickover?" Paige asked.

"No, that's not the question," Veliotis said. "The question is how is he going to get along with me!"

Both men laughed heartily.

From May to October 1977, Veliotis's team members worked in the boarded-up conference room at Quincy, collating intelligence they had gathered from their briefings and from the ship schedules and weekly man-hour estimates that MacDonald's clerks were sending north to them. The picture emerging of the shipyard terrified Veliotis. The cumulative cash flow deficit at Electric Boat had reached the $300 million mark and was growing at a rate of $15 million per month. Very simply, the yard had exhausted the government contract payments for the first of the 688-class submarines and now was paying—out of pocket—the cost of completing the ships and the salaries of several thousand workers assigned to them.

MacDonald had gone on a hiring spree, putting thousands of new and untrained workers on the payroll with little supervision in hopes that he could get more men working on the ships and thereby increase productivity. But the crush of men added to the work gangs on the ships had not helped productivity and, in some cases, had hurt it.

A survey of Electric Boat by a corporate team revealed a massive "failure of the system to provide the planned manpower, materials, paper and resources to the right place, at the right time to complete work to a schedule supporting the next operation. The division is being raped of its [personnel and material] resources without a proportionate amount of progress on the submarines."

It had not been quantity MacDonald needed, but quality.

The week before the late October takeover, Veliotis flew to St. Louis for the regular quarterly management meeting. During one of the breaks, Veliotis and Lewis stepped into Lewis's corner office overlooking the St. Louis skyline in the distance. Veliotis said the shipyard was a disaster and the cost overrun was much larger than MacDonald had been reporting. It was on the order of $1.1 billion.

"Oh God," Lewis exclaimed. "I didn't know it was that bad."

The $544 million claim would never cover such an overrun, Veliotis said, and there did not appear to be much substance to the claim to begin with. Most of the claim was for delay and disruption, but given the bad management at Electric Boat, Veliotis said he could not imagine how the company was going to prevail.

Lewis appeared shaken. He looked as if he were hearing the estimate for the first time. Later Veliotis would remember the look on his face. It was a look of shock and surprise and Veliotis had no suspicion at that moment that Lewis could have been acting, that he might have already known the horrible truths Veliotis was discovering.

The schedules for delivering the ships were wildly optimistic, Veliotis continued, and MacDonald had reported more construction progress on the ships than existed. The first Trident was more than a year later than the delivery schedule the company was standing behind in public, and the last 688s would be two years later than the schedule indicated.

"They have been lying to you, Dave," Veliotis said. He wanted to clean house and fire E.B.'s entire senior staff, Barton included, replacing them with the team he had brought with him from Quincy. They had done their homework on the shipyard. They were ready to take full responsibility.

But Lewis cautioned Veliotis to wait. "Take your time," he said. There was no rush. Lewis said he wanted Veliotis to really dig in, to come up with a comprehensive report on the costs and schedules of the ships. It would take him a good ninety days, Lewis said. "Don't listen to Barton," Lewis said. "Make your own estimate."

That was not the way Veliotis wanted to do it. "Dave, the fourth decimal place in the estimate may change," Veliotis objected, but the billion-dollar overrun was there, immutable and inevitable. "I am your expert, Dave," he said. The costs were the costs. They might change a little, but not enough to matter. However, if Lewis wanted him to take ninety days to report on it, he would do so, because he was an organization man.

That's what Lewis wanted and Veliotis sensed the obvious reason: if the billion-dollar overrun estimate surfaced before the end of the financial reporting year, Lewis would have been forced to declare the biggest loss in the company's history. And once he did that, there was no way the navy was going to feel any pressure to settle the $544 million claim. Taking the loss was, in effect, accepting responsibility, and it would take the pressure off the navy to settle. The company line was still that a loss could be avoided by productivity improvements and a successful claim. After his five months of study Veliotis knew that the company line was a cruel hoax.

Lewis said the best thing to do was to get the costs under control while he and the board negotiated a settlement with the navy. It was not the right time to fire Barton or the others. Given the delicate nature of the negotiations with the navy, it was no time to take a chance that Barton, if fired, might run straight to the navy and cause trouble. The solution to the increasing overrun, Lewis said, was filing more claims against the navy. The drawing revisions and changes were continuing. The company could update its claim to $1 billion if need be.

For the first time, Veliotis realized how far out on a limb Mac-Donald had climbed. Now, after he had confided the truth to Lewis, Veliotis had an uneasy feeling about Lewis's instinct to keep the lid on because it forced Veliotis to embrace the same strategy.

Veliotis returned from St. Louis to Quincy. On his last day there, he awarded an additional $12 million in contracts to Frigitemp Corporation for joiner and insulation work on natural gas tankers under construction. In return for the contract award, the Frigitemp vice president who had been paying kickbacks into Veliotis's Swiss bank account for three years communicated his assurance that another $500,000 would appear there in short order.

Veliotis told himself that he had a job to do. On October 24, 1977, just as the morning shift was streaming toward the waterfront, he steeled himself and put on what he called his "imperial" bearing— what you show to men you intend to lead, or fire. The Quincy Eight had established control and assembled the entire management staff for the 8:00 a.m. meeting. The second-floor conference room was dead silent as each man took a measure of Veliotis's authority. He introduced himself. Dispassionately, he told them that he had a job to do and they were being demoted. Each of them was getting two new bosses: first, himself as general manager, and second, one of the Quincy Eight managers inserted over each of their departments. By implication, they might be fired as soon as Veliotis evaluated their performance. He did not have to tell them that he found their performance lacking—why else was he there? He was the expert, Mr. Shipbuilding. He knew what he had to do.

Veliotis asked if there were any questions. There were plenty, but it was the kind of moment in which you knew that if you stuck up your hand you would pull down a stump. No one moved as Veliotis walked out of the room and down the stairs to the general manager's office. Over the next hour, the Quincy Eight called in the department heads and told them the shocking news: Veliotis was going to lay off more than four thousand workers immediately to cut more than $100 million out of the shipyard's overhead. The days of the welfare state at Electric Boat were over. Veliotis wanted a day's work for a day's pay.

If anyone did not give it to him, he would personally show them the gate.

It was a simple strategy—cut costs and improve productivity. That's how Veliotis looked at the production process. He had told Joe Pierce years before that the problem at Electric Boat was obvious: too much work at the wrong price and on the wrong schedule. For Pierce, there had been no solution. But Veliotis intended to run a much sterner strategy. He was going to cut and chop ruthlessly, then he was going to automate the hull-cylinder construction, computerize the shipyard's inventory of steel and parts, and minimize idle time by changing work rules. Veliotis knew he could not save the overrun that already had accumulated. You don't regain time lost on a ship under construction. The only hope was to break even on the ships whose keels would be laid over the next four years and to pull in some new ships under better contracts.

The Electric Boat managers were stunned by the size of the cut he was ordering and each felt the panic of slicing that deep into their organizations. It was going to be mayhem—good people with mortgages and tuition payments were going to be on the street by Friday. Each department head was given his quota of layoffs to meet by the end of the week. Each was told that the numbers had been arrived at after careful study. They were not negotiable. If MacDonald's managers could not come up with a roster of names to meet the quota, the layoffs would be made for them at random.

This message was delivered in a tone that conveyed the harsh reality of Veliotis's first day: the job of every man in the shipyard was on the line, especially those in management.

Veliotis had brought with him from Quincy a Yale-trained engineer named Bim Holt to run the waterfront as director of operations. It was Holt's task on that first day to deal with the fate of MacDonald's director of operations, Hal Foley. Aside from the general manager's job, Foley's had been the most important post in the shipyard. The Trident manager and the *688* program manager both reported to him.

Foley had imagined himself taking over the general manager's job one day, but he had the misfortune of having been identified as MacDonald's "yes" man. When MacDonald broke the news the previous Friday that he was returning to St. Louis, Foley had been crestfallen. "What about us?" he asked plaintively, invoking the team they had formed.

But MacDonald said it was not the time to talk about it, and left.

After the 8:00 a.m. meeting, Holt followed Foley back to his waterfront office. Holt did not relish his task, but neither did he perform it delicately. He walked into Foley's office and asked him for a list of the ten most critical problems facing the shipyard. Foley quickly complied with a memorandum and sent it up to Holt's office. When Holt returned, he didn't say anything about the memorandum, he just told Foley that he was sorry. "You are through as of right now."

"I don't understand," Foley said. "Why me?"

Holt offered no explanation. The decision had been made.

Foley asked about some other position in the shipyard. After all, he had worked there since 1963.

"You don't understand," Holt said. "It's not a question of taking another position. You're through. If you want to appeal, you'll have to go see Veliotis." But Holt said it wouldn't do any good.

Foley went to see Veliotis. He asked again, "Why me?"

"Because you didn't do what MacDonald told you to do," Veliotis replied sternly. The answer did not make any sense to Foley and it was not true. But there was no further remedy and the outrage of the moment just froze Foley into a useless apoplexy. MacDonald had fled back to St. Louis. This was it. This big Greek who had taken charge had thrown him out. There was nothing he could do. The security chief sent a guard down to watch Foley pack his personal things in his office, then escorted him to his car and watched him drive out the gate.

Foley was the only member of Electric Boat's management to be fired. He was emotionally crushed and embittered by the experience. He had told MacDonald a few weeks earlier about the large new home he had purchased. Neither Lewis nor MacDonald had warned him what was coming. They had cheered his efforts and imagination in the yard against impossible odds. When they asked for commitments for improved productivity so they could support their optimism in the boardroom, Foley had delivered. He had come up with construction schemes that had never been tried before. They looked great on paper—and one of the first things Veliotis did was throw them all out.

Veliotis had fired Foley for effect. He wanted Electric Boat's managers to fear the consequences of nonperformance. People were motivated by fear, and Veliotis needed motivation to bring about the changes that had to occur to complete the ships. Veliotis was a simple man. He instructed his managers to go into the shipyard and line up the supervisors, give them specific production goals for the week, then line them up again at the end of the week. He told them to pick out the three worst performers and suspend them without pay or, if need be, fire them.

In many respects, Veliotis operated like Rickover. He understood that fear proved a very efficient motivator when you did not have time to rebuild a workforce from the ground up or to pare it down by attrition. He was willing to impose the brutality of mass layoffs because his agenda, his goals—the corporation's salvation and the chairmanship—were that important to him.

Everyone had expected Veliotis and Rickover to tangle viciously, and Veliotis had even created the mystique that he would put Rickover in his place from the start. The weekend before he took over, Veliotis received a letter from Rickover insisting that he adhere to all past agreements and understandings between Rickover and previous general managers. Veliotis had no idea—and Rickover had not bothered to tell him—what any of these agreements and understandings were. "He must be kidding," Veliotis said, and he instructed Electric Boat's general counsel to draft a polite refusal. Veliotis had the letter delivered to Rickover on his first day. It was his way of establishing himself with Rickover.

Veliotis expected the legendary admiral to be his biggest obstacle, especially if he did not assert himself early and forcefully. He intended to be polite to Rickover and, in truth, he admired all that Rickover had done as a propulsion engineer. But Veliotis better than most people understood the bullying side of Rickover, and no one was going to bully Veliotis in his own shipyard. He did not need Rickover—as MacDonald had—to tell him how to run the place. Veliotis was the expert. He had his plan, his people. Rickover was an inspector for the government as far as he was concerned. He would treat him cordially and give him the respect he was due, but he would hit the old man with a two-by-four, if need be, to establish who was going to be in charge.

Rickover expected a daily telephone call from each of his shipyard managers, but Veliotis quickly defied the tradition: "Why should I call him every day?" he said to his deputies. "I don't even call my mother every day."

So Rickover called Veliotis. It suited his purpose to ignore the small acts of defiance. Rickover had no intention of challenging Veliotis's authority because if Veliotis didn't save Electric Boat, it was going to look just as bad for Rickover as it was for General Dynamics. If Veliotis was good—and Rickover judged him to be a strong shipyard manager—Rickover was going to be his biggest supporter.

From the moment Veliotis arrived at the shipyard, he and Rickover established a relationship that was marked by mutual support. Their common and desperate goal was the rescue of the *688* program. For Rickover, Veliotis was the tough manager he had been waiting for to fire the idlers and get the ships built. And for Veliotis, Rickover was the father of the nuclear navy whose legacy enriched Veliotis's immigrant pride. It reminded him that he had arrived at the center of the shipbuilding universe. But their cordial surface relationship was constantly at risk in the larger state of warfare between General Dynamics and the navy. Rickover was mounting a righteous and holy crusade against the company's cost-overrun claims. He had told David Lewis that he was going to take the company on, and Lewis had told Veliotis that he should prepare for the worst from Rickover.

Yet when he arrived, Veliotis found different circumstances. Rickover scrupulously avoided attacking Veliotis's management—as long as Veliotis stayed out of the claims fight and as long as Veliotis did not blame the cost overruns on the navy. Veliotis was only too willing to accept these ground rules. He was there to rescue the yard and that would take all of his energy.

"I want to talk to you about what's happening . . . on the *Omaha,*" Rickover opened one of their first conversations.

After five years of construction, Electric Boat had delivered only one of eighteen submarines under contract to the navy. U.S.S. *Philadelphia* had been commissioned the previous June, and the yard frantically was trying to get U.S.S. *Omaha* ready for her sea trials. The navy crew already had moved on board, but the crewmen had found dozens of imperfections in workmanship.

"Of all the ships we've had over many, many years, this one is acting up the worst," said Rickover. "I'm not complaining, I just want to tell you a problem you're going to have. We have too many things happening . . . I don't think we can ever get her on trials. Some of it is your fault and some of it is not, like the turbine. But the lesson of it now, and I mention it to you, you can make a lot of changes in the organization, you can let excess people go, but the basic thing is there's got to be excellence up there. And that has deteriorated a hell of a lot. See what I'm getting at?"

"Yes, I understand that," Veliotis said.

Rickover said that he had been quoted in one of the local newspapers and wanted to read the quote to Veliotis: "'For many years there has been a large amount of loafing at Electric Boat. I have personally observed [it] in both shops and ships during my inspections and recently I have received reports that loafing is so bad that some workers do not even make the effort to appear busy.' I just wanted to tell you what my public statement is on that."

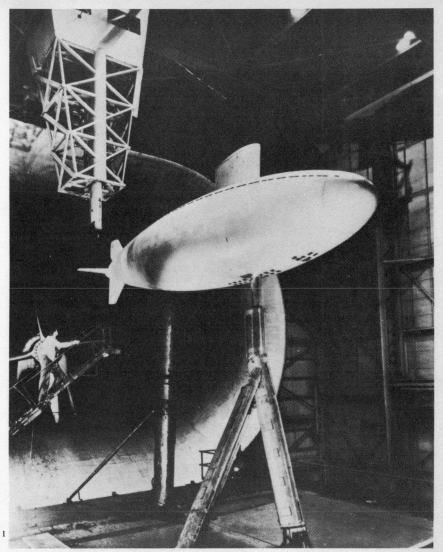

1

A little-known experimental high-speed submarine, U.S.S. *Albacore*, was designed and built in 1952 with a revolutionary hull shape, round and tapered like a porpoise, and had a single propeller for thrust. According to classified studies, nuclear submarines of the future built along *Albacore*'s lines and powered by nuclear reactors could achieve speeds approaching fifty knots—sixty miles per hour under the ocean!

Vice Admiral Hyman G. Rickover, father of the nuclear navy, aboard U.S.S. *Tecumseh*, a Polaris ballistic missile submarine commissioned in 1964. He understood that to win in the maddeningly large Pentagon bureaucracy, a player needed a variety of tools: stealth, cunning, good intelligence, political muscle, and, on some days, just a bully's club to make mush out of the opposition. He used them all to seize power for the nuclear navy.

Since the early 1960s, Rickover had begun to fear that the United States would lose its edge in the silent war against the Soviets. As the navy added weight and size to new classes of its submarines, the fleet was losing precious speed. Rickover began in 1964 to develop higher-powered nuclear reactors for submarine use. At the same time, he fought to convince his superiors that the Soviets were developing high-speed submarines to challenge the American armada—the aircraft-carrier battle groups.

4

5

6

Some conspicuous intelligence reports indicated that the Soviets had deployed the first of a new class of high-speed submarines, the *Victor* class (bottom), in late 1967. On January 5, 1968, a Soviet *November*-class attack submarine shattered all previous speed estimates for its class by pursuing the nuclear-powered aircraft carrier U.S.S. *Enterprise* in the Pacific at a sustained speed of 31 knots. The impact of the *Enterprise* episode rolled thunderously through the back channels of the defense establishment in Washington.

L. Mendel Rivers, chairman of the House Armed Services Committee, was among the Southern Democrats who believed that the country could not afford to lose its military edge over the Soviet Union just because Vietnam was draining $80 million a day in budget resources.

7

Chief of Naval Operations Thomas H. Moorer, who had chased German U-boats during World War II, was inclined to accept Rickover's view of the Soviet threat. Moorer, among the most shrewd and conservative CNOs of the postwar era, was also a good politician who wanted to reap the benefits of Rickover's influence in Congress. That was good for the navy.

8

During Defense Secretary Robert S. McNamara's long tenure at the Pentagon, he delegated great authority over weapons procurement to a group of "systems analysts." In the final months of 1967, they refused to include funding for Rickover's high-speed submarine prototype. McNamara's men argued that Soviet submarines were crude, noisy, and vulnerable. But Rickover knew better.

9

The Soviets were building nuclear submarines in unprecedented numbers at industrial facilities that dwarfed the U.S. shipbuilding base. With the help of reconnaissance satellites, such as the one that took this photo of Nikolayev South shipyard on the Black Sea, U.S. intelligence analysts were able to monitor the Soviet naval buildup. The evidence showed that the Russians were innovating, experimenting with new designs, and, more alarmingly, that their submarine program had the highest national priority.

10

11

12

Senator Strom Thurmond of South Carolina and Senator John Stennis of Mississippi were part of the military-congressional alliance Rickover forged to win funding for the "High-Speed Nuclear Attack Submarine." Said Thurmond: "I am of the opinion that if we are going to stay ahead of the Soviets— whose every thought, every move, every action is to become superior to us and dominate the world— we should no longer quibble about a few million or a few hundred million dollars."

John S. Foster, Jr., under secretary for defense research and engineering, was the person before whom all new weapons systems had to pass muster. Foster fought Rickover's high-speed submarine prototype because it would cost twice as much as the *Sturgeon*-class submarine, and because it still might not break the thirty-knot barrier.

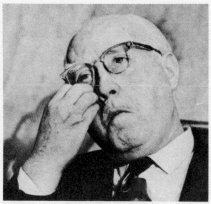

13

14

Deputy Defense Secretary Paul H. Nitze, who had been tangling with Rickover for years, made an effort to block the *688* design from becoming a new class of submarines, though aware of the political forces arrayed against him.

Representative Chet Holifield's hearing on June 21, 1968, gave the high-speed submarine its final boost. Rickover rewarded Holifield by recommending that the U.S. Navy christen the first ship after Holifield's home district, the city of Los Angeles. The navy had always named its attack boats for fish, but as one Rickover aide put it, "Fish don't vote."

Rickover benefitted beyond his wildest dreams from Richard M. Nixon's election as President in November 1968. He had known Nixon since the 1950s, when he had accompanied the then Vice President to the Soviet Union as a science adviser. After the election, the *688* prototype grew from a class of 12 ships to 23 ships.

15

A panel of seven submarine commanders made the fundamental and fateful compromise that would haunt the *688* class until the end of the century. By shaving the thickness of the hull, the panel got most of the weight savings they were after to ensure that the boat would break thirty knots. But in so doing, they substantially decreased the depth of ocean in which the submarine could operate—no deeper than 950 feet.

16

17

Henry Crown: "The colonel" wanted to remake General Dynamics into a giant of the defense industry.

18

Lester Crown oversaw Material Service Corporation, the Crown family business that merged into General Dynamics.

David S. Lewis was one of the most successful aerospace executives in the country when he was recruited by Crown in 1970. His Charleston manners were disarming; he fancied himself an actor always on stage and his eyes made fond, brotherly contact that set you immediately at ease.

19

20

Nathan Cummings: The grocery magnate was the most troublesome and meddlesome member of the Crown group of directors because he had so much at stake personally.

21

Albert E. Jenner, Jr., the Crown's lawyer, protected the family's interests as a member of the executive committee.

22

Hilliard W. Paige: Recruited by Lewis from General Electric, Paige was looking for a collegial environment and a chance to get back to managing basic engineering industries. He quickly found that he had made a horrible mistake.

23

The geography of The Boat had been cramped by nature, backed up against a bluff that overlooked the Thames River. The waterfront machine shops and building ways for the ships were jammed together on a narrow strip of shore that formed a continuous series of piers and drydocks, which made the best use of precious space. An old ferry served as the cafeteria. By late 1973, Electric Boat was in the midst of what some believed was an institutional nervous breakdown, a kind of gridlock that swamped the yard managers with so many new problems every hour of every day that they lost track of them. The cover-up of what was happening at Electric Boat began toward the end of 1974.

24

Joseph D. Pierce: He grew up on the waterfront and rose through the ranks to become general manager of Electric Boat. Having played up to Rickover, he ironically became a victim of the admiral's wrath.

25

Arthur M. Barton: Some of Rickover's people considered him the prototype of the new generation of contractor accountants whose sharp pencils looked for ways to gouge the government.

26

A lot of men who worked on U.S.S. *Philadelphia* would later say the ship was built twice because just about everything installed on her was ripped out at least once due to faulty workmanship, changed plans, or improper sequence. She was far from ready when her launch date arrived in October 1974, but General Dynamics, fearing a public relations disaster if the deadline was missed, sealed up the *Philadelphia's* hull and let her slide down the ways, then pushed her into drydock and resumed work the following week. It would take three more years to complete the ship.

27

Edward Hidalgo, the man chosen by the Carter administration to end the war between the navy and the shipbuilders, pursued a covert strategy of accommodation which he forever after denied.

28

Admiral Elmo R. Zumwalt, Jr., the ambitious and innovative naval officer who, as chief of naval operations, became Rickover's greatest nemesis.

29

The first Trident ballistic missile submarine, nearing completion at Electric Boat, was a key element in the Carter administration's strategic weapons policy. David Lewis told members of Congress that a shutdown of the *688* program could substantially disrupt the Trident production line. It was a less than subtle threat to hold the Trident program hostage until a ransom was paid on the *688*s.

30

Representative George Mahon told David Lewis that no one was sure whether General Dynamics was to blame for 20 percent or for 80 percent of the problem. Mahon said that Lewis had better take the deal that had been offered him, or "I wouldn't come back up here again."

31

Representative Christopher Dodd witnessed the kind of blunt and final exercise of power that only men of long tenure and high stature can wield without explanation and without appeal.

Takis Veliotis had planned the takeover of Electric Boat like a military operation. He walked through the shipyard with an imperial bearing. Laying off more than 4,000 workers, he spoke to those who remained about the need to perform, to get the yard moving again. He told them he would make the system work and he would be there for as long as it took. He knew what he was doing, he said, because he had been building ships for as long as many of them had been alive.
32

33

The welding and quality control crisis was the beginning of the end for Veliotis. In a nuclear submarine, the suspicion of a defect was as bad as a defect. That's what the navy had learned from the loss of U.S.S. *Thresher* in 1963. You couldn't be 99 percent sure that all the welds were there. Veliotis had inherited both the crazy system and the ships —half-built time bombs of poor workmanship— and now they were exploding his plans for real achievement. The navy took a hard and aloof position: Don't ask the navy how to fix it; show the navy how you intend to guarantee the ships' integrity. It was going to take a year or more and Veliotis was going to have to rip apart a half-dozen ships.

34

The bailout of General Dynamics energized Rickover for the last campaign of his career—indeed, of his life. He was determined to punish David Lewis for the slick and treacherous public relations campaign that had wounded Rickover in Congress. When Veliotis saw it coming, saw that he would be in the middle, saw that Lewis would be standing behind him not as his backer but as someone who needed a shield, Veliotis understood that it might be up to him to defeat Rickover, to kill the old man for good, or perish himself.

35

During the July 1981 sea trials of U.S.S. *La Jolla*, Rickover fell into the trap Veliotis had laid for him, and the old man never really recovered. In the five or six minutes that *La Jolla* was out of control at Rickover's hand, the big submarine nearly dived into the sandy bottom 600 feet beneath the surface of the Atlantic. It could have been another *Thresher*, this time at Rickover's hand and with Rickover aboard. He had been wrong and he had no business going out on trials at age 81.

36

In 1985, David Lewis was pummeled in Congress—accused of lying, accused of cheating the government. Triple bypass surgery had sapped his stamina and he had stepped down as chairman after 15 years, but he remained unrepentant about the business decisions of the past. He had been, perhaps, "wrong, naïve," even "stupid," but he clung to his firm belief that "the navy screwed this thing up." His greatest misjudgment: "Veliotis."

37

38

Rickover had been overwhelmed by history and by his own hubris. He was in charge of the U.S. submarine program at a time when the Soviets had made submarine advancement a national priority—similar to the U.S. effort to put a man on the moon. The Soviets had spent tens of billions of dollars on the fastest and deepest-diving ships in the world, while Rickover had had a couple of billion to build a competitive fleet.

Veliotis, fugitive and witness. The flaw in his judgment appeared with dreadful clarity; he had compounded his ambition with unthinking greed, not knowing how it would lead to his undoing in the end, not knowing how it would steal from him the opportunity to ascend to the top of the American defense establishment, and not knowing how much he would regret the criminal allegations that stick like a horrible tar to a man's reputation when the day of reckoning comes.

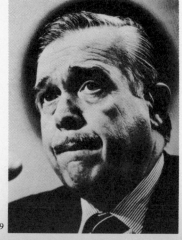

39

Lewis believed that his reputation had been crushed by the impact of the first round of Veliotis revelations. But a second, more devastating round was coming, this time in Congress. Lewis and Gorden MacDonald had traveled down the road together. MacDonald had gone to Electric Boat with no shipbuilding experience and he had made a mess of it. When the first hearing was called before Representative John D. Dingell of Michigan, Lewis and MacDonald spent an entire day at the St. Louis Club in rehearsal, complete with hot lights and hostile questions, because Lewis had never testified before Congress. He had never been called to account for his performance as chairman of the largest defense contractor by the elected representatives of the taxpayers, who paid the bills.

James Ashton became a secret informer against Veliotis. It was a conspiracy born of Ashton's naïveté, and doomed from the beginning because of the partnership that existed between Lewis and Veliotis to keep the lid on at Electric Boat while they tried to shake down the navy for more money.

42

43

44

What remained were the submarines, heading out on silent patrols in the silent war, gathering intelligence and making torpedo and mine-laying runs along the Kola Peninsula and out beyond the great northern rim of the Soviet landmass. The consequences of the political trade-offs and the ad hocism that had sown the weak seam into their diving armor would radiate out across the decades. The existential moment awaited them like a distant coordinate somewhere in the future, where the latitudes of war and the limitations of machinery would intersect for the final test. Only then would they confront the brutal physics of survival in combat.

"Admiral, you don't have to tell me that, I just came back from the shipyard and I can see it. I can see what's going on, Admiral."

"But they are still loafing?"

"They are loafing very much."

Rickover warned Veliotis that the workers would try to fool the new general manager by appearing busy when he walked down the hill to the waterfront.

"It's easy to hide on a submarine. They're all notified when somebody comes aboard."

Veliotis agreed. "The signal goes out. The level of noise and activity increases."

"And they all look busy," Rickover said.

"Oh, yes."

Rickover liked what he was hearing. "We'll give you all the help we can, but you must understand that we cannot tolerate [it] when General Dynamics' people go to Congress and testify that everything that's wrong up at E.B. is the navy's fault. We're not going to take that."

"Admiral, I have said to my staff—yesterday—I got them in a very short staff meeting—I am a man of very few words—I said, 'Stop complaining about the customer. Get off your asses and start performing!' "

"If you find anything that we're doing that's wrong, I wish you'd let us know," Rickover said.

"We will let you know, Admiral, but I haven't found anything and I have asked them. I said, 'Give me an instance where the customer has stopped you from working. Give me an instance where the customer told you to walk around, not to work, to promenade.' "

"It's always the customer's fault," Rickover said. "They've been saying that for so many years and they keep on. But we want to help because, after all, you're building our ships and we have a lot of expertise. . . . But you have undertaken a job which is very, very difficult. It'll take a long time. You can stop the loafing all right, I think you can, but to create excellence is another matter entirely."

"And we have to create excellence and we have to get the pride back in the people so that they do their job and they are proud of what they are doing."

"Well, I don't think you are ever going to get that with American workers," Rickover said. "I think you're kidding yourself. You're not going to get pride. Very rarely do you get that. The only way you're going to do it is to have an organization and a system where men have specific jobs to do and you can measure whether they do it or not. . . . In my opinion you're kidding the hell out of yourself if you think you're going to get thousands of people up there to have pride. You've seen what goes on up there. A bunch of them are slobs!"

"I have seen it, but I have seen also at Quincy the way it was and the way it turned out."

"Oh yeah, but it isn't necessarily pride, it's what kind of supervision they have. If you get the supervision, you don't have to worry about pride."

"We made the supervision there, we trained them," Veliotis said, again reminding Rickover of his accomplishment at Quincy.

"Then you're going to have to do a hell of a lot of training at Electric Boat. But don't forget that all these things I'm telling you I have been telling for years to your people from St. Louis, been telling them, and telling them. . . . It's been going on for years and we keep on pointing it out, but no action was taken. They just blamed the navy for everything. You ought to investigate why so many things are failing on the *Omaha* because it will give you an inkling into some of the things that are wrong and you can put your finger on the people concerned."

"Okay, Admiral, I will do that."

It was quiet in Veliotis's office. He had put Rickover on the speakerphone because Veliotis was increasingly deaf in his right ear and the hearing in his left was not what it used to be. The other reason was the speakerphone made it easier to tape-record the conversation. Veliotis had paused after the call, then reached over to the credenza behind his desk to rewind a little bit of the tape to see if the machine had worked properly. It had. He pushed the record button again and spoke softly into the recorder, "Conversation with Admiral Rickover." After ejecting the cassette, he dated it and placed it in his desk drawer. He was playing defense. He knew the tapes might be valuable if they ended up at each other's throats. For the moment he and Rickover were allied. There were seventeen 688s to get to sea along with the first three Tridents. But they were also bitter adversaries whose institutions were on a collision course over the $544 million claim, over future claims, and over a long list of outstanding disputes. Both men understood that any of these overlying tensions could pit them against each other in public, in the federal courts, or in the Congress.

The desktop Sony tape recorder next to the telephone was the only personal artifact that MacDonald had left behind. Veliotis was intrigued by the suggestion that MacDonald had taped his telephone calls; it fed his suspicions about MacDonald's tactics as an infighter in St. Louis. Perhaps MacDonald had left it behind as a warning.

Art Barton had met Veliotis on few occasions before the take-over. Then one morning Barton arrived at the shipyard to find that he had been kicked out of his office on the first floor and moved into smaller quarters upstairs to make room for the Quincy Eight. Barton's new boss was Gary Grimes, Veliotis's financial whiz kid, who had the disposition of an angry Doberman and who already was making Barton feel like he would be bodily thrown out the front gate. Banished as he was to the attic, Barton had not expected to be summoned to the general manager's office on the first day, but he soon found himself returning Veliotis's cool and unfriendly gaze. Grimes was present, a Marlboro in his hand and his eyes boring a hole in Barton's temple. It was a brief conversation.

Veliotis wanted two pieces of paper on his desk by the following morning. They should contain the man-hour and cost estimates for the two *688* contracts, he said.

Barton momentarily blanched. How much did Veliotis know? What had MacDonald told him? Did Veliotis know what Barton had been keeping locked away to prove that he had told Lewis and MacDonald exactly how bad things were?

Veliotis sent Barton back to his office, where he could privately rage against his circumstances. Did Veliotis want more delusion? Faced with the terror of his future, Barton quickly realized that there was only one safe course with Veliotis—tell him everything he wanted to know. Help him to find the truth for himself, because it was Barton's best defense. If MacDonald or Lewis tried to reach out from St. Louis and swat Barton for telling the truth, so be it; but Veliotis was closer and a much greater threat. Barton was an organization man. He knew little about Veliotis, yet he knew enough that he was not about to deceive or challenge him.

The following morning, Barton returned to Veliotis's office with the two sheets of figures. He handed them over with the anxiety of a man wearing a blindfold. Would he be thanked for his honesty or fired?

On the first seven submarines, Barton projected an overrun of $515 million. On the eleven submarines of the second contract, he projected the overrun at $709 million, for a total overrun of $1.22 billion, more than double the value of the original contract.

Veliotis studied the figures for a moment. When he looked up at the comptroller to speak, his voice was full of scorn.

"You ought to be in jail," he hissed. "I ought to fire you right now. Why didn't you tell Lewis, goddammit, huh, why didn't you?"

Barton's face was flushed. He was angry. "I did tell Lewis."

"I ought to fire you," Veliotis said, ignoring his answer. "I talked to Lewis. He had never heard of these figures. He said to me, 'Oh God, I didn't know.' Now, why shouldn't I fire you?"

"That fucking Lewis," Barton blurted out. He started to unleash his frustration. The words rushed out of him in an emotional torrent: about Lewis cutting the bid, about Curtis dictating the estimates for the man-hours, about Curtis telling Barton to keep out of the cost projections, about MacDonald coming in and shutting down all cost reporting based on actual performance.

"That fucking Lewis, I told him at every step of the way."

Veliotis did not let up. He threatened over and over to fire Barton, and shouted, "Show me!" every time Barton said he could prove that he had told Lewis and MacDonald what the cost figures were. Finally, he dismissed Barton, seeing that the comptroller was in a state of terror for his job and that's what Veliotis wanted. He wanted to find out the truth about this monstrous overrun and why someone hadn't done something about it. Sometimes you had to scare the truth out of people.

With Barton gone, Veliotis turned to his deputy, Grimes, and said, "The way that fellow Barton talks, you would think that Dave Lewis had been baptized 'That Fucking Lewis.'"

Both men laughed, but Veliotis had been riveted by Barton's assertion of "proof." If Barton had an incriminating file, Veliotis needed to know it for his own protection. But there was more to it than that. He had nothing but contempt for MacDonald over the mess he had left at the shipyard. The two sheets of paper Barton had produced convinced Veliotis that MacDonald had been covering up a huge overrun at Electric Boat.

What concerned him was how much Lewis had known. Why hadn't Lewis confided in him before he took over the shipyard? When Veliotis was at Quincy, he sent almost daily memoranda to Lewis about costs on the tankers. Yet Lewis had sent Veliotis into Electric Boat unprepared, without the detailed knowledge and history that Lewis was carrying in his head. Veliotis's mind flashed back to the week before, to the look on Lewis's face when he said, "Oh God. I didn't know it was that bad."

Lewis knew—he knew everything! The realization hit Veliotis with a thunderous certainty and he felt a twinge in his stomach that the man for whom he would go through a brick wall had not leveled with him. Why? To protect MacDonald, or to protect David Lewis? Was Veliotis being set up to take the fall for the overrun that had been kept off the books? Did they want him to cover up also? Obviously they did: Lewis after all had told him to take ninety days to prepare cost estimates that already existed.

For the first time Veliotis fully understood the stakes of the game that he was playing: no one could tell the truth because they might all go to jail for covering up something so large for so long. The only thing to do in the short run, Veliotis believed, was to keep the lid on. After all, he intended to turn the shipyard around and save the corporation from disaster. But he had to protect himself. He had too much to lose. He would have to rely on the tape recorder. And he had to remain an organization man, because if he pulled it off—if Electric Boat got the ships delivered and managed somehow to shake enough money out of the navy to cover the overrun—Veliotis would be on top.

David Lewis's only chance of surviving the year was in threatening the U.S. Navy with the most ruinous act he could think of until it surrendered cash.

Lewis, the actor, did not like to play the part of bully, but he was desperate. He would do almost anything for cash. Veliotis had been only half the solution. He could stop the hemorrhage at the shipyard and find a way toward a profitable future, but that would not solve the immediate problem. The searing reality was that General Dynamics was dropping $15 million month after month after month. A vein had been opened and no company could survive that kind of bleeding for long. Already, Wall Street was beginning to get the scent of failure. The defense analysts warned of the "substantial risk" the 688 program posed for the company, and Arthur Andersen was planning to qualify the company's financial statements for a second straight year.

The company's stock was searching for the bottom. From a high of $65 a share in 1976, its value fell through $50 during October 1977.

Over six years, Electric Boat had absorbed all of the cash generated by all other divisions of General Dynamics. The drain had left the company so anemic that the market value of the eleven million outstanding shares of common stock was barely equal to the $544 million claim the company had filed against the navy the previous December.

Worse, Barton's estimates of the overrun at Electric Boat were nearly double the equity value of the entire corporation.* If that terrifying fact had been known in the investor community, General Dynamics might well have fallen under the weight of the disclosure.

The $544 million claim was being carried on General Dynamics' balance sheet as a hard asset of the corporation, as a bank carries a performing loan. But more and more, as the navy refused to make any provisional payment under the claim, General Dynamics' reliance on

---

*Even on an after-tax basis, Barton's estimate of the overrun would have roughly equaled the value of shareholders' equity.

the claim as a bankable asset was becoming a fiction. There was an acute awareness in St. Louis that if the claim was not worth anything, then General Dynamics would be forced to declare a massive loss.

The claim had thus become a symbol. If it had no integrity, then the financial position of General Dynamics had no credibility, and by extension, neither did its chairman.

That was why, when David Lewis got private word from his Washington office that the navy was going to issue a formal "finding" stating that General Dynamics' claim had little value, he threatened to shut down the nuclear submarine program in the United States unless someone in power stopped that disclosure.

Someone did: Edward Hidalgo, the Assistant Secretary of the Navy for Shipbuilding, and the man designated by the Carter administration to end the war between the navy and the shipbuilders.

The pressure had started mounting on Lewis at the end of the summer. The rigid admiral in charge of the evaluation of the $544 million claim refused to consider the company's demand for a $120 million provisional payment to stem the cash flow drain until the navy evaluation was complete. The navy would not pay, and was demanding cause-and-effect analyses to justify the huge amount of money claimed. The admiral refused to pay for unsubstantiated "delay and disruption."

One Lewis operative summed it up bluntly: "The navy intends to dispute the majority of the amount we have claimed."

Lewis rushed to Washington to take his own soundings. He discovered that only the political appointees in the navy secretariat could settle the claim for the kind of money General Dynamics needed, and they could do it by going to Congress.

Lewis had not realized the distinction. He thought the Navy Claims Settlement Board was his only remedy, his only forum to get cash.

He went to see Hidalgo, whom he found cordial and open. The new attitude in the navy secretariat, Hidalgo said, was that there had been entirely too much acrimony in the past. The political realities of the day seemed to cry out for an equitable settlement.

This was a man Lewis believed he could deal with.

Lewis's opening gambit came on September 21, when he flew to Washington and met with the Carter team leaders, Deputy Defense Secretary Charles W. Duncan, Jr., and Navy Secretary W. Graham Claytor, Jr.

The delays in processing the company's claims had become intolerable, Lewis told them, and the company was running out of patience. The board of directors was considering legal action. If forced to, Lewis would file a notice stating that the navy had defaulted on the *688* submarine contracts, and—he paused to light the fuse of the bomb he wanted to explode in their minds—this would be accompanied by a suspension of work on the ships.

The civilian secretaries were shocked that Lewis was talking about such drastic action. Claytor insisted the claim would be processed by the end of the year and that Hidalgo already had decided to seek congressional approval for special funding allowing the navy to offer a larger cash settlement to the shipbuilders. In the meantime, Claytor said, the Navy Claims Settlement Board was preparing to offer a provisional payment that might alleviate the company's cash flow crisis.

Lewis thought it was a successful confrontation. He had bluntly stated the company's resolve, yet he was clear on the point that catastrophe could be avoided if the Pentagon came through with a lot of cash. That's all he wanted.

Two weeks later Lewis was stunned when word was flashed from the Washington office that the provisional payment being offered by the Navy Claims Settlement Board was $13 million, plus an additional $7 million that would be paid out over the remaining years of construction on the submarines. Thirteen million out of $544 million!

"This will destroy investor confidence in General Dynamics," Lewis complained bitterly in a telephone call to the navy secretary. "After ten months of work, this board comes up with 3.67 percent of the total amount of the claim as a reasonable settlement?" Lewis reminded Claytor of the assurances he had made during their meeting and asked, "What are we supposed to do now?"

Claytor was just as surprised as Lewis that the settlement board had found so little merit in General Dynamics' claim. But he did not have an answer except to reiterate his earlier assurances. He counseled Lewis to be patient. Hidalgo was going forward as fast as he could with a broader settlement proposal to Congress, and in that context, whatever the settlement board did was irrelevant.

But the assurances were not enough. The fiasco over the provisional payment forced General Dynamics to go privately to Hidalgo, drawing the Office of the Secretary of the Navy into the company's strategy, which would keep Wall Street and the company's shareholders from finding out the truth about the navy's official evaluation of the $544 million claim.

Rickover was stoking the congressional fires of criticism over the claims and the pressure on the Navy Claims Settlement Board to complete its task was building. The rear admiral in charge had been constant in his private assessment, which had begun to leak outside the navy: General Dynamics' claim was worth but a fraction of its face value. If that judgment was issued before General Dynamics closed its books for the year, Lewis's strategy was dead. The legal requirement to record an enormous loss would be unavoidable. Worse, the navy would feel no incentive to take responsibility for the overrun if General Dynamics already had eaten it.* Lewis believed that in recording a loss, he would be cutting his own throat, and he would never recover that money from the navy.

On October 5, General Dynamics' executive committee held one of its longest sessions trying to find a way out. Lewis, Crown, and the other members debated the escape routes all afternoon and into the night. The meeting carried over from the boardroom to the dinner table at the St. Louis Club on the fifteenth floor of the office tower adjoining General Dynamics headquarters. At the end of the evening, the committee members were still at a loss for a solution, but they had come up with a plan to send MacDonald on a delicate mission to sound out Edward Hidalgo as to whether he would help.

The morning after the meeting, MacDonald placed a call to Hidalgo's office at the Pentagon. He told the assistant secretary that the board had been meeting to consider shutting down the production line at Electric Boat. After long deliberations, MacDonald said, the executive committee had agreed to withhold filing a notice to stop work on the submarines, but only if the navy stated its intention in writing to settle the claim by requesting additional funds from Congress, and—this was the key condition—provided that the navy agreed in writing not to make a "finding" on the merit of the $544 million claim until well into the next calendar year.

There was a momentary silence on the line.

Hidalgo understood the financial crisis that General Dynamics was facing. He had practiced law on Wall Street and he realized the ramifications of what MacDonald was proposing. And Hidalgo knew

---

*One report prepared for MacDonald in October 1977 crystallized the areas of crisis:
　　"—S.E.C. required disclosure arising from failure to achieve productivity improvements [at Electric Boat].
　　—Effect of loss recognition on negotiations with the navy.
　　—Effect of shutdown on costs currently on balance sheet."

the settlement board had found little merit to the claim.* It would be an enormous risk for Hidalgo to put such a pledge in writing. He would jeopardize his own reputation and that of the entire Pentagon leadership.

Yet Hidalgo wanted desperately to prevent a shutdown at Electric Boat. He told MacDonald that he could agree to all of the board's conditions except the one about the "finding." He would have to review the matter further. That was the best he could do for the moment.

The board members tried to read between the lines of Hidalgo's response. They decided to wait. Maybe Hidalgo could deliver. Two weeks passed and Lewis decided he could wait no longer. The company was living under constant threat that the Navy Claims Settlement Board would finish its work. The Washington office was sending intelligence reports to Lewis that a "finding" might be imminent. The terror and anxiety of these weeks of waiting preyed on Lewis. Everything seemed to be in the balance for him. The struggle over the claim was the struggle against failure for Lewis—the failure of his management and of his vision.

On October 18, Lewis and MacDonald met with key members of Congress and announced the company was going to walk out on the *688* program, shut down the largest submarine production line in the country because, Lewis said, the navy had materially breached its contracts with the company. The company regretted taking the action, he said, because it would throw thousands of workers into the streets and unemployment lines. The only thing that could dissuade General Dynamics' board from taking such a drastic step was more aggressive action by the navy to settle the corporation's claims.

The telephones in the navy secretariat lit up with congressional inquiries about what the navy intended to do to head off the crisis. The company's strategy was planned in close consultation with the former Secretary of Defense, Clark Clifford, one of General Dynamics' Washington lawyers. General Dynamics' goal was to put the maximum political pressure on the Pentagon to act; to blind-side the Carter appointees in the most important forum in Washington. Lewis

---

*Hidalgo denies that he knew the settlement board had found little merit to the claim. However, Admiral Rickover, in a November 28, 1977, meeting with Hidalgo, pointed out that the board appeared to have reached this conclusion, according to Rickover's memorandum of the meeting. Also, the board's chairman, Rear Admiral Manganaro, said in an interview that he informed Hidalgo regularly in 1977 that the board had come up with very little value to the items that composed the company's $544 million claim. And General Dynamics officials who were in frequent contact with Hidalgo indicated at the time in their own internal records that every indication pointed toward a low evaluation of the claim's worth.

shaped the issue in a way that made the company's position appeal eminently reasonable, responsible; made in good faith. By confiding in the congressional leadership his concerns over the imminent confrontation, Lewis established himself as a patriot first and businessman second. He wanted to give the Congress an opportunity to head off the crisis—for the good of the country.

The fact that General Dynamics had precipitated the crisis was lost in the vagaries of its explanation that the company had no choice due to its cash flow crisis. Everyone, even congressmen, understood cash flow. They also understood that the first Trident submarine was nearing completion at Electric Boat, and Trident was a key element in the Carter administration's strategic arms policy.

How would the shutdown affect Trident? the congressmen asked.

Lewis's expression was grave, his tone somber. He talked about the extensive disruption in the shipyard from massive 688-program layoffs. Under labor union rules, those workers with seniority on the 688 program could "bump" less senior workers on the Trident program. It would be a real mess and could take months to sort out at great expense. The disruptive effects were hard to predict with any accuracy except that they would be substantial.

In fact, it was a less than subtle threat to hold the Trident program hostage until a ransom was paid on the 688s. It was a form of blackmail against the new administration, revealing a deep cynicism in the relationship between the businessmen who were running a key defense industry and the Pentagon.

At the end of the day, Lewis led his four-man team to the Pentagon to meet with Duncan, Claytor, and Hidalgo. The timing was perfect because it had allowed for the wave of political inquiries to wash through the Pentagon and the national security bureaus in the State Department and White House.

Lewis repeated that the company was shutting down the 688 program, pulling the men off the ships. The navy had breached the 688 contracts. This was it.

Claytor said the navy still very much wished to avoid a confrontation. But, he added, if the stop-work notice was filed, the navy was going to play hard ball. The navy would sue General Dynamics for breach of contract and for damages for not delivering the ships. At the same time, Claytor threatened, the navy would pull the unfinished ships out of Electric Boat and place them in other shipyards. The navy would then ask the court to force General Dynamics to pay the navy's costs to complete the submarines.

In fact, Claytor's threat to build the ships elsewhere was hollow since there were no other American shipyards qualified to build them except Newport News, and it too was at war with the navy. But there was metal in Claytor's voice and Lewis did not want a fight if he could avoid one. All he wanted was cash.

The Carter appointees were over a barrel. It was Hidalgo who finally gave Lewis the assurance he wanted to hear:

The Navy Claims Settlement Board would not complete its work until after the first of the year. Hidalgo would see to it. And there would be no "finding" on the value of the claim in the interim. Hidalgo would go to Congress for the big money General Dynamics needed, and they would work together to find a politically acceptable settlement.*

That was the deal Lewis had wanted. Apparently it was a deal that Hidalgo was willing to make, because it cost him nothing in the negotiations he was about to commence and gained for him a debt of goodwill from General Dynamics that he would later need. By the end of 1977, Hidalgo knew he would never get enough money from Congress to satisfy all of the shipbuilders' demands for cash; therefore each one of them—with General Dynamics taking the lead—was eventually going to have to declare the large and painful loss it had been avoiding for years.

It was easy for Hidalgo to say that a private agreement with

---

*Whether it occurred during the meeting or outside it is not clear, but Lewis, in an interview, acknowledged that a pact was made. According to Lewis, Hidalgo told company officials: "We will hold this finding in abeyance, if you will continue to work." Lewis said he extracted this private agreement from the navy out of fear that the Navy Claims Settlement Board would refuse to negotiate with the corporation and would issue its evaluation of the claim as a contracting officer's "finding," which could not be reversed without an appeal to the Armed Services Board of Contract Appeals. Lewis said he learned that Hidalgo had concluded that the settlement board's chairman, Rear Admiral Manganaro, was under Rickover's direct control. Lewis asserts that the private pact General Dynamics made with the navy secretariat was therefore a proper counterstrategy to thwart Rickover's assault on the company.

For his part, however, Hidalgo absolutely denies entering into any such agreement with General Dynamics and asserts that it was an act of "destiny" that he later confiscated the General Dynamics claim from the settlement board's offices before the board could issue any finding. Hidalgo said that there were sound organizational reasons to pull the claim into his office, where his staff could apply uniform standards to all claims under review. Hidalgo asserts that up to this point, he had repeatedly urged the settlement board to quickly complete its work in the fall of 1977, and therefore it is impossible to construe his actions as trying to block the board's evaluation of the General Dynamics claim. However, Hidalgo's later testimony before Congress shows that when the evaluation of the claim was finally completed in early 1978, the results were not released publicly by either the navy or General Dynamics. The dollar amount was held privately until mid-1978 and it did not figure into General Dynamics' calculation of profit and loss on the 688 program for the 1977 financial reporting year.

The head of the settlement board, Rear Admiral Manganaro, said in an interview that he had never known of this pact. He asserted that the settlement board was never under Rickover's control and scrupulously maintained its independence in evaluating the General Dynamics claim.

General Dynamics—one that allowed the corporation to forestall the disclosure of massive cost overruns—was no more than a reorganization and schedule adjustment that was within his discretion and wholly unrelated to General Dynamics' financial predicament.

But in fact, by making this private pact with General Dynamics, the navy played right into the company's hands in one crucial respect: Had the navy forced General Dynamics to take its loss up front by publishing the claim evaluation as a finding of the settlement board, there would have been much less to deal with at the bargaining table. The company would have already swallowed the loss the navy saw as essential to a settlement. But fearing the calamity of a shutdown, and the political fallout over massive layoffs and delay to the Trident program, the navy pursued a strategy of accommodation on the timing of its crucial finding. And Hidalgo forever after denied that he had been its architect.*

It fell to Gorden MacDonald to brief Veliotis on the marathon negotiation with the navy. It was important that Veliotis know the company line and what Lewis had told the directors about the claim, because Veliotis now was in the inner circle, part of the cover-up.

Lewis had decided to hedge against the discovery of the $1 billion overrun by stating in the company's third-quarter earnings report that "the thousands of drawing revisions and changes imposed by the navy, which forms the basis of our present claims, are continuing at a high rate. This continues to impact production . . . and will result in additional substantial claims."

MacDonald telephoned Veliotis on November 4.

"Dave wanted to make sure I took you through this," MacDonald's guttural voice said over the speakerphone on Veliotis's desk. "I had sat down with Arthur Andersen [the accountants], I guess it was last week, and went through with him where we stood with the claims, with the Secretary of the Navy and Duncan, and so forth. And that we

*Hidalgo's superior, Claytor, said such an agreement was never discussed in his presence and added that he would have considered such a pact as stock fraud. Yet the minutes of the November 3, 1977, board meeting of General Dynamics show that Albert E. Jenner, Jr., member of the General Dynamics executive committee and Crown family attorney, explicitly summarized the terms of the agreement: "(1) In view of the urgings of Messrs. Claytor, et al., that the corporation not discontinue performance under the 688 contracts, (2) their affirmative representations respecting their intentions . . . to process the corporation's claim diligently by Admiral Manganaro to the end that his recommendation with respect thereto will be forthcoming early in 1978, (3) their assurances that the navy contracting officer will not make a finding as to the corporation's 688 claims while the course of action they plan to undertake is being pursued . . . the directors ratified and approved the actions taken by Mr. Lewis and the executive committee."

were satisfied that we didn't want to give no decision—and then of course acknowledge that the [man-] hours are well above the [man-] hours on the first flight, but that the changes had grown from twenty-seven thousand changes when we submitted our claim to thirty-five thousand, and that the people were looking at the claim to possibly update it, or approach the claim deal maybe different than we did before—if we didn't do it the right way, you know—if we should have done it another way using hindsight."

MacDonald was a master of doubletalk.

Veliotis was laughing to himself. He could hear MacDonald squirming on the line, trying to say something and yet not say something. He was trying to tell Veliotis what Veliotis already knew. Mac-Donald had altered the schedules on the submarines to get the amount of the claim down from the $1 billion level it should have been to $544 million to keep the banks and Wall Street from pulling the plug on General Dynamics.

That's why the schedules were all wrong. If MacDonald had admitted that it was going to take two additional years to complete everything in the shipyard, he would have had to add two years' worth of man-hours, and Barton's cost-overrun estimate of $1 billion would have been staring him in the face again. By putting off the day of reckoning, MacDonald now had to eat crow and talk about "updating" the claim. The only way he could justify filing a new claim was to blame something new—like more drawing revisions—on the navy.

MacDonald was still talking.

"So then we had an audit committee meeting of the board. . . . Our big argument, Taki, was that our problem was not in the third quarter, the problem was going to be at the end of the year. What do we do?"

Veliotis thought it was an excellent question, but he chose not to answer it, as if to emphasize that it was MacDonald's problem. The board of directors by now had to know what the potential loss was. The whole lot of them were walking a tightrope. For a moment, the monstrous challenge in the shipyard did not seem as frightening to Veliotis as the anxiety level that must have been gripping the board of directors. Veliotis thanked MacDonald for the briefing. He made it clear that he already understood the company line about the plan to keep the lid on for the remainder of the year.

"I spoke with Dave myself and I told Dave that I need at least three months from next week before I have a cost to complete."

"Right, that's what he had said, too," MacDonald interjected.

But Veliotis did not want to let MacDonald off the telephone without having some sport and without getting some things on tape.

"You know," Veliotis said, "I told the same thing to the Arthur Andersen people who were here. They leveled all kinds of I-told-you-so's. They started by saying, 'We told MacDonald to cut twenty-five hundred people from the overhead and he didn't do it.' We talked about material control. . . . And, well, they say nobody told them anything. . . . And they had asked me, 'Will the claims grow?' Of course they're going to grow, the claims. A certain time elapses, there will be more claims."

Then, in an aside to MacDonald, Veliotis added, "Although what I heard from the engineers, the differential—seven thousand or eight thousand more [drawing] revisions—they are more revisions than changes, you know. They are very small and very negligible. But we'll see what we have to do."

The words hung in the air: *"They are very small and very negligible."*

Veliotis paused to see if MacDonald would respond. General Dynamics had recently stated that on the basis of those seven thousand to eight thousand revisions it intended to increase its $544 million claim to perhaps $1 billion. The statement was a warning from Veliotis that he knew the game being played. If he was going to participate, it was going to be with the stated knowledge that, in his opinion, any new claim based on the "negligible" impact of the navy drawing revisions would be a fiction, a contrivance. Veliotis had said it for the tape recorder and dared MacDonald in the silent moment afterwards to challenge it.

But MacDonald let the comment pass. He did not try to defend the company's position that the drawing revisions were the root of all evil at Electric Boat. Veliotis after all was the company's most expert shipbuilder; what was MacDonald going to say?

"Okay, well, I just wanted to make sure I passed that on, Taki."

"Okay, Gorden."

"Take it easy."

"Okay, my friend, bye-bye."

The political storm gathered swiftly over the layoffs. The local press already had dubbed Veliotis's arrival as "Black Monday" and there were horror stories about the hardships of sudden unemployment. One woman said she had been home sick when she received a telephone call from her supervisor. "They wanted me to come in, they said it was an emergency. So I got dressed and went in, and when I got there, they told me I couldn't have been sick after all, since I was well enough to come to work. So they fired me."

A shipyard supervisor recounted how one of Veliotis's "hench-men" had come to his office and said he wanted the names of ten people to be dismissed in his section. "He came back and asked for the list, then he asked me why my name wasn't on it. I told him I was the supervisor. He told me it didn't matter. I was fired, too."

The congressional delegations of Connecticut and Rhode Island raged against General Dynamics on every television and radio station within a hundred miles of Electric Boat. Senator Lowell Weicker accused MacDonald of lying about the layoffs and demanded an apology.*

Representative Christopher Dodd revealed at a news conference that the layoffs had been planned months in advance and in secret to foil any attempts by the unions and by federal or state officials to block them. President Carter was called upon from the floor of the House of Representatives to "reverse the catastrophic consequences" of the layoffs.

On day two of the takeover, Veliotis had flown to Washington to meet with the entire delegation. Senator Abraham Ribicoff borrowed the office of the Senate Majority Leader just off the Senate chamber. When Veliotis walked into the room, it was crowded with reporters and photographers who had been invited in to record the confrontation. He moved slowly around the room. He was courteous, reserved as he shook hands with each member. He settled on the side of the conference table across from Ribicoff, who waited for the clicking of camera shutters to ebb and then said, "I thought we would start off with a private discussion with . . ." He paused, turned to Veliotis, and said, "I'm trying to pronounce your name."

"Vell-eee-O-tis."

The reporters left for the private part of the meeting. One by one, the congressmen attacked Veliotis and demanded that he restore the jobs he had lopped off. Weicker fumed at the duplicity of company officials and Dodd was furious that no humanitarian considerations had been taken into account. Had there been some warning, state officials could have arranged for emergency unemployment assistance, he said.

But Veliotis had been prepared for the onslaught. He told Weicker that he would not reverse his decision. He told them that if they were interested in protecting the employment base of Connecticut and Rhode Island, they ought to support what he was doing, be-

---

*As MacDonald was leaving town, he had been asked whether General Dynamics planned to close the shipyard. MacDonald had given Weicker and others firm assurances that no such measure was contemplated. There was some confusion on whether he had been asked about massive layoffs.

cause if Electric Boat did not recover from its financial crisis, it faced extinction. Instead of three thousand workers on the streets, the congressmen would have to contend with twenty-three thousand.

His presentation was matter-of-fact and some members of the delegation understood his position, but as a group they nevertheless called the press back in and repeated their attacks for the record. Veliotis understood the political dynamic they were acting out. Thousands of constituent jobs had been lost. They could not congratulate Veliotis, and Veliotis knew it. So he sat there and took it. He listened intently and kept his hands on the table in front of him as the congressmen one by one criticized his actions. When they were finished, he thanked them and left.

Before Veliotis left Washington, he paid a courtesy call on Rickover. The admiral was very curious about the reaction Veliotis had received on Capitol Hill. Rickover said he knew something about the Congress and that he had been gathering his own political intelligence about the members of the New England delegation. He wanted to help, he said, and when Veliotis got back to Groton, Rickover was on the telephone to report: "What I'm telling you privately is that there are some people in the delegation who understand the position. And here's what I've told them. If this loafing keeps on and the place doesn't become productive, General Dynamics is not going to pay out their money, their own money, just to take care of the unemployment situation in Connecticut, see. And I think it's understood and you're not going to get in trouble over that. I think that's going to die, and, furthermore, if the new manager up there doesn't straighten out the place, there won't be any Electric Boat. See?"

Veliotis thanked the admiral for his intelligence report and marveled at Rickover's political network.

"Admiral Rickover called me to thank me for the Sarah Lee cakes that I sent him."

Nate Cummings couldn't resist sticking his nose into Veliotis's tent during those critical first weeks.

Cummings, one of the oldest and richest of General Dynamics' directors—and Colonel Crown's investing partner—was on the telephone. He wanted Veliotis to know that he had spoken with Rickover and that the old admiral had said nice things about Veliotis. He thought Veliotis would appreciate hearing it since Rickover was supposed to be such a terror on new general managers.

Nate Cummings also was working the telephone because he

had so much at stake personally, financially, in General Dynamics, and the corporation was deep in crisis. Cummings couldn't help but meddle in management. He had meddled when Hilliard Paige was president and he had been meddling ever since. Veliotis thought he was harmless, but he was mindful of his power in the boardroom. It was amusing to hear the petty way in which Cummings had been trying to curry favor with Rickover, sending him coffee cakes of all things.

"You know I've been sending a shipment to his wife, not to him, but to his wife, and he went on to tell me how good they are and so on. And I said we're bringing out a new one called Light & Fluffy and it doesn't have any butter in it and therefore no cholesterol. . . . Then all of a sudden he switched over and he said, 'You know, Mr. Veliotis, whom I've met, I'm very pleased with meeting him, and he shouldn't have laid off three thousand people, he should have laid off five thousand.' "

"Well, we know that, Nate," Veliotis said, a little irritated already at Cummings's indirect dig that he could have laid off more. "We know we have to lay off another two or three thousand people more. But we have to do it slowly because of the politicians."

Cummings agreed. "At the board meeting, they read us a letter from one of the senators, which was pretty rough."

"You see," Veliotis continued, "my plan was to lay off the first four thousand, four hundred ten people. But you know, there's no other way to do it. There's no other way to do it, Nate. If you start having people come in and you call them all together, and you say, 'I'm going to lay off within two or three weeks four thousand people,' then the pressure starts building on you. I've decided to cut clean, you know, and I cut thirty-two hundred people out, and every day I'm getting fifty, one hundred [more]. . . . This, Nathan, is going to give you about $100 million a year on the overhead."

"You're obviously on the right track, but you're being subjected to a lot of criticism, which you'll get over."

"What do you want me to do? I can be a nice guy, I don't want to be a bad guy . . . I have big problems here . . . because, hey, we are not doing well. The situation was worse than I thought. But we can do it. I brought good people from Quincy, they are with me. Give me now a year, a year and a half at this place, there will be so much change that you will not recognize it."

"I believe that you have the courage," Cummings said, and then asked, "Are you keeping in close touch with Dave and Gorden? Do they know what you are doing?"

"Oh yes, I keep in close touch with Dave, yes."

Veliotis did not want to acknowledge that he had any reporting responsibility to MacDonald, but Cummings caught the slight.

"Well, you ought to keep in touch with Gorden, too, because, after all, he's our financial man, if you know what I mean."

"Oh yes, of course, of course. Don't you worry, don't you worry."

Still, since Veliotis was taping the conversation, he was not going to let the opportunity pass without criticizing MacDonald on the record to one of the directors. He told Cummings that it appeared to him that Rickover was not the problem at Electric Boat and never had been.

"We created the situation ourselves. We had bad management for many years here," Veliotis said.

"That's right, you're curing it, that's what you want to do."

"Well, we should have tried a couple of years ago, you know."

"Looking back isn't going to help us," Cummings said paternally. "It's going forward, the way you are now, that's going to help us."

Veliotis did not press it further. He had made his point.

Some people said Electric Boat was headed for violence during those first tense weeks when thousands of workers got their pink slips. The resentment over the loss of jobs and the tension over strict new work rules combined to create a potentially explosive mixture.

The local newspapers carried accounts of shipyard workers who said the bilges of the submarines were filling up with urine because Veliotis had cracked down on workers leaving their stations to loiter in the restrooms. He was getting persistent calls from reporters and from city and state officials to respond to the rumors that the yard was going to be shut down in December. A kind of hysteria was in the air and Veliotis was concerned that it could turn into a wildcat strike or something worse.

Some of the congressmen, particularly Chris Dodd, were trying to inject themselves as players in the layoff crisis, and their offices had become clearinghouses for rumors that were getting magnified out of proportion. Veliotis thought Dodd particularly was fanning the flames until the company started paying attention to him. Every new piece of information or rumor that Dodd picked up in Washington seemed instantly to be telegraphed to the local press.

One afternoon, one of Dodd's aides telephoned Veliotis and announced, "We've been picking up persistent rumors that you're going to be announcing a two-week temporary layoff of a considerable number of people at Electric Boat and we wanted to confirm or deny that with you before, you know, it happens."

"Well," said Veliotis, "you know I'm getting calls from you and the congressman about rumors. The last rumor that you got was that I was going to close the yard entirely, for good, and I told you it's not so. What we're talking about is we have to take inventory. While we'll be taking inventory in certain areas of the yard, we cannot have people there. But that will not affect everybody in the shipyard. Now, you know, I'm not interested in the rumors you are hearing."

"I understand, sir."

"I mean everybody . . . gives you people a telephone call. The newspapers—they say everybody is pissing in the submarines now—did you read that?"

"I have not read that, sir."

"Well, I'll send you the newspaper. And now the big rumor here is that everybody's pissing in the submarines because I don't let them go and piss in the pisshole. I mean, what have we got up here?"

"Okay, I just called to ask because . . . in this instance there were government sources who claimed to see the printing of fifteen to eighteen thousand layoff slips and when we get a rumor like that from people who are reliable and it could affect numbers of people in our area—that's why we called you."

"Well, I appreciate that, but whoever gives you that information, it's not correct."

"I understand."

"And tell the congressman I'm still waiting to hear from him about when we are going to go out for dinner. I talked to him last week and he said we'd get together and we haven't and I'm going on sea trials Monday and the next week is Thanksgiving and pretty soon we'll be getting together for Christmas drinks."

No sooner had Veliotis hung up than he received a telephone call from the police commissioner's office.

An aide to the police commissioner asked, "I wonder if we could talk off the record?"

"Yes, of course," Veliotis said.

"We had a call from Washington today. They told us to hitch up our belts, that we were going to get hit with big, big layoffs and problems at the Electric Boat Company this weekend."

"I don't know who called you from Washington."

"Well, I'll be very candid with you. As I said, I'm talking off the record. We had a call from one of the congressmen to try to find out. Now the only thing we're interested in, sir, is [preventing] bloodshed. That's the only thing we're interested in."

"We don't intend to lay off people," Veliotis replied. "But if the congressman knows better than I know . . ."

"I'm sure he doesn't, that's why we're calling you."

"Well, I mean if the congressman wants to run the place, that's entirely different. But I don't have a plan for . . ."

"If we can talk about it," the police commissioner's aide said, "I'll tell you exactly how the conversation went. The conversation went in this respect: that because of the holidays coming up, there was going to be a two-week vacation-type closedown, starting tomorrow."

"Well, again, I'm saying tomorrow morning I'm going to be here working myself and I expect the people to come in and work. If they come in and they don't work, I'm going to kick them out. It's as simple as that."

"Okay."

"And somebody else told me that I printed eighteen thousand layoff slips. You know, they tell me what I do that I don't know."

"Okay, but you have to understand our problem."

"I understand your problem."

"We're interested in mobilization in case there's going to be something happening down there, we can't get caught short. You know, we have an obligation to protect the public."

"Exactly."

"We have to stabilize anything like that if some of those people get radical or something like that, that's the only reason for calling you. It's a police matter which is of no interest to anybody else but you and us. Nobody."

"Okay, for your information, I plan no layoffs whatsoever tomorrow. Not the day after tomorrow, not the day after. I don't plan to shut down the plant for the holidays for two weeks, no. I'm going to be working here tomorrow all day and I hope the people are going to come in and work."

Veliotis confronted the threat of violence. Some said he tempted it by his arrogance, but during the first shift on most of those early days he took his white hardhat and walked purposefully down the hill to the waterfront. He would not wear overalls. He wore his best three-piece suits among the grimy welders and mechanics. It was part of his imperial style. He wanted them to believe that if he got grease on his suit, he would throw it away.

Many of the shipyard workers who had survived the first round of layoffs were in awe of this tall Greek, who projected fearlessness and a sense of absolute control. Some of them vilified him as the uncaring butcher who had thrown their friends out the gate like used machinery. Most of them feared him, and that was all right with Veliotis. People with anxiety worked harder.

Veliotis wanted to be seen in the yard. The local newspaper had said the mood of the workforce was very bad. Said one welder, "There's going to be violence in that place soon. The next time somebody tells me to get a pass before I can go to the toilet, I'm going to punch him in the face."

Veliotis moved slowly through the South Yard, his head up, shoulders square. He casually scanned the buildings, cranes, machinery, and men. He walked across the gangway to the deck of U.S.S *Omaha* and climbed through the hatch and down the ladder. The engineers had told him that morning that one of the bypass valves in the main steam system had been improperly welded. The defective weld had been passed by an inspector and improperly certified. Now the valve had to be cut out and rewelded.

Other defects were popping out by the score. The forward weapons loading hatch on the U.S.S. *New York City* had been misaligned so badly that the navy would not be able to load its Mark 48 torpedo through it. One of the giant engine-room foundations in the U.S.S. *La Jolla* had been built backwards, but was still installed. It would have to be ripped out.

Veliotis walked through the submarine forward and aft, stopping to question welders about their jobs, making small talk with some of the tradesmen. Some were hostile, others welcomed the promise of better management. They told him about the problems getting material and training the green laborers. Some complained about the foul working conditions on the boat. Veliotis told them about the need to perform, to get the yard moving again. He told them that he would make the system work and he told them he would be there for as long as it took and that he knew what he was doing because he had been building ships for as long as many of them had been alive. Veliotis's tour of the shipyard was widely observed and word swiftly reached Rickover's representative on the Hill.

"A friend has told me about your visit, and the important thing from my standpoint is I think you're beginning to see that it isn't the government's entire fault for everything that's wrong at Electric Boat," Rickover called to say.

"I know, I know," Veliotis replied, "that's what I'm telling my people here, but for the last twenty years those people here they have been brainwashed. . . . I went on the ship yesterday, the *694* [*Groton*], and of course I went in from one side and by the time I was at the other end of the ship the noise was so much I couldn't stand it anymore. You know, people start working when they see you."

"Oh, yes. In fact, there's a story about that, it's called the duty riveter. You've heard that story, I'm sure?"

"Of course, sir."

"At lunchtime when people get off and stay off a long time, they assign one guy to make noise. That's a famous story in shipyards."

"Oh yes, oh yes."

"I'm glad you're fighting that because it's so easy to say Rickover's doing this and Rickover's doing that. You notice we shy away from running near you. You notice every evidence we don't want to run the yards. In many cases we have had to. You know what I mean?"

"I appreciate that, too," Veliotis replied.

"Yes, we have had to. Look at the people you've had in there."

"I appreciate that," Veliotis said and changed the subject. "I had an incident yesterday. You know we found one of the main valves on the main steam system for the *692* [*Omaha*] defective."

"I know, the bypass valve," Rickover said.

"I'm horrified, you know, at what happens. Every moment something new happens. I paid good money for an inspector. The inspector was supposed to look at the valve and check [it] with the diagram. The fellow didn't do his job. Well, I don't need people like that around. I called them in yesterday. I said the inspectors sign and say that they did the inspection and it is correct. They use my signature with their name. It is my integrity. The quality and the technical excellence we're going to achieve is my integrity and I'm not going to take it lightly."

"I understand that," said Rickover. "You don't have to tell me. I know what you're trying to do, but you're the first guy they've ever had in that goddamned place that has tried to run the thing as a technical proposition instead of a political proposition."

"It is a technical proposition."

"YOU THINK I HAVEN'T KNOWN THAT?" Rickover roared. "But what the hell can I do about it? I can't tell the company who to put in charge. I can't do that. I suppose everybody says I was responsible for the guys being put in. I was not. When they put Curtis in there, I wasn't asked. . . . But I want you to realize that I am ready to help you anytime you need help, if it's within my power."

"I appreciate that."

"I don't want any attitude of antagonism between the government and the contractor. That's wrong. We also realize that when a contractor makes mistakes, the government ultimately pays."

"Exactly."

"You know that."

"I know that," repeated Veliotis, "I know that too well. I know that too well, but do you know it's a good thing I brought quite a few people with me so we can see that things that we say will happen, will happen."

"Well, you notice we haven't stepped in at all to tell you how to run your place."

"No, sir, you have helped me a lot."

"We will not do that."

"Thank you very much, Admiral."

"Thank you."

The memo was on Veliotis's desk when he returned in late November from the *Omaha* sea trials, where he and Rickover had spent two days together on the 360-foot submarine running the crew ragged as they put the ship through stressful dives and drills in the cold depths of the Atlantic.

It had been an opportunity for the two men to take a measure of each other and Veliotis boasted to his deputies about how he was in the middle of his dinner one night when Rickover sent one of his runners to announce: "The admiral would like to see you forward right away."

Veliotis had looked up from his plate and said, "Is it an emergency?"

"No," the messenger had said.

"Then tell the admiral I will be there when I am finished eating."

It was their own silent war. Rickover never mentioned these little tests of will between them, but he clearly was testing Veliotis.

Altogether, the trials were disappointing. Veliotis had been amazed at the deficiencies that were detected throughout the ship, and he was relieved to get back to his office. That's where he found the memo.

Art Barton probably had saved his job by bringing Veliotis the proof. It had taken weeks to compile, but Barton and his staff had catalogued all of the memos, reports, and meetings in which Barton had presented the man-hour projections to Lewis, beginning with the review in the fall of 1974, the one in which Barton first projected an overrun in the neighborhood of $800 million. That was three years ago. Barton had decided he was not going to lose his job protecting Lewis or MacDonald.

In the month since he had taken over, Veliotis had subjected Barton to the worst kind of treatment. He had threatened over and over to fire him, and he had turned Grimes loose in the comptroller's office, picking through the bones of every file cabinet, treating Barton like he would soon be history.

Barton's memos and cost reports showed the history of the bid for the "flight two" submarines and how almost every quarter after the contracts were awarded Barton had gone to St. Louis with a bleaker projection of the man-hours needed to complete the ships. Veliotis took some notes, but mostly he was just astounded by what he heard. Lewis had known. Lewis had known everything.

Barton showed him the handwritten forecasts he had kept in his drawer during the two years that MacDonald had told him to stay out of cost forecasting. He had some memos from just a few months before Veliotis's arrival. In one note, dated June 21, Barton had urged MacDonald to "Do more thinking" about reporting the enormous cost growth in the first six months of 1977. "No bullshit," Barton had added in the note, "[we] must do something about it." But MacDonald had refused.

With the documents, Barton also presented an updated cost-to-complete estimate for the *688* contracts. It showed that the overrun could go as high as $1.5 billion. Veliotis's heart sank. In little more than three weeks since Barton had bared the truth about the forecasts, the overrun projection had climbed $300 million!

Veliotis realized the record Barton had secretly maintained was devastating for Lewis, for MacDonald, for the corporation. The self-delusion, the deception, whatever it was, appeared to have deceived the outside accountants, the board, the shareholders, and the navy. Barton had covered his own ass very well, Veliotis considered. No wonder Lewis had warned Veliotis not to fire him. But Barton's projections also showed that he was an insightful numbers man who understood the cost, schedule, and manpower dynamics of the shipyard better than anyone.

Veliotis was full of conflicting feelings: fear that what was hidden could easily be discovered by a thorough audit; resolve to save Electric Boat and claim his reward; contempt for MacDonald for having done so little to stop the rampant deterioration that went on for two years; shaken confidence in Lewis, who knew everything and who—unmistakably—had misled Veliotis. In addition, there was the ever-present gnaw from the Frigitemp kickbacks.

Veliotis started thinking about getting legal counsel.

It was crazy, but during the early days of discovery, Veliotis at times felt more kinship with Rickover than he did with corporate headquarters.

What was all new to Veliotis, Rickover had been watching for years, and what Rickover did not know about the cost overruns, he could guess. Rickover appeared to have liked MacDonald, but understood what a poor manager he had been in the shipyard.

"The general impression there about MacDonald," Rickover told Veliotis in one of their daily exchanges, "was that he wasn't running the place at all."

"He was not because he didn't know," Veliotis said.

"Well, he didn't know, but . . ."

". . . he had good intentions," Veliotis finished the sentence, knowing that Rickover found it difficult to be too harsh on MacDonald.

Rickover was full of suggestions in those opening weeks.

"You've got a problem," he warned one morning. "You're going to have to lay off more people. Do you mind my making a suggestion to you?"

"No, sir, go ahead."

"I'd get those [union] guys together pretty damn quick and tell them, 'Look, if you guys don't help and get some employee discipline, you're going to lose a lot of jobs here.' "

"Very good, sir. That's a good idea. We'll do that."

"Look, I think you're beginning to realize, I'm all for you."

"I appreciate that."

"You're the first goddamned guy we've had up there that has made any attempt to run the yard."

"I cannot do it without your help, sir. I passed the four thousand mark already and . . ."

"You're not saying that [publicly], are you?"

"No, I'm not saying anything at all."

"How far are you going?"

"Maybe six thousand."

"Good."

"Maybe sixty-two hundred fifty, that's the number we have."

"When are you going to be finished with your six thousand?"

"February," Veliotis said.

"Well, isn't that going to get known up there?"

"Well, it will be known."

"Well, so what?"

"Well, that's what I'm saying, so what? But this is why I need your help."

"Why do you need any help?"

"Well, they will come to you . . ."

"LET 'EM COME TO ME, GODDAMMIT!" Rickover shouted. "I will say, 'What do you expect?' The state of Connecticut has people on their relief rolls and they say, 'If you don't go and work for Electric Boat, we'll cut off your relief.' Electric Boat took in all the guys who didn't want to work. They had to go up there or they'd get nothing, and then you're starting to get all the absenteeism. They didn't want to work. You see, they only wanted to stay in the yard long enough to get the same amount of money they got on welfare. That's not going to happen. You're in a much stronger position than you believe you are, I'll tell you that."

"Well, let me talk to the union Monday morning."

"I would talk to them and tell them pretty damn plainly what the situation is. They know how many people you've laid off, don't they?"

"No, they don't. Nobody knows."

"But you tell them. If you don't get their help, there's going to be some horrible consequences around there."

"The situation, really, it is bad," said Veliotis. "It is very bad. I mean, you look at the cost to complete the ships. . . ."

"I know, I've got the figures," Rickover said. "All I can tell you is that anything you do to try to get discipline in that goddamned place, I will help you."

Veliotis agreed. He said he had given his waterfront foremen thirty-day work goals; if the goals were not achieved, they had better have a good reason or he would suspend them.

"We cannot afford to have nonperformers here. We just cannot afford it. The loss, Admiral, is so great we cannot afford to waste a penny anymore. How can I explain it to you? My heart bleeds here. When I see what has gone on here, my heart bleeds. . . . I came here last night," said Veliotis, "it was two-fifteen in the morning. I came here because I go to the hotel and I can't sleep there and so I woke up. I came here. . . . I went around and I spoke with the night superintendent, and the guy was amazed, you know: 'You are the boss?'

"I said, 'Yes.' He says, 'What are you doing here?' I said, 'What do you want me to do? If I didn't come here, who the hell is going to come here?' I found a few things that were not right, too many riggers on the night shift. . . . So this morning, I'm suspending the night-shift superintendent. I'm going to suspend him for a week. And I don't like to suspend people. I'm a kind person, Admiral. I don't like to do things like that, but the guy shouldn't have had so many riggers. Why should he have all those riggers if he doesn't need them?"

"What was his answer?"

"Well, his answer was, you know, 'We're waiting for materials.' And I'm a peculiar person. I said, 'Now, tell me exactly what materials. Show me. Get your plan here. Show me the material you are waiting for.' Well, he could not show it to me. I don't say he was lying, but he practically lies and I don't go for that."

Rickover applauded Veliotis's attitude and encouraged him to run more spot inspections in the middle of the night to keep the anxiety level high in the workforce. That was what Rickover did. He had developed the most proficient inspection teams of any organization over the years, he boasted.

"Did you ever hear the story how I told Pierce there was a fire in Electric Boat?"

"No, I didn't."

"I was talking to my guy one day, my representative, and he happened to look out the window, and he said, 'My God, it looks like there's a fire in the yard.' So I hung up and called Pierce and told him there was a fire in Electric Boat. How do you like that? He didn't know it. That's a true story. He got a call from me saying 'There's a fire in your yard.' How do you like that?"

"Pretty good, pretty good."

The news had come over the Dow Jones ticker about noon on Tuesday, November 29, and sent people flying out of their offices at General Dynamics headquarters. Henry Crown was due in the boardroom for the executive committee meeting in a couple of hours, and the last thing Lewis and MacDonald needed was a run on the stock triggered by bad press reports from Washington.

The company was on the brink of disaster; the SEC was asking questions about the $544 million claim and now this: two rear admirals were saying the Trident program was in trouble.

Everyone in the country had known the *688* program was in trouble, but General Dynamics had been booking profits on Trident all along. It was a great contract. You almost couldn't lose. But when the two rear admirals told reporters at a Pentagon briefing that the first Trident was behind schedule and over budget, the telephones in St. Louis lit up. The stock analysts were nervous. They wanted to know what the hell was going on—was there another big overrun brewing?

Trading in the stock increased immediately after the press conference and there were more sellers than buyers.

At 2:00 p.m., MacDonald telephoned Veliotis to ask if he'd heard about the release.

"What release?" asked Veliotis.

"It says, 'Delivery of the navy's first Trident strategic missile submarine will be delayed about a year . . . because of productivity problems at General Dynamics' Electric Boat division. Rear Admiral Donald Hall, the Trident project engineer, explained that the General Dynamics unit has found it more difficult than anticipated to construct the submarine, the largest ever built by the navy. As a result, the cost of the initial submarine has risen to $1.193 billion, about $400 million more than the initial estimate when the program began. However, Admiral Hall said the General Dynamics unit could still make a profit on the first submarine if the price does not rise further.' "

"Who put that out?"

"The navy," said MacDonald. "I just wanted to know if you were aware of it."

"No, this is the first time I've heard about it."

"This apparently hit right at noon, just an hour ago."

"That's the first time I've heard about it. We have no report on the Trident ourselves . . . until I conclude my studies. So I don't think it came out of here. 1981, they say now?"

"It says 1981, right."

"I don't know, Gorden."

"Okay, well, I can just tell the board that it came out of the navy."

"A lot has come out of the navy. . . . I think we should be calling Admiral Hall and giving him shit."

"Yeah, I'd like to, I just don't want to interfere," MacDonald said.

"No, you're not interfering at all."

"Okay, I'll do it then."

"Get to Admiral Hall and tell him to fuck himself."

"Right."

"It's not our date."

"Okay," said MacDonald.

"Don't give him any dates, though."

"No, I won't. Real good, Taki."

"Okay, bye-bye."

Thirty minutes later, MacDonald called back. He had not reached the Trident project manager, but he had talked to the chief of navy shipbuilding, who said the reporters might have confused the date the navy expected the Trident to be delivered to the navy—April 1980—with the date the ship actually joined the fleet—sometime in 1981.

MacDonald was relieved. He could tell the board that the press screwed up and thereby discredit all the negative reports coming from Washington.

But Veliotis didn't really care about the press reports. He was more concerned that, if anything, the admirals had understated the problems of the Trident program. With the tape recorder running, Veliotis listened as MacDonald explained the disaster of the Trident schedule.

"December 1978 was the 'best efforts' schedule that the company agreed to when they signed the [Trident] contract," MacDonald said.

"Yeah," Veliotis replied sarcastically, "the navy knows and we know that it won't be before the end of 1980."

MacDonald ignored the remark and continued. "I told them, I guess it was in July, that it was not going to be December 1978, it was going to be October 1979."

"Well, you told them about a year and two months too early." MacDonald ignored this remark also.

"And, ah, they said, 'You're too optimistic,' and I said, 'That's probably true, but that's all we're willing to go to now.' "

Veliotis's tone turned angry. "Why is that all we were willing to go to? Why not tell the truth from the beginning, when everybody here knew that it cannot be done before the end of 1980?"

There was a pause on the telephone line. MacDonald had to consider that Veliotis might be taping the call and he would not want to expose himself in any way to Veliotis. He had been telling people in the corporate office that Veliotis had a "hard-on" for him.

"Everybody up there says that?" MacDonald asked.

"Everybody. There is a letter they have sent to you. They say they told you it won't be before the end of 1980."

"Foley never agreed to that," MacDonald said, invoking the name of the operations director Veliotis had fired on the first day.

"I beg your pardon?"

MacDonald decided not to rest his case on Foley and quickly substituted another authority.

"Ed Lindahl never agreed to that." Ed Lindahl was the Trident program manager at Electric Boat and had reported to Foley.

"Ed Lindahl is an asshole, if I may tell you, sir, an optimistic asshole," Veliotis said, louder, angrier. "He spoke with me, Gorden. He doesn't know what it's all about. He doesn't talk to you, he talks to me now. He was going to man the ship with 2,750 people. He must be an idiot and I told him so. And now he realizes he cannot do that."

"Uh huh."

"So the ship is not forty percent complete, the ship is only thirty-five percent complete."

"Uh huh."

"And the man-hours are not going to be twelve million hours, they're going to be about fifteen million hours."

"Uh huh."

"And Lindahl is the optimist. He will do it with blood and sweat. How many times did he make good on his promises to you? Never!"

"You're right," said MacDonald.

The flare in Veliotis's temper passed after a moment.

MacDonald welcomed the reprieve. "No, that isn't the point," he said. "The point was that since that announcement hit the wire, we've already lost another one and a half points on the stock."

There was MacDonald's real concern, Veliotis thought. MacDonald wanted Veliotis to help cover up the bad news about the Trident schedule so the stock would not go down.

Veliotis thought the crisis had passed until two-thirty the next afternoon, when the corporate public relations man from St. Louis, Frank Johnson, telephoned to read him the press release Lewis and MacDonald had drafted: "General Dynamics does not agree with the magnitude of the overrun estimated by the navy" and "General Dynamics believes that the first Trident and all of the Tridents currently under contract will be completed on a profitable basis. . . ."

It was the last section of the press release that Veliotis reacted to.

"With regard to schedule, General Dynamics has advised the navy that it expects the first ship to be delivered in October 1979, approximately six months after contract delivery date. The navy believes that an April 1980 delivery date is more likely."

That was it. The company was sticking with MacDonald's delivery date, which was wrong.

"That's our statement," Johnson said.

"Well, I don't know who gave you those deliveries, but they're not mine."

"That was [from] a statement that was issued back in August," Johnson replied. "We haven't given the navy any later dates, have we?"

"No, I haven't given the navy any later dates and I told them I won't be able to before the end of January, beginning of February. But I know they are going to be later than what you are saying."

"Oh, I see. Okay. Ah, is it going to be later than what the navy is saying?"

"Yes, it will."

"Okay."

"So, you know, I don't know what 'Okay' means," Veliotis said a little indignantly, "but the way we are putting it out, it gives the impression that we are going to meet an April 1980 delivery."

"That's right."

"Well, that is not what I know yet. I don't know, but I don't think we can meet that. See what I'm saying?"

"I will tell that to Dave."

"You tell that to Dave. And [tell him] I don't think MacDonald knows what it's all about."

"Okay, okay, I will tell him that, Taki."

Johnson said the company was working with Hidalgo to get the navy to put out a similar press release to clarify the cost figures on the Trident. "And it will all be out on the street by three o'clock."

Veliotis looked at his watch. It was just a few minutes before three. He wondered if Johnson was wasting his time.

"If it's going out by three o'clock, you have already sent out that message about the deliveries. You cannot change anything now."

"Well, we haven't sent ours out."

"Then you tell Dave what I said."

"Yeah, we'll do that."

An hour later, MacDonald telephoned back and announced to Veliotis that "We made a release about an hour ago."

"Yeah, your fellow Frank read me the release."

"Oh, good."

"Yeah. Did he come back and tell you that those dates that you give there, they're not real?"

"Yes."

"He told you that?"

"Yes."

"But you still wanted to go ahead?"

"Yes, Dave wanted to go ahead anyway."

But Veliotis protested that the shipyard could not deliver the ship by April 1980: "There is no chance of doing that." He paused, adding for emphasis, "No way. *It's not real.*"

"And we understand that, too," MacDonald replied. "And Dave understands that. But he wanted to go ahead only to stop our stock from sliding."

"At some time we have to tell people the truth, you know."

"I know it."

"At some time, we have to come out and say what the delivery is. And I don't know what the stock will do at that time, but we have to do it."

But MacDonald filibustered. Better to wait until after the first of the year, he said, when Veliotis would complete the ninety-day review he and Lewis had agreed upon.

Veliotis was angry. It looked like he was adopting MacDonald's schedule, which he was sure was wrong and he didn't want to be associated with it. But the damage was done. He wondered whether the SEC—if it knew what was going on—would consider him part of the cover-up.

In early December, Veliotis sought legal advice. Could he be held personally liable by shareholders for not disclosing to the SEC what he had discovered about the schedule manipulation at the shipyard, he asked the shipyard's attorneys in Boston.

The lawyers wanted to know the extent of what he had learned.

Veliotis told them that, based on what he had discovered, it appeared that General Dynamics' claim might be based on a serious misrepresentation of the ship-delivery schedules. He wanted to know whether his legal duty as a corporate officer required him to disclose what he had discovered.

The lawyers supplied him with a legal memorandum. It concluded that a fuller investigation was warranted because there were "several areas in which further investigation may turn up real problems for Electric Boat division. . . ."

The lawyers' memo said,

Most of the possible problems raised . . . involve possible misrepresentation of facts concerning Electric Boat Division's work progress, intentions, or costs. If there have been any misrepresentations (and we should be careful to keep in mind that the documents we have do not amount to firm evidence that there have been any), they might result in Electric Boat Division's being liable to the navy, or in a reduction or even rejection of Electric Boat Division's contract claims; or (if the possible misrepresentations relate to matters which are material to General Dynamics Corporation's financial condition or its published statements of income) they might result in liability to General Dynamics Corporation for having published misleading financial statements.

Veliotis threw the lawyers' analysis on his desk. Their final conclusion was that Veliotis had a duty to disclose what he had discovered to his superiors. But they already knew!

"Fast Eddie"—that's what they called Assistant Secretary Hidalgo in the navy shipbuilding command—struck on Thursday, December 1, by issuing a one-sentence order to the chief of naval material: Seize the files and documents of the Navy Claims Settlement Board.

The settlement board had a suite in one of the Crystal City office towers and the chief of naval material sent in uniformed navy clerks who boxed everything up and took it to the Pentagon. Frank Manganaro, the admiral in charge of the settlement board, was furious, but there was nothing he could do. Hidalgo was his civilian boss.

The day Hidalgo struck, the board was about two weeks away from completing its evaluation of General Dynamics' $544 million claim. Confiscating the board's files was a heavy-handed power play, but Hidalgo had no choice. If he did not fulfill his private commitment to General Dynamics' board of directors, the company would shut down Electric Boat, and that would set off the political dynamite of congressional outrage, lost jobs, massive litigation, and paralysis in the navy shipbuilding program. The other shipyards might follow suit and it would be a first-class disaster for the Carter administration.

So Hidalgo seized physical control of the settlement board, and in so doing the navy secretariat kept its bargain with David Lewis and General Dynamics. The company would be spared the devastating "finding" that the $544 million claim was worth very little, and Lewis could avoid posting a massive loss in 1977.

Rickover immediately raised a cry against Hidalgo's unexpected act: "I was not informed of any plans to terminate the . . . [board's] efforts on the Electric Boat claims," he complained in a letter to Hidalgo, adding, "The Navy Claims Settlement Board should be permitted to complete its analysis."

Hidalgo tried to keep a low profile. A few more weeks and the pressure would be off; General Dynamics spared from the ruinous disclosure. He did not think Rickover could get him reversed before the deadline passed. He replied to Rickover curtly:

Driven by circumstances of the highest importance which have been carefully analyzed and seriously affect both the shipbuilders and the navy, and therefore the national interest, the decision has been made to undertake separate discussions with . . . Electric Boat aimed toward possible resolution of complex, longstanding problems. It was the consensus of those directly interested in the foregoing decision, that sound organizational reasons dictated that the Electric Boat claims should be withdrawn from the NCSB [Navy Claims Settlement Board] during the pendency of such discussions and awaiting their eventual outcome.

"Gobbledegook! He's a feather merchant!" Rickover raged, then he dropped his own bombshell. He was preparing a report for the navy inspector general documenting examples of "apparent fraud" in the Electric Boat claim. Rickover's letter to Hidalgo was leaked to the press within days of its writing. Senator William Proxmire of Wisconsin announced that he would hold investigative hearings on Hidalgo's decision to remove the claim from the settlement board.

Rickover's twelve-page report on fraud in the claim was the first specific indictment against the claim's integrity and added to the panic in St. Louis that the claim would come unraveled before the books were closed for the year. But the report stayed bottled up in the confidential channels of the navy inspector general's office. In it, Rickover documented more than a dozen examples of the alleged fraud. In most of these cases, Electric Boat claimed it had not been prepared for the complex construction requirements on specific parts of the 688s. But in each instance, Rickover showed that the shipyard had received the plans and detailed design data on each part of the submarine cited six months to a year before the company had submitted its bid to the navy.

Fraud, Rickover noted to the inspector general, was defined by the shipbuilding command procurement manual as "any willful means of taking or attempting to take unfair advantage of the government, including but not limited to deceit, either by suppression of the truth or misrepresentation of material fact."

Before the month was out, Hidalgo was called to account by Senator Proxmire. In the congressional hearing, Hidalgo denied "absolutely" that he had been motivated by any knowledge that the settlement board was going to deflate the value of the claim when he seized the files. When he was questioned about his intention to settle the claims, Hidalgo was evasive:

Q: Mr. Secretary, is it your present intention to propose to Congress a bail out of one or more shipbuilders?

A: I am going to have to give you a hypothetical answer, Mr. Chairman, to the best of my ability. If the discussions with Electric Boat and Litton . . . lead to a consensus as to how not only we can resolve all the pending claims but also the underlying problems, that is, there is continuous cash shortfall, a negative cash flow that these shipbuilders have in the construction of vital navy ships . . . if the only way we can resolve the underlying problems is through some modification of the existing contracts, then I say to you that extraordinary relief under Public Law 85-804 may be invoked at that time.

By the time Hidalgo made that statement in Congress, he had twice met with senior General Dynamics officials seeking their assistance to write a tale of financial woe that would persuade the Congress to bail out the company.

"Gentlemen," he had said to MacDonald and to Max Golden, General Dynamics' vice president for contracts, as they were seated in his office on December 8, "I would like to have your thoughts about how we go forward from here and I hope this meeting can be treated as an off-the-record discussion." He said he needed a "rationale" to go to Congress with, something along the lines of: if General Dynamics does not get relief, it will face a financial disaster leading to bank-ruptcy.

Wait a minute, MacDonald said. The General Dynamics board would probably not go along with that. Whatever happened, he asked, to the rationale that the troubles in the 688 program stemmed from inequitable contracts, navy design changes, and delays at Newport News?

That approach was unacceptable, said Hidalgo. "We'll get opposition from you know who"—Rickover. It was best to plead in Congress that General Dynamics was a failing business, in the same way Grumman and Lockheed had argued earlier in the decade when they were going under due to massive overruns on defense contracts. Hidalgo even had pulled from the files the "rationales" those companies had included in their bailout requests. Failing business, Hidalgo emphasized, was the rationale he intended to use—for General Dynamics and for Litton—and, he added, he couldn't go to Congress with different rationales for each company. He wanted one neat package: the bailout petitions of all the shipyards in one big ball of wax. His tone lectured them, reminding them that he had taken a serious step in removing the claims from the settlement board. It was time to go down the road together.

MacDonald and Golden said they would have to consult with Lewis.

By the way, Hidalgo said before they left, he'd heard the overrun at Electric Boat might be as high as $800 million. Was that so?

Yes, it was, MacDonald replied. It could be even higher—maybe $1 billion.

Hidalgo was shocked at the size of the company's problem. It would make his task all the more difficult when it came time to force the company to declare a loss as part of the bailout.

But he was no more shocked than Golden, who reeled at the disclosure MacDonald had made so casually to someone outside the company. After all, General Dynamics had not told its stockholders the overrun was that high. Golden telephoned Veliotis later that day and the two men commiserated about the appearance of a cover-up and MacDonald's attempt to protect the stock: "We don't want the SEC to get [the figures] before we actually go public on this," Golden said, "and, in effect, he's telling them that our information may be contrary to what the hell we have published. . . ."

Veliotis said he had to agree.

"Yeah," Golden continued, "if while you're discussing this [with Hidalgo], you say for example that your overrun or your loss is $800 million or $1 billion, Jesus Christ, if you spent six months discussing it with the navy, or three months, well, what about shareholders who buy and sell stock?"

Veliotis then recounted what one shipyard manager had told him about MacDonald's manipulation of the delivery schedules and his stated purpose to protect the stock.

"How can he say a thing like that?" Veliotis asked.

"I don't understand it," Golden replied.

When Lewis heard the course Hidalgo was trying to chart for the bailout, he was incredulous: "How could we let this happen?" he asked Golden and MacDonald. General Dynamics was not a Lockheed or a Grumman, he said. Hidalgo had to get off that track. After all, the company had been telling Wall Street for how many straight quarters about record earnings, record backlogs of funded orders for new weapons, and the financial strength that was evolving from the F-16 program, the Trident program, and the new Tomahawk cruise missile program. How could the company argue out of the other side of its mouth that it was on the brink of bankruptcy?

On the Wednesday before Christmas Lewis flew to Washington to confront Hidalgo.

It was just not in the cards for General Dynamics to base its petition for relief on financial disaster, he said. Hidalgo would have to come up with a better rationale, like the one used in 1976: inequitable contracts, et cetera.

"Listen," Hidalgo stopped him. It was time for Lewis to "get down to the real world." Hidalgo had taken "a serious step" in removing the Electric Boat claim from the Navy Claims Settlement Board and he was taking a lot of heat for doing so. "Rough seas are ahead," Hidalgo said. "We're in the floodlights." He said that all of them would get into "serious trouble" if they tried to plead the merits of the claim—inequitable contracts and poor administration by the navy. Hidalgo's way was the only way to go; otherwise, Hidalgo said, the settlement would be "blown off [Capitol] Hill."

That just wasn't acceptable, Lewis said. The company was considering filing new claims because the design changes and drawing revisions were still driving up the costs at Electric Boat.

Hidalgo was a little perturbed that Lewis was trying to push him around. After all, he had developed a plan that would help the company and the navy, but Lewis wanted it both ways. He wanted to be bailed out and he wanted the navy to say General Dynamics was a financial Gibraltar. But Hidalgo feared someone would ask: If that is the case, why should the navy bail! Lewis out?

Go ahead, file new claims, Hidalgo told Lewis, and Hidalgo would immediately refer them to the Navy Claims Settlement Board, where they would sit for at least a year getting the most careful analysis Admiral Manganaro could give them. Hidalgo's sarcasm conveyed his threat. If Lewis was not going to cooperate, Hidalgo could also become uncooperative. And so Lewis abandoned this ploy.

Lewis then asked if there was any possibility that the $544 million claim would be returned to Admiral Manganaro. The company was still a few weeks away from closing its books for the year. Lewis could imagine getting clobbered by disclosure at the last minute. Could it be that the nightmare could still occur?

"Not as long as I am in this job," Hidalgo reassured him, but added that he was fending off pressure from a number of congressmen who had counseled him in the strongest terms to return the claims to the settlement board.

Hidalgo believed Lewis was now ready to listen to some sense. He said his assistant, who was sitting in on the meeting, just happened to have copies of the old Lockheed and Grumman petitions for financial relief. He gave them to Lewis as a guide for drafting General Dynamics' petition. "[We] need a story on financial impairment," Hidalgo's assistant emphasized, and in effect, he was asking General Dynamics to help write a script that would scare Congress. Hidalgo suggested they emphasize the drastic nature of their cash flow drain and how it would affect the company's ability to continue building naval warships in the future and also the cross-over impact on the company's other major weapons programs.

But Lewis was not going to cave in. Such a strategy "could destroy our stockholders," he protested.

Hidalgo would not budge either. He had three "boxes" to fill on his strategy sheet, he said. First, the settlement board would fix the amount of actual "entitlement" from its analysis of the claim. They all knew that would not be much. The second "box" was a precise determination of the loss the company was facing at Electric Boat. Veliotis would have to provide that number after his ninety-day review. Hidalgo insisted that the company get financially "naked" so he could assure the Congress that the government was not getting snookered. Finally, the third "box" would be how much of a fixed loss the company would take as part of the settlement. That figure, Hidalgo said with a smile, would likely be the subject of a good deal of negotiation.

It was an astounding scene, the spectacle of an Assistant Secretary of the Navy trying to convince the chairman of his largest defense contractor to contrive a story of financial disaster against his will. But worse, Hidalgo's settlement strategy had suddenly crossed another line of demarcation that affected government policy in a fundamental way: it seemed that he no longer cared how much Electric Boat was entitled to as a matter of law and contract. He had decided that the only way to get a settlement was to determine the size of the total overrun at Electric Boat and then negotiate how much the government could cover. The rest General Dynamics would have to absorb as a loss.

As a negotiating strategy, it was simple and practical. As a matter of public policy, it was indefensible. With little or no analysis of the history of poor management at Electric Boat and with no congressional review, Hidalgo had acted out the scenario that Rickover had most feared. He had abandoned the contracts the navy signed with the shipbuilders in 1971 and 1973 as if they were meaningless documents, ill-conceived in prior administrations, and for which he bore no responsibility.

David Lewis marked off the final days of the calendar year in quiet desperation over whether Hidalgo's raid on the settlement board would hold. The company's financial condition was so fragile—as the Trident press release crisis had shown—that any additional bad news could have triggered a cataclysmic reaction on Wall Street, where the stock had lost five more points since October and was teetering at $45 a share. The onset of the Christmas holidays improved the odds that the year would close with no new surprises. But Lewis could not rest because the corporation's books would not be closed for at least another month. After New Year's, he flew immediately to Washington to appeal Hidalgo's strategy to the Deputy Secretary of Defense, Charles Duncan.

Lewis dreaded a Pyrrhic victory in which General Dynamics finally recovered a big cash settlement but also was saddled with a verdict of management failure. He was not going to accept such a judgment. Lewis showed Duncan an overrun estimate of $800 million, and explained that General Dynamics would only have to extend its credit lines by $200 million to cover it; therefore, the company would be "out of the banks" by 1981, based on increased revenues coming from the F-16 program and from Trident.

The overrun, however, was much higher—and Lewis knew it. Without a government bailout, it would take at least $400 million in additional credit to save the company, and that was more credit than the banks had ever extended to General Dynamics.

Duncan had no way of knowing the true cost projections buried in General Dynamics. He was persuaded by the figures Lewis showed him. The failing business rationale would have to go, he said, and Hidalgo would have to come up with something different.

On January 3, 1978, Lewis rushed back to St. Louis in time to announce the good news to the executive committee.

For months, Rickover had suffered the small indignities of Takis Veliotis. No daily phone call. No weekly letter of self-criticism.

But when one sentence in a Veliotis press release echoed the hated allegation that the navy and its thousands of change orders and drawing revisions were the root of all evil, Rickover pounced so fast and so hard that it startled Veliotis. The release blamed the yard's inventory-control problems on "the difficulties and burdens imposed on us by the thousands of changes in designs and specifications ordered by the navy." That charge had been picked up by the local newspapers and reached Rickover's desk in Washington on January 4, 1978, by the time Veliotis got to his office at the shipyard.

Rickover's voice was low and calm, the tone that worried Rickover's staff.

"I thought you had told me you were laying off this claims business and you were just confining yourself to your work. Now you're getting involved. Now you're becoming a protagonist blaming the navy. Fine. So we're going to take that issue on. . . . A lot of the changes in the drawings are nits. You don't have many changes. And, we have to have some changes. Some of them are caused by what you guys do."

"I appreciate that."

"A lot of poor workmanship."

"I appreciate that, Admiral."

"I'm not aware that there are any excess changes coming."

"I have been advised here there are thirty-two thousand revisions."

Rickover screamed at the top of his lungs: "ALL RIGHT, MR. VELIOTIS! YOU BETTER BY A GODDAMNED SIGHT FIND OUT WHAT THE HELL YOU'RE TALKING ABOUT!

"FIND OUT WHAT THOSE THIRTY-TWO THOUSAND CHANGES CONSIST OF!

"GO AHEAD!"

The admiral paused for a moment, then calmed down.

"You're falling into the same trap. You find out! You started out right, but people complained that [Rickover] was telling you what to do. You called them on it. I hate to see you get started on that circuit."

"Admiral, I'm . . ."

"I wish you would not interfere with this. Now you're going ahead."

"I haven't said you're interfering with me at all."

"Of course we're interfering. We've tried to help you."

"Yes, fine."

"We will continue to do that unless you keep on with this god-damned attitude like your predecessors that it's all the navy's fault. That's a lot of nonsense." Rickover's voice roared again. "I'M GOING TO TAKE YOU ON ON THIS ISSUE. I DON'T WANT TO."

Veliotis was getting a little angry. He had let Rickover make his point. "Well, all right, if you want to take me on . . ."

"I will. If you keep on blaming the navy for everything that's happening in that goddamned yard, we'll take you on! Now you can make up your mind how you want to operate. You want to get help from us, or do you want to operate to keep blaming the customer for every goddamned thing that's wrong up there?"

"Let's put it in the right perspective," Veliotis said, looking for a way out of the confrontation. He felt the vise he would always feel as long as there was a claim and as long as there was a dispute over who should pay. And in this dispute, he could see his future with Rickover: he would always be the ally in the search for technical excellence in submarine construction, but the moment Veliotis got over his head on the cost side, Rickover would transform into the formidable, scream-ing adversary now on the telephone. Though he once had said it him-self, Rickover could never accept the notion that the customer always pays.

"Well, you go ahead and try to put it in the right perspective," Rickover was saying in his most menacing tone.

"Thank you," Veliotis said. "I haven't blamed the customer for everything."

"The hell you haven't. You're talking about the thirty-two thou-sand changes. Go ahead and look into that. Find out what they are, really."

"Very good."

"All right. I'll give you some advice from my standpoint. We want to help, but if you keep on this way, you're antagonizing the customer. Now you have read in the newspaper that I reported [in the Proxmire hearing] there are potentially or possibly fraudulent claims. You know that, don't you?"

"I read that."

"Don't think I would put just a bunch of goddamned gossip in there."

"I read the transcript. They sent me the transcript."

"Do you think I would write a letter like that to my superiors without knowing what I was doing? And you should use the same care in starting talking about thirty thousand changes and fifty thousand pages. You ought to know what the hell you are talking about."

"Well, are you telling me that there is fraud?" Veliotis asked.

"I didn't say there was. I said I testified there is possible fraud. That's all I said."

"Admiral, if there is fraud, I don't want to be associated with it."

"I can't help it, but don't kid yourself . . . , I'm giving you good advice. Be goddamned sure you know what you're talking about."

"Well, I will know what I'm talking about. But you tell them that you know what you're talking about; therefore, there must be fraud."

Rickover erupted again: "LOOK! I AM PUTTING MY NAME AND CAREER ON THE LINE WHEN I SAY THERE IS POSSIBLE FRAUD ON A CONTRACTOR. IT'S OFFICIAL BUSINESS. DON'T YOU UNDERSTAND THAT GODDAMNED THING?"

"No, I don't."

"I'm putting my career on the line when I do that. And you ought to feel the same way when you make these statements without knowing the facts. That's what I'm talking about. You get the point? I hope you're keeping a goddamned record of this conversation so you can tell it to your goddamned board. YOU UNDERSTAND?"

Rickover slammed the phone down hard. Veliotis reached over and turned off the tape recorder.

If Rickover wanted to take him on, fine. Veliotis believed he had evidence that could send Rickover to jail. During January 1978, Veliotis set out to document carefully the illegal gifts of jewelry Rickover had received the previous summer from MacDonald.

William Pedace, the special projects director at the shipyard, confessed to Veliotis's team that he had hand-delivered the jewelry to Rickover and then covered up its purchase with phoney invoices. Pedace also had recounted the historical care and feeding of Rickover. Veliotis was not impressed with most of the perks the shipyard had arranged for the admiral. He thought most of them fitting for an officer of Rickover's stature, and they were not unlike the perks the navy lavished on its officer corps at naval installations. He found some of the special favors bizarre, the laminated $50 bills for a party for Mrs. Rickover, the shower curtains Rickover had fancied at a New Jersey hotel, the gold-plated fruit knives with water buffalo handles.

But Veliotis had come from the commercial shipbuilding world where ship sponsors routinely were given expensive gifts at ship launchings. A $5,000 gift was not unusual in that setting. However, the two pieces of jewelry MacDonald had sent Rickover the previous summer were in a special category. They were privately delivered to Rickover's office and had nothing to do with a ship launching. Rickover was the military officer supervising contracts at Electric Boat. Both Rickover and MacDonald were vulnerable to a charge of bribery, Veliotis felt.

Pedace had blurted out the whole story to Veliotis. At the end of his confession, he said that he would not commit perjury about his role in the jewelry affair.

"I have no interest in you committing perjury," Veliotis had replied in surprise. "Why would you make such a statement?"

MacDonald, Pedace said, had told him he might be expected to lie about the gifts if they were ever discovered.

Veliotis dismissed the nervous special projects officer. Then he ordered one of the Quincy Eight to quietly conduct an investigation of the Rickover gifts and anything else that occurred during MacDonald's tenure that looked suspicious.

All during the ride from the Pentagon to the White House, Hidalgo fidgeted in the back seat of the government sedan.

He had no way of knowing whether the President of the United States was going to praise him or take his head off for how he was handling the shipbuilding claims. This, after all, was the President who had worked for the father of the nuclear navy, who had dined privately with him, and who had spent a day with him aboard U.S.S. *Los Angeles.*

Hidalgo knew the White House had gotten involved in the political backlash that followed his raid on the Navy Claims Settlement Board. In January, Defense Secretary Harold Brown and Duncan had told Hidalgo to send the claim back to the board because there was no use taking so much heat over it. By then it didn't matter. Hidalgo had insured that there would be no public disclosure of the board's finding. General Dynamics would be able to close its books for the year without declaring a loss. And so, Hidalgo had quickly complied with the order.

Hidalgo's big concern was still all of the trade-offs and concessions he was having to make. He had lost the battle to force General Dynamics to plead financial disaster in its petition for a bailout. That left him with little to argue beyond the obvious: General Dynamics was an important defense contractor and the shutdown of its shipyard at Groton would deny the navy its 688-class submarines.

On that basis, just about any defense contractor could walk in and demand that the government pick up its overruns or it would shut down.

It was getting to the point where someone in Congress was going to ask the cosmic question: If General Dynamics was not failing, if the company could absorb virtually all of the overrun, and if the Navy Claims Settlement Board said there was very little merit to the claim—and if Rickover said there was fraud in the claim—then why on earth was the government working overtime to bail out General Dynamics?

The briefing team consisted of Duncan, Claytor, Hidalgo, and Vice Admiral Russell Bryan, the chief of navy shipbuilding. The one-hour session with the President was remarkable because the leadership of the Pentagon straightforwardly told Carter how little merit there was to the shipbuilding claims, but how politically expedient it was to settle them.

The companies were not on the verge of failure, Duncan said, as was the case with Lockheed and Grumman during the Nixon administration. It looked like the shipyards had been "hungry" for business when they took on large orders for ships, then failed to achieve their management goals of finding tens of thousands skilled tradesmen to meet the construction schedules in the contracts.

But a settlement was desirable, Duncan said, because there were "negative perceptions" in the defense industry about the navy's shipbuilding management capability; and it was the sense of key congressional leaders—Senator Stennis in particular—that an adversary relationship between the navy and the shipbuilders was not productive. He told the President that David Lewis had predicted a negative cash flow of $500 million by the end of 1978 if there was no settlement.

"Negative perceptions," "cash flow." Never had a Pentagon official proposed to give away so much of the U.S. Treasury based on so little evidence of government liability.

Hidalgo gave a detailed rundown of each shipyard. When he

got to Electric Boat, he told the President more than any General Dynamics' stockholder knew at that time: the overrun at Electric Boat was $900 million to $1 billion, a loss of $55 million per ship.

Hidalgo listed the alternatives for Carter.

The first was litigation. Since 1975, he said, the navy had spent $50 million in prime human resources evaluating and contesting the claims. The shipyards, he estimated, had spent even more. But the human and financial resources were only part of the chaos. How were the navy and the shipbuilders to continue constructing ships while fighting each other in court for five to ten years? Litigation was a certainty unless a settlement was achieved, he concluded.

The second option was to take over the shipyards as part of a settlement and operate them as government facilities under contract to one of the shipbuilding companies. Hidalgo knew that this was the alternative most favored by Rickover, and so he spent a greater amount of time shooting it down. Hidalgo said he had serious questions about proceeding this way. If the government took over Electric Boat, for instance, where General Dynamics had invested $150 million of its own money at the navy's behest, was that fair? The navy already had eight shipyards and was spending $1 billion to modernize them. Who was the navy going to find to run Electric Boat? If the navy declared the yards in default under the contracts, it was facing the same problem. Litigation and possibly a required takeover by the government.

The last alternative, Hidalgo said, was the one he had recommended to Claytor, Duncan, and Brown, and which had their concurrence: a settlement under Public Law 85–804, the Bail Out Act, which would be coupled with a requirement for each of the shipbuilders to take a substantial fixed loss to acknowledge their own deficiencies in performance under the contracts.

The President was smiling at Hidalgo when he completed his script. He asked several questions about the ships under construction, then turned back to Hidalgo and said, "Eddie, when are you going to know one way or the other when you're going to settle the claims?"

"How does June 30 sound to you, Mr. President?"

"Fine. Why don't you just keep going and do the best you can."

Hidalgo was lightheaded with relief.

The President stood up, signaling the end of the meeting, but before he turned to leave the room, he gave Hidalgo another of his Georgia smiles and said, "And by the way, if you could come up with a settlement that would be acceptable to Admiral Rickover, that would be all right, too." Then Carter disappeared through the side door that led back to the Oval Office.

Everyone laughed nervously. The comment appeared to have been intended in jest, but the conventional wisdom in dealing with presidents is that when the chief executive says something, even in jest, he is *saying* something. Whatever it was, it ruined the afterglow of the briefing.

Veliotis could no longer sleep through the night.

If he was not stalking his hotel room at Norwich, he drove to the shipyard and paced his office or roamed the waterfront, where the floodlights turned the submarine hulls into gargantuan creatures, at once ominous and serene as the Lilliputian work crews swarmed over them. Some nights he told his driver to take him back to his large Tudor-style home at Milton, Massachusetts, where he sank into a black-leather recliner in the den and closed his eyes—never sleeping—trying to work through the long chain of threats and strategies ahead.

Takis Veliotis was living in a perilous state, filled with uncertainty over whether the shipyard could survive the onslaught of the fraud investigation unleashed by Rickover and at the same time perform the Herculean task of getting the remaining ships to sea in record time. He was haunted by the prospect of collapse and calamity.

Above all was the threat that the still-buried secrets of Frigitemp might be exposed. He had the most to lose in the Frigitemp kickback scheme, whose science had seemed secure, but whose random upheavals were conspiring against him.

By early 1978, a Frigitemp vice president had paid more than $1 million into Veliotis's bank account in Lausanne, Switzerland. But Frigitemp Corporation itself was skidding toward bankruptcy, with $20 million in outstanding claims against shipyards that had stopped payment due to their own overruns. Several Frigitemp officers had been looting the company through kickback schemes, siphoning off millions of dollars into their own foreign bank accounts and into the accounts of key executives in the shipyards they serviced. A bankruptcy would only bring in the creditors and their bloodhound lawyers, who would start following the trails of any suspicious cash transfers. Then it would just be a matter of time.

At the same time, Rickover's allegations of fraud in Electric Boat's claim were attracting the attention of Congress. Senator Proxmire was preparing for investigative hearings. The Securities and Exchange Commission and the Justice Department were being queried daily by newspaper reporters seeking to know the government's response to the fraud allegations. Investigations by both agencies seemed imminent.

Veliotis felt trapped by Rickover's assault on the claim. Though it had been prepared under MacDonald's direction and signed by MacDonald, Veliotis had inherited the legacy of the claim and was forced to defend its integrity by the very fact that he was general manager. When fraud allegations were reported in the newspapers, Veliotis's name appeared, not MacDonald's, as the guardian of the claim. Each allegation deepened Veliotis's contempt for MacDonald. It was a poisonous circumstance because Veliotis understood the claim's critical weakness, and being saddled with it fed his suspicion that the corporate office might be setting him up.

These were Veliotis's ghosts. They walked with him every evening and spoke to him each time he thought his mind could rest, each time the cacophony of the yard was stilled by his fatigue, each time the wail of Rickover's siren faded in his ear, and each time the melodious drawl of David Lewis dissolved into the sounds of the night.

David Lewis had aged and there were deep circles under his eyes when he arrived with Max Golden at Electric Boat on February 9, 1978. He had come to receive the long-awaited Veliotis cost estimates for completing the 688s and the first Trident. These were the ninety-day numbers, the numbers Veliotis had known from the second day he had taken over the yard.

Lewis now needed to soften the blow of Veliotis's estimate because it was going to become a key factor in the negotiations with the navy. The larger the overrun projection, the greater the loss General Dynamics would have to accept as part of the settlement with Hidalgo and the greater the damage to Lewis's reputation on Wall Street. So Lewis had sent messengers to Veliotis to let him know that he expected the shipyard's most optimistic number, a number that reflected a commitment to do better, to perform the miracle the Lewis was counting on.

It had all of the echoes of the past, but Veliotis could not turn Lewis down and maintain the compact between them, the compact of general and field commander. And in cutting the estimate, Veliotis had confronted those horrible realities: to cut too deeply he would have to play MacDonald's game of wild and blind optimism; to refuse to cut he would have to break faith with Lewis. So he had pushed hard against both sides of the vise that gripped him. He pushed down Barton's estimate of a $1.2 billion to $1.5 billion overrun to just under $1 billion. That was the best he could do; he was resolved to go no lower.

They met in the second-floor conference room where Veliotis

had assembled his senior managers, including Art Barton and Gary Grimes. Lewis was on stage, jovial and avuncular to his division troops, knowing that in a few minutes he was going to have to lean on them to knock the numbers down some more.

Veliotis was warm to Lewis, deferential and respectful, but as division manager he chaired the meeting, leading Lewis through the viewgraph presentation of the new estimates.

Lewis looked at the figures and shook his head. Nine hundred eighty-two million, he said. He could not believe it. He had never known it was that bad.

Veliotis marveled at Lewis, realizing that in front of his assembled division staff Lewis had chosen this moment as the moment he "learned" the awful truth about the numbers at Electric Boat. Everything was so well staged: the ninety-day review; Lewis's representations to the board, to the auditors. It all fitted neatly into the artificial time frame Lewis had constructed: the company had investigated the costs on the *688* program, and because of the change in management it had taken a while for the new man to get a grip on things. Lewis looked across the table at Barton and said earnestly that MacDonald had never told him the numbers were so horrible.

From where Veliotis was sitting it looked as if Barton could have choked Lewis. The expression on Barton's face was the same one Veliotis had seen months before when Barton had raged: "That fucking Lewis. That fucking Lewis."

Lewis was going on about how very disappointed and frustrated he was at the productivity problems the shipyard suffered for so many years. He reminded Veliotis of the mess he had found when he took over the Quincy shipyard in 1973 and how he had turned it around dramatically. Soon Lewis was lecturing Veliotis and his managers about the need to do better. He was confident they could achieve higher levels of productivity. Lewis turned to Barton, knowing that Barton's expertise in predicting costs was an important influence on how Veliotis had set the estimate. After all, history was proving Barton had been right all along.

But Barton was in a state of exasperation. His job had been on the line for months; he did not take this kind of pressure well to begin with and the past three months had seemed more than he could endure. Now Lewis was backing him into a corner. At that moment, Barton considered that the only person who knew the truth and who could back him up was Veliotis. If he caved in to Lewis, Barton would have to face the wrath of Veliotis as soon as Lewis's jet lifted off from Groton Airport.

He strained in his chair, his face flushed. He let the anger and frustration well up inside him, then he burst out, "Fuck you, David Lewis."

Lewis stopped speaking, his face showing his complete amazement. The room was silent except for Barton, who raced through his indictment of Lewis. It was horseshit that Lewis had not known how bad the overrun figures were because Barton had told him at every step of the way. And as for the new estimate, it was the plain truth about the costs in the shipyard. The overrun at current performance levels was well over $1 billion and the division management was taking on a heavy burden in making a commitment to bring those figures down by substantial margins. For Lewis to say that was not enough, that the division could do better, was a mistake—the same mistake that had been made in 1973 when Lewis had forced the shipyard to bid too low on the flight two submarines.

Veliotis silently enjoyed the show, but for Lewis's sake he made reproachful sounds at Barton. Lewis struggled to regain his own composure by chuckling about how Art could lose his cool, poor Art, the volcanic conscience of the division, the prophet of gloom and doom. But Veliotis had taken the opportunity while Lewis was on the defensive to reinforce the message. He was unwilling to give any more ground. He already had made a substantial cut in the estimate. Lewis could expect no more.

"Dave," Veliotis stressed in the most personal way, "this is if nothing whatsoever goes wrong" during the remaining six years of construction on sixteen 688s. It assumed there would be no labor strikes and that the growing number of defects that were being found in the submarines could be eliminated in the future. A man had to be a believer to make such a commitment, but Lewis had wanted at least that much, and Veliotis had given it to him. But no more, he said by his tone.

Golden had been silent, although he knew that Lewis expected him to jump in and try to turn around the momentum of the meeting. Lewis did not like to lose a negotiation and this was not going Lewis's way. But Golden sounded more sympathetic to his friend Veliotis when he nudged Veliotis and asked limply, "Come on, big guy, can't you do a little better?" Everyone in the room knew it was over; the line had been drawn. Veliotis had a way at times of outselling Lewis by saying, "No, Dave, I cannot recommend that to you," in a voice of unchallengeable loyalty that conveyed this sentiment: "I must protect you from this misjudgment. So I will stand firm out of loyalty to you." It was hard to destroy that kind of argument, and after a while, Lewis finally gave up.

Lewis stayed over that night. During dinner at a little restaurant overlooking the Mystic River, Veliotis said he would like to see Lewis privately the next morning. When they were alone, Veliotis showed Lewis for the first time the evidence that MacDonald had given jewelry to Rickover and that the purchase of the jewelry had been covered up as "retirement watches." Moreover, Veliotis's investigation showed that MacDonald had certified to Arthur Andersen & Company that no "sensitive disbursements" had been made to government officials during his tenure as shipyard manager. The certification was part of SEC-required controls to combat bribery of government officials.

There was additional evidence, Veliotis said, that MacDonald had improperly charged tens of thousands of dollars in charter-jet travel for personal trips to the company as "entertainment of division guests" and only reimbursed the company after the charges were discovered.

Veliotis pointed out that MacDonald had charged a number of flights from Groton to Chicago initially as business trips, then amended the record stating they actually had been personal trips. Veliotis suspected, and believed that Lewis would share the suspicion, that MacDonald had regularly flown to Chicago to report directly to Henry Crown about operations at Electric Boat.

If Lewis was angry at another indication of MacDonald's disloyalty, he did not show it. He tried to discount the discoveries. Rickover had been a problem for years, he said, and had made all kinds of quirky demands on the division. He told Veliotis to make sure that the jewelry had not been charged to the government as part of the 688-construction contracts and told him it was best to let the matter lie. As for the MacDonald flights, his reimbursement had resolved the situation. Lewis agreed to transfer Pedace to another division.

Veliotis said he wanted to make sure that Lewis was aware of the discoveries in case an audit turned something up in the future. As Lewis got up to leave, he told Veliotis: "You shouldn't put that kind of stuff in writing."

But after Lewis left, Veliotis resolved to document every aspect of MacDonald's jet travel and gift-giving to Rickover. One week later, he completed a formal memorandum to Lewis with attachments that included all of the details.* In the cover memorandum, Veliotis told Lewis:

*Lewis denies ever having received the memorandum, though he acknowledges that he was aware at the time of virtually all of the details included in it, except the cover-up of the jewelry as retirement watches. Lewis said he and MacDonald have different memories as to whether MacDonald informed Lewis of the gift-giving as it was occurring. MacDonald said Rickover requested the jewelry, but this request was not mentioned by Pedace when he wrote his nearly contemporaneous account of the episode in his memorandum of January 31, 1978. MacDonald denied he had any improper

I do not know the number or the extent of unusual or sensitive matters that may have occurred. However, the present atmosphere of rumor, innuendo, and offers by such persons as Mr. Pedace to provide unusual information, is quite unsatisfactory.

It is my strong recommendation that appropriate staff from the corporation's internal audit group be assigned to review thoroughly the disbursements described in this memorandum, including all information of irregular actions that may be disclosed as a result.

The evidence Veliotis had gathered against MacDonald and Rickover could only strengthen his hand against whatever discoveries lay ahead.

"Good morning, Admiral Rickover, this is Taki Veliotis speaking. Admiral, a few minutes ago I was instructed and I delivered to Captain Martin a letter . . . of notice . . . to discontinue performance on the *688*s."

March 13, 1978, was the second time in six months that General Dynamics had decided to go to the brink. This time Lewis and the executive committee of the board took a formal vote and the lawyers drafted a detailed letter of default. Veliotis printed up more than ten thousand layoff slips. Lewis had to show the navy this was war. The company was going to hold the U.S. nuclear submarine fleet—including the first Trident—hostage until the navy met Lewis's demands. The company was going to lay it all on the line because Lewis knew he had to play the wildest game of chicken to find out how deep the navy would go into its pocket to bail him out.

After four months of wrangling with Hidalgo, there was still no settlement of the $544 million claim and Hidalgo, crying that he had only so much money from Congress, had sprung on Lewis the horrible financial reality that the navy expected General Dynamics to take a $550 million loss as part of the bailout deal.

It had started three weeks before Veliotis's call to Rickover.

Hidalgo had summoned MacDonald and Golden to Washington and revealed to them that the Navy Claims Settlement Board had stretched its evaluation of the claim to $125 million. It was delivered to Hidalgo in a sealed envelope. It was the maximum "entitlement." But Hidalgo was willing to request from Congress a total bailout package of $431 million for General Dynamics. It was a substantial amount of

_____

intent in giving the gifts, but acknowledged that he hoped Rickover would go easier on the company afterwards.

money, nearly three times the amount that General Dynamics had been so eagerly willing to accept in 1976.

But instead of jubilation, Hidalgo's offer had "shocked" and "outraged" Lewis and his board of directors. The reason was simple: the mathematics had shifted since the year before. Hidalgo was offering $431 million, but Veliotis had identified the overrun as $982 million. That meant Lewis was going to have to declare the difference—$550 million—as a loss. Such a loss would rival the largest financial debacle in the corporation's history. Lewis was crazy at the thought of taking such a bath. The goddamned navy was going to have to do better or he would bring the house down.

As soon as Lewis heard the figures, he telephoned Hidalgo and berated him. He called the offer and the rationale behind it horrifying. "We really went down the road on this one," Lewis said, adding in accusing tones, "You have defaulted on your obligation." Lewis had then telephoned the Deputy Secretary of Defense, Duncan. He denounced Hidalgo, arguing that Hidalgo did not know enough about business to understand all the financial data General Dynamics had provided him to come up with an acceptable offer.

Duncan, however, was firm with Lewis. Coming from the corporate world, he understood Lewis's predicament. But there was only so much money from Congress to go around and Hidalgo had to settle with all of the shipbuilders.

"Dave, you're a strong company and you can stand it," Duncan had said, adding, "We must have a winner" to get the settlement through Congress. That meant General Dynamics was going to have to take a large and painful loss.

But Lewis would not even entertain the point. He had said that the two sides desperately needed a negotiator who was a businessman to get into the dispute in depth and understand the problem. "We are worried that Claytor will support Hidalgo, who doesn't understand. Someone must spend the time and learn," he argued.

Duncan held out little hope for Lewis. He said he had to back his negotiating team and they were operating within the constraints that Congress had set for them. Hidalgo had barely $1 billion to settle the backlog of nearly $3 billion in claims filed by the shipbuilders.

The General Dynamics executive committee met on March 8. Lewis was erect in his chair, his voice clear with resolve. The navy, he said, would have to improve its offer to avoid a confrontation. Management, he said, had made it clear that it would recommend shutting down the shipyard on this point. Lewis in fact was desperate, and his argument to the board conveyed as much as anything his indignation that accepting a $550 million loss was a judgment that the debacle of the *688* program was his fault. It was the goddamned navy's fault, Lewis kept saying. Rickover's fault. Newport News' fault. And he was not going to open his belly with a long deep cut just because the secretaries in the Pentagon could not get all the money they wanted from Congress. He could not believe that John Stennis, Tip O'Neill, and Jim Wright wanted him to die this way and he was putting his personal reputation on the line over this settlement.

The executive committee was willing to back him. After all, it was the return on their investment that was at stake. But Colonel Crown and the others were determined to take every possible step to show the company's reasonableness. They could not appear to be impetuous. That would turn the Congress and the defense establishment against them. The committee sent Lewis back to Washington to meet with Claytor and Hidalgo before the full board met on the afternoon of the next day. But when Lewis returned, he reported that Claytor had only marginally improved the navy's offer by suggesting the government might find another $50 million, but absolutely no more. Lewis had told the board there were only two choices: to accept the offer, or file the stop-work notice. Lewis recommended brinksmanship. They had nothing to lose. They could always accept the settlement offer as it stood. Lewis had brought all of his senior staff into the board meeting to back him up. Lewis said he was fighting for General Dynamics, but he was really fighting for Lewis.

The board then authorized Lewis to inform the navy that Claytor's amended offer had been rejected. If the navy did not improve its terms dramatically, the board authorized Lewis to shut down the *688*-construction program at Electric Boat and lay off eight thousand or more tradesmen assigned to the ships.

Claytor and Hidalgo knew the limits of their support in Congress and drew the line. They told Lewis they could not improve the offer.

On Sunday, March 12, the members of the executive committee were flown by private jet to Miami for a final meeting with Henry Crown at a suite reserved in the hotel near his apartment. Of the twelve-member board, those voting were: Crown and his attorney, Albert Jenner; Robert Reneker, the Swift & Co. executive; Lewis and MacDonald. Nathan Cummings was consulted by telephone in New York and reported his concurrence long distance.

Veliotis was on the sidelines, a spectator in awe of how far Lewis appeared willing to go to prevent the bloodbath his reputation would suffer from failure. But Veliotis did ask to handle Rickover personally after the shutdown vote had been taken. It was his way of communicating to Rickover that the war over the claims was being waged on a different level, a level that had nothing to do with the common struggle Veliotis and Rickover shared to get Electric Boat rolling again.

So Veliotis placed the call to Rickover's office Monday morning, March 13, just after he returned from hand-delivering the formal stop-work notice to Captain William Martin, the navy's supervisor of ship-building at Groton.

Rickover was calm: "Just the *688*s?" he asked.

"Just on the *688*s and just a few minutes ago," Veliotis replied.

"What is the main reason, the settlement of the claims?"

"Yes, the settlement of the claims."

"What does the company request?"

Veliotis explained that the letter suggested that the claims dispute be submitted to the Armed Services Board of Contract Appeals. In the interim, General Dynamics would agree to continue work on the ships if the navy would pick up the shipyard's full costs—including the $15 million per month the shipyard was losing because it had exhausted its contract funds on some of the ships.

"They want the government to pay whatever it costs?"

"From now on."

"From now until the termination of the contracts?"

"Yes, that's the idea."

"In other words, they ask that the contract be changed to a cost-plus contract."

"Yes, you can put it that way."

"Well, on that basis, does the government have anything to say about running the yard?"

"I don't know, Admiral. It's all strange to me. I tried to stay out of it entirely. They asked me last night about eleven o'clock, Mr. Lewis, to be at the yard early in the morning."

"All right, thank you very much."

"Admiral, thank you very much for listening to me. I didn't want you to find out from anybody else. I took it upon myself."

"Well, you're carrying out [the] orders of your company."

"I took it upon myself to call you because I didn't want you to find out from another source."

"This has been a very pleasant conversation," Rickover said.

"Thank you very much, sir."

Veliotis's courtesy did not soften the attack Rickover had been planning to launch against General Dynamics in Congress.

By the end of the week Rickover was before the House Defense

Appropriations Subcommittee. He had found so many instances of apparent fraud in the claims, he testified, they all ought to be referred to the Justice Department.

"Most senior defense officials," Rickover told the members without naming Hidalgo, "came from industry or from law firms. Some may be reluctant to pursue the false claims issue, for fear of being criticized for not promoting 'good relations' with contractors; or for scuttling a potential claims settlement; or for not seeing the 'big picture.' Some may be reluctant to devote the time and effort needed to complete a thorough investigation. Others may be unwilling to face the great pressure corporations can bring to bear in these cases."

Before he finished his testimony, Rickover said he opposed the award of any further 688 or Trident submarine contracts to Electric Boat for at least two years and perhaps three—shutdown or no shutdown. Then he added for emphasis, "Certainly not for two years would I put anything—even a BARGE!—into Electric Boat.

"Not even a barge!"

Veliotis was incredulous when he heard from the Washington office how Rickover had attacked his management before Congress. It was one thing for them to spar in private, but Veliotis had a reputation in the shipbuilding business. He was turning the shipyard around. He was cleaning up the disgusting mess that MacDonald had left him. How dare that asshole of an admiral say he couldn't build a barge!

When Veliotis finally got Rickover on the phone, he let him know how he felt about the statement.

"How could you say you wouldn't trust me even with a goddamned barge?"

Rickover protested he was not referring to Veliotis.

"I don't blame you for blowing up," Rickover said. "As I told you, I do it all the time myself. And I think you understand that that does not affect my personal attitude toward you or Electric Boat or anyone else."

"I am that way, too, Admiral," Veliotis said, trying to calm down.

"Now the claims are not your business, the production is. It is said that I am running down Electric Boat. Everything I've said about Electric Boat is in testimony."

"Okay, Admiral."

"There are other people making statements about Electric Boat and it's not me, but I'm being blamed for everything. There are statements being made about your productivity, but that's not my job."

"Admiral, I . . ."

"You don't have to apologize."

"I don't have to apologize. I said that I don't like what you said when you said there was 'apparent fraud.' "

"Wait a minute. You're not involved with fraud. I didn't say there was fraud. Look! Let me get that goddamned thing straightened out once and for all. I told the Secretary of the Navy there was potential fraud. The Secretary of the Navy apparently also thought there was potential fraud because he was the one who sent it around to the Justice Department, not me. Let's get that straight."

"Okay, but just the same I don't like it and I said so."

"Now wait a minute. You told me at the beginning you are staying the hell out of this claims business."

"But I work for the company that's being accused."

"I can't help it. I work for the government."

"I understand that."

"I am bound by law, if I think there's potential fraud, to point that out. And I have done it. And that has nothing to do with you in any way."

"And then you say you aren't going to trust me even with a barge," Veliotis fumed again.

"That's absolutely correct. I don't mind you telling me as long as you don't do it enough so you get sick and it interferes with your work. Outside of that, I don't give a goddamned. I can yell better than you can."

"We're not going to go through a yelling contest now," Veliotis said, the harsh tone gone from his voice.

"I don't care," Rickover replied indifferently.

"I care. I respect you too much," said Veliotis. He knew the argument was over. They had both made their points; neither really wanted to fight on a personal level. Veliotis truly respected Rickover for the technical achievements of the nuclear navy and Rickover respected the tough Greek who had come to the shipyard as the first manager in more than a decade who seemed strong enough to fire loafers, who was not afraid to talk back to politicians, and who refused to be bullied, even by Rickover. In many ways they were alike and they knew it, and in many ways they were struggling to defeat each other.

So the two men danced a difficult minuet, while the claims crisis swirled around them, while litigation and work stoppages were threatened by their superiors, and while they faced, together, the formidable task of completing the largest part of the nuclear attack submarine fleet which Congress had allowed Rickover to purchase and which Rickover had allowed Electric Boat to build.

It was a fatiguing battle. At times, Veliotis and Rickover leaned on each other like two punch-weary fighters who felt the bond of their marathon struggle. Rickover was seventy-eight years old: had Veliotis worked for Rickover, he would have put him on the same pedestal that Veliotis reserved for the strong paternal figures who had been most important in his life. Rickover for his part regarded the younger man as a hard worker in the immigrant tradition the two of them shared. Both were survivors.

"Look, I'll tell you right now," Rickover said, "anytime you want to yell at me—my own people yell at me all the time because I yell at them. That's the way we work. Except I can yell louder than they can. Now have we got that squared away?"

"We do."

"I don't want you to get worked up because I have a better constitution than you have. We Jews are better that way than the Greeks. We've had to stand for more than you have."

"Well, I don't know about that. I know my history very well."

"I know your history just as well as . . ."

"My family, from my mother's side and my father's side, they live over a hundred years."

"A hundred years? Well, mine went up to a hundred and three."

"I don't believe that," said Veliotis, enjoying the jostling with the old man.

"Well, I don't care if you don't believe it."

"My mother is eighty-four years old," Veliotis said. "She came all the way [from Greece] to visit me and she gave me hell the other day because I was not dressed properly."

"You're goddamned right, and if she knew the truth about you, she'd give you more hell. Tell her I said that," Rickover said.

"I will tell her, Admiral."

"I know all about the Greeks and I like them. I like particularly the ancient Greeks. Say, Jean," Rickover yelled to his secretary in the next room, "send that Greek up at E.B. that speech I made in Athens."

Rickover allowed as how the ancient Greeks had built good ships, ships that lasted a long time.

"They knew one thing that the people in Washington don't know," Veliotis replied. "When the Persians were about to attack Athens, the orders spoke of wooden walls. In other words, have a navy, have a big navy. If you have a big navy, you can control the world. You can control freedom and democracy."

"The next time you come down and talk to the Congress, you ought to tell them that," Rickover suggested.

"Well, I don't talk to Congress. They don't talk to me, they talk to you."

"They don't talk to me, I talk to them," Rickover corrected him.
"You do a very good job with the Congress. You are the master."

Rickover changed the subject. "I still want to tell you I think Jews are better than Greeks." And so the friendly banter continued, both men enjoying the brief escape from battle.

By mid-May, Rickover's campaign in Congress against the shipbuilders was building momentum, the only counterbalance against the drive by the civilian leaders in the Pentagon to settle the claims and against General Dynamics' lobbying on Capitol Hill.

On the 19th, Rickover convinced the chief of navy shipbuilding, Vice Admiral Russell Bryan, to go before Senator Proxmire's panel to debunk once and for all the fallacy that drawing revisions could cause billions of dollars of cost overruns among the shipbuilders.

The idea of thirty-five thousand drawing revisions had a simplicity to it that anyone could relate to, and General Dynamics' public relations campaign had taken very effective hold in Congress. It had caught the navy without an effective rebuttal that could show with equal simplicity how little substance there was to the allegation.

But Bryan told the Senate panel that misleading information had been released by General Dynamics. Bryan explained how the plans for a ship were updated as the skeleton and hull are erected, followed by the interior finishing work. "Drawings serve a number of purposes," Bryan said. "Primarily, they are the way engineers and technicians tell the workmen how to make and install every bit of a ship, from its hull and frames down to the precise details of how to make the millions of electrical connections in all the switchboards and weapons systems. Further, they form the living record of general technical instructions to all those who construct and inspect every part of that . . . ship.

"They serve as the means to record every lesson learned throughout the design and construction process so that errors noted and problems encountered are corrected or avoided in subsequent ships. Every time a drawing is modified . . . that . . . drawing modification is carefully recorded and is issued with a revision coding so there can be traceability and accountability for the actual set of plans to which each ship is built," Bryan explained.

"This basic procedure . . . is called a drawing revision. It is a system proven over the years for naval ships and commercial ships." Bryan paused before making his key points.

Electric Boat, he said, which had designed the 637-class attack submarine, had issued an average of five revisions to every drawing used in the construction of the fleet. Thus, the total number of Electric Boat revisions a decade earlier rivaled the thirty-five thousand drawing revisions it was complaining about in the *688* class. The revision issue was a fantasy and Bryan's straight comparison had proved it.

But there was an even more damning statistic, Bryan said: "The estimated shipbuilders' cost at completion of the first five SSN 688 class submarines at Electric Boat averages about $50 million more for each ship than for the first five ships at Newport News. These ships are being built to the same design, with the same drawing revisions, with the same changes, and in roughly the same time frame."

Rickover was delighted with Bryan's testimony, and in his daily telephone call to Veliotis, he said, "The thirty-five thousand drawing revisions are being exposed for what they are. This morning, there is testimony by Admiral Bryan, who is telling just exactly what the hell these thirty-five thousand changes are."

"Well, you read the General Dynamics annual report, no doubt," Veliotis said sarcastically—referring to Lewis's statement to shareholders that the navy's drawings for the ships were "replete with error which led to more than thirty-five thousand revisions to these plans and specifications being imposed on Electric Boat by the design agent through the navy."

"That's in their annual report?" Rickover asked.

"Yes, and Lewis says thirty-five thousand drawing revisions. And MacDonald says . . ."

"One thing I can tell you right now," Rickover interrupted, "Bryan's pointing out the number of drawing revisions are no different for the *688* than they've been for other classes of ships. He's also pointing out that the total changes represent five percent of the cost of the ship. But General Dynamics is using this and I think they're making a big mistake . . . it's a very foolish thing to do in my opinion. MacDonald or his lawyers started that thirty-five thousand changes stuff."

"Well, MacDonald said that he counted the revisions himself."

"Well, I don't say that he didn't, but MacDonald didn't know what they meant. Now this is being brought out in testimony this morning and I'm glad it is. My advice would be if General Dynamics is wrong, to stop playing that game."

"I think MacDonald should go and testify too," Veliotis said scornfully.

"I don't know."

"Maybe Lewis should go and testify," Veliotis added, but Rickover was not connecting with Veliotis's dark humor and cynicism about the corporate office.

"The truth is gonna all come out eventually."

"Absolutely right," said Veliotis.

David Lewis had roamed miles of corridors in the Senate and House office buildings. He had button-holed dozens of congressmen. He had made his speech a thousand times about how the navy had made a mess of the shipbuilding program and how he was dead serious—he hated to be, but he was—about shutting down Electric Boat the minute the deadline arrived unless somebody improved the navy's offer.

Lewis thought he was doing pretty well in Congress. In fact all the sentiment was running against him and he was blind to it. So he took every sign of sympathy in the voices on Capitol Hill as fervent support for the company position. He just could not face the alternative. A half-billion-dollar loss was the kind of thing that no executive could survive.

Lewis prepared for his best performance, realizing that the only way to win was to outsell the Carter appointees before the most important audience in Washington. He had gone to Clark Clifford's law offices as part of his preparation and soaked up some good advice about where to push the buttons on Senator John Stennis and Representatives George Mahon, Robert Giaimo, and Joseph Addabbo, and the others who controlled the defense budget. He believed that if he could keep claiming strong support on Capitol Hill, he could turn the Carterites around on the settlement.

One person Lewis was not paying a lot of attention to was young Representative Christopher Dodd, the second-term congressman whose home district in Connecticut encompassed Electric Boat. Dodd was not what you'd call a powerhouse, but he was very ambitious and worked very hard to get to the center of issues that affected his district. His father, Thomas Dodd, had been a powerhouse in the Senate for a long time until he got censured for mishandling campaign funds. Partly because of that old trauma, Dodd and Hidalgo had fallen into close alliance. Hidalgo had practiced law at Cahill Gordon & Reindel in New York, the firm that defended old Senator Dodd during the censure vote. Hidalgo invoked this old connection and latched onto the young congressman as one of his operatives to drum up support for the settlement among the young reformers in the House.

Christopher Dodd wanted a settlement. It was life and death for his district, and he had come to believe that Hidalgo had a winning financial package that could get through Congress. The only remaining impediment was David Lewis's ego. So Dodd had taken as his mission in life the conversion of David Lewis.

He appealed directly to Lewis, but at the same time he also worked the back corridors of the Capitol in hopes of finding a way to get the message through to Lewis that he was going to have to cave. The critical problem, Dodd had tried to explain to Lewis, was that General Dynamics was trying to sell a huge bailout to a bunch of young, post-Watergate reformers who did not want to be involved in any bailout of a big defense contractor. Dodd was working hard, he had told Lewis, to push the deal the navy had put together, but few congressmen were inclined to go along. To those who did, Dodd was having to encumber himself by asking for their support as a personal favor, which, of course, obliged Dodd to return a lot of favors some day. Lewis had to realize that the kind of settlement he wanted would suck up most of the funds available in Congress for *all* of the shipbuilders' claims.

Dodd thus painted the political realities as he saw them, but he always got the feeling that Lewis looked at him as a kid who was playing over his head.

One day in May, Lewis went to see the Speaker of the House and later stopped by Dodd's office to boast, "Boy, we're in great shape."

Dodd inquired why Lewis thought so and Lewis explained that he had laid out the company's case to Tip O'Neill and the Speaker had responded by saying, "Well, Dave, you make a good case."

Dodd stared at him for a moment. "Dave, just because the Speaker said you made a good case doesn't mean that you've solved the problem or that Tip is going to support you." Dodd wondered whether Lewis was deluding himself intentionally or whether he just had a poor instinct as to how to read the Congress. After all, the public image of the General Dynamics' claim already was tainted. It was being attacked as the largest overrun settlement proposal in the history of the U.S. military. Rickover was portraying the claim as fraud-ridden and the settlement proposal as ill-conceived, bad policy. Didn't Lewis understand that the natural political instinct was against such a settlement?

But Lewis kept pushing and working the Hill.

As a last resort, Dodd started working to orchestrate a final, powerful act of conversion. On June 1, the tension had not broken, no one had caved, and the deadline, which had been extended once and which everyone knew could not be extended again, was a week away. For the first time it looked as if the two sides were locked into the cataclysm. The lawyers were drawing up briefs for the showdown in court, where the government would seek a temporary restraining order forbidding General Dynamics from shutting down the navy's nuclear attack submarine program.

Right before the Memorial Day break, Dodd went to the men he thought could turn Lewis around, and after these discussions he called David Lewis and suggested that he return to Washington and talk to House Majority Leader Jim Wright or to Representative George Mahon because they controlled the budget and, therefore, the funds available for a bailout. Dodd warned him that the mood of the Congress was poor. Hidalgo had called asking that Dodd pass along to Lewis the message that Hidalgo's last offer of splitting the $719 million difference between them in half was "the last mile I can go." Hidalgo wanted an answer within a few days because in a week's time they would be at the brink of a shutdown again and the navy was getting ready to go into court.

Lewis's limousine arrived at the East Front of the Capitol. He climbed the half-dozen steps to the swinging brass door that opened onto the long, tiled corridor leading to the office of the House Majority Leader. Lewis and Jim Wright were old friends, which was why Lewis had chosen Wright as the man to whom he would make his final plea. Wright's district was home to thousands of General Dynamics workers employed at the mile-long air force production plant in Fort Worth, where General Dynamics built the F-16 Falcon.

Wright stood up to greet Lewis warmly, then Lewis suddenly realized that he had walked into more than just a private session with the Majority Leader. The other men in the room were Mahon of Texas, who had been in the Congress since 1935 and who chaired the appropriations subcommittee that controlled the defense budget, and Giaimo of Connecticut, who was completing his tenth term in Congress and who sat as a ranking member of Mahon's subcommittee as well as a ranking member of the House Budget Committee. Off to the side was young Chris Dodd.

The three principals spoke for the defense establishment in Congress. Instinctively Lewis knew this was his final performance. It had to be his best. He began the speech he had given so many times, putting what he hoped would be convincing new emphasis on how the navy had mismanaged the shipbuilding program and how General Dynamics was being made to pay, unfairly, for the navy's mistakes.

Dodd was watching the faces of the listeners. He grew anxious when he saw the impatience gathering in Mahon's expression. The elderly Texan glanced at his watch; then suddenly, when Lewis paused in the middle of a sentence, the chairman stood up and said, "I'm sorry, but I have to go." Dodd was panic-stricken. The meeting looked like it had fallen apart because Mahon did not have the patience to sit through Lewis's long-winded sell. Lewis looked startled and embarrassed at Mahon's blunt move for the door.

But after Mahon was on his feet, he cocked his head and addressed Lewis as if to emphasize the brevity of his advice.

"Mr. Lewis, this is an election year," he said with a touch of West Texas drawl. "There are too many people who believe that you are partly responsible for this, and nobody knows whether it's eighty percent or twenty percent or what, but this is an election year and the Congress will not vote to bail you out for this large amount of money. I have to tell you, you can count on our support provided you take a very painful part of this."

Mahon paused for a moment, looked away, then cocked his head again and said, "Mr. Lewis, if I were you, I'd take this deal or I wouldn't come back up here again."

Dodd was in awe of Mahon, and he realized that he had just seen power exercised in a way he had never before witnessed. It was blunt and it was final and it was the kind of power that only men of long tenure and high stature can wield without explanation or appeal. They were the men at the top of the defense establishment, the men whom Clark Clifford got paid to interpret for outsiders, the men who controlled the budget and who could tell someone like David Lewis how things were going to turn out for him and so he had better reckon with it.

The finality of Mahon's words sent a chill through Lewis. He looked into the faces of the men in the room and saw the unity of their expressions. A sense of despair washed over him. The long months of performing were over. He had tried so hard, but had lost before the most critical audience and, truly, there was no appeal.

By the time he slumped into the rear seat of his limousine, David Lewis was weeping.

Navy Secretary Graham Claytor had taken a long weekend to return to his family home in the rural Virginia countryside. He enjoyed the solace of the lakeside home, where the warm June sun had induced him to stay over until Monday. When the telephone rang in the afternoon, Hidalgo was on the line. He explained that he was flying to Glenview, Illinois, just outside Chicago, the next morning, and had arranged to meet with Lewis. Hidalgo had gotten a report from Dodd on Lewis's encounter with the House leadership. He thought the time was right to play a final card in the negotiations and he wanted Claytor to come along to close the deal.

The expiration of the sixty-day extension of Electric Boat's stop-work order was a week away. This might be the final chance.

Claytor was pessimistic. He thought the negotiations were hopelessly deadlocked and that both sides would be in court by the end of the month.

"What do I want to do that for?" he growled.

"Don't be so negative, Graham. I think we can turn the final trick by raising the issue of front-end money." Under normal settlement terms, any settlement from the government would be paid out over years as work was completed on the submarines. Paying settlement funds up front was like giving the company an interest-free loan.

Hidalgo's strategy was to meet privately with Lewis and tell him the navy was sticking with its last offer. "But our bargaining chip will be a front-end payment," Hidalgo said, adding, "Come on, Graham, I need you for this one."

Claytor protested. He had a full schedule the next day.

"No, you don't. I looked at your schedule and you don't have anything important until the afternoon. I can have you back by then. Besides, I've canceled your morning appointments."

Claytor growled again and started packing.

The next morning they met Lewis and Golden in a large conference room whose windows overlooked the line-up of military jets and cargo planes at the Glenview Naval Air Station.

"Gentlemen," Hidalgo opened, "the deal is $359 million or no settlement. But if you are willing to meet our figure, we would consider making an advance payment that would be recovered [from progress payments] over the unexpired term of the contract."

Lewis and Golden asked some questions about how the advance payment would work and how much it would be. Hidalgo said he was thinking along the lines of a hundred million or so, but was willing to discuss it.

Lewis decided to make a last play for a larger overall settlement. He told Hidalgo that his offer of an advance payment wasn't very good since the company was being asked to take a horrendously unfair loss to begin with. But all of the men in the room realized the benefits of an interest-free advance payment. At going rates, General Dynamics could earn tens of millions of dollars a year on a large lump-sum payment. The company's bankers would be ecstatic to have the use of the money.

After a few more questions, Lewis announced that General Dynamics would have to consider the offer and get back to the navy men.

During the afternoon, Hidalgo received a telephone call from Golden, who said he and Lewis had gone straight to Henry Crown's office after the morning meeting to confer with the colonel about the offer. Golden said the company's final position was that it would accept the $359 loss only if the settlement included an advance payment of $300 million. He said the company's banks and other lenders, which included Crown, believed $300 million up front was the magic number.

Hidalgo had been willing to go to $300 million all along. He told Golden he thought he could swing it, and they agreed to talk later.

The next day, however, Hidalgo's military aide received a message from Golden: "Tell the secretary that the deal is off."

Hidalgo suspected that Colonel Crown was behind the last-minute ploy. After Hidalgo had suddenly sweetened the deal with a $300 million advance, hopes had been raised at General Dynamics that the navy had not reached the bottom of its pocket. The corporation could always accept the $359 million at the eleventh hour, and so, tactically, fifty years of deal-making had taught Henry Crown patience. Maybe if the corporation waited a little longer, the navy would come up with another $50 million. There could be a big return on an investment of just a few more nerve-wracking hours.

But Hidalgo had truly reached the limit. The only thing he could do was wait out Crown and the executive committee. He sent a message to Max Golden: "So be it."

The company got the message. Later in the day, Golden called back to report that the deal had been approved as outlined in Glenview, with a $300 million advance payment and a fifty-fifty sharing of any additional overruns up to $100 million.

The eight thousand layoff notices that Veliotis had prepared were canceled and he flew to Washington on Friday, June 9, to meet Lewis and Golden in Claytor's office for the signing of an "aide-mémoire" drafted by Hidalgo to memorialize the agreement. In the corporate office in St. Louis, there was great relief. The company had ended the long battle and Lewis took credit for improving the terms of the settlement substantially by winning a $300 million advance payment and a navy commitment to cover half of the next $100 million in overruns.

On Friday afternoon, Lewis, MacDonald, and the other top

managers in the executive offices organized a betting pool on how the
settlement announcement would affect the company's stock. When
the market opened the following Monday, it was clear that the winner
would be James M. Beggs, who had bet that the stock would soar.
Trading was heavy from the outset and within two months, the value
of General Dynamics' stock had increased by 50 percent.

In October, President Carter signed the defense bill authorizing
the settlement, and the $300 million advance payment check was
rushed by limousine to a Virginia bank for wire transfer to Chicago. A
copy of the check was flown to the Chicago office of Henry Crown,
where it was framed for the wall of his office.

In the end, there was an illusion that the navy and General
Dynamics had split the difference, but it was only an illusion. The
claim had been $544 million, yet by the time the navy finished paying
under all the terms of the settlement, the government had given General Dynamics a total of $639 million in cash. The last-minute sweeten-
ers that had been added by Hidalgo—half coverage of additional
overruns up to $100 million and the $300 million advance payment—
wiped out *all* of General Dynamics' financial problems.

In the whole process of filing and evaluating the claims there
had been no time for men like Senator John Stennis to find out the
truth about them. He wanted to support any reasonable settlement.
He left others to arbitrate reason. Stennis had urged the parties to
avoid even the use of the word "claims" in the spirit that they were all
good patriots looking after the nation's defense.

Representative George Mahon was left to dispense rough justice behind closed doors when he told David Lewis that no one was
sure whether General Dynamics was to blame for 20 percent or 80
percent of the problem. It seemed Solomon-like to cut the baby in
half.

But the notion that the navy somehow cut the baby in half to
settle with General Dynamics wilted before the final comparison of
the $544 million claim and the $639 million navy payout.

As part of the settlement, General Dynamics declared a $359
million one-time loss, but the U.S. tax code allowed the corporation to
deduct half the loss; so in the end, the charge against earnings was
only $180 million. The loss, in effect, was split with all U.S. taxpayers.

And finally, the interest generated by the $300 million advance
payment amounted to a respectable sum over six years. Assuming that
Crown, Lewis, and MacDonald were shrewd enough to invest the

money for a 10 percent return each year, the total benefit would amount to another $180 million.

Thus in settling the $544 million claim in the manner it did, the navy provided cash, tax, and interest benefits to General Dynamics of $1 billion or more.

It was no wonder that, some weeks after it was all over, Edward Hidalgo got a warm and personal letter from Henry Crown congratulating him for his skillful negotiating tactics, and letting him know there were no hard feelings at General Dynamics.

IV

THE FINAL ASSAULT

The bailout of General Dynamics—and the subsequent bailouts of Newport News and Litton—energized Rickover for the last campaign of his career, indeed, of his life. He would soon be eighty years old, but he still got up early and worked all day, stopping only at lunchtime to run in place for fifteen minutes at his desk, flapping his arms like a bird to get the blood circulating.

He was determined to punish David Lewis for the slick and treacherous public relations campaign that had wounded Rickover in Congress; it had sown pernicious doubt and had called into question Rickover's vision and judgment in the minds of men like John Stennis and George Mahon. Had not Mahon said as much when—in an act of political expedience—he had apportioned blame on both sides: navy and industry? The settlement, fair or not, had left Rickover saddled with a recognizable measure of guilt for the industrial disaster at the shipyards. In his effort to strike back at Lewis, Rickover attacked the only thing he could, the only precious asset that he had worked hard to nurture and to perfect, one of two precious assets capable of giving nuclear-powered submarines to Rickover's nuclear navy: he attacked Electric Boat.

When Veliotis saw it coming, saw that he would be caught in the middle, saw that Lewis would be standing behind him not as his backer, but as someone who needed a shield, Veliotis understood that it might be up to him to defeat Rickover, to kill the old man for good, or perish himself.

Veliotis understood that Rickover—at any time he chose—could become the greatest obstacle to Veliotis's plan for triumph in General Dynamics. Veliotis could cut the costs and he could streamline production, but no boat could go to sea, no boat could be "finished" until Rickover said it was finished. He had seen the poison that Rickover was capable of injecting into the navy's relationship with

Electric Boat. Before the settlement, it had gotten so bad that the shipyard deliberately was installing defective snorkel assemblies on several 688s because Rickover would not let the navy process any change orders requested by Electric Boat in the midst of the claims controversy. The shipyard was forced to cut up the ships after the settlement and before the boats went out for trials. It was an insane way to do business.

In the months after the settlement, Veliotis found himself pitted more and more against an angry and embittered Rickover. He was learning that if Rickover decided to take you on, if he decided you were no good, he would just keep coming at you like a fighter with an iron jaw. In late 1978, Rickover wrote a series of memos to the navy secretariat charging that the settlement had done nothing to prevent the shipbuilders from filing large claims the next time they got into financial trouble. Rickover asked for a formal meeting at the Pentagon to present his case to Claytor.

In the secretary's office, Rickover attacked Electric Boat and Veliotis for changing the shipyard's method of doing business in a way that, Rickover charged, was destined to produce more claims. He came prepared with examples. He sat on the couch across from the civilians while his aides laid out the charts to demonstrate what he was talking about.

In one instance, the navy had requested Electric Boat to drill a one-and-a-half-inch hole in radiation shielding boxes on the Trident submarines. Electric Boat had notified the navy that the change would cost $1,000 for each hole drilled. That was outrageous, Rickover said.

In another case, the navy asked for a wire rope to be added to each of the Trident hatches to secure them in the open position. The wire ropes could not have cost more than $5 to fabricate. But the shipyard had taken the position that each wire rope would cost the navy $1,400—as well as a two-week delay charge, which could total more than $100,000. Overall, Electric Boat had notified the navy that in order to process any change, the shipyard was adding a 50 percent cost-increase factor for delays in other work and a 25 percent cost-increase factor for the alleged decline in productivity while change work was done on overtime.

Rickover said the navy should not submit to such outrageous charging methods. Electric Boat under Veliotis, he said, had begun "banking" these unresolved change orders against the day when the shipyard got into more financial trouble and needed another bailout. Then all the unresolved changes would be wrapped into one large omnibus claim for millions of dollars and filed against the navy.

Near the end of Rickover's presentation, Claytor was buzzed by his secretary and he excused himself from the meeting. At that moment, Rickover stood and addressed Hidalgo, who had said nothing during Rickover's presentation. Vice Admiral Bryan, who represented the shipbuilding command at the meeting, saw the sneer on Rickover's face and knew what was coming. He wished he was elsewhere.

Rickover started out in a low voice. "You know, the mess we have in shipbuilding today is primarily the result of the civilians in the navy secretariat who don't know what they are doing and who are unwilling to consult their subordinates who have greater experience. The problem is that some civilians in senior jobs are more concerned about future employment than they are about looking out for the taxpayers' interests, and therefore they try to settle claims by finding ways to pay the shipbuilders what they want. These civilians," Rickover continued, "are not well regarded by their subordinates, but a few of them have the courage to speak out."

Then, looking straight at Hidalgo, Rickover said loudly, "I am particularly referring to you, Mr. Hidalgo, when I say these things and when the secretary returns, I am going to repeat what I just said in front of him."

The blood had drained out of Hidalgo's face. The room was silent, but there were inaudible groans constricting the faces of the witnesses to the embarrassing attack. The chief of naval material and the chief of navy shipbuilding saw their boss's humiliation. Hidalgo wanted to lash out at the sneering old man, but he was plagued by the thought of enlarging the scene already created. Hidalgo stood up, put on the most dignified expression he could muster, and walked out of the room.

After that day, Hidalgo refused to speak to Rickover and he resolved, along with Claytor, who soon heard of the outburst, that if they could convince President Carter to retire Rickover, they would do it.

Hidalgo and Veliotis also became natural allies against Rickover—it was an alliance of necessity. Hidalgo had pledged to Congress that he had not only settled the claims but also solved the underlying problems that led to massive overruns in the shipyards. He thus had a vested interest in the continuing profitability of the shipbuilders, and especially of Electric Boat, which had received the largest of the settlements, the largest in navy history.

Hidalgo believed he could prevent future claims, or at least minimize them, by establishing himself as the guardian of a healthy business relationship with the shipyards. He had told Claytor that if the shipbuilders were determined to file claims for their cost overruns, there was little the navy could do to prevent it by writing new terms or conditions into contracts. If a shipbuilder tried to take advantage of the navy and if the navy harbored an attitude that all shipbuilders were crooks, the relationship would never improve. The message to the uniformed navy, therefore, had been to get along. In effect, Hidalgo became the representative of the shipbuilders against the uniformed navy. And any blue-suiter who complained about the shipyards was labeled a stooge of Rickover by Hidalgo.

To Veliotis, Hidalgo's support was crucial to the salvation of Electric Boat. Veliotis may have been able to stop the runaway costs, but to make money, he needed more ship contracts. By the time the first eighteen ships were completed, Electric Boat's production line would be a well-oiled and cost-efficient machine. It would then be poised to take new contracts under realistic schedules and, with a shrewd bid strategy, Electric Boat could finally start recording profits on the 688 class. Hidalgo appeared determined to steer those ships to Electric Boat. But there would be no profits while Rickover was opposing new construction contracts for Electric Boat.

Rickover for the moment had solidly frozen Electric Boat out of navy business. Veliotis counseled Lewis to ignore the old man. The navy would have to come back to Electric Boat eventually because Newport News could never handle all the submarine construction that lay ahead on top of its heavy commitment to surface ship construction. Still, Veliotis piled insult upon insult at Rickover's door. He had gone over Rickover's head to propose a new and more innovative attack submarine to the navy, one that would cost less than the 688s, one that employed the latest computer technology to automate shipboard systems and cut down on the crew size—a critical factor in the overall size of the submarine.* He turned his engineering department loose to investigate titanium as a building material for future submarines and to once again consider advanced propulsion concepts.

Veliotis challenged Rickover's authority across the board. He told the admiral that if he expected Veliotis to call him every day, to meet his plane at the airport, to check with him about promotions and table settings at ceremonies, then he had better get all of that written into the contract for the ships because that was the only way Veliotis

*This proposal for a "Two-Thirds" submarine—two thirds the size of a 688—was prepared with the guidance of Vice Admiral (Ret.) Joe Williams, Jr., who served as Veliotis's deputy operations director after leaving the navy. Williams and Rickover clashed violently over the submarine design proposal, which remains highly classified, but which would have reclaimed the depth lost in the 688 class and would have applied technology that only today is being considered for a new generation of attack submarines.

was going to comply. All of these things were driving both Rickover and Veliotis mad. Veliotis began to believe that Rickover was bent on destroying him because that was the only way Rickover was going to hang on to his empire for a few more years.

"Let me tell you something, I don't intend to put in for any more claims," Veliotis tried to tell Rickover over the telephone in October 1978. "How can I explain? You are an intelligent person." Veliotis asserted that his cost-saving measures already were paying off in the shipyard, and that he had shaved $5 million off the cost of U.S.S. *Groton* and U.S.S. *New York City*. Under the terms of the settlement, just as the navy picked up half of any additional overrun, it also split the savings from any underrun.

But Veliotis's assurance had a hollow ring to it. He knew there were still hidden overruns in the shipyard and his only hope of covering them was the cash infusion new contracts would bring.

Rickover was no longer buying Veliotis's sincerity.

"Have you seen any examples where I'm out to screw you on money or anything?" Rickover asked.

"I don't think I will discuss that, Admiral. Look, we understand each other. I won't discuss that. I'll tell you one thing, that I got very mad with you, if I may say so. It's not nice that I got mad with somebody, but you wrote to the Secretary of the Navy and you told him that he shouldn't give us any additional work."

"I told your boss, I told that to Lewis."

"Yes, you told my boss. You told Lewis. You told the Secretary of the Navy, the newspaper, Proxmire, and the world that we shouldn't be getting any more work. We have a morale problem here."

"I got a morale thing, too," Rickover replied.

"Well, I don't know. If it is that bad, maybe we should get a divorce," Veliotis said sarcastically.

"I have control over certain work where I can make a decision where it goes," Rickover said, laying down the law with Veliotis.

"Well, we expect that if our price is good, and the terms and conditions are good, to be given a fair shake."

"I WON'T LET IT GO TO ELECTRIC BOAT," Rickover shouted, and then after a pause added, "until we feel that the thing is open and above aboard where I can control it."

"AND WE ARE GOING TO FIGHT YOU, ADMIRAL, THE BEST WAY WE KNOW," shouted Veliotis with equal power.

Rickover came right back. Why was Veliotis cutting off the flow of routine information about progress on the ships and why was he interfering with Rickover's ability to monitor the shipbuilding program? He was not going to recommend any new work, he repeated,

"Until I feel that myself and my representative are treated as customers. I will NOT . . . !"

"Don't get excited now," Veliotis goaded him, glad that Rickover had lost his temper.

"Do you realize that my representative up there is the guy you should see? He is there. He is my representative, and I will NOT have my representative treated the way you're trying to treat him."

"I treat him very nicely," Veliotis said, feigning surprise. "I address him very nicely. I call him 'Mister.' Etiquette is very nice."

"It isn't etiquette," Rickover snapped angrily. "It isn't. We've gotten ourselves into a position where my representative is not paid any attention to and I WILL NOT TAKE IT! I'll tell you that!"

"Admiral, do you have a deal? Give me a choice."

"I insist on being treated like a customer."

"Admiral, I am treating you like a customer. What else do you want me to do?"

"I'm suggesting one step in the arrangement at least to treat my representative as the customer's representative. What you do with the navy supervisor, that's another matter."

"The supervisor is the customer. Your representative is the representative of the Department of Energy, right? Is the Department of Energy the customer, too?"

"Yes, sir!" Rickover asserted.

Veliotis's remark was another slap at Rickover. The Department of Energy, which included the reorganized Atomic Energy Commission, did not have a contract with Electric Boat, but Rickover's authority to supervise and monitor all aspects of nuclear propulsion flowed from the Atomic Energy Act and the regulatory authority of the Department of Energy. The actual customer for the submarines was the navy, and the navy was represented by the supervisor of shipbuilding, who did not report to Rickover.

"I didn't know that," Veliotis taunted. "I thought the customer was the navy. The Department of Energy is a regulatory agency."

"On account of the nuclear project, absolutely, on any part of that propulsion, that's my responsibility."

"I appreciate your explaining to me, I appreciate that very much," Veliotis said, his voice thick with mock sincerity. "But we're talking about the customer. The customer is the navy."

"Just a minute! The navy pays for the ship, but I have the responsibility. . . ."

"Yes, like any other inspection agency."

"I am not an inspection agency. I AM RESPONSIBLE," Rickover yelled into the phone.

"Fine, fine," Veliotis relented, again content that he had set off Rickover's temper.

"You see, we're getting into goddamned semantics," Rickover said, sounding frustrated and a little weary. "We'd better stop it, because every time I get to a substantive point, you don't want to treat me like a representative of the customer."

"Admiral, I treat you like a customer, and don't say I don't treat you like a customer, don't feel bad about it. I treat your representative like a customer, but there is no point [in] working out with him any arrangement for reciprocal visits."

"Well, we're right back to zero. So let's stop it." Rickover hung up.

With Hidalgo as his guardian, Veliotis saw the opportunity to outflank Rickover in the years after the settlement. Hidalgo was working to isolate the aging admiral as the shrill voice in the wilderness and, as long as there were no claims, no one was going to pay attention to his sounding brass of discontent. Thus naturally joined, Veliotis and Hidalgo cultivated their relationship. Both were men of ethnic origin, Hidalgo having been born in Mexico City in 1912. Like Veliotis, Hidalgo practiced the style of leadership as much as the substance. He was an extremely courteous man, a well-traveled internationalist. Years as a trial lawyer made him somewhat theatrical in conversation. His metaphors were sweeping, and he sprinkled discussion with contributions from his native Spanish and acquired French. He wore dark pinstripes, smoked a pipe, and his silver hair and tanned complexion gave him a proper Castilian bearing.

One morning in February 1979, Hidalgo telephoned Veliotis to ask: *"Dites-moi, est-ce que vous avez reçu un nouveau r.f.p. pour deux bateaux?"*

The question was whether the navy had solicited a bid from Electric Boat for two 688-class submarines authorized by Congress for the following year's shipbuilding program.

"On n'a pas rien reçu," Veliotis replied.

"Je ne crois pas que vous allez le recevoir, mais j'aimerais bien savoir si vous le recevez," Hidalgo said, pointing out that he did not believe the Rickover "stooges" in the shipbuilding command were going to send the bid request to Electric Boat, but asking that Veliotis notify him immediately if any bid request was received. Hidalgo had been pressuring the admirals to send the bid request to Electric Boat. Once they did, he knew Veliotis would aggressively go after the business. Veliotis thanked Hidalgo for staying in such close touch.

"Merci beaucoup, Monsieur le Ministre."

"Très bien. À bientôt," Hidalgo replied. "Let's keep in touch, huh?"

"Oui, oui, we will, sir," Veliotis said.

"Très bien, au revoir, Takis."

The following month, Hidalgo was successful in overruling Rickover's opposition to soliciting a bid from Electric Boat, and in April 1979, Veliotis won the bid competition for the two *688*-class ships. It was a great victory for the alliance against Rickover, although Veliotis knew Electric Boat needed more than two ships to return to profitability. Nonetheless, it was a strong start, and it had proved that Veliotis and Hidalgo could be effective against the Rickover machine in the navy and in Congress.

On a raw day in December 1979, Evelyn Small made her way down the hill toward the waterfront, clutching her clipboard and the sheaf of plans she carried for the audit she was assigned to perform on *SSN 698*, the sixth submarine of the *688* class under construction in the South Yard at Electric Boat. She had tucked her dark hair beneath the rim of her hardhat. It was bitter cold and as she leaned into the icy blast sweeping up off the river, she pulled at the collar of her parka before she scurried across the gangway to the foredeck of U.S.S. *Bremerton.*

Small, a civil service employee of the navy, was one of dozens of inspectors working for SupShip-Groton, as they called the navy supervisor of shipbuilding at Electric Boat.

What she found that day in the torpedo room of *Bremerton* was the beginning of the end for Takis Veliotis.

The submarine sat low like a long, still whale in the frosted river. Small hurried across the narrow steel deck to the forward hatch. The ship was in the last stages of preparation to go out on sea trials. The audit was part of the navy's final regimen to check the quality of the shipyard's work before accepting the submarine and commissioning her as a combatant in the Atlantic fleet.

Bremerton's keel had been laid in May 1976, the month that Gorden MacDonald became general manager, and she was launched in July 1978, a month after the big claim settlement. Electric Boat had delivered four *688*-class submarines to the navy by the end of 1979, and ten ships were in various stages of construction at the shipyard. The keel-laying ceremony for U.S.S. *Albuquerque* was scheduled for two days after Christmas. The purpose of the *Bremerton* audit was to select from the ship's plans a random series of welds and inspect them. Were they in the right place? Were they ground to specification? Did they appear to have any flaw that would warrant further testing?

Small stepped quickly through the hatch, using her free hand to grab the hand holds to steady her descent through the sonar and control rooms, then down past the officers' quarters, before reaching the torpedo room on the lower level. The crew was living on board and the torpedo room was well lit. Small sorted her plans and neatly laid out the drawings for the sixteen-foot torpedo skids. The "skids" were polished steel trays, convex in shape so the torpedo would not roll if the ship went into a banked turn.

The welds Small had chosen to inspect were buried back up under the trays where the supports and foundations met the hull. She got out a mirror and an extension bar and squatted down to look under the tray. She lay flat on the deck and shinnied sideways, the mirror in one hand, a flashlight in the other. She twisted and craned her neck to line up her vision with the mirror and the light, and then she got still. She lay there for a minute, jostled with her gear again, and was still for another moment. Then, slowly, she crawled out of the tight space.

The welds were not there. A whole series of welds, just not there. The supports for the torpedo skid were there and enough welding had been done to hold them firmly in place during normal operation, but a series of welds that were supposed to give the skids extra support to sustain the shocks of a depth-charge attack or a nuclear detonation in the distance were nonexistent. The skids were weaker than the navy specs called for—and everything in the specs was there for a reason.*

The Electric Boat work authorization and sign-off sheets said the welds were there and had been verified by company inspectors. Something was terribly wrong and Small rushed back through the shipyard and was still huffing when she told the chief of quality control for SupShip-Groton that Electric Boat had falsified its welding inspection reports on *Bremerton*.

When his waterfront managers brought him the news, Veliotis was heartsick. He realized the implication immediately: if Electric Boat's quality-control records showed welds had been completed when in fact they did not exist, the integrity of the whole system was suspect. In a nuclear submarine, a suspicion of defect was as good as

*In April 1968, the nuclear submarine U.S.S. *Scorpion* was lost in the Atlantic with all hands when, according to a navy report declassified in 1984, one of her torpedoes exploded inside the ship. SOSUS sensors had picked up the explosion and the sound of the hull breaking up. The navy was never been able to determine what caused the torpedo to explode, but the accident heightened safety concerns in the navy about all aspects of torpedo handling and support inside the ship.

a defect because everything had to be perfect. That's what the navy had learned from the loss of U.S.S. *Thresher* and her crew of one hundred twenty-seven men. You couldn't be 99 percent sure that all the welds were there. It was going to be a nightmare, and Veliotis was full of despair. He was sure Rickover would try to murder him over the discovery—and he was right.

Veliotis was angry because he saw the history of sloppy management at Electric Boat as the unaccountable villain in his tragedy. Shipyard inspectors had been signing off on work that was half done or not done at all—and what was equally shocking to Veliotis was the fact that the hundreds of navy inspectors who swarmed daily over the shipyard had been accepting and certifying the same faulty workmanship for years. He had inherited this crazy system and these ships—half-built time bombs of poor workmanship—and now they were exploding his plans for real achievement. Veliotis saw no personal responsibility in the welding disaster, but he would have to account for it and accept its bitter consequences for the division's reputation and—more importantly to the watchful board members—for its earning power. But there was evidence that Veliotis bore some of the responsibility. After all, his punishing style of management, the layoffs, the fearsome threats against the idlers and nonperformers had driven a small percentage of the workforce into short-circuiting safe construction and inspection procedures. It wasn't necessarily Veliotis's fault, but it was a direct result of his management and for that, some believed, he shared responsibility for the crisis.

The phrase they liked to use in the navy was you had to "pull all of the threads" once you found a weakness in the system. A full inspection was ordered for *Bremerton* and then for all the other 688s in the shipyard. Then they started on the Tridents. At the beginning of 1980, work effectively came to a halt as navy and Electric Boat inspectors found thousands of welds that were either missing or defective and that had been improperly certified by the shipyard's inspection force. At the same time, inspectors discovered that inferior grades of steel had found their way into parts of Electric Boat's inventory, requiring reinspection of thousands of pieces of steel that had come from the tainted stockpiles.

Prior to Evelyn Small's discovery, it looked as if Veliotis could have met the cost projections and the schedules he had set for himself as goals and as his commitment to Lewis. If he had brought the last of the eighteen ships in on budget, he would have been a hero. And, if he had picked up a few more contracts from Hidalgo for additional 688s and Tridents, the board of directors and Henry Crown would have thought Veliotis could walk across the Thames River.

He had automated key portions of the production line at Electric Boat and had brought a science to the shipyard's management that it had never seen. The automated frame and hull-cylinder facility at Quonset Point was finally going to give Electric Boat the production capacity to do what the shipyard had promised to do from the beginning: build at a rate of three 688s plus two Tridents per year. The completion of a mammoth land-level facility for Trident construction and its lake-sized floating drydock had added critically needed space and had restored efficiency to the waterfront. Everything had finally come together—state-of-the-art manufacturing facilities, control systems, discipline, and a battle-tough management staff under Veliotis. A half-dozen 688-class boats were virtually completed, all tightly scheduled to go out for sea trials during the first half of the new year . . . and now this.

In the last weeks of 1979, with the onset of the welding crisis, Veliotis went to Washington to meet with the chief of navy shipbuilding, Vice Admiral Bryan, the chief of naval material, and the chief of naval operations. He asked them, "What do you want me to do?" But they were ready for the question. "Tell him nothing," Rickover had warned. It was not the navy's job to tell Veliotis how to solve the crisis. It was the navy's job to insist that its warships were constructed with absolute integrity to meet the stringent building specifications laid down for them.

Rickover infected the navy hierarchy with the fear that if they told Veliotis how to go about reinspecting and recertifying the more than eighty thousand welds on each of the ships, Veliotis would treacherously slap the navy with a large claim asserting that their advice amounted to a "change order" in the contract. There was precedent for this fear. The shipbuilders had been banking and successfully litigating "constructive" changes for years, alleging that anytime a navy official injected himself in any way in the construction process at the shipyard, it amounted to a change in the contract for which the shipyard should be compensated.

All of those years of sharp claims strategies were coming home to roost on Veliotis's doorstep. Instead of the best minds being pooled for the best technical strategy to ensure that the submarines were safe, the navy withdrew from the process and took a hard and aloof position: Don't ask the navy how to fix it; show the navy how you intend to guarantee the integrity of the ships, and if that method is deemed satisfactory by the navy's technical experts, the plan will be approved.

The realization washed over Veliotis like a spasm of nausea: he was going to have to rip apart a half-dozen ships. It was going to take a year or more to guarantee the integrity of the submarines in the shipyard and those already at sea. Many of the suspect welds were in the forward section of the ships, where the sound isolation "cocoon" was delicately constructed to stop any noise from the crews' quarters and control rooms from reaching the outer skin of the ship. The cocoon was a hull within the hull. The ten-inch gap between them was filled with sound-baffling material laid in to absorb all the interior noise. In this manner, the outer skin of the ship was sound-isolated to become a sensitive acoustical membrane, studded with passive sonar sensors able to hear distant noises in the ocean and feed them to the fire-control computer.

It had taken months to fit up the cocoon just right, and there were thousands of welds on its frames and light-steel plating. As more and more structure was fitted up and equipment moved in, the cocoon became virtually inaccessible. Ripping out the cocoons to check all of the welds was a monstrous task, and over the long months of 1980 it cost the shipyard hundreds of thousands of man-hours.

If he was nothing else, however, Veliotis was a fighter, a survivor who never gave up until the lights went out in the stadium. He resolved that he would not let the welding crisis defeat him or interfere with his personal goals and ambition in General Dynamics. He still had a powerful ally in Edward Hidalgo, who had been named Secretary of the Navy in late 1979 as President Carter shuffled top jobs in the administration: Hidalgo replaced Claytor, Claytor replaced Duncan as Deputy Secretary of Defense, and Duncan moved over to the Department of Energy to replace James Schlesinger as secretary. Hidalgo had more power, and he and Veliotis drew closer during the welding crisis. But Hidalgo was powerless to buck the uniformed navy over a safety question in the nuclear submarine fleet, and that's what the welding crisis threatened, safety. Since *Thresher*, safety was motherhood. The only thing Hidalgo could do was help keep the lid on the bad news. He instructed the uniformed navy not to mention the possibility of new claims and to minimize the problems at Electric Boat in testimony before Congress. The welding crisis was minor and troublesome, but Veliotis was handling it. That was the company line established by Hidalgo for the navy. Hidalgo could not control Rickover, but as long as there were no claims, he was still able to isolate the old man.

Despite the growing hostility between Veliotis and the uniformed navy managers who oversaw the submarine construction program, Hidalgo appeared to cultivate Veliotis's friendship, and some of the senior uniformed officers took private affront at it. Veliotis and his wife, Paulette, were among the guests at Hidalgo's home for a reception before the navy relief dance, and Mr. and Mrs. Veliotis rode the Navy Secretary's private train car from Washington to Philadelphia for the Army-Navy Game.

Hidalgo's policy was that any new bids for *688* construction were going to go to Electric Boat because he also knew that the infusion of new cash from new contracts could help Veliotis defray the mounting costs of the welding repair work. But the uniformed navy dragged its feet, largely because Rickover wanted to starve Electric Boat. When Lewis and Veliotis were ready to accept Rickover's leadership again and to treat him with respect, Rickover said, then, and only then, would he agree to put more work into the shipyard.

The relationship between Veliotis and Rickover in early 1980 reached a nadir of open hostility and rage. It seemed something of an understatement to say that each man had become dedicated to the destruction of the other. Veliotis relished each opportunity to tweak Rickover or his representative in the shipyard. Rickover took each offense personally and an insult to one of his men was an affront to Rickover's name and his legend.

"When I had him go around to see you last Friday, you said you thought maybe you didn't want to see him anymore," Rickover challenged Veliotis in a February 1980 call.

"I will tell you what I told Mr. Hansen, Admiral. I said, 'Mr. Hansen, you came to see me three times yesterday. The first time you came to see me, you brought me two items which I already knew about and which we had discussed before. And the second time you came to pass me a message about how many welds were wrong on some of the ships. It was a garbled message. The third time you came back to collect that message and you passed a message which I did not understand at all.'"

Rickover tried to interrupt, but Veliotis cut him off.

"May I finish please? Let me finish. Please, let me finish, I haven't finished. Please. Let me finish and then you say whatever you want to say. I said, 'Mr. Hansen, if it is something important, barge right in here. Just come in anytime you want. I don't mind. Day or night, if it's something important. If it is something that is not important, don't. Give it to me on a piece of paper, write to me like any other businessman and I will answer you.' He came to see me yesterday. He brought me an item and I said, 'I am aware of that item. Thank you very much for bringing it to my attention.' This is all I told Mr. Hansen."

"All right, fine," Rickover said, "I think we're both on the same track. In the first place, he has a legal right to see you, you know that."

"Admiral, I don't know what legal rights he has."

"WHY DON'T YOU TRY IT OUT!" Rickover shouted. "If you don't agree with that, why don't you refuse to see him and see what happens if you want to try it out?"

"Admiral, Admiral, I'm not here to try it out. If he has a legal right to see me, tell him to see me. I'm not saying he doesn't have the legal right to see me, what I'm saying, when you come and see me, have something important to tell me. That's all I said to him."

"But who is to decide whether it's important? Let me tell you this. You cannot settle anything. If you think that he ought to see you only on limited things, why don't you write down what they are?"

"I am going to write NOTHING, Admiral."

"All right, I advise you not to," Rickover said with a tone that suggested if Veliotis put anything in writing, Rickover was going to use it against him.

"I am going to write NOTHING, Admiral."

"We're all together on that, but let me tell you this. He represents the government, he represents the Energy Department, and you cannot have a situation anywhere where a representative of the Energy Department cannot see his top guy."

"I have not said that."

"Maybe he thinks it's necessary."

"Well, okay, that's fine. Anytime he thinks it's necessary and if he comes to see me for things I believe are not necessary, I am going to tell him so."

"Fine."

"And then you find somebody who knows what is necessary and what is not necessary."

"I'm not arguing with you, fella. I'm only saying that he has a right to see you anytime he thinks it's necessary."

"If he has a right to see me anytime he thinks it's necessary, he can come and see me, and if he comes to see me for things that are not . . ."

"Can we stop the conversation at this point?" Rickover interrupted, believing he had won the argument.

"I will stop. Thank you very much."

"We're both in agreement, is that right?"

"I don't know what agreement we had, we had no disagreement to start with," Veliotis goaded.

"We don't need an agreement because it's required, that anytime he thinks it's necessary to see you, he can come and see you."

"Well, Admiral, if you say so. If you say it's so, and it is so, who am I to say . . ."

"Why don't you let me know that you don't agree with it?"

"Admiral, Admiral, I don't have to let you know what I agree with and what I don't agree with. I have no argument with you. I have no quarrel with you."

"Well, then we terminate the discussion."

"Thank you very much."

"All right, goodbye."

"Bye."

Veliotis hung up the telephone and looked over at his deputy, Gary Grimes, and his general counsel, William Gorvine, both of whom had listened to the conversation. The three men laughed at how well Veliotis had taunted Rickover. They were cheering their leader on because all of them believed that the company would have to pursue a strategy of terror and guerrilla warfare against Rickover to keep him from burying Electric Boat in the rubble of the welding crisis.

February 1980 was one of the worst months in Veliotis's life. One morning he counted twenty-six lawyers going through the filing cabinets at Electric Boat, earmarking for photocopying hundreds of thousands of pages of documents that were under subpoena from the federal grand jury sitting in Hartford or from the SEC in Washington. The investigations that Rickover had triggered seemed endless. Art Barton, the comptroller, and half of the senior staff at Electric Boat had been called before the grand jury and questioned about Rickover's allegations that the company's cost-overrun claims had been fraudulent. It looked as if the FBI agents and prosecutors could go on forever digging into the company's files, and Veliotis lived in horror of what they might discover there. The SEC was gathering documents to determine whether General Dynamics had violated disclosure laws in 1976 and 1977 on the 688 program.

People were sweating because it looked like the FBI, which was working on the case in conjunction with Justice Department prosecutors, was pressing for indictments based on the evidence it had gathered. The company was doing everything it could to protect itself. To deal with the Justice Department in the grand jury investigation, General Dynamics had retained Thomas G. Edwards, a former federal prosecutor who was close friends with and had been the immediate superior of Jo Ann Harris, the chief of the Justice Department's fraud section in Washington, where the final prosecution decisions would be made.

Veliotis was terrified about the boxes of documents going out the door. He stayed late some nights going over files he thought might contain sensitive material, and he confided in his deputy, Grimes, that all it would take was some cross-eyed clerk in Washington to put all of the documents together and prove that the overrun had stemmed from bad management and the claims were manufactured to cover the losses.

Then, at the end of the month, Veliotis was served with a subpoena to give testimony under oath in the bankruptcy proceedings of Frigitemp Corporation. The chairman of Frigitemp had fled the country and the law firm hired by the creditors of Frigitemp had soon heard the rumors about kickbacks. Veliotis was getting his legal advice from Foley, Hoag & Eliot, the Boston firm that handled both Quincy's and Electric Boat's outside legal affairs. Veliotis had maintained that he knew absolutely nothing about the kickbacks, and General Dynamics' lawyers accompanied him to the deposition in an office building in downtown Boston on February 28. He also was accompanied by the general counsel for the Quincy shipyard. Veliotis was argumentative with the bankruptcy lawyer during the day-long deposition. And when the question was asked, after four hours of back and forth, "Mr. Veliotis, did Mr. Davis ever give or transfer any sums of money to you?" Veliotis replied in a clear voice, "No, sir."

Davis was the Frigitemp vice president who had paid the money through intermediaries into Veliotis's Swiss bank account from 1974 through 1978. The questions for which Veliotis was later charged with perjury all came in rapid succession at the end of the deposition. Veliotis was strong when he looked into the lawyer's eyes and denied categorically four more times that he had ever received money. A lie was not a lie until you were caught. And if you were tough and smart and crafty—and Veliotis was all of those things—you never got caught.

Still, Frigitemp and all of the investigations seemed to be closing in on him. After the deposition, Veliotis told Rickover in one of the few civilized telephone conversations they had during the month, "The situation here is very tense. It's a nightmare. It's a real nightmare because people have been called at the grand jury and they come back and they tell the stories, and right now they are so careful about what they do that they don't do anything at all without a firm of lawyers."

In the midst of these crises, Lewis did something that deeply disturbed Veliotis. He hired Oliver Clark Boileau as the new president of General Dynamics Corporation. It was an act that was very close to a breach of faith in Veliotis's eyes. It was embarrassing to him, since he had confided in his closest deputies that Lewis had made a commitment to him about the chairmanship.

Lewis tried to soften the blow by explaining to Veliotis that he had been without a president since Paige had departed in 1973. Henry Crown and the rest of the executive committee thought it would look better on Wall Street, since Lewis, at sixty-three, was too much of a solo figure at the top of General Dynamics.

Boileau was an aerospace executive who ran the Minuteman project for the Boeing Company and had risen to become president of Boeing Aerospace. He was big and jolly and said things like "gee whiz" and "gosh" and you knew right away that his nickname was Ollie. Lewis made clear that Boileau was not necessarily his successor. Boileau would have to prove himself and compete for the job just like everyone else when the time came, but Veliotis did not like the looks of it and from the moment Boileau entered the company, he set out to intimidate and dominate Boileau where he could.

Lewis had not broached the subject of the succession to Veliotis since that day at Quincy in May 1977. There had been no reason to speak about it. "The succession" was one of the most sensitive topics in any large corporation. Unless Lewis or a board member raised the subject, subordinate managers were out of place in doing so. Veliotis believed the commitment had been made to him, but he also understood that only he could create the image of shipyard savior and leading contender, both of which were necessary to bring Lewis and the board to the realization that Veliotis was the only logical choice to become chairman of the board.

Veliotis knew the chairmanship still was within his grasp and he was going to eat anyone alive who tried to become a contender for the job. Boileau had been with the company barely a week when Veliotis had attacked him, making it clear that the marine division belonged to Veliotis and that he did not deal with anyone except Lewis.

Boileau had gone to Washington for a series of get-acquainted meetings with General Dynamics' customers at the Pentagon and quickly found himself in the midst of the welding and quality-control controversy. The admirals in the shipbuilding command vented their long list of complaints against Veliotis. Boileau, who knew nothing of the history, listened attentively. But when word of the meetings reached Veliotis, he roared to his staff that he was going to give the new president a piece of his mind.

The opportunity soon arose. Boileau and Ted LeFevre, the company lobbyist who had set up the meetings, telephoned Veliotis a week later to give him a report on their conversations.

"Hi, Taki, this is Ollie," the high-pitched voice came over the speakerphone on Veliotis's desk. He listened to their report for a moment, noting the care they took in saying they did not comment during the meetings on the fight Veliotis was waging against Rickover's navy. But Veliotis didn't believe them and he was angry at the presumption of the new executive.

"Well, you couldn't have had any comment," he snapped, "because both of you didn't know what it was all about. How the hell could you have had any comment? How the hell could you have carried on any discussion with them?"

"We were in a listening mode," Boileau tried to explain.

"I have no problems with that, Mr. Boileau, you and Ted can go and see anybody you want to see. Nobody's going to stop you. You can talk about anything you want. You want to tell me about it, you tell me about it. Go ahead. You can go see Queen Elizabeth, it doesn't bother me."

Boileau tried to change the subject: "I'd like to take you up on your invitation and come up there and learn the business."

"Well, fine, try and come and learn the business, and if you learn it, well, you can replace me, too. It's as simple as that. Let me tell you something, Mr. Boileau, life is too short. Life is too short. . . . You are the president of this company. But if I were you—and I'm saying that for the record—I would go to the fellow who was involved. I would call Veliotis as a courtesy. There are people in the navy who like me and there are people in the navy who hate my guts. I cannot tell you what to do. But let me tell you, we may have to work together, we may not have to work together. But from me you're going to hear it straight. If I don't like something, I will tell you so."

When LeFevre tried to take the blame for setting up the appointments without checking, Veliotis cut him off.

"Ted, don't. Mr. Boileau can speak for himself. Mr. Boileau doesn't need you. Mr. Boileau can speak for himself."

"I'm listening . . . I'm getting the input," Boileau said slowly, warily. And when he mentioned a second time that he would like to visit Electric Boat, Veliotis was anything but hospitable.

"Now look, Mr. Boileau. You are the president of the company. I am only one of the vice presidents. Any time you wish to come, let me know, I will try to be here. Tell me what you want to discuss and we will make everything available to you so you can do whatever you want to do. And I hope I will grow to like you, it's as simple as that."

It was the worst encounter a new president could expect to

have with one of his most important division managers and Boileau could not have understood what was motivating Veliotis.

Rickover's instinct that Veliotis was going to hit the navy with a new round of claims was absolutely right. The idea for how to do it took shape gradually and sounded outrageous to everyone the first time they heard it. But in the end, everyone in General Dynamics embraced it, albeit awkwardly like a long-lost derelict cousin. They embraced it nonetheless because it was the only card the company could play to avoid taking another painful bath.

In the opening months of 1980, when Veliotis realized that the welding crisis was going to cost tens of millions of dollars, perhaps $100 million, he resolved that he was not going to pay for it. He was not going to take the fall for the history of bad management at the shipyard. He could not accept responsibility for the loss and at the same time create the image that he had saved the shipyard from disaster. He had to find a way.

The welding crisis was an expensive mess, and someone had to pay for it.

The navy would only pay for it over Rickover's dead body, and that left one alternative: the insurance underwriter. The ships were defective and the insurance might cover that.

It surprised a lot of people that the insurance company that underwrote the risk of fires, floods, and other acts of God while the multi-million-dollar attack submarines were under construction turned out to be the United States Navy. Builders' risk insurance had been part of maritime commerce since the Middle Ages and protected shipyards from the ravages of everything from fires to pirates. The large underwriters, such as Lloyds of London, insured shipyards around the world against such losses. A typical premium for such insurance had been 2 percent of the value of the contract. But since World War II the navy had insisted as a cost-savings measure that it would insure the yards against "all risks" of accidents, fires, floods, and other calamities. The navy had been receiving the benefits of the cost savings for forty years.

Even David Lewis had been incredulous when Veliotis told him privately that he had assembled a team of lawyers and legal experts to lay plans to file an insurance claim against the government of the United States, asserting that the navy was responsible for paying the cost of Electric Boat's poor and negligent workmanship on the submarines. Such a claim had never been filed in forty years, but Veliotis said that the "all risks" clause in the insurance rider of the contract could be legally stretched to include poor workmanship by the shipyard. Such a claim ran strongly against established precedent in the marine insurance industry, but Lloyds of London had recently settled a claim at a New Orleans shipyard in which poor workmanship had been a factor.

Subjectively, it looked like one of the most colossal insurance scams of the century and it seemed inconceivable that General Dynamics could get away with such an arrogant and cynical act against the Pentagon and the taxpayers. But in the real world of defense contracting, both Lewis and Veliotis knew that it was their only chance to avoid another harsh, financial setback—another judgment against both of them. And so the insurance claim was added to their compact of mutual self-interest. They would at least use it as a bargaining chip against the navy and if they were lucky—as they had been on the last claim—the navy would see the benefit of settling the dispute by finding some more money to give General Dynamics.

On March 3, 1980, Rickover sounded the alarm in the navy by writing a formal memorandum to Hidalgo warning that Electric Boat was getting ready to hit the navy with another large claim to cover the company's negligence and poor workmanship. It was the I-told-you-so memorandum Rickover had been waiting two years to write. Rickover reminded Hidalgo of their meeting in Claytor's office after the claim settlement and of Rickover's warning that the settlement "would not preclude large, inflated claims in the future."

Rickover's memo was timed to precede the spring round of budget hearings on Capitol Hill. Veliotis could not contain his rage at the admiral's preemptive strike. He immediately drafted a reply letter. It was the strongest personal attack on Rickover that General Dynamics had ever put in writing and was addressed to the Secretary of the Navy. As he prepared to send it, Veliotis telecopied a draft of the letter to Lewis, who was quickly on the telephone to head off a disastrous and public confrontation. Lewis hated confrontation.

"The point is a good one," he said to Veliotis. "His letter is a real low blow, and, as you say, it's an undisguised attack on us primarily. But it seems to me that we'll be lowering ourselves to his level on this thing and in a way that we can't win, because in spite of the fact that he's a sorry bastard and all that, he still has a lot of friends in Congress."

Added Lewis for emphasis: "We don't want to expose ourselves to launching a major battle. I don't think we can."

"Well, it's not a question of winning a major battle, Dave. You know, I have been dealing with the man now close to three years. And this is Rickover. Unless you shoot him back, he will do it and do it again. . . . Rickover tried to take flight five [two *688* subs] away from us. I mean we have to get after him," Veliotis said with urgency. Getting after him meant attacking him with the full force of the company. "As a matter of fact, I had decided myself that if you didn't want to, I will quit and I will get after him, and I have planned to get after the man."

Veliotis was almost breathless. The panic he felt pushed him to pressure Lewis, to force Lewis to back him in the strongest possible way with the most brutal assault the company could mount against Rickover.

Lewis tried to calm Veliotis, suggesting that he go to Hidalgo with a "white paper" response to Rickover and also with the draft of a tough letter. "Sit down with him on both and discuss the value of each one, which is the most valuable."

"Well, okay, I can do that."

"We just have to ride out a lot of his abuse and just ignore it as you've been doing and, you know, most people know the man is over the hill. Most of his congressional cronies know that but they're not going to nail"—Lewis paused—"uh, they're sympathetic to him, and they don't want to have his reputation wrecked after thirty or forty years of service to the navy. And I think that's my real point. And if they're not going to listen to him, they're not going to take flight five or flight six from us, as long as we don't destroy the man's reputation—even though he deserves it. That's the real feeling I have."

"Well, Dave, if I wanted to destroy the man's reputation, I have enough on file here to put him in jail."

"Yeah?" The tone of Lewis's voice dropped noticeably with apprehension.

"I have enough on file here. I have sworn statements here—I don't have them here—I have my own safe deposit box—about all the gifts and everything else that I can put him in jail on. I don't want to destroy the man. I appreciate and I recognize that all of us should be grateful for what he did in the past, but right now that man has one objective in life: Destroy General Dynamics. Dave, he is mad because we got the settlement. He wrote letters to the Secretary of the Navy and everybody else not to give us any additional work. He went out in the press saying not to give us any additional work. He went out in the press saying not to give us even a barge. He has been abusing me all of the time. I have been taking it from him. You know, the man is crazy. There are no two ways about it, and I believe it's about time for us to go out and say how we feel about it."

"Well, he's attacked us, but they've [Congress] ignored him," Lewis said, avoiding Veliotis's reference to the safe deposit box file on Rickover.

Lewis said he had drafted an alternative to the harsh personal attack Veliotis had made on Rickover. He asked if he could read it to Veliotis.

"By all means, Dave."

The letter was much tougher than Veliotis had expected from Lewis. It cited the history of Rickover's attempts to dominate Electric Boat's management, and accused him of "trying to regain dominance over the day-to-day operations of the shipyard," an event which the company could consider a "disaster" for employee morale.

"I like it," Veliotis said.

"You do?" Lewis seemed surprised and relieved that he was not going to insist on a harsher attack.

"I like it," Veliotis repeated, his confidence restored that Lewis would stand behind him for an attack—albeit a milder one than Veliotis might have preferred—against Rickover. They were still operating as a team, Lewis and Veliotis, and even with the arrival of Boileau, theirs was the most important partnership in the company because Electric Boat still represented the largest management challenge in General Dynamics.

With the onset of the welding crisis, Veliotis was becoming the lightning rod for the company, just as he had when the company laid off more than four thousand workers in 1977. The difference this time was that Rickover was no longer an ally but an enemy. Veliotis had become the sword that General Dynamics was going to wield against Rickover, whose every tactic seemed to be geared to the financial devastation of Electric Boat. Lewis shrewdly stayed above the fray, but was deeply involved in charting Veliotis's strategy. Veliotis was Lewis's toughest warrior and Lewis treasured his toughness. There was no need for Lewis to bloody himself unnecessarily in the war over who should pay for ripping apart the submarines. If Veliotis wanted to try to hustle the navy for the money, Lewis was willing to back a winning proposition that would save the company's bottom line, but he was going to hedge his bets by letting Veliotis lead the attack. Veliotis accepted the position. He believed he could do anything as long as Lewis was backing him.

Veliotis took the letter and the company's white paper to Hidalgo, who then explained to the congressional committees that, while he had never said there would *never* be another shipbuilder claim, he expected that the welding crisis at Electric Boat would be resolved through businesslike negotiation.

Because no claim actually had been filed, Rickover's alarm failed to provoke a congressional reaction in early 1980. Still, Veliotis was in a rage at the old man and wanted to deliver a crushing blow to

Rickover. The evidence of gift-taking was his strongest and most secret ammunition, and he thought seriously about exposing Rickover
to the Justice Department. When Veliotis checked, his lawyers told
him that he had an obligation to disclose the gift-giving under a clause
in the submarine construction contract that forbid the giving of gratuities to government officials.

Veliotis probably would have tried to put Rickover in jail during those tense months if his deputy, Gary Grimes, had not pointed
out that to turn in Rickover he would first have to turn in MacDonald,
and that would put Veliotis at war with the corporate office. He
couldn't get Rickover without cutting his own throat.

So Veliotis did what he could to harass Rickover, and he did it
with all the energy and the spitefulness he felt for him. The old man
could talk a blue streak—that was one of the ways Rickover wore you
down, but Veliotis had the same kind of power and he was determined
to grind Rickover down every chance he got. He knew there was no
way an eighty-year-old man had the stamina anymore to win.

On March 27, Rickover got word that Veliotis was canceling the
longstanding weekly meeting between the Electric Boat general manager and the skippers of the nuclear submarines that were under construction or repair in the shipyard. The meetings were a forum for
Rickover's commanders to raise any issue about progress on the ships
with the top man in the shipyard.

"I get in one of the reports that you plan or you have knocked
off the weekly meetings with the commanding officers of nuclear
ships. I'd like to ask you, what are you planning to do? Are you gonna
knock it off or are you gonna keep it going?"

"I answered that. The supervisor wrote me a letter and I
thought I answered it."

"You said you were considering."

"Yes, yes, I'm considering it."

"When are you gonna make up your mind?"

"Soon."

"How soon?"

"Well, you know, soon."

"Well, a week? A month? A year or something like that?"

"What does it matter?"

"Well, it matters to us, we just want to know what you propose
to do."

"I will let you know in due time, Admiral."

"But if you're gonna do it, how long does it take you to make up
your mind on a thing like that?"

"I don't understand it. I mean, what is the purpose of this discussion?"

"Well, can you make up . . ."

"What is the purpose of this discussion?"

"Because we're interested."

"Well, you're interested. You know, this is for my benefit, and it's me that has to decide, and I told that supervisor that you have across the street there."

"You told him you were considering it."

"Yes."

"Then maybe he ought to go back with a formal letter and ask you when you are gonna make up your mind. We're trying to get the thing settled without a lot . . ."

"There's nothing to settle, there's no argument to settle, there's nothing to settle."

"Wait a minute. You told him you're contemplating to knock it off, because I'll have to take some action before . . ."

"If that's what you want to do, go ahead and do it."

"I don't . . ."

"Hey, go ahead and take any action you want right now, Admiral."

"Mr. Veliotis, I'm asking you a very . . ."

"Hey, look, don't threaten . . ."

"I'm not threatening you at all. I'm talking very politely."

"Go ahead, you can threaten politely."

"Yeah, fine."

"You want to take any action, go and take any action you want."

"Wait a minute, just a minute. What do I do with an answer like that? I asked you . . ."

"Do anything you want to do."

"You're contemplating knocking this thing off so the first question I ask is: Are you gonna knock it off? And you say . . ."

"The answer is, I don't know. I told you I don't know."

"Wait a minute, I'm asking you."

"When I know, I said I'll advise you, and I don't know when I will know so I will keep you posted. Now, if you don't like that answer, Admiral, and you want to do something else, do it."

"Mr. Veliotis, stop it. Look, I'm trying to conduct a simple . . ."

"We cannot, you and me, we cannot conduct any business because, you know . . ."

"You know I deal with a hell of a lot of other contractors and I don't . . ."

"Oh well."

"Take this from any other contractor in the United States."

"Well, that's too bad."

"Well, all right."

"That's too bad."

"I will send you a record of this conversation and here's what I will say. I note that you are contemplating whether you should or should not stop these things, so I said, well, so I asked you, are you gonna stop it, and you can't answer that. Then I asked you when are you . . ."

"You can say any self-serving statement you want," Veliotis interrupted.

"Wait a minute, then tell me what you say."

"You are looking for an argument again."

"I'm not arguing."

"I have more serious problems here than to argue with you, Admiral."

"I have one question: Do I have the right to ask you that question?"

"I don't know what rights you have."

"Then why don't you ask . . ."

"Why do you ask me if you have the right? If you have the right, you have the right. Why do you ask me that?"

"Just a minute. I'm responsible for all this stuff."

"Well, yes, you are responsible, what do you want to do?"

"Well, I'm asking you a question. You said you were contemplating knocking it off. Now this is what I'm gonna put in my record of this, I noted that you are contemplating . . ."

"I could not care less, Admiral. I couldn't care less what you put in your record. I don't have to agree."

"I'll send you a copy."

"I don't have to agree or disagree, you don't send me copies of everything you say. You are a master at presenting things . . ."

"I'm no master at anything."

"You are master at presenting things to serve, to serve your purpose."

"Mr. Veliotis, you are compelling me now to go to your superiors."

"Well, if that's what you want to do, be my guest! If that's what you want, be my guest, Admiral! GO TO MY SUPERIOR RIGHT NOW, AND I WILL GO SOMEWHERE ELSE RIGHT NOW! If that is what you want, Admiral, I will do it. Go ahead. Don't ask me. Go to my superior! Don't ever talk to me anymore! Talk to my superior from now on!"

"Now look, calm down a bit," said Rickover. "I've been calm during this whole conversation. You're the one that's getting worked up. I asked you a simple question."

"And I gave you a simple answer."

"You didn't give me a simple answer."

"I told you I don't know."

"Fine, then I asked you the next question."

"When I know, I will let you know."

"Well, about how long will that take?"

"And I tell you, I don't know."

"You don't know. Could it be a month?"

"It could."

"Could it be a year?"

"Could be a month, or less. Could be a month. Could be less."

"And you will not say when you're gonna make a decision. Then I assume it's gonna keep on going the way it is?"

"You can assume whatever you want to assume."

"Thank you very much for your attention."

"Don't mention it at all."

It was just too much of a coincidence for Veliotis when he discovered that the new president of General Dynamics had returned to Washington for another round of private meetings with the uniformed navy hierarchy—including a three-hour meeting with Rickover and his deputies—to discuss the navy's complaints about how Veliotis was handling the welding crisis.

Veliotis knew by instinct that Boileau could not be operating behind his back without the knowledge of David Lewis, and that thought troubled him most deeply. Veliotis needed Lewis's backing if he was going to survive the welding crisis and continue fighting Rickover. If Lewis had for some reason decided that he was now expendable, Veliotis did not have the stomach or the inclination to continue. If it was so, it meant that he was dead in the corporation anyway. If that was the case, he was not going to continue laboring on behalf of men who only wanted him to finish the job so they could throw him over the side.

In the meantime, Lewis had said some things to Veliotis in subsequent telephone conversations that were disquieting, admonishments such as, "Somewhere up and down the line, we've got to get back to a working relationship [with the navy]." Lewis's support seemed all too tentative. He said he agreed that the navy bore responsibility for the cost of ripping the ships apart, "but in the final analysis, we have to get our own place shaped up."

The words had stuck in Veliotis's craw. They were words of criticism. They were words that reflected failure or bad management, and these were judgments Veliotis was not willing to accept. So when Veliotis caught Boileau sneaking back to Washington for private meetings with the shipbuilding command, he had to find out where he stood with David Lewis and the only way to do that was to put everything on the line. He did it in a four-page letter.

"I am deeply concerned that recent activities of Mr. Boileau in the marine area have virtually destroyed my effectiveness in dealing with the navy," he wrote, reminding Lewis of the earlier problem with Boileau and of Boileau's promise not to engage in further discussions with the navy without consulting first with Veliotis. Now this. The letter continued:

My first reaction was total disbelief . . . Dave, [and] as one businessman to another . . . for a newly appointed top executive with no background in the subject matter to meet with key navy officials to discuss the relationship between Electric Boat and the navy, and at a most crucial time in this relationship, demonstrates a lack of judgment that I can only describe as appalling. I am particularly aghast to learn of Mr. Boileau's meeting with Admiral Rickover since we both know that . . . he really respects only strength and determination and he interprets accommodations on the part of any company he deals with as signs of capitulation to his demands.

Since I must assume, Dave, that you were aware of these meetings and that they took place with your concurrence, I am deeply hurt and thoroughly upset by what I regard as a complete emasculation of my position in dealing with the navy.

He concluded: "Since these same events make it unequivocally clear that Mr. Boileau and I are totally incapable of working together, I would appreciate it if we can make the necessary arrangements for the orderly transfer of my duties and responsibilities to my successor. I regret the difficult situation this puts you in, Dave, but I am sure you will appreciate that its origin was not of my doing. I know you will always do what is in the best overall interest of General Dynamics."

Lewis got Veliotis's letter at his home outside St. Louis on Saturday, March 29, 1980, and reached Veliotis Sunday by telephone.

"God, I'm stunned and shocked. I tried to call you last night when I first read it, but gosh, all I can say is that all your conclusions with regard to me and Boileau are a hundred and eighty degrees from what we intend, what we think our corporate organization is. I can see how you're upset. But golly, this is all—it isn't funny but it's obviously a comedy of errors, but I would like to go through it with you if we could."

"By all means, David."

"Is this a good . . ."

"Yeah, it's a good time. I'm alone in my office."

"Uh-huh. Maybe I can come up and talk to you about it."

Since Veliotis was taping the conversation, he tried to discourage this suggestion.

"Well, no, I can come and talk to you. You don't have to come and talk to me. But the situation is very simple: I don't know why the man will do things like he did and why not talk to me? I made it very clear to him the first time, if he goes and sees Rickover, and doesn't tell me before, doesn't tell me after, what am I supposed to do here?"

"Well, I agree with you," Lewis said. "Can I go back to the beginning?"

"Of course," Veliotis said, as he filled a glass with ice cubes and poured a can of Tab over them.

Lewis had a way of defusing a tense situation by talking it to death, starting at Genesis and going on for thirty minutes with so much history, context, and tangential material that by the time he was finished, it was difficult to remember the offending act. That was how he handled Boileau's meddling.

"Rickover had his standard group there," Lewis said in an almost sing-song tone to pour monotony over the event, "and they went into the same old crap about the radiation and all that and Boileau swears he didn't say a word. And Rickover said that what they were worried about was . . . that we were going to overrun the 688s, a $100 million overrun . . . and that we were building up another claims issue."

Lewis said that when he heard about it, he had written off the whole encounter—"without doing it consciously in any way to try to hide anything from you . . . [but] every new man that comes in here is going to get scrubbed up by Rickover."

Veliotis was not satisfied. He wanted to put Lewis over a barrel by threatening to go out the door right then.

Lewis protested: "I will absolutely guarantee you, Taki, Rickover will never have any influence over Boileau or me at all, other than as you and I discussed—that we've done some things to sweet-talk him and kiss his boots, which neither one of us wanted to do—but Boileau is not interested or capable or in any way qualified to participate in anything to do with the management of the marine division, nor does he want to. And you have my word for that."

Veliotis was still playing coy. He wanted a stronger commitment and he wanted it on tape.

"Well, I don't know, Dave, I don't know Boileau well, but from what I have seen, what I have heard about him, he will have a hell of a time to fill your shoes if ever he fills your shoes."

But Lewis would not take the bait and discuss his own succession.

The real problem, Veliotis said, was that the company had to stand united, to speak with one voice, and Boileau was creating the impression that there was a route around Veliotis.

"Well, no one in this place is gonna speak with a different voice than yours. I'm behind you one hundred percent. You will never get any undercutting from us, any of us. Now I really feel badly about this, Taki. You're extremely valuable to us."

"Dave, I feel bad because—ah—forget about it, because I like you, I told you I like you, whatever I did, I do it for you, I will go through a brick wall for you. I won't work for anybody else but you. Maybe I'm a peculiar person. You have treated me very well and have given me your confidence and you trust me."

"Well, everybody does, Taki."

"I don't care about everybody. I care about you. You are the one who has treated me properly, and now this fellow comes in and, you know. . . ."

"Well, that's a screw-up."

Veliotis waited during the long pause and then asked, "What do you want me to do?"

"Well, tear up the [letter] and make him [Boileau] prove himself . . . ride it out, but I don't think you'll ever have any concern about his integrity—maybe his brains or something—but never his integrity."

Veliotis had as strong a vote of confidence as Lewis was capable of giving and he had it on tape. He may have wanted more and he may have imagined that it was more than it was. But at a minimum, it encouraged him. In a showdown, Veliotis believed, Lewis would cut Boileau out of any role in the marine division to keep peace with Veliotis. He decided not to wait for the showdown. Boileau was scheduled to come to Electric Boat in mid-April. In the weeks before Boileau's arrival Veliotis was vigilant for the tiniest infraction. He discovered one in early April: a consultant Boileau hired to look into shipyard economics. Veliotis was not informed and he was on the telephone like lightning to Boileau: "If you come down here, you'd better find a way in, because I will tell the gate not to let you in. And you will have to get me out of here before you get in."

Boileau tried to apologize, but Veliotis would not let him.

"I'm trying to learn the job," Boileau protested, feeling the humiliation of a company president pleading with a subordinate—a mad Greek whom he had met barely a fortnight before and who seemed determined to engage him in a bloody duel for power.

"I don't know what you are supposed to do," Veliotis said indifferently, "nor do I care what you are supposed to do. I didn't hire you. I don't know what you are supposed to do. I don't care. Right now is not the time. You have done enough damage to me by going and talking to Washington. People now think somebody else speaks for the marine division, we don't have to talk to him. Now the navy is pulling all kinds of things. You were naive, that's all I can say. You walked in and started talking with the Rickover commission for three hours. You were naive. You were not prepared. And pretty soon, Rickover will be chasing you down in the bathroom, he will be working you over at midnight until such time as you tell him to get off your back. Please let me do my job and it won't be long. My tenure here is short. I will fuck off and then you can come and do anything you want. Please in the meantime let me do my job, or else, if you don't want to, let me go right now."

"All right, I guess there's nothing more to say," said Boileau, the resignation heavy in his voice.

General Dynamics failed to deliver a single ship from its Electric Boat division to the navy during 1980. The cost overruns built quickly, and before the year was out General Dynamics was facing another loss, but Veliotis and Lewis kept the lid on. Lewis used the same formula he had used during the 1970s when the overruns had mounted: he told the Arthur Andersen accountants that whatever overrun there might be would be offset by claims the company would file against the navy under the builders' risk insurance clause in the contracts.

For Veliotis, the Boileau episode temporarily had shaken his confidence in Lewis, but he emerged from the confrontation with his power over the marine division unchallenged. General Dynamics continued to speak with one voice to the navy, Veliotis's voice. By winning the skirmish with Boileau so convincingly, he had demonstrated to all other contenders in the corporation that titles were meaningless in the competition for Lewis's job. As czar over the marine operations of the company, which were the largest contributors to the sales and earnings of the corporation over the previous five years, Veliotis was first among equals in the line-up of division managers. And owing to his domineering personality, the size of his staff, and the budget resources he controlled, Veliotis eclipsed all other management figures in the corporate office save Lewis.

Banning Boileau from the shipyard quickly became part of the Veliotis mystique in General Dynamics and it crippled Boileau's effectiveness as president of the company. He tried, almost plaintively, to arrange for a trip to Groton and thereby signal an end to the embarrassment, but Veliotis—having taken the stand—quickly became vested in the notion that he could humiliate the most visible competitor for the chairmanship. When Boileau telephoned to try to schedule a later visit, Veliotis found some excuse to keep him away.

"Let me get those two ships out of here first, Ollie. I'm not trying, you know, I'm not trying to insult you, I'm trying, you know, to work with you. I don't think it will be good because, you know, I had some problems of backfire from all of those visits down in Washington. And, you know, I think the best thing for you is to stay out of here for some time. Let me get the 698 and 699 out and then you have all the time to come here."

"All right, fine," Boileau had said weakly. His continued lack of access to the most important division in the company was conspicuous in the corporate office and on the board of directors. Lewis made no effort to back Boileau's attempts to become president of the company more than in title, and that was a reflection of the same competitiveness that Lewis had shown with Paige. Because Lewis would not delegate the day-to-day running of the corporation, any president who served under him was on his own to find some useful function. As with Paige, Lewis ended up using Boileau as an extra division manager who could be plugged in where help was needed. Later, when General Dynamics purchased from Chrysler Corporation the M-1 tank program, which operated government-owned factories in Detroit and Ohio, Lewis sent Boileau out of the corporate office to run the new division. Lewis did not need a president.

Meanwhile, Veliotis constantly focused Lewis's attention on the notion that he was again thinking about retirement, an act that would leave Lewis in the desperate situation he was in before Veliotis agreed to take on Electric Boat in 1977. During all of their discussions, Lewis did not mention the chairmanship and he did not act like a man two years away from his own retirement. But he flattered and cajoled Veliotis about his importance to General Dynamics and about how Lewis had big plans for him. Lewis charmed Veliotis. At the end of one of their conversations that spring, Lewis suddenly added, "One last very important item."

"Sir?" Veliotis replied.

"That picture you sent down here for the annual report, I don't know whether you've looked at it . . . [but] it makes you look like the meanest man in the world. You need one that's got a smile on it."

"I will try to smile, Dave," Veliotis said, making the picture a metaphor of his troubled outlook on the future. It was Veliotis's way of reminding Lewis how hard he was working for Lewis, not for General Dynamics, but for Lewis.

Lewis was doing what he could. He elevated Veliotis to the title of executive vice president, nominated him to a seat on the board of directors at the annual meeting in May 1980, and started talking about the need for General Dynamics to build a truly international sales and marketing division to sell its line of weapons in Europe, the Far East, and to Third World countries. If Veliotis wanted to leave Electric Boat, Lewis said he was determined to create a province for him in the corporate office to keep him challenged. The idea was attractive to Veliotis. Also, it was clear by the middle of 1980 that the threat from the Frigitemp investigation had receded and, along with it, the prospect that Veliotis might have to make a swift exit from the corporation. The kickbacks appeared safely shielded by the confidentiality of Swiss banking laws.

To give Veliotis a taste of the future, Lewis made a corporate jet available and sent him on a business hunting expedition to London, Cairo, and Athens, where he helped lay the groundwork for F-16 sales in Greece and Egypt, and presented the Greek government with a "global proposal" to sell airplanes, telecommunications equipment, naval warships, and coal from the Crown mines.

Veliotis broadened his reach in the company by drumming up new business proposals to incorporate the new Tomahawk cruise missile into the 688 fleet and to build giant submarine tankers to carry natural gas under the North Pole. Veliotis was a good promoter and the idea of taking over the corporation's international operations appealed to him. He knew Canada, Europe, and the Middle East intimately. His French was elegant, and he stood out as a sophisticated businessman against the relatively bland backdrop of General Dynamics' executive staff. In Washington, he arrived at his appointments by limousine, and he logged more miles on the Grumman II corporate jet than anyone except Lewis. As a board member, he insisted that the corporate office arrange for a king-size bed when he attended board meetings, just like Henry Crown. Despite the troubles at Electric Boat, Veliotis had created the imagery that he was the leading contender to replace Lewis. He had joined the inner circle and devoted his full concentration to seizing the center stage at General Dynamics to perform before the most influential audience, the aged Crown and his son and heir, Lester.

With the inauguration of Ronald Reagan in January 1981, a new administration took office. The restoration of American military power was the most important item on the Reagan agenda: the imminent buildup was the hottest topic in the Washington defense establishment. And the navy was going to be at the center of it. Ships were the most expensive capital items of military procurement and so a bright young Navy Secretary, John F. Lehman, Jr., suddenly became the key architect on the Pentagon team presided over by Caspar W. Weinberger. The thirty-nine-year-old Lehman had trained in the disciplined national security bureaucracy of Henry Kissinger.

Shipbuilding was going to be the largest single component of the Reagan defense procurement budget, where one dollar in every four was needed to get the worldwide fleet back up to six hundred ships to protect American power in the more dangerous world seen through the eyes of Reagan, Weinberger, Alexander M. Haig, Jr., William J. Casey, Jeane Kirkpatrick, Edwin Meese III, and Richard V. Allen, the core of Reagan's national security advisers.

The uniformed navy had waited patiently for Edward Hidalgo to leave office. Then the blue-suiters, under new direction from Lehman, blind-sided General Dynamics in Congress within weeks after the inauguration. The new chief of navy shipbuilding, Vice Admiral Earl B. Fowler, Jr., went before the House Armed Services Subcommittee on Seapower and called what had happened at Electric Boat a "breakdown" of quality control on one of America's most sophisticated weapons systems.*

Lehman was briefed on the paralysis at Electric Boat; he soon realized that unless he could whip the shipbuilding industry into shape, the new administration would never achieve the buildup. Rickover had been at the front of the line to warn the new secretary about a fresh round of claims and how General Dynamics—particularly Veliotis—was conspiring to commit an act of fiscal piracy against the

*Veliotis asserts that Hidalgo and Fowler had struck an agreement with Electric Boat to award two 688-class construction contracts under favorable terms in return for Veliotis's pledge to file insurance claims only for poor workmanship that postdated the 1978 settlement, which Hidalgo was still defending as having "solved" the shipbuilding mess. This deal was rejected, Veliotis asserts, by the new Reagan appointees in the Pentagon. Hidalgo denies any deal-making with Veliotis. Fowler declined an interview request.

navy. Lehman was shocked to hear that Veliotis was weeks away from filing insurance claims against the navy for the poor workmanship at Electric Boat. If Lehman really wanted to help the navy, Rickover said, he'd stop any work from going to Electric Boat until the company foreswore filing such claims.

Fowler went before the seapower subcommittee on March 12 to lay out the indictment against Electric Boat's "breakdown." His white dress uniform was radiant beneath the television lights as he summarized how the inspectors had found the flaws in the submarines at Electric Boat and then started pulling all of the threads. In the wake of the discoveries, Fowler said, the navy had audited the records of eighteen thousand welds that had required magnetic particle inspection to ensure that they contained no impurities or cracks. They found that no records existed for eight thousand of the welds, he said. As a result, Electric Boat reinspected 6,900 of those that were accessible and found that 45 percent of them were defective and required repair work.

Hidalgo had told the committee the previous year that all of the problems at Electric Boat were being handled in a cordial atmosphere of open and constructive dialogue, but Fowler detailed the wrenching tug-of-war that the navy had waged to force Electric Boat to undertake a full-scale review of all the submarines to ensure their safety and structural integrity.

"In summary," Fowler told the chairman, "a review of the defects identified during the weld reinspection program indicated a serious breakdown in workmanship and quality control in structural welding. Not only were plan requirements not followed and jobs left incomplete, but deficiencies that affected all ships under construction were not detected by the quality-control procedures at Electric Boat."

The chairman of the committee, Rickover's longtime supporter, Representative Charles Bennett of Florida, said he was appalled by the litany Fowler had recited. "I must say, this is one of the most distressing hearings, if not the most distressing hearing, that I have experienced in more than thirty years I have been in Congress. . . ."

The reaction to Electric Boat's plan to charge the navy for its own defective workmanship was even stronger. Fowler said that navy lawyers had determined the government could win a court fight over any attempt to make the navy pay for poor workmanship under the builder's risk insurance clause in the contracts.

"The attitude of this member of the committee is that the navy won't pay the claim," declared Representative Charles F. Dougherty of Pennsylvania.

On March 17, Lehman dropped the other shoe. He canceled the

request for bids that had been sent to both Electric Boat and Newport News for the three *688* submarines in the 1980–81 budget. Lehman said the navy would negotiate on a sole source basis with Newport News.

The sudden decision outraged Veliotis, who was on his way to delivering more submarines in one year than anyone believed possible. The navy had accepted his new quality-control system and he was confident that the shipyard's problems had finally been put behind him. That's why Lehman's act was so hateful and why Veliotis believed all of the rumors that Lehman had diverted the new contracts to Newport News out of gratitude to Senator John Warner of Virginia, one of three powerful men who had told Ronald Reagan in no uncertain terms that young John Lehman was the only man for the Navy Secretary's job in the new administration.

In a formal letter to Lewis, Lehman justified the drastic action, saying, "The basis for this . . . is my fully considered determination that the award of these submarines to Newport News is necessary in the interests of national defense so as to have Newport News available as a supplier of SSN 688-class submarines at levels necessary in the case of national emergency."*

That was not the real reason. Lehman told David Lewis that he pulled the submarine bids from General Dynamics to get the company's attention and to send a signal to the shipbuilding industry that the new Reagan managers were not going to tolerate gamesmanship in contracting. They wanted performance. In return, they would make sure the shipyards got a good profit, but above all they needed performance to get to a six-hundred-ship navy. Lehman called Lewis to Washington to tell him pointedly and privately that General Dynamics would get no more ships from the navy while John Lehman was Navy Secretary if it filed insurance claims for poor workmanship. The policy decision had come down from Weinberger. Paying off poor workmanship was a Pandora's Box that the Reagan team was not about to open.

During the lunch hour on Tuesday, March 24, thousands of Electric Boat workers gathered at the gates of the shipyard to cheer Veliotis as he left for Washington to defend their honor.

It was like a high school pep rally as Veliotis, dressed for the

*Newport News in 1981 was still full of ships under construction and was in no danger of losing money or going under had it lost the new submarine contracts in competitive bidding. Lehman's use of his national security "exception" authority to steer these contracts to Newport News was a bureaucratic contrivance to punish General Dynamics.

halls of Congress in his most formal pinstripes, walked out of the administration building and through the crowd of workers who had formed a cheering corridor to the gate. Some wore T-shirts proclaiming that Electric Boat was the best sub builder in the world; others pressed forward to shake Veliotis's hand and told him to give the people in Washington hell. Veliotis stood proudly among them. He had terrorized them and fired more than four thousand of their number, but they cheered the struggle, or the struggle as he had defined it: to save the shipyard; to restore excellence; to protect freedom and democracy with the deadly submarines they constructed by their labor on the filthy New England waterfront.

The public relations department admitted reporters and photographers from the local newspapers to witness the send-off. The police cordoned off the road into the yard so the crowd of workers could escort Veliotis's limousine out of the gates and on his way to Groton Airport where the corporate jet was waiting to take him into battle.

Veliotis's testimony had been printed in a thirty-six-page glossy color booklet like an annual report and thousands of copies were printed for distribution to the press and to members of Congress and their staff.

The next morning at eleven o'clock, Veliotis settled at the witness table in the seapower subcommittee hearing room, which was brightly lit under the television lights. His half-frame reading glasses were perched on his nose, and the text of his testimony, printed in block letters, was before him. His deep accent filled the room:

I am P. Takis Veliotis, general manager of Electric Boat Division and executive vice president for marine operations of General Dynamics Corporation. In addition, I am on the General Dynamics board of directors. I am here today, on behalf of Electric Boat's twenty-five thousand men and women, to respond to the criticisms which have been made against us. I am proud of these men and women. I am proud of our product and our role in the nation's defense. We have had our problems. That cannot be denied, but we have faced them squarely and put them behind us.

Veliotis had insisted on putting the truth in his testimony about the history of bad management at Electric Boat. The lawyers had asked him to include a paragraph that blamed everything on the navy because the grand jury investigation still was under way; but beyond that paragraph, he stated for the record that

At the time of the management change in 1977, Electric Boat was a company with a number of serious problems resulting from its continuing efforts to meet SSN 688-class schedules which had clearly become unrealistic. . . . Since the primary cause of our problems was unrealistic scheduling and rapid manpower build up to attempt to meet such schedules . . . we devised and established new schedules and budgets which were achievable but, at the same time, called for significant and challenging performance improvements.

Veliotis then attacked Fowler's testimony about the use of defective steel. "Now let me tell you what Admiral Fowler did not tell you. On the *Ohio*, with full navy technical agreement, only forty-one pieces of steel weighing fifty pounds ended up being replaced. Fifty pounds. Do you know how much steel we bought for construction of the *Ohio*?—23,600,000 pounds. Fifty pounds out of 23,600,000 pounds. Now, I am not saying that we did not have a problem with non-conforming steel, but I am saying that we discovered it, we addressed it and we solved it."

Veliotis paused for effect and then looked to Bennett. "I have brought with me, Mr. Chairman, those pieces of steel so you can see them for yourselves and really see what the problem was." With that, Veliotis stood and dumped a box of steel parts onto the hearing-room table. Camera shutters fired like muted machine guns as more than a dozen newspaper and wire-service photographers jostled to record Veliotis's dramatic demonstration.

Seated again, Veliotis turned to the welding problem. The figures that had been used by Admiral Fowler with regard to the percentage of defective welds on the U.S.S *Bremerton* were incorrect, he said. "Let me tell you that the total number of welds which require magnetic particle inspection on an SSN 688-class submarine is approximately 74,100, not 17,792 as you were told."

While it was true that twenty-five hundred welds on *Bremerton* had to be repaired or replaced in the course of the reinspection program, Veliotis said, the replacement rate was not 45 percent as Fowler had claimed, but rather 3.4 percent.

To cover the high cost of the reinspection program, Veliotis said Electric Boat intended to file up to $100 million in insurance claims under the legal theory that builders' risk insurance protected the shipyard from the poor performance of its workers. Since the navy had set itself up as an insurance company, Veliotis said he had nowhere else to go to file his claim:

If you have collision insurance on your new car and you get involved in an accident, the insurance company will pay, regardless of whether or not the accident was your fault. Similarly, if you fall asleep while smoking in bed and as a result your house catches fire and burns down, your home owners insurance will pay, even though in this example it is obvious that you were at fault. . . . When the government chooses to go into the marine insurance business in order to save premium costs, that would not change the result either—nor should it. The fact that the government became underwriter should not deprive the insured of the coverage he would have had if the underwriter had been a commercial insurance company.

After Veliotis completed his prepared remarks, Representative Bennett said that he had given an effective and impressive response to the navy's testimony.

"Mr. Veliotis, now that we have heard your explanation of the situation at Electric Boat, what is your suggestion as to how the navy should proceed to get on with the 688 and the Trident?"

It was the kind of softball question that Bennett was famous for and Veliotis had been waiting for it.

Well, Mr. Chairman, I have asked myself this question several times. . . . I believe that the navy should immediately award two 688s to Newport News from the fiscal year 1980 and 1981 program rather than the three announced by the Secretary of the Navy last week. The navy should also immediately award the other two 688s to Electric Boat. . . . Mr. Chairman, I believe that you have seen that Electric Boat is not the shambles that you and apparently Secretary Lehman were led to believe it was. . . . Withholding awards now penalizes rather than helps us, regardless of the arguments used to explain the actions.

He noted that Electric Boat had been the low bidder for the three ships before Lehman pulled them back for noncompetitive award to Newport News. "From the standpoint of overall national interest, I must agree with Secretary Lehman that the United States should have two shipyards building 688s, both Electric Boat and Newport News. I cannot agree that preservation of the industrial base for submarine construction at Newport News should be accomplished by destroying an irreplaceable portion which already exists at Electric Boat."

None of the members of the committee made the extensive inquiry that Veliotis expected on the legal theory of the insurance claim. But Charles Dougherty, the Republican from Pennsylvania, reflected the skepticism of some of the members. "I have heard your testimony this morning, Mr. Veliotis, and I do not mean to be argumentative . . . [but] the most important part of the whole debate and discussion today is what is the navy going to pay in the future to settle up for the problems that existed in the past and how are those dollars going to impact on our overall defense budget. . . . You are now telling us today you are going to file for reimbursement requests for the welding problems which were related to worker mistakes."

"Let me tell you," Veliotis responded, "I am not asking the navy to pay me that in its capacity as my customer."

"No, you are not. I know you are not."

"The navy went into the builders' risk insurance business in competition with free enterprise."

"I understand that, Mr. Veliotis. I understand it completely. You made a very good point of it in your prepared testimony today. The navy as far as you are concerned is your insurance company and the navy should, therefore, pay up. Some of us do not buy it."

It was an impressive performance, and soon thereafter Veliotis went to the Pentagon to meet Lehman and to criticize his decision to punish Electric Boat. Lehman was flanked by the Chief of Naval Operations, Thomas B. Heyward, and the Chief of Naval Material, Albert Whittle. Veliotis explained that the navy's attack on Electric Boat might have been warranted a year earlier when the shipyard was in the midst of the welding crisis, but that was ancient history now. Lehman, however, took a hard line. He replied toughly that the decision to pull the three submarines bids from open competition and award them to Newport News was irreversible. He repeated the warning he had delivered to Lewis: If the company filed insurance claims to recover the costs of poor workmanship, Electric Boat would not get any more ships from the navy, period.

But Lehman also showed that he was willing to be conciliatory. He said he was setting up a committee of navy and Electric Boat officials to give him a detailed report as to whether the shipyard truly had put its quality-control problems behind it and whether it was capable of producing three 688s and a Trident every year. Lehman reminded Veliotis that Electric Boat had delivered no ships to the navy during 1980 and asked whether the shipyard could make up the lost ground.

For Lehman's information, Veliotis said, Electric Boat was going to deliver six 688s to the navy during 1981 as well as the first Trident. It was going to be the most impressive production feat in the shipyard's history.

Lehman turned to Admiral Whittle and asked, "Can he do it?"

"I don't think so," Whittle replied. "I don't believe he can."

Veliotis exploded, "How do you fucking know I cannot do it? How do you fucking know?" Veliotis was angry and frustrated, and no longer cared whether he insulted the top admirals in front of their civilian boss. If he was going to win, he was going to have to do two things: deliver those ships and make the customer pay, pay for everything. He believed the men in the secretary's office hated his guts, but it didn't matter to him. He had lost the three submarines and their profits, and he was facing a bitter fight over the insurance claims. These men were trying to corner Veliotis and he was determined to fight them—all out.

After his outburst in Washington, Veliotis felt he no longer should deal directly with senior navy officials. He would just lose his temper again, and that would only make matters worse. So he sent three of his senior managers on March 31 to meet with John Lehman. Veliotis told them to deliver a simple message to Lehman: If the navy was not going to give the shipyard any more business, Veliotis would slow down the production line to produce only two *688* submarines per year instead of the three required under the contract schedules. "We cannot destroy our industrial base. We cannot throw our people out in the street the way he wants us to do . . . I have to balance my trades, and I'm telling you, after we deliver the six ships this year, from there on, the only way for us to go on until 1985—because whatever they give me now will be for delivery after that—I have to go two per year. It's as simple as that."

"Okay, I'll take care of that, Taki," said William Gorvine, his negotiating team leader.

"I'm very upset with that fellow, the Secretary of the Navy," Veliotis added, as the team prepared to enter another round of talks with Lehman.

"Well, I don't blame you for that," said Gorvine. "But at this stage of the game, Taki, in effect, the damage has been done, as you point out, and they are not going to say, 'Look, we goofed, we knew it was fake, we screwed up.' "

"Why doesn't he tell his boss, you know, to stop changing the foot in his mouth?" Veliotis asked, referring to Weinberger's public criticism of the Trident program at Electric Boat.

"Well, that's a good question," Gorvine replied, trying to humor Veliotis but at the same time convey that he expected the most realistic outcome as one in which the navy, having punished Electric Boat by taking away contracts, would now return to doing business with the shipyard after a decent interval.

Veliotis said he didn't believe them. He told them to return to Lehman and catalogue the shipyard's complaints against the navy in a forceful way and to find out what Lehman was going to do for Electric Boat. "Where's the carrot?" Veliotis asked. "What do I get, one ship? At the moment when I was pushing the Secretary of the Navy, he said, 'I can accelerate the fiscal year 1982 ships and give you three at the same time.' Is he going to make that commitment? Is he going to give us three ships? I know they're under pressure. I know [Senator John] Chafee's calling him to award us the Trident ship. I know that [Senator Lowell] Weicker is after him."

He paused for a moment, then told them to return to Lehman with a more vigilant attitude. "You go ahead the way you are going, but keep in your mind, you know, that my asshole tells me that they are going to screw us again."

"You know as I have said to you before," Gorvine replied, "I regard that as a very valuable asshole in terms of . . . warning about things."

"I have a feeling they are setting us up," Veliotis said. "I have a feeling they want to change their strategic balance of weapons. I have a feeling they are going to come around and say, 'Veliotis tells us Electric Boat cannot build two Tridents a year so we're stuck with getting one Trident and we will have to go some other [strategic weapon].' This is what worries me very much. They say they will give you a seven-hundred-ship navy. I'm telling you, those fellows are not going to get a seven-hundred-ship navy. I don't believe them. They increase it from one day to the other, from six hundred to seven hundred ships. I mean, why not eight hundred? Those fellows there, they have thought it through very carefully. Weinberger is not that stupid."

"I must confess, I think he is that stupid, actually," Gorvine interjected.

"This is a ploy. My concern is that this is a ploy because they are not honorable men. You know, I'm an old person you can call a prostitute. My asshole has been so many times fucked, I don't feel it anymore."

"As far as what his game is," Gorvine replied, "I think I would have to say at this moment, Taki, that remains to be seen. If it's a sinister game, it is not obvious yet. And we're going to proceed."

"Have your eyes and your ears open and all of your senses and put your hand on your asshole, that's all the advice I can give you," Veliotis said, adding that he did not want to meet with senior navy officials who planned an inspection tour of the shipyard. "I don't want to be involved. That's why I kept out of this one because I would be taking them apart. . . . They would like to see me out of here and I would like to go right now."

James Ashton became a secret informer against Takis Veliotis in the following manner: Ashton was near the crest of his fourteen-year career at General Dynamics' Fort Worth plant, where the F-16 Falcons rolled out like clockwork every month. His title was assistant general manager in charge of production. Then one day in July 1980, Veliotis and his chief engineer, Spencer Reitz, showed up at the plant for a tour. Ashton's boss asked him to spend the day with the visitors, and that evening, Veliotis invited Ashton and his wife to dinner. Veliotis was a big man in General Dynamics and Ashton was flattered by the attention and readily accepted. During dinner, Veliotis invited him to come to Quincy the following month for the christening of one of the natural gas tankers.

Ashton traveled to Boston for the festivities and, on the morning of the launching, he was pleasantly surprised when David Lewis asked him to take a walk with him through the Quincy shipyard. Lewis was sixty-three and Ashton thirty-eight. They walked, just the two of them, and the older man's tone was avuncular. Ashton had strong aerospace training. If he was ambitious to go higher in the company, he should try to broaden his base. Veliotis was talking about retiring, Lewis said.

"I hope to talk Taki out of it," he added, but in the meantime, he needed to get a strong manager under him to learn all the skills that Veliotis had developed during his long and successful career as a great shipbuilder.

In his search for an apprentice and potential successor to Veliotis, Lewis had once again gravitated to the aerospace side of General Dynamics. There were probably two reasons for this. First, he believed that the aerospace industry was on the cutting edge of manufacturing technology, and that the shipbuilding side of the company could benefit from the highly evolved production-line systems that had been applied to aircraft and missile production. Second, Lewis would have preferred to groom a successor at Electric Boat whose loyalty was more closely tied to himself. The other candidates inside the company were all members of Veliotis's Quincy Eight team, where Veliotis ruled and David Lewis was the outsider from corporate headquarters.

After they finished their tour, Lewis guided Ashton into the large conference room. It was quiet. Even a whisper stood out.

Lewis smiled at Ashton and told him that if he made the right move and went to Electric Boat, where Veliotis had agreed to take him under his wing and train him, Ashton would be on a fast track to come to the corporate office someday and take on even greater challenges.

"You could someday be a chairman of the board," he said. Lewis did not promise the general manager's job, but he told Ashton he would be in the best position to get it if he accepted Lewis's advice. It was enough for Ashton. In October 1980 he left his wife behind in Texas where she was pursuing a doctoral program at the University of

Texas. They agreed that on alternating weekends she would make the trip from Austin to Connecticut and he from Groton to Austin.

Ashton arrived at the shipyard driving a pumpkin-colored Corvette Stingray. He had a bit of a swagger and projected the aura of a man who reported directly to Lewis and soon would be taking over from Veliotis. His title was assistant general manager for engineering, but he showed an interest in every department at the shipyard.

To his shock, the Veliotis who had been so charming in Fort Worth was not the same man Ashton found in Groton. Far from being taken under his wing, Ashton was shunned by Veliotis and ridiculed by some of the senior managers, such as Grimes, who saw themselves as Veliotis's successor. Veliotis gave Ashton a total of fifteen minutes of his time during the first three months, and by the end of 1980, made it clear that Ashton was persona non grata by totally ignoring him.

"Dave Lewis thinks that fellow is going to take my job," Veliotis said one day to a deputy. "But I know different."

Ashton just happened to be in the wrong place at the wrong time. He was Lewis's guy and for that reason alone Veliotis was going to assert his independence by ignoring him. Ashton came from an aerospace background and Veliotis scoffed at the aircraft engineers who thought they were superior managers in any technology. Lewis was not intellectually or emotionally equipped to understand waterfront production operations, Veliotis preached to his deputies. If and when Veliotis left Electric Boat, he planned to install someone from his own management team. That's what he had done at Quincy and that's what he intended to do at Electric Boat.

By early 1981, Ashton was convinced that Veliotis hated him and would never relinquish control over the shipyard. The vision David Lewis had planted in his mind of a meteoric rise in General Dynamics was melting away and the sick dread that he was trapped in a hostile environment settled over him. He believed he had to fight to change his circumstances, and the only leverage available was his intimate knowledge that Veliotis was covering up a massive cost overrun.

On the day Ashton decided to go to Electric Boat, Lewis had told him that everything was great in the shipyard; Veliotis had fixed the welding problems and was predicting he would underrun his 1978 estimate on the first eighteen submarines by $100 million.

But Ashton found a much different situation. He had dug into the cost reports coming out of the comptroller's office and had plotted the shipyard's performance: Veliotis was overrunning his budget on the ships by 250,000 man-hours per week and was losing three days off the schedule during every ten-day period. Ashton believed any twelve-year-old math student could have seen it. Electric Boat was headed for another overrun on the *688* program of between $170 and $200 million.

Ashton was convinced that Lewis did not know. He cast Veliotis in the role as villain and resolved secretly to undermine him. Going up against Veliotis was a dangerous thing to do, but Ashton believed that his only escape was by turning Veliotis in, going to the chairman and telling him everything he knew or suspected, and hoping that Lewis would reward his integrity and good citizenship. It was a conspiracy born of Ashton's naivete—and it was doomed from the beginning because of the partnership that existed between Lewis and Veliotis to keep the lid on at Electric Boat while they tried to shake down the navy for more money.

Oliver Boileau was nominally Veliotis's superior, so Ashton closed the door to his office one day in March 1981 and dialed Boileau in St. Louis. The stories about Veliotis banning Boileau from the shipyard had reached even Ashton's isolation. That made going to Boileau easier. Boileau was friendly. Ashton laid out his problems with Veliotis and told Boileau about the cost overruns in the shipyard. He added that he realized what he was doing was not going to be good for his career, but he had decided to lay out the whole story in a letter to Lewis. He wanted to force the issue since it appeared to him that nothing was happening and Veliotis was treating him like a pariah.

Boileau cautioned Ashton not to write the letter, knowing the allegations would then take the form of a document and documents could be dangerous, especially one created by someone outside the inner circle of top management. "Why don't you sit tight," Boileau advised him. A cost-estimating team from the corporate office was scheduled to visit the shipyard the following month to look at the Trident program. He would make sure the team met privately with Ashton to go over his overrun projections on the *688* program.

The audit team did not show up for weeks, and in the meantime Ashton also placed a private call to Gorden MacDonald and laid out the problem in the shipyard and his concern that Veliotis was covering up cost overruns. MacDonald instantly counseled Ashton to sit tight—don't do anything drastic and let the corporate office handle it. Ashton waited nervously for the team and thought about what he would do if Veliotis discovered his perfidious activities. He could only hope that Lewis would protect him. After all, Lewis had big plans for him.

The cost-estimating team finally met Ashton in April at the motel where he was living in temporary quarters. He was delighted to find an old colleague from Fort Worth heading up the group. Ashton made his presentation. The audit team took the comptroller's reports and noted the assumptions he had used about productivity in charting the overrun. The entire exchange was handled in secret as the group returned to St. Louis.

A month later, Ashton got word that everybody in the executive suite had been briefed on the numbers and Ashton glowed with anticipation. He was sure it would be just a matter of time before a grateful Lewis would be on the telephone.

During the July 1981 sea trials of U.S.S. *La Jolla*, Rickover fell right into the trap that Veliotis had laid for him—and the old man never really recovered.

The incident reports prepared for the Chief of Naval Operations and the Secretary of the Navy reconstructed the events of that night this way: *La Jolla* was the fourth of the six *688*s Veliotis pledged he would deliver to the navy in 1981, and her sea trials had been set for July 26–27. Rickover flew up from Washington on Saturday evening for the Sunday morning departure. It was one of those surreal routines that kept on going in the midst of the war of words and the war of wills. Rickover would give a speech, somewhere attacking Veliotis and Electric Boat, then by the end of the week he would be sharing quarters with a couple of dozen E.B. engineers on a nuclear submarine.

With one or two exceptions, every nuclear ship in the navy had gone on trials on a Sunday because that was the day Rickover took *Nautilus* to sea in 1954. The official reason was that Rickover did not lose any work time by going to sea on Sunday, but unofficially a lot of people thought Rickover was superstitious. Everyone had mustered at Building 118 on the South Yard waterfront and those who needed them picked up their seasick pills.

There was wind on the Atlantic and a few whitecaps measuring about a Sea State Three, which meant there was enough broad-band ambient noise in the ocean so *La Jolla* could conduct most of her maneuvers without fear of detection and eavesdropping by the Soviet intelligence trawlers that patrolled the North Atlantic to monitor the trials of U.S. warships. The trawlers recorded propeller noises where they could and scooped up satellite and radio communications for analysis. For months the Soviets had been more active than usual in the North Atlantic because U.S.S. *Ohio*, the first Trident submarine, had gone out for trials. The Russians were intensely interested in recording and studying the propeller noises of Trident, whose advance billing was that she would be so quiet as to be virtually undetectable.

La Jolla's crew first checked the SINS (Ship Inertial Navigation System), which operated redundant sets of delicate gyroscopes and accelerometers to measure the movement of the submarine over the earth's surface. American attack submarines were capable of going out for sixty days without surfacing and always plotting their position from their point of departure. SINS was accurate to within a hundred feet or so anywhere in the world. And if there was ever any doubt about the ship's position, the captain could poke a single antenna through the waves from periscope depth and double-check the precise longitude and latitude from the naval navigation satellites sitting in high stationary orbits above every ocean.

The crew worked through a lengthy checklist while they were running on the surface for the first few hours: they checked the high-frequency radio, then they ran an uplink-downlink test of the SIXS (Satellite Information Exchange System) equipment that bounced *La Jolla*'s test message off a satellite transponder in space, down to COM-SUBLANT in Norfolk, Virginia, and back—all in less than a second at the speed of light. Technicians tested the electronic countermeasures equipment that could send false signals through the hull and into the water to confuse Soviet sonar equipment.

The crew operated the 6,000-gallon-per-day water distillation plant and its back-up, a 10,000-gallon-per-day plant. All of the on-board life-support systems were monitored, oxygen generators and filters. In the engine room, technicians inspected the teeth of the huge "bull" reduction gear to see if they meshed properly with the teeth of the high-speed pinion gears from the turbine shaft. The resonance changer, which killed the vibration the propeller shaft conveyed to the hull, had to be "groomed" to make sure its layer of oil was flowing properly at the thrust bearing.

It took about three hours for the crewmen to work through the checklist before the captain gave the order for the submerged run and the crew rigged the ship for a dive. The ballast tank vents were opened and the captain ordered a down angle on the diving planes until they reached periscope depth and then *La Jolla* set a level trim. The crew tested the ship's three-inch launch tubes by firing test probes from them. Submarines had been equipped with three-inch launch tubes since World War II. They were first used to send up colored dyes as a coded message to friendly vessels that there was a friendly sub below. But as technology evolved, the three-inch launchers gave the sub drivers a whole range of electronic capabilities, from sending out noise-making decoys to checking the salinity and temperature of the ocean current. From a depth of six hundred feet, a skipper could float a probe on a wire all the way to the surface and get a precise picture of his environment so he could find the best layer in which to hide from enemy sonars. Change in salinity or temperature could block or deform a sonar beam just like a wall.

During the initial dive, the crew checked thoroughly for leaks around the propeller shaft seals before taking the ship any deeper. Sometime after midnight, Captain James R. Lang gave the order to the senior reactor engineer to bring the S6G plant to one-half power. An engine-room technician opened the main steam valves to the turbines, and the reactor went supercritical to keep up with the demand for more steam. *La Jolla* ran at half power for sixty minutes. At the end of the half-power run, Lang ordered full stop so the engineers could inspect the "bull" gear again. The tests continued, and in the early morning hours of July 27, *La Jolla* conducted her full-power surface run on the starlit Atlantic.

One hundred miles off Long Island, the ship rendezvoused with her sub tender to check the communications equipment again before preparing for a series of deeper dives and high-speed submerged runs. Shortly after 2:30 a.m., *La Jolla* dove to 360 feet and Lang rang up flank speed on the annunciator. The S6G surged to supercriticality and the G.E. turbines whined on their rubber-encased deck until they reached six thousand rpm. Like those of her sister ships, *La Jolla*'s sleek hull had cut blindly through the black ocean at just over thirty knots.

Rickover was out of the captain's quarters before 6:30 a.m. They were coming up on his part of trials, where he put the entire ship under maximum stress. He made his way aft, through the shielded tunnel that traversed the reactor compartment and into the engine room to what was called the "maneuvering" area.

At 6:41 a.m., *La Jolla* had been running at full power for four hours.

At 6:43 a.m., Rickover gave the "crashback" order. The helmsman threw the submarine into high-speed reverse to bring *La Jolla* from full forward speed to a quick stop. It was like stomping on the brakes of a 7,000-ton truck in the middle of a freeway. Every piece of equipment in the engine room went to full stress as the turbines and gears reversed direction and strained against the forward momentum of the ship. The chief Electric Boat engineer, Pete Hill, was taking detailed notes of the submarine's performance as Veliotis had instructed him to do. He noted that under the pull of full reverse thrust, *La Jolla* slowed quickly.

Rickover was in charge of giving the order for "all ahead" after the ship came to a full stop. If he was even seconds late in giving the order, the full reverse thrust of the propeller would instantly drag the submarine into reverse speed. Submarines were not designed to go backwards. Sternway, as it was called, was dangerous because the stern of the ship was where all of the weight was packed, and a little down angle could quickly drag the submarine too deep too fast.

"Ship dead in the water" was reported over the public address system from the executive officer in the control room. But there was no "all ahead" order from Rickover. *La Jolla* quickly developed five knots of reverse speed and the depth of the ship slipped sixteen feet. "All ahead" was heard over the speakers, but the order had not come from maneuvering. Someone had usurped Rickover's authority. Rickover bellowed from his station in the maneuvering area to conduct the test again. Goddammit, he was going to give the order.

The whine from the turbines built slowly. *La Jolla* went to flank speed again, cutting through the ocean at nearly forty miles per hour.

After a few minutes of high-speed running, Rickover gave the crashback order a second time and the submarine lurched into the braking position. When speed had decreased to three knots, the navigation center announced "Ship dead in the water" over the ship's public address system.

But Rickover waited. And waited. His silence dared anyone to give the "all ahead" order before he was ready. Seconds passed and the crew members who knew what was going on were perspiring. *La Jolla* continued full reverse thrust for one hundred eighty seconds. The reverse speed indicator climbed over ten knots, then past eleven knots to nearly twelve knots. The angle of the ship was noticeable. They were going down at the stern, going down fast. The newcomers aboard flinched visibly as the hull popped loudly. It was the pressure loading across the steel skin. The Atlantic tightened its grip as they slid deeper and deeper. Finally Rickover ordered forward speed, but the whiplash action of the change in water flow over the diving planes threw the nose of the submarine into a diving angle. Within seconds, *La Jolla* was plummeting again through the Atlantic in a bow dive that was forty degrees below the horizontal. Loose gear and equipment crashed and clanked to the deck throughout the ship, the noise tearing at raw nerves and adding to the feeling of panic. Crewmen lost their footing. Some yelped with pain as elbows, shins, and knees slammed into metal to break their fall. Even Rickover was surprised and reached for hand holds to keep from losing his dignity on the deck of the engine room.

In the five or six minutes that she was out of control, first sliding down by the stern and then in the hard dive by the bow, *La Jolla* had fallen another 240 feet to a depth of 600 feet. They had nearly dived into the sandy bottom and that might have been the end for all of them.

She had only made one dive to six hundred feet, the day before, under extremely controlled conditions. You didn't mess around at six hundred feet because you were within a ship's length of your limit and any failure of the diving planes or the ballast system could send the ship quickly to her death. It was dangerous to run at more than half-speed at such a depth because there would be no time to recover from a sudden accidental dive. It was just a fact of life in the *688* fleet.

La Jolla was one submarine length away from the lower limit of her operating depth. In a few more seconds the ship would have been up against her crush depth, and that would have been it—another *Thresher*, but this time by Rickover's hand and with Rickover aboard.

He had been wrong to do what he did, and everybody knew it, but they treated it delicately because it was Rickover and because he was eighty-one. That was the point. What the hell was he doing putting nuclear attack submarines through full stress maneuvers at that age. Was his memory going? Had he forgotten to give the "all ahead" order? Had he forgotten that a *688* could not dive to thirteen hundred feet as the *637* class could? It was more likely that he was being bull-headed, that he was only thinking about asserting his authority and not about how quickly the loss of control could throw the ship to a depth where the ocean would find a chink in the pressure hull and bore through it with a cutting power that could split a man in two and part steel like butter.

At the end of the trials, the Electric Boat engineers assembled in Veliotis's office to give him a detailed report. Memoranda and letters were drafted. The lawyers looked them over, then Veliotis got on the telephone to Lewis. Together, they edited the final draft of the letter Veliotis would send to the Chief of Naval Operations. The letter made no reference to Rickover by name. Lewis wanted it that way, and to prove it, Veliotis played a tape recording of his telephone conversation with Lewis to Bim Holt, the director of operations, and to the other senior managers working on the Rickover project. Lewis wanted the navy to discover the details about Rickover from the attachments to the letter, the blow-by-blow accounts that would raise the hair on the back of their necks.

Veliotis had evidence from an earlier sea trial of an instance in which Rickover had allowed the ship to develop nine knots of reverse speed, without losing control of the ship. Those memos also were in-

cluded in the report, along with the assurances senior navy officials
had given six months earlier that they would not allow it to happen
again.

The whole indictment was delivered to Admiral Thomas B.
Heyward on July 31. "I wish to bring to your attention a matter of
utmost concern to us at Electric Boat," Veliotis opened. Then he recounted both incidents in disastrous detail to the CNO, evoking the
emotional trauma that had tormented the navy for a decade after the
loss of *Thresher*. He concluded:

While the operation and control of a nuclear-powered submarine undergoing
sea trials are clearly in the hands of the navy, the ship has not yet been
delivered to, and accepted by, the navy. Consequently, I still feel a deep personal responsibility for the safety of the ship and the personnel aboard, many
of whom are Electric Boat employees. I also feel personally responsible for
safeguarding the reputation of this company in the marine area. In order to
fulfill these responsibilities, I request that you advise me, prior to the . . . trials
for SSN 702 . . . what specific actions the navy is taking to preclude recurrence
of the kind of incident that took place on SSN 701.

The letter had the desired effect. In public, uniformed navy
officials vigorously defended Rickover, saying there had been no danger to the ship and crew from the routine maneuver. Navy officials
discounted Electric Boat's complaint. Veliotis's motives were questioned because of the blood feud between him and Rickover.

But privately, senior navy officials issued discreet instructions
that the skippers of submarines on sea trials in the future must ensure
that the crashback maneuver not result in reverse speed, even if it
meant countermanding Rickover. Even Rickover's most loyal staff
members in the Naval Reactors Branch were concerned that he was
vulnerable because of his age. His reappointment was up again in the
fall and his enemies would surely cite the episode and argue that it
was in the national interest to retire Rickover before he did something
that would tarnish the legend.

Veliotis had landed a very effective blow. He had struck at
Rickover's fitness to stay on the job, giving Lehman or Weinberger the
kind of ammunition they could use if they wanted to throw Rickover
over the side.

And it wasn't long before they decided that they did.

In open defiance of the navy, General Dynamics during June
1981 filed the first installment of its insurance claims against the navy.

The company demanded $19.8 million for the cost of repairing the defective welds and steel on U.S.S. *Bremerton,* and announced that future claims would be filed as additional ships were delivered.

The filing of the claim amounted to a declaration of war. John Lehman summoned Lewis to the Pentagon on June 29 and said the navy would sue General Dynamics for breach of contract and for the loss of ships' service to the fleet while they were tied up during 1980. Lehman warned that the navy would not award any *688*s or Tridents to the shipyard if the company persisted in the insurance claims. Encouraged by Rickover, Lehman began to talk publicly about finding another builder—even offshore—for Trident submarines. To this, Veliotis replied mockingly that the only offshore shipyards capable of building the Trident were in the Soviet Union, and with the Russians as his builder, the Secretary of Defense would get no guarantees on price or delivery.

The confrontation became more public as the summer wore on. Veliotis told reporters on July 18 that it was "idiotic" for the navy to carry on a vendetta against Electric Boat. "They are not destroying us, they are destroying the defense of the nation."

Edward Hidalgo, out of office, but unofficially playing adviser to General Dynamics, told a Democratic congressional group in Connecticut that it was "devastatingly stupid" of Lehman to have yanked the three *688*s away from Electric Boat. Hidalgo noted that in doing so, Lehman had lost all bargaining leverage over Newport News in awarding the submarines on a sole source basis and, therefore, the navy was going to get stuck with higher-priced ships.

Lehman did not acknowledge his predecessor's criticism. The navy soon announced that it had concluded price negotiations with Newport News for the three submarines. The price figures were not included in the press release, but a comparison of the final figures showed that the navy had allowed Newport News to substantially improve the terms of the contract.*

The contract with Newport News was designed dramatically to

---

*Under the direction of Lehman's Assistant Secretary for Shipbuilding, a former shipping industry executive, George A. Sawyer, the submarine contracts were restructured to set a higher ceiling price and a "share line" of fifty-fifty instead of the decade-old seventy-thirty split under which the government picked up 70 percent of cost growth between the target and ceiling prices. The critical gain for Newport News from the new fifty-fifty arrangement stemmed from the fact that Newport News had been building *688* submarines for ten years, and the navy's acceptance of a higher base price ensured that Newport News could underrun the contract and split the underrun with the navy on a fifty-fifty basis. By allowing higher contract prices, Lehman created artificial underruns in which the shipyards took a greater share of the reward than ever before. General Dynamics officials monitoring the Newport News negotiations calculated that Newport News improved its profit margin on each ship from 14 to 18 percent, an increase of 30 percent.

increase the shipbuilder's profits as an incentive to step up production. It was a policy that was denied publicly by Lehman—a policy to
purchase a six-hundred-ship navy by throwing money at the shipyards. The contract changes were sold to Congress as cost-saving de-
vices, but in fact, they were profit-generating machines for the defense
contractors.

The Newport News contract negotiation was the crystallization
of Lehman's shipbuilding strategy. After a very few months in office,
the young Navy Secretary and his advisers realized they would never
achieve the military buildup they sought—never see a six-hundred-
ship navy—if they locked themselves into a confrontational and disruptive duel with their key industrial shipyards. Having drawn the line
with General Dynamics over the insurance claims, Lehman and his
chief shipbuilding deputy worked assiduously in private to find a way
to buy their way out of the battle while maintaining a tough and
uncompromising posture in public.

On August 14, Lewis and the board of directors released General Dynamics' earnings statement for the second quarter of 1981
without mentioning the overrun of nearly $200 million at Electric
Boat. The pressure was mounting to resolve the dispute with the navy
by the end of the calendar year, when the Arthur Andersen accountants would have to be told about the loss and how the company intended either to offset it with other revenues, or to charge it painfully
against earnings. For Lewis, it was the same pressure that had motivated him in the fall of 1977 to threaten a shutdown unless the navy
got busy with a bailout proposal that would save General Dynamics
from red ink at year's end.

During those fretful weeks, Lewis arranged to see presidential
counselor Edwin Meese III at the White House. He hoped that by
cultivating a visible friendship at the top of the Reagan administration, Lehman and Weinberger would feel the pressure to settle the
insurance claim in a way that let Lewis and General Dynamics escape
another financial embarrassment in the submarine program. Meese
was friendly and listened carefully as Lewis summarized the company's frustration in dealing with the new Navy Secretary. Lewis also
complained that Weinberger would not meet with him—an official
and embarrassing snub that persisted throughout the Reagan administration. The meeting with Meese lasted only fifteen minutes, but
Meese accepted the company's one-page briefing paper and said he
would look into the problem for them. That was all Lewis wanted

because he knew his visit would result in telephone calls from Meese's office to Weinberger and to Lehman. John Lehman was a young man, and not as secure in his job as the Californians who came east with Reagan to join the new administration. A call from the President's closest adviser, even if just a few questions were asked, could have a big impact on the navy secretariat, in Lewis's view.

Lewis also sought out Clark Clifford, the former Defense Secretary, whose counsel had been so valuable during the company's confrontation with the Carter administration. Clifford did not like the insurance claim any more than Lewis did, and he counseled Lewis that General Dynamics would wreck its long-term relationship with the Pentagon if it tried to recover from the government for poor workmanship. That was a box that had Pandora's name on it. There was only one thing to do: try to bluff the Secretary of the Navy. Make him think General Dynamics would press the claim. See what he would give up, then drop the claim as quickly as possible before the Reagan administration decided it had to make an example out of General Dynamics and drag the company into an ugly confrontation in court.

Lewis played the bluff on August 25 in a meeting prearranged to follow the inquiries from the White House. It lasted for more than an hour, and as soon as Lewis and his Washington lobbyist left Lehman's office, they got on the speakerphone in Crystal City and gave an accounting to Veliotis.

"Ted and I are here on the speaker, muddied but unbowed," Lewis said.

"I beg your pardon?" Veliotis said, not understanding Lewis's attempt at humor.

"*Muddied but unbowed!*" Lewis repeated exuberantly, and loudly enough to vibrate the speakerphone, but Veliotis could not understand the antebellum colloquialism.

"Yes?" he said in a deadpan voice.

Just before the meeting at the Pentagon, Lewis said, Ted LeFevre (the company lobbyist) had met with Hidalgo to seek his advice on how to handle the new secretary. "Hidalgo told me," Lewis related, 'Don't make any deals with this man.' "

They had arrived at Lehman's outer office at ten o'clock sharp. "I was very cool, cold, you might say, just shook hands in a very cold manner, and [Lehman] said, 'I asked you to come here because we want to talk about the progress in the yard and the manning on the ships and then I want to talk a little bit about the insurance problem."

Lewis said he bluntly replied to the secretary's opening: "Goddammit, did you get us down here to talk about that? It would be a hell of a lot easier to talk about progress in the yard if one or the other of you knew what the hell you were talking about. This meeting could far more constructively take place up at Groton or Quonset Point."

Lehman replied bluntly that he had to be satisfied about the progress in the shipyard before he could do anything.

Lewis said he fired back, "Yes, I read that in your speech," referring to Lehman's remarks a week earlier at the National Press Club where he had blasted General Dynamics' insurance claim as "preposterous." Lewis gave Lehman his blunt assessment of the speech. "I just want you to know at the outset here that I consider that an absolutely insulting and degrading speech, insulting to our company and to our people."

"Well, I had to get across how seriously we felt about the issue," Lehman had responded.

"You've told me that before. You don't need to go to the goddamned press and say those terrible things about us. Our company's been working with the navy for more than fifty years and trying hard to maintain a position of ethical conduct. You're inferring something that isn't true, that we'll go for any excuse to turn the lawyers loose to get money. I've personally been working with the navy for forty years, longer than you've been on this earth. And I think generally my reputation is reasonably good. And your suggestions I don't like at all."

Lewis paused and told Veliotis, "God, he was kind of ashen at this point. Could hardly say anything." Lewis turned to LeFevre for affirmation. "Wouldn't you say that?"

"Right," chimed LeFevre. "He started laughing and Dave just [verbally] slapped him in the face and said this is no laughing matter."

Veliotis listened without commenting. It sounded to him like Lewis was slurring his words and might have fortified himself with a stiff drink before placing the call. Lewis was no longer at ease with Veliotis. When he telephoned, he usually had someone else on the line just so there would be no intimate conversation, the kind that made Lewis uncomfortable. The reason was that settling the claims dispute put Lewis in the middle between Veliotis and the navy. They still were on the same team, united against Rickover and allied to keep the lid on at Electric Boat; but the alliance was becoming increasingly uneasy. The navy—goaded by Rickover—was out for Veliotis's blood and Lewis was on a tightrope.

Lewis was still talking. Lehman, he said, had defended his speech at the Press Club by saying it was important for the navy to state publicly what its policy was with regard to the insurance claims.

Lewis continued, "And I said, 'Listen, I want you to know something right now. We have merit in this case.' And Hidalgo told me to say this:", Lewis added as an aside, "the previous secretary had a study made of the validity, legal validity of our claim. And I know that record is in the file, and if you don't believe it, you'd better dig it out."

At that point, Lehman "started snickering again," but Lewis cut him off. "I am not kidding. I know that's there, and it doesn't say that our case is ironclad, it doesn't say the navy's case is zero, but it says that there is merit and substance to this [claim]."

The description of what Hidalgo had leaked to General Dynamics drew a rise from the new Navy Secretary. Lewis quoted Lehman as saying, "What I'm trying to tell you is that we cannot afford to let this thing be tested. We have a policy that comes right down from the Secretary of Defense that we cannot afford to let this thing go forward." Lewis understood what he was saying. It was the same thing Clifford had said about opening Pandora's Box to contractors who did sloppy work.

" 'So you're blackmailing us.' I used just that word," Lewis said.

"Very good," Veliotis interjected over the speakerphone.

"And he said, 'It isn't blackmail,' and I said, 'What the hell is it?' He said, 'I never used the word "blackmail" in that speech,' and I said, 'No, but you told me personally that we would not get any more business until we withdrew that claim. Now,' I said, 'what do you want me to do now, since you have offered us nothing?' I said, '[The claim is] a real asset for us, which we don't want to push the navy in a hole on, but it's worth something and it's worth something for you to get rid of it and not have it tested.' I said, 'All I've been offered is the opportunity to come in here and withdraw this [claim] and I can see it now, coming in this office and groveling on the floor with a picture of you standing there with your hand raised on high saying that you brought us to our knees.' And he said, 'Oh no, God no,' something like that."

Lewis related that he had pointed out to Lehman how generous Lehman had been to Newport News. "I said, 'Hell, you've given those guys eighteen percent earnings . . . ,' I said, 'Hell, that's terrible,' " but Lewis had just as quickly added, " 'And if you want to do that with us, that's fine, too.' "

"Well, we argued and bitched and hollered a while." Lewis's Southern drawl was becoming a little deeper with the slur. "I said, 'Hell, you haven't offered us one damn thing.' Well, he cut in, 'I want you to know, very earnestly . . . we're running out of money and there's a great deal of pressure [on the defense budget]. The Sea Command knows I don't want to go to Mare Island [and reopen the shipbuilding facilities there]. Secretary Weinberger doesn't want to go to Mare Island. I don't want to do it. It will cost us money and take time, but we have to view this as a viable opportunity, a viable option.' "

" 'That's just more blackmail,' " Lewis related, " 'You know goddamned well that to do that is going to cost you a hell of a lot of money. You'll get ships later, it will cost you more. And then outfitting that yard, there's another example of what settling this issue is worth to you. Right there, just in dollars and cents.' "

Lewis said the first part of the discussion went on for a little more than an hour. He said he had blistered Lehman more than he had intended to.

"Taki, I'll tell you, we're in a hell of a goddamned"—Lewis paused, then resumed—"we just somehow got to inch together."

"I agree, Dave, yeah, we have to get together, you know, but if getting together is to tell them that from now on we are not going to claim for the bad workmanship . . . well, we can do that," Veliotis said in a tone which showed his disapproval.

"What . . . they're driving for is to eliminate the specter of any insurance [claims]," Lewis explained.

"Yes, Dave, and they found a way with Newport News where you say they increased their profit to eighteen percent—but he [Lehman] doesn't give us anything at all. He wants us to give up the . . . insurance provision we have right now for nothing. Why doesn't he increase our profits? I don't think he is reasonable at all."

"Well, Taki, we've got to find a way out. I just can't fight this thing being in a nutcracker here."

Veliotis started to speak, but Lewis regained his composure and continued. He said Lehman left the room for a while and the discussion had continued with Lehman's assistant secretary, George Sawyer. "And I said, 'Look you've got other ships coming along here.' I said, 'On the first of October, you have either three 688s or four available to give somebody.' I said, 'You've got a hell of a contract with Newport News. The terms are reasonable. We like the terms. We're willing to step up to one hundred thirty percent, and as long as we get earnings that go with the high risk of a fifty-fifty [share line].' Then," Lewis continued, "I said, 'Well, why in the hell don't you come in and make a proposal to us?'

"And [Sawyer] said, 'Well, those opportunities are there,' and I said, 'Well, you're going to have to come up with something.' And I guess we talked about four or five minutes more, and then Lehman came back. He said, 'Look, we don't need a settlement where anybody loses. We've got to have a settlement where you give up something and we give up something, and if we have a picture, it's got to be of people shaking hands and nobody groveling and tearing up paper.' "

As an aside to Veliotis, Lewis pointed out, "Now this was an hour after I'd made that statement about groveling. So I said [to Lehman], 'Now you're saying what we've been saying. This thing is valuable as a pain in the ass to you, and you ought to be willing to give up something to get rid of it. And just telling us that you'll send us the request for proposal for the ninth Trident is not enough.' And so he said, 'Let's keep working,' and I said, 'Well, I hope from now on your communications are with me or with our people and not with the press.' He just kind of grinned and didn't promise anything."

LeFevre interrupted to add, "One thing he did say, that it's going to be up to Sawyer to decide whether or not you guys are ready to accept more work, and that means whether or not Sawyer is convinced that the manning in the out years is enough to keep the schedule that you're working toward. So he left it pretty much in Sawyer's hands, and Sawyer said, 'Well, I've got to go up to visit Mr. Veliotis, spend some time up there.' And right at the moment, Sawyer seems to have the action, Taki," LeFevre concluded.

Lewis picked it up from there. "I said, 'That's a constructive move. Go up there and go through the whole program and you'll have a feel. And I think if you spend some time up there, you'll make up your own mind.' And so we've got [to do] a hell of a convincing job on how well we're doing," continued Lewis.

Then he added, "Sawyer wants to settle, I'll guarantee that, and I'll come back to what happened later."

Lewis had disclosed to Veliotis all of the key portions of the conversation with Lehman—except one. Lehman had reminded Lewis that he and Weinberger were planning to recommend Rickover's forced retirement when his commission came up for presidential extension in January 1982. Lewis was well aware of the many previous unsuccessful attempts to retire Rickover, so he avoided either endorsing or opposing the suggestion. He merely replied, "Oh, that's interesting."

Now Lehman had raised the issue again. "We're going to try to do this, and we think we can get the President to go along, and we want you at the same time to bring oil to the waters and agree to get Veliotis out of the shipyard." Lehman said the feud between Veliotis and Rickover had poisoned the entire relationship between Electric Boat and the navy. The chaos and flame throwing between them had filtered down to lower levels, Lehman said, but his characterization was incomplete.

The feud between Rickover and Veliotis was indeed bitter, and the La Jolla incident had shown that Veliotis was capable of drawing blood. But, in fact, the welding crisis and the quality-control problems at Electric Boat were both well in hand, and a settlement of the insurance dispute would have removed the only major irritant remaining in the relationship. The submarine production line at Electric Boat was becoming the well-oiled machine that Veliotis had promised and he had gotten the costs under control.

But Lehman was shrewd enough to know that if he wanted support in the uniformed navy and in the Congress for easing Rickover finally into retirement, the appearance of a trade for Rickover's chief adversary would make the transaction much more politically palatable.

This "trade," as it came to be known, was never more than a charade for the navy and for General Dynamics. Undisclosed to Lehman was the fact that Lewis and Veliotis already had agreed that Veliotis would leave the shipyard after the Trident was launched at the end of the year to take on additional corporate responsibilities, overseeing both the marine and international operations of General Dynamics. Still, Lewis preferred to lead Lehman to believe that Veliotis was a bargaining chip if that would help dislodge Rickover, and he didn't want to do anything to discourage such an attempt. Without saying anything explicit, Lewis conveyed to Lehman during their Pentagon meeting on August 25 that a trade would be acceptable. Knowing Veliotis's certain outrage at being thrown onto the bargaining table to help win a settlement, Lewis mentioned nothing about the discussion.

"So anyway," Lewis continued on the speakerphone, "we went out of the office and . . . by the time we got down to the parking lot, we were in the car and Sawyer runs out and asks for a ride over to Crystal City here. And he said, 'Look, we've got to find a solution. This is just between us, and we've got to figure out a way to sit down here and negotiate some contracts, give you some stuff that maybe we can do to find a solution.' And I said, 'Fine. That's what we're asking you to do.' I said, 'We're not giving this stuff up and I hope you understand it, without something in return.' And he said, 'Okay, I'm going to go to work. I can write you a contract for the 688 with options [for three more 688s] right now, priced options . . . with terms like those we've got with Newport News.' And he said, 'I can give you the ninth Trident without priced options for the tenth and eleventh.' And I said, 'What about the price, you're talking about terms. That goddamned Sea Command will drag out our option price of last March and we couldn't start there, we're not interested.' "

"And he said, 'No, you've got to trust me. I will see that that does not happen. I want to have terms that get you out of this problem.' "

"That's a quote," Lewis added for emphasis, and continued, "I said, 'We're open-minded, we'll sit down and talk orders any time.'

"So this is the first time now," Lewis told Veliotis, "they're coming around to what we were talking about yesterday. And as you said, I'm going to stay out of it and let Ted [LeFevre] handle it."

"I think you should stay out of it," Veliotis replied, "the same way Lehman stays out of it."

"But anyway, that's what we accomplished. We left and we didn't show, as far as I can tell, any yellow feathers. Only thing I told him was that I know the best interests of everybody is to settle it, but we're not going to throw it in. Do you think that's a fair summary, Ted?"

"Yeah, I think that's pretty good. I'll tell you, they're looking for a way here, Taki, no question about it."

"They got mad with us," Lewis added as an afterthought, "because we went to see Meese . . . and I said, 'You bet your ass we went around to see Meese. We were not getting any satisfaction from you. We had to go up there.' So we didn't back down one iota, and neither did they, but it's obvious to me that somebody told them to settle," Lewis concluded, implying that his trip to the White House had paid off.

"That's good," Veliotis said. "Well, if they give us what they will give us—the four ships and the Trident—who are we to say no, Dave?"

Jim Ashton believed that he could not wait for Lewis any longer. In mid-August he began trying to get a telephone call through to the chairman of the board. It took several days. Ashton told Flo Stark, Lewis's secretary, that it was really important. Stark told Lewis that the young executive sounded upset. On the evening of August 18, Ashton was sitting in the bedroom of the Madison, Connecticut, home he had moved into after living for months in a hotel. When the telephone rang, Ashton was relieved finally to hear David Lewis's friendly voice.

Ashton didn't quite babble, though his emotions were ready to burst out of him. He recounted how he had come to Electric Boat expecting to work closely with Veliotis to learn the shipyard operations and then ascend quickly to the general manager's office. It was obvious to him—and he wanted to point out to Lewis—that none of his expectations had been fulfilled. He said he was sure that if Veliotis had a vote, he would never get the general manager's job. Everything had bogged down and he found himself in isolation from Veliotis, he thought because he had challenged the cost figures on the submarines and the schedules. He wanted advice: Did Lewis want him to stay? Or should he go find something else to do in the company at another division?

Lewis said the problem was mostly of Ashton's making and it was up to him to resolve it. Veliotis respected strength. The best thing would be for Ashton to have it out with Veliotis and try to get the relationship back on a good footing.

They talked for an hour, Ashton sitting on the edge of the bed, distressed and near tears at times. He told Lewis that he didn't think it would do any good, but he would try it if that's what Lewis thought was best. Lewis said he did.

The next morning at work, Ashton wondered if there was any real way to repair the damage. At eight o'clock his secretary appeared at the door to tell him his brother-in-law was on the line. Ashton frowned. He picked up the telephone and heard the Southern drawl of David Lewis. The company chairman chuckled and told Ashton that he had used the ruse so as not to alert anyone to his call. He didn't want Ashton to get into any more trouble with Veliotis than he already was in.

Lewis said he had reflected further on their conversation the night before and decided that it was not the time for Ashton to have a confrontational meeting with Veliotis. It was a particularly delicate point in the negotiations with the navy, and a lot of things would be happening in the next thirty days. It was best to leave the issue of Ashton's future alone for a little while longer until the crisis with the navy was settled. "Just sit tight," Lewis said, and signed off.

George Sawyer, the Assistant Navy Secretary for Shipbuilding, made his pilgrimage to Electric Boat on September 8. He received an hour's briefing from the navy officials and a shorter briefing from Veliotis. It was the hasty culmination of the "exhaustive" analysis he was to make of the shipyard before clearing the way for new submarine contracts. A week later, the navy announced that it had begun negotiations with Electric Boat to award the ninth Trident ballistic missile submarine, even though the first ship had yet to be delivered and stood two years behind schedule and $400 million over budget. Lehman refrained from any more harsh comments about Electric Boat in public. He said the dispute with General Dynamics had "nearly disappeared," and that navy officials were trying to resolve their differences and "get more work into the yard . . . but we are not, however, at the point where I can say we have resolved differences."

The deal that Lewis had been hoping for took final shape in the first week of October 1981, and was the result of a series of private discussions between Sawyer, LeFevre, and Lewis. It would give General Dynamics at least three 688-class submarines—one firm and two options—which would generate more than $100 million in additional profits, thus offsetting the bulk of the company's loss and allowing General Dynamics to gracefully drop its insurance claims in a public demonstration of good faith.

Sawyer had been acting on behalf of Lehman, and Lehman, by all of his public statements, was intent upon showing that he had backed down General Dynamics in a tough confrontation. Indeed, he cultivated the image of the brash young public servant who was going to whip the contractors into shape in order to get the six-hundred-ship navy that he deemed so critical to Ronald Reagan's defense buildup. It was the Rickover prototype, only Lehman was rebuilding it in a different time and for a different purpose. He wanted his six-hundred-ship navy and he believed in it as a monument to his own vision; but Lehman did not have time to do it the hard way. And so, through the artful contract-juggling of his deputy, Lehman was going to buy peace privately with General Dynamics while in public he would always assert that he had brought the company to its knees as an uncompromising servant of the Reagan administration.

When the news reached Lewis of how Sawyer planned to implement their private compromise, he quickly reported the good tidings to Veliotis.

"[Sawyer] says that this plan, this entire thing, is already approved by Lehman . . . and that when Lehman signs this [document certifying Electric Boat is ready for more navy work], this is the cue or the green light that we're going to get [new submarine contracts]. Now, I said, 'How are you going to handle this?' . . . We went into great detail about how the [uniformed navy] system could beat him the way they beat Hidalgo. And he said, well, he didn't believe that this could happen, that this plan had been approved by [Admiral Jack] Williams [chief of naval material] and [Admiral] Fowler."

"And lots of captains," added LeFevre on the phone line.

Lewis said he and Sawyer had talked in depth about pending navy shipbuilding programs that might provide future business for General Dynamics' Quincy shipyard, including giant navy warehouse ships that Lehman wanted to build to support the rapid movement of U.S. troops to trouble spots in the world.*

---

*Sawyer did indeed come through for General Dynamics. A series of navy warehouse ships was awarded to Quincy beginning in 1982 under construction contracts that

"That is real work," Veliotis agreed. "And then, perhaps, you know, David, they can give it to us."

"I think they can and I hope they will. We know these people lead a transient life down here [in Washington and] I don't know when all these [new ships] will be coming up for the taking."

Veliotis knew it would be some time, but he was sure that Lewis had built an important new relationship with Sawyer.

General Dynamics settlement discussions with Lehman and his deputy continued in total secrecy. As the date approached in early October on which Lehman planned publicly to announce a reconciliation, Lewis was haunted by the same anxieties that had plagued him four years earlier when the world seemed to hang in the balance as the days counted down to his salvation.

And as Lewis sweated out every detail of the settlement, Veliotis grew more and more concerned that Lewis was ignoring the all-important transition at Electric Boat in which Veliotis would be declared its savior and his new corporate station prepared in St. Louis, where the chairmanship still beckoned him.

After all, he had done what the admirals had said was impossible: he had delivered six 688s and the first Trident in a single year. The shipyard had survived the most rigorous series of sea trials on each one of them—each aggravated by Rickover's insistence on perfection beyond perfection. And though Veliotis's achievement was marred by the welding crisis that had frozen deliveries in 1980, the enormous task of ripping apart the ships and certifying their integrity in excruciating detail while keeping the production lines going was an engineering accomplishment that distinguished the entire management and workforce at Electric Boat.

But there was no accolade for Veliotis. Instead, there were rumors of a deal in which Veliotis was being "sacrificed" to bring peace with the navy. Every new hint that such a deal had been struck drove Veliotis into a private rage against Lewis, whom he dared not confront out of fear that his anger would explode at what Lewis had kept from him. If Lewis's deal with Lehman included his sacrifice, how could

---

were the most lucrative ever signed by the shipyard. In early 1983, Sawyer decided to leave the navy, and among his first suitors was David Lewis and the board of General Dynamics. Sawyer joined the company as an executive vice president in June 1983 at a salary of more than $200,000 a year. Sawyer's failure to disclose his private job talks with Lewis and his failure to disclose travel expenses paid by the company during his last months in office led to his criminal indictment in late 1985. He was acquitted of the charges during a two-day trial in December 1985 after Lehman took the witness stand and praised Sawyer as someone who had been tough on the contractors—especially General Dynamics—and who had saved the taxpayers millions of dollars.

Veliotis play the spoiler now without turning the board of directors against him? He was a prisoner of his reliance on Lewis's assurance that he would ascend to the chairmanship. Whatever game Lewis was playing, Veliotis knew he was powerless to intrude until Lewis confided what he had not yet confided. But it was torturing Veliotis to know that Lewis might be making concessions about who would run Electric Boat—even disingenuous ones—at his expense.

Veliotis wanted a neat and tidy announcement about his departure, his promotion, and the succession at Electric Boat, and he wanted it put out with careful timing after Veliotis triumphantly turned over U.S.S. *Ohio* to the navy in November. But Lewis was dragging his feet, and a messy announcement would just feed the rumors that Veliotis's departure was part of some kind of deal. He and Lewis still were circling the question when Veliotis saw the hand of Jim Ashton in an October 4 newspaper article suggesting that Veliotis would depart unceremoniously and that the shipyard was facing big cost overruns on the *688* and Trident submarines. Veliotis exploded, and decided it was high time he fired Ashton. For months, Veliotis had suspected Ashton of leaking shipyard cost figures to navy project officers. On Veliotis's orders, Electric Boat's chief of security had put Ashton under surveillance, an invasion of his privacy that turned up nothing more than a detailed accounting of his nighttime pursuits. Still, Veliotis was determined to fire the swaggering Texan.

The newspaper article described Ashton as the leading contender to replace Veliotis. The shipyard meanwhile was facing at least a $145 million loss on the *688* program, the article reported. In the midst of Veliotis's investigation to determine the sources for the offending article, *The Wall Street Journal* reported from its St. Louis bureau that Veliotis was being sacrificed in a "peace gesture" to the navy after a long feud with Rickover.

Veliotis got the corporate public relations man on the telephone and accused him of giving credence to the rumors that were flying in Groton and Washington: "You son of a bitch! You have ruined my reputation. . . . You have put this story out to the newspaper. . . . After all of my contribution to General Dynamics, after solving all of the problems at Electric Boat, after not sleeping at night with all of the problems, you go and ruin my reputation. You asshole! You goddamned son of a bitch! I will do everything in my power to get you out of this company." Veliotis slammed down the telephone.

The public relations man, Fred J. Bettinger, was so shaken that he went home early, took his wife out to dinner, and told her he probably would be fired because one of the most powerful men in the company had decided to go after him over the newspaper article.

Lewis, his attention still riveted on the pending settlement, did not realize what was happening until he suddenly received a telefaxed memorandum from Veliotis announcing that he intended to fire Ashton immediately. The memorandum put Lewis in a panic. Veliotis did not know Ashton as the secret informer he had become over the past year. But Lewis realized that if Ashton could blow the whistle on Veliotis, he could just as easily blow the whistle on the whole corporation for what it had been covering up.

The only way Lewis could head off Veliotis was to tell him the whole story. It was a risk. Lewis had known of Ashton's treachery for months and had not bothered to tell Veliotis. But he had to do something and quick, so he gathered round him two other officers, MacDonald and Warren Sullivan, the chief of personnel, and had his secretary place the call: "Taki?"

"Yeah, Dave."

"On the speaker here is Gorden and Sully. Ah, with respect to Ashton, I wanted to make sure we all knew what everybody knows . . . and what one of our real concerns is about triggering action on Ashton right away. I agree with the conclusion, but . . . that has kind of a history that you may know all about or may not know any of. But at one stage of the game, we began to get stories back here that he was making some analyses of the cost to complete the 688. . . . And one day he called Gorden, and he started telling him about the fact that he was concerned that the cost-to-completes were not right and that we were optimistic and he felt it was his duty to bring this to somebody's attention."

Veliotis listened, his anger rising. Evidently Ashton had been going behind his back to the corporate office and Lewis was just now getting around to telling him about it. It was just like the Boileau episode—Lewis suddenly bursting with information only after Veliotis tripped over the deception.

"Gorden told him," Lewis continued, "and Gorden is listening here, and he reported this to me—told him to go the hell back to doing his engineering job, and that he was not a skilled or professional cost estimator and, furthermore, that you were making an analysis that you had told us would be finished by whenever it was . . . and that the normal annual review was being made . . . at the same time, and he ought to get the hell out of it.

"What really scared us about this," Lewis continued, "if this silly bastard starts popping off—and this is what motivated Gorden to try to get him out of it and not have it come up as a point of controversy—and that if he starts talking that we've got a big loss on the 688, then we bring Arthur Andersen in, immediately, saying, 'Well, now, look, if this is the true story, we've got to record a loss, you know.' We didn't want that issue to even arise.

"So he called back again, called Gorden a week or so later, a few weeks later . . . and said that he was putting in all this time and he was . . . [not] getting anywhere in the division, and Gorden told him to go back to work. . . . This is no time to be rocking any boats. I know how you felt at that time [when] I suggested that maybe we ought to do something about Ashton and you said, 'Well, we had better look a little longer [for a better candidate].'

"But then he called me on a Friday night, and I was in a meeting or something, and he was very upset, according to Flo. So I talked to Gorden, and we were again really concerned about him popping off, in the public, or going to the navy or . . . writing a letter to Henry Crown, or writing a letter to Arthur Andersen, doing something stupid, really stupid. I called him at home that night, and he was talking about how hard he was working and nobody liked him and he wasn't getting anywhere. And I took the same identical approach that Gorden had taken of saying, 'It's up to you to win these people over and it's up to you to convince Taki you're doing a good job. And you ought to stay out of this cost area, that's none of your business.'

"And he said, 'Well, I just feel like we ought to be doing more than we're doing, and I don't think Taki realizes how bad things are,' and so on. And I said, 'Go back and do your job.' He said, 'Well, I don't know what's going to happen. I'm not going to get this job.' And I said, 'Well, I don't know whether you will or not, that's up to Taki.' "

Lewis said his telephone conversation with Ashton had been some time earlier, perhaps five or six weeks earlier. "Now we've later heard," Lewis said, "and this is the part you were bringing up, that he's been going around telling people that he's going to be the new general manager. You know that, I'm sure."

"Yes, I know that," Veliotis said, "and I know other things too that he has been saying. He has been talking to the newspapers and supplying some information. Go ahead."

"All these things—I just wanted to make sure you knew whatever we know, and I thought you probably already knew it. But my real concern here is if we give him the gate today, which I think would be a good idea except for this one factor, he is very likely to run, (a) to the navy, and (b) to the newspapers, or both, and I think this could have an upsetting influence on—what you mentioned yesterday when we talked—that he had been throwing off on the quality of our insurance issue."

"Well, he has been talking about the company being unethical, and he has been talking to people, et cetera, et cetera," Veliotis said.

"Well, that's the point. And I think if he starts popping off like that, it might slow up a little bit on our settlement activities, playing into the hands of the Sea Command, who take exactly the same position."

"I agree with you one hundred percent, what you say, but the man is going to do it either way. He is precipitating that situation. The man is going to do it."

"Well, let me ask you this," Lewis said, "as a suggested course of action, instead of just saying today, 'You're not going to get the job and go back to the chief engineer or do whatever you want to do,' what would you think of telling him something like this to try to hold him at bay for another three weeks, at least? To say, 'Jim, I understand that you have been talking to some people here at the yard, maybe other places, that you're going to be selected for general manager. I don't think you ought to do that and I don't think you ought to talk about it. We have not made that decision yet. I will say you're on the list, but there are others on the list and . . . until we decide, I think it can only be harmful to you and to the morale of the division . . . for you to be talking this way. And in fact it's not good for you.'

"And if he says, 'I haven't said that at all,' then just let it go. But in any event, it might defuse him until we can actually decide who we want to put in the job, and make the announcement, and tell him an hour before."

"Well, the day we make the announcement," Veliotis said, "he will do all those things that you said he may do right now."

"But then it's sour grapes," Lewis interjected.

"Yeah, well."

"At least it's sour grapes. And he may do it. . . ."

"He will do it, he will do it," Veliotis warned. "I have been told what he has been saying, what he has been doing, he will do it. I have no doubts in my mind that Jim Ashton will go out and do it and say all kinds of things. If we tell him today, he will do it today; if we tell him three weeks from now, he will do it three weeks from now. The other thing is to say to Jim Ashton absolutely nothing. We can leave it the way it is. If he comes and asks me, then I can tell him what it's all about. If he doesn't ask me, just let it go like the way it goes, and three weeks from now, tomorrow, whenever, we decide to make the appointment, we make it."

"Well, that would be my second choice," Lewis said, "because I again think we are very concerned about Arthur Andersen, and if we can at the time all this blows up say, 'Okay, now we've got in our program accounting . . . a Newport News–type contract deal on the 688,' and if we got those new two options, the problem is over. Then we've got something. If we can get the letter contract before this announcement is made, we would have Arthur Andersen in a position where they would be much more relieved and pay little or no attention to this."

"Yeah, Dave, I agree with you, but you have to appreciate that Jim Ashton has started all that, he has precipitated all that. I'm pretty sure, I don't have all the proof, I'm pretty sure he spoke to [Dan] Stets [a newspaper reporter] several times, although he said he hasn't talked to Stets. He wants a confrontation. What I'm worried about, if I go and talk to him and tell him all the nice things that you told me to tell him, I have no problems, I can tell him that, [but] I suggest that we tell Jim Ashton nothing. Leave it the way it is, and then after the announcement, we say, 'Yes, Jim, you were considered, but, you know, you did not win, another man won.' "

"Yeah," Lewis said unenthusiastically.

"But you know, I'm easy, one way or the other way, but, you know, Ashton is determined to do something. . . . The man wants to come here, punch his ticket as general manager so he can come over to the corporate office and take over your job."

"Yeah," Lewis repeated.

"He's not mature. A man who did what he did, he's not mature . . . and he made a fool of himself."

"Yeah."

"He's not a mature person. He has in his mind that he wants to be the chief executive officer. He thinks this is the right step for him, as I say, punch his ticket and go up higher."

"Well, I don't think we disagree at all with what we finally do with him, we're in agreement on that, and that's the big thing."

"But the situation, the way it is right now, we have to make the announcements now as soon as possible because if we don't make them, people are going to think that my departure was something that was not planned a year, year and a half ago."

"Yeah."

Veliotis said he was "very upset" with Lewis's public relations man, "because he's the one who spoke with [*The Wall Street Journal*], and he told [them] that I was not available, and he gave him the perception that you offered me, you know, as part of the deal."

"Were you bothered by that story?" Lewis asked.

"I was bothered by that story very much, Dave, because if you look at the headlines and the first paragraph, what it says, it says that, you know, the wolves in Washington, they scream for blood and you threw me in. And it will not be very good for anybody else we're going to be hiring from the outside. . . ."

"Yeah, well, I know good and well that Fred [Bettinger] never told him that," Lewis said.

"Well, Fred may not have told him that, Dave, but that is what the fellow understood. And Fred, you know, I told him this morning, 'Let me make up my mind with whom I will talk or not. . . .' Everybody is trying to find out if there is a rift between you and me, and I said, 'No, this is something that Dave Lewis and I have agreed on.' But you know, sometime, we have to tell how things are and take our chances with Ashton perhaps, but we can't afford to have people polarizing here. There are people here, they hear stories: Ashton is going to be general manager. He's going to fire [John] Rannenberg. He's going to do this. He's going to do that. The man hasn't been mature."

"You don't think it would be a good idea to tell him to cool it?"

"What? To talk to him and tell him to cool it? To give him sort of hopes that he has been considered? If you want to do that, I will do it. I don't think it's the honest thing to do, but I will do it."

"It isn't the honest thing to do," said Lewis.

"But I'm not," Veliotis said quickly, "you know, Dave, I'm not trying to wave the flag of ethics here. You know, the organization comes first, this is the way I was brought up. It may be old-fashioned, but this is the way I am. But I will tell him that. The only thing he will do—knowing Jim Ashton—he will go out and say, 'Well, yeah, I just spoke with Veliotis. He told me I'm in the running.' And then he will start putting the rumors out. He has done a very good job of putting those rumors out and trying to get the job. But if you want me to do it, I will do it."

"We ought to talk about it, consider it. If you think it's a bad idea. . . ."

"No, no, I don't. Dave, look, at this stage of the game, you know, it's six of one, half a dozen of the other. I believe the thing that we have to do is make up our minds what we will do with this place here. Dave, what is it going to be in the years to come? It's going to be a production factory. Somebody will be building the same ship. They're not going to design new missile-carrying submarines. They aren't going to design newer-type submarines. They're going just to continue those. . . . Now we've got to get somebody strong in production."

They were back to the same argument.

Lewis wanted a good public relations man to run the shipyard, someone who could charm the admirals in the Sea Command. His last concern seemed to be production. Veliotis knew the problems that remained at the shipyard. They were three years away from finishing the first eighteen submarines, and they had yet to achieve the production level they had promised the navy at the beginning of the decade.

"Dave, we don't have the luxury anymore of months to go and wait. We'll have to do it and do it fast, and we have to make it nice and clean. And for me, too, you know, Dave . . . I want to be in that commissioning [of U.S.S. *Ohio*] and then go. . . . You know, I have said I will support you, but you know, on the other hand, I have to protect my reputation."

The script was acted out just as Lehman's assistant had guaranteed. On October 16, the navy's contracting officer ruled that General Dynamics' insurance claim had no legal validity. Six days later, Lewis and Lehman appeared at a Pentagon news conference to announce that the company and the navy had patched up their differences. The company agreed to drop its insurance claim and the navy agreed to negotiate the award of a contract for a 688-class submarine with options to purchase two additional 688s that had been funded by Congress.

Reporters asked Lehman what had changed in the short period of time since he had railed against General Dynamics, but Lehman insisted that a review of the record would show that Electric Boat had made great strides toward demonstrating that it was ready for additional work.

At the end of October, Veliotis hand-delivered an official letter to the navy supervisor of shipbuilding, turning over U.S.S. *Ohio*, the first Trident ballistic missile submarine, three years late. The commissioning ceremony was set for mid-November. At the beginning of the month Lewis telephoned Veliotis to say that he wanted to preside over the ceremony because Vice President George Bush was going to be there and Bush was important to the corporation. But Veliotis insisted that "This is my show, Dave. You may come as my guest, but the general manager represents the builder at commissioning." Lewis was miffed by Veliotis's insubordination and did not attend the commissioning of the first Trident.

There was bile between them, always just below the surface. It was the bile of unfulfilled expectations and promises, of the poorly planned succession at Electric Boat, and the spin that someone in St. Louis had put on Veliotis's departure as a "peace gesture." Lewis, by his silence and inaction, had soured the triumph. There was no celebration, which Lewis easily could have orchestrated for Veliotis's benefit. There was just talk of sacrifice and peace gestures. Veliotis had made good on his pledge to deliver six 688s and the first Trident in 1981, yet in an instant the triumph he felt so deeply disappeared, and it was all over the press that Lewis had thrown him to the wolves. If Lewis had really intended to support Veliotis for the chairmanship, wouldn't he have been leading the victory parade? Instead, Lewis was coy and said nothing about his own retirement or the succession.

These thoughts preyed on Veliotis's mind and his mood turned black. Lewis had stolen the victory. He had become the voice of reason, the great compromiser who had built new bridges to the navy where Veliotis had burned the old ones. In a real sense, the welding and quality-control crisis had killed Veliotis's hopes and ruined his strategy to become chief executive. Ripping apart those completed hulls had ignited the overrun and forced Veliotis to bludgeon the customer until the customer accepted the submarines. But the daily violence had poisoned everything, turning the whole navy against him. In leaving Electric Boat, Veliotis presided over little more than the scorched earth where he had battled one of the company's most important customers.

He had soldiered for Lewis, yet there was no hero's welcome. Just a sense that he had fought brutally beyond the truce and become more of a problem than a solution. Lewis had become the corporation's negotiator with the Reagan administration and had done more to pull the company out of the fire than anyone. Lewis had stood calmly between a snarling Veliotis and the entrenched uniformed navy. Lewis had incredible luck. He had wrung a host of concessions and new contracts from Lehman and Sawyer. He had brought home the bacon where Veliotis had brought home more bile.

After the commissioning of *Ohio*, Veliotis went on vacation. Lewis sent the corporate plane down to Fort Lauderdale to pick him up so he could attend the December meeting of the board of directors. There still was an open agenda item on whether to declare a loss for the year because the overrun was large and Arthur Andersen had to be told what the company intended to do. By a conservative estimate, Lewis suggested that dropping the claim and taking the settlement Lehman's assistant had worked out for the company would bring in about $150 million in additional revenue, probably enough to offset the loss.

Veliotis turned argumentative. In front of the other directors, he challenged Lewis's assumptions and questioned the prudence of going forward on the unwritten promise of Sawyer, a man whom Veliotis did not trust to begin with. He questioned the wisdom of signing a pledge never to file builders' risk insurance claims on the ships in the yard. What if one of the submarines fell off the building ways? But the executive committee had met the day before and the Crown interests had recommended going with the package Lewis had negotiated. The full board was not going to go against the grain. Some of the members had been surprised at Veliotis's performance, and one of them leaned over to Veliotis and murmured, "Taki, we have to back our chairman."

The scene on the corporate jet afterwards was ugly. Lewis and his wife were going down to Deer Run, their antebellum farm in southern Georgia, and Veliotis was returning to Fort Lauderdale. Dorothy Lewis had her feet up and was smoking a cigarette when Lewis came aboard, and in front of Veliotis and the crew, he snapped at her to put out the cigarette and take her feet off the seats. Dorothy Lewis turned red with embarrassment. At that moment Veliotis thought Lewis a coward for venting his anger at his wife and not at Veliotis, the person he really was mad at.

Lewis's strategy for avoiding a loss at the shipyard fell on its face when Arthur Andersen & Company said it would not go along with using anticipated revenues from new contracts signed in 1982 to offset losses on contracts signed in the early 1970s. Now Lewis had to face up to the loss. Using some optimistic assumptions, the overrun was set at $90 million, half of which the government had to pick up under the terms of the 1978 settlement. General Dynamics wrote off $45 million against 1981 earnings.*

The day after the announcement about Veliotis moving to the corporate office and the appointment of one of his deputies, Fritz Tovar, to take over the yard, Jim Ashton got a call from the chief personnel officer at corporate headquarters. "You weren't a team player," the personnel man said. Ashton thought he was being transferred, but a few weeks later the personnel man made it clear there was no room for him in the company. He had been fired.

During that same momentous week in November, Admiral Rickover got a telephone call at his desk from his wife. She said she had heard on the radio that President Reagan had decided to retire him. The old man just sneered and said, "Is that so?"

No longer were there a hundred men in Congress to stand up and decry the decision. Many of Rickover's supporters had died, been

*In August 1982, Lewis faced the remainder of the loss and wrote off another $84 million on the first eighteen 688s. Ashton's original projection had turned out to be very accurate.

defeated, or retired and gone home. The ones who were still there were hardpressed to fight the decision by the popular new President. There were rumors about Rickover being a little senile and the *La Jolla* incident was fresh in everyone's mind. The week U.S.S. *Ohio* joined the fleet, Rickover was summoned to Weinberger's office, where he was told by the secretary and by Lehman that the President had decided not to reappoint him. They said a lot of nice things in his honor, but when it was Rickover's time to speak, he just got up and walked out.

Rickover saw his own martyrdom in the firing. And when that same week he received a telephone call from the chief of the Justice Department's fraud section, Jo Ann Harris, who informed him that the department was closing its criminal investigation of General Dynamics, he was convinced that sinister forces in the Reagan administration had cut a deal with the defense contractors. While there was evidence of fraud, the department had not been able to find a "smoking gun" document or witness who could testify that the company had falsified its $544 million claim with criminal intent.

Rickover wrote a letter protesting the decision to Attorney General William French Smith, but it didn't change anything. When the President of the United States called Rickover to the Oval Office on January 8, 1982, for a farewell meeting, Rickover found Reagan standing with Caspar Weinberger and John Lehman. It was his sixty years of service and his great contribution to naval propulsion that gave him the right to demand to meet alone with the President. Weinberger and Lehman awkwardly excused themselves. Then Rickover turned to Ronald Reagan and told him he was being poorly served by the Secretary of Defense and the Secretary of the Navy. They were afraid to take on the shipbuilders for filing false claims; the only reason they were trying to get rid of Rickover was because he had the courage to speak out.

Reagan fumbled for words. He didn't know anything about the shipbuilding claims, but he had been warned about Rickover. The President made some assurances about being against fraud, and spoke highly of Cap and young John Lehman. Then he walked Rickover to the door, congratulating the older man on the marvelous achievements of his lifetime. Rickover went out talking about fraudulent claims.

Weinberger and Lehman were stung by Rickover's attack. When friends of Rickover requested a military band for the banquet honoring Rickover the following month—a banquet to be attended by Richard Nixon, Gerald Ford, and Jimmy Carter—the Pentagon turned down the request. Rickover also believed he had a pledge from Lehman to name one of the two nuclear-powered aircraft carriers in the Reagan defense budget after the father of the nuclear navy, but with Rickover out the door, Lehman quickly switched signals and announced publicly that the navy would honor Rickover's distinguished career by naming a 688-class submarine after him. Upstaged as he was by the announcement, Rickover was powerless to protest.

Of the three, Rickover, Lewis, and Veliotis, the three who had the greatest impact on the nuclear submarine fleet that would stand watch in the oceans until the end of century, Rickover, the oldest, once the strongest, was the first to fall. He turned his back completely on the submarine program, saying he would give no advice because he had been fired. But he carried the torch over the claims, working the back channels with congressional staffers, navy analysts, and federal law enforcement officials who still believed that David Lewis and the others had gotten away with murder.

It had been fourteen years since the *November*-class submarine had chased *Enterprise* between San Francisco and Hawaii. The U.S. shipyards had completed fifteen of the first twenty-three high-speed submarines that Rickover had gotten authorized in Congress between 1968 and 1972. Fleet construction in the United States had proved truly glacial and the new generation of nuclear submarines was proving so complex, so sophisticated as to rival in scope the great medieval cathedrals of Europe, where tradesmen passed their tasks from generation to generation, each hoping he would be among those to pray inside.

Somewhere in the midst of all the chaos, the United States lost so much ground in the silent war with the Soviet Union that by the early 1980s no one could say with any certainty who was ahead. Only one thing was sure: the Soviets had outbuilt the United States by more than two to one; the Russians had a definite numerical advantage in fast submarines capable of diving deeper and of firing a variety of stand-off weapons—putting the U.S. aircraft carrier battle groups in substantial jeopardy in wartime.

The *688* class, it was becoming increasingly clear, was not the answer to protecting the carrier task force. Just as Rickover was making his exit, the Soviets deployed a massive cruise missile–firing submarine, the *Oscar* class, which was fitted with twenty-four low-flying birds—nuclear-tipped or conventional—that could strike at the carrier groups from more than five hundred miles away.

New Soviet submarine designs slid down the ways almost every year. For the first time the Soviets—already superior in speed, power efficiency, and diving range—began sending nuclear submarines to sea with thick ablative coatings on their hulls to dampen the noise generated by their power plants and machinery. Other new classes sported tail assemblies for retracting the long, towed-array sonar systems that would give them better eyes and ears across great distances of ocean.

More alarming, the Soviets appeared to have begun experimenting with their own radar satellites in hopes of rendering the oceans transparent before the United States. In one incident monitored by the U.S. intelligence, a Soviet satellite passed over a U.S. submarine running submerged. After the satellite pass, a Soviet submarine-hunting airplane flew from its base to the precise area of the U.S. submarine's patrol. The incident deeply disturbed officials, who speculated that the satellite might have tested one of the new electromagnetic-detection technologies. If that was the case, the United States might lose the invisibility of its seaborne nuclear deterrent, the Trident fleet, before the end of the century.

Rickover had been overwhelmed by history and by his own hubris. He was in charge of the U.S. nuclear submarine program at a time when the Soviets had made their nuclear submarine fleet a national priority—similar to the U.S. effort to put a man on the moon. The Soviets had spent tens of billions of dollars on submarines, while Rickover had a couple of billion to build a competitive fleet. He had felt this disadvantage deeply and often complained that he would rather be running the Russian submarine program than the American one because the Russians had so much more to work with. His was the disadvantage of history. To his credit, he took responsibility for it, which was why he had so terrorized anyone who stepped into his path.

But when he was defeated, he went out swinging at the shipyards, as if they had somehow defeated his destiny. It was not true. Rickover had been defeated by the relative resource commitments of the superpowers in the silent war.

Had he been granted the resources of the Russians, there still was no guarantee that he would have built superior ships. In his last two decades of navy service he had shown the all-consuming reach of a man imbued with his own notion of legend. He had jammed three submarine prototypes through the defense bureaucracy—*Narwhal*, *Lipscomb*, and *Los Angeles*—each of them flawed in a fundamental way. It was to no one's credit that one of them became a class that soaked up all of the budget resources for attack submarines over two decades. Had he not been so keen on crushing the last vestiges of opposition to his primacy in the nuclear submarine navy, Rickover could have used the talent and design base that was available to him in the community of submarine engineers and naval architects he had been so intent on defeating after the loss of *Thresher*. The odds are, they would have given him a better ship at a better price.

History proved that Rickover was more conservative than the Russians and that his expertise did not go far beyond the propulsion chain. More important, there was no towering figure at the top of the navy with the longevity of Rickover, and so there was no one to keep him in his place. There was no one to give the U.S. submarine fleet the broad reach the Soviets had achieved across the spectrum of technological advance. So Rickover, with his rigid but proved ideas on propulsion, had prevailed, and his power had grown out of all proportion. In the end he used it to attack the industrial base that could never measure up to the standards he had set for it. That it had cheated him and the navy was a given, but it could not be blamed for the larger failure.

Indeed, by the end of the century, it may seem providential that the United States did not overcommit its defense resources in nuclear attack submarine construction, because by that time both superpowers may have solved the technological limitations to detecting submarines from airborne platforms or from outer space.

The prospect that he might be indicted hit Veliotis just after the beginning of the new year in 1982.

He had gotten busy putting together an international marketing organization for General Dynamics when the Frigitemp case suddenly exploded. By a fluke, an assistant U.S. attorney in New York got hold of the records that showed the wire transfer of kickbacks to Veliotis's account in Switzerland. The Frigitemp case had been in the U.S. attorney's office since 1978, but it had just sat there like so many cases where there were allegations of kickbacks, but no smoking gun and too few legmen to run down all the leads.

Veliotis was undone by one of those crazy acts of fate. He and the others had almost gotten away with it. The Frigitemp vice president, who had been raking off all the money, settled with the bankruptcy trustee for $1.4 million in the summer of 1981, and everybody involved had reason to breathe a sigh of relief. But the crooked vice president then got into a fight over money with his accountant/partner in Canada. The accountant had been the accomplice who moved the kickback money around for the conspirators. That fight was a big

mistake because the accountant flew to New York and walked into the
Federal Building at Foley Square, where he showed one of the assistant U.S. attorneys the wire-transfer records for all the Frigitemp kickbacks to Veliotis, going back to 1974.

The next thing Veliotis knew, a young assistant U.S. attorney in
cowboy boots wanted him to come in for questioning. Veliotis had
been getting his legal counsel from the Boston firm that represented
the Quincy and Electric Boat shipyards. He had maintained to company officials that he did not know anything about kickbacks.

But on February 24, 1982, Veliotis went to New York and hired
John H. Gross, a onetime prosecutor himself in the Manhattan U.S.
attorney's office. Bert Jenner, Henry Crown's lawyer, had tried to steer
Veliotis to one of Jenner's friends, an ex-federal judge in private practice; Veliotis, however, needed a lawyer who was not beholden to the
Crowns or to General Dynamics. He needed advice on matters that no
one else could know about.

Veliotis met with the lawyer, but with the Swiss bank records
already in the prosecutor's hands, it was just a matter of time. The
only thing Veliotis could do was mount a delaying action against the
inevitable indictment. And when that occurred, the company would
be forced to turn on him in the name of the shareholders.

On April 29, the prosecutors insisted that Veliotis come in to
give handwriting samples, to sit for photographs, and to produce his
U.S. passport. That was it for Veliotis. You could have smelled it coming. On May 3, he wrote a memorandum to Lewis saying he was
shocked at how badly his successor, Fritz Tovar, had managed Electric Boat in his first six months, and predicting "catastrophic financial
consequences to the company" from Tovar's inept performance. In a
challenging tone, Veliotis added, "I consider it essential that you be
fully aware of the entire situation since it cannot be allowed to continue without having a disastrous effect on General Dynamics." Veliotis had created the fight as a pretext to leave.

The next day, Lewis telephoned Veliotis to talk about Electric
Boat. Veliotis attacked Tovar, saying he was not tough enough to line
up the nonperformers and "get after them." The navy was pressuring
Tovar to hire more men to increase the manning of the ships, and
Tovar was caving in. The overhead costs were creeping up again. Veliotis said he did not have time to rescue Tovar. He had to return to
Greece. His aged mother had died the previous year, and the probate
lawyers were fleecing the estate. He had decided to retire, he said, to
return to Greece and attend to his mother's estate.

Lewis's tone was sincere as he pleaded with Veliotis to take
some time and think about it, but Veliotis believed that Lewis would

be delighted to see him go quietly and amicably. General Dynamics was headed into some golden years of high profits from the maturing F-16 and Trident programs. There was no reason for Lewis not to stay for another five years basking in the warm light of his achievement. He had left little room for Veliotis at the top. Without a big expansion in General Dynamics' overseas markets, Veliotis would be left to crash about the corporate office in search of battles to fight for a commander who no longer desperately needed his services.

Veliotis told Lewis he would think it over some more and let him know in a day or two.

There was no discussion of Frigitemp. Lewis only asked once whether Veliotis intended to testify, and Veliotis asserted, "I am eager to testify."

On May 5, Veliotis's attorney, John Gross, met with the prosecutor in charge of the Frigitemp investigation. The assistant U.S. attorney said he was intensely interested in Veliotis and wanted him to appear before a grand jury investigating the kickback case. Two days later, in a twelve-line letter to Lewis, Veliotis announced that he had decided to retire from General Dynamics.

"My association with General Dynamics and with you personally has been an exciting and challenging time which I will always remember."

At the end of May Veliotis's attorney notified the prosecutor that Veliotis was outside of the United States and would assert his Fifth Amendment rights against self-incrimination in declining to testify before the grand jury. The prosecutor expressed concern that Veliotis was trying to skip the country permanently. Three days later, the young prosecutor in cowboy boots called Gross downtown and showed him the Swiss bank account records the government had obtained. The prosecutor then revealed that Veliotis was, in fact, a target of the grand jury investigation.

When John Gross informed General Dynamics' general counsel in St. Louis of the position he had taken with the federal prosecutors, the general counsel became alarmed. The prospect of Veliotis taking the Fifth would be too much for the board of directors. "That's a big problem," he told Gross. "We're a high-visibility defense contractor." It was a big problem because if word leaked out that General Dynamics was standing behind an executive who was taking the Fifth Amendment, the press, the Congress, and the Pentagon all would land on the company with charges of cover-up. Almost immediately, Lewis instructed his general counsel to stop paying Veliotis's legal fees. Shortly thereafter the federal prosecutor met privately with company officials and showed them the Swiss bank account records. There was nothing else Lewis could do. From that point on in the fall of 1982, General Dynamics cooperated fully with the New York grand jury.

It took the prosecutors more than a year to put their case together. During that time, Veliotis returned to the United States regularly and maintained his home at Milton, Massachusetts. In November 1982, Tovar and Grimes threw a farewell party for Veliotis at the Ritz Carlton Hotel in Boston. Veliotis also was Electric Boat's guest at the meeting of the Society of Naval Architects meeting that fall. Grimes, as the new general manager of Quincy, had written to Veliotis during the fall to say, "On Friday, September 17, 1982, we received congressional approval for the first two ships of the TAKX program. We now have a real, funded program which should grow to five ships and make 1984 and 1985 good years for Quincy." George Sawyer had been the architect of these contracts. Veliotis believed that Lewis was going to reward the Assistant Navy Secretary with the job Veliotis had left behind.

Edward Hidalgo, too, had been rewarded. On Veliotis's recommendation, Hidalgo was given a $50,000 consulting fee for traveling to Spain to assist with the sale of the F-16 Falcon to the Spanish air force.

In May 1983, the same month that George Sawyer was hired as an executive vice president of General Dynamics, the assistant U.S. attorney in New York informed Veliotis's lawyer that the government had prepared an indictment against Veliotis, alleging conspiracy, wire fraud, racketeering, and perjury in connection with the kickbacks. Veliotis had until June 6 to make any argument on why he should not be indicted.

John Gross traveled to Foley Square and argued that his client should not be indicted because there had been no conspiracy, because Veliotis had never done anything for the kickbacks he was alleged to have received, because the alleged perjury had not taken place in New York, where the indictment was being drawn up, and, furthermore, the government should not bring a racketeering indictment because it was just a regular kickback case, not the kind of continuing criminal enterprise defined by the anti-racketeering law. The lawyer had known ahead of time that none of the arguments would prevail. The prosecutors believed they had a solid case and had invested an enormous amount of time and money on it. They were going to go for it, even though their primary target might be a fugitive for years.

In Greece, Veliotis realized that the indictment was just weeks away. He authorized Gross to tell senior Justice Department officials in Washington that they had missed the boat in their aborted four-year investigation into General Dynamics cost-overrun claims. The claims were fraudulent, Veliotis said, and he had important information that would show obstruction of justice and perjury by General Dynamics officials. If the government would agree to hold off on the indictment, he would meet with prosecutors in Greece and give them the information.

Gross relayed Veliotis's offer to Stephen S. Trott, assistant attorney general in charge of the criminal division, but Trott turned the offer down. He said the government would be glad to meet with Veliotis after the indictment, and then only in the United States. John Gross thought he had to be kidding. In a series of last-minute telephone calls, Veliotis sharpened the offer through Gross. Veliotis argued that the government had paid nearly $700 million to settle the claims filed by General Dynamics; he alleged that those claims had been fraudulent. He was saying Rickover had been right. The government was only after a couple of million dollars in the kickback case against Veliotis. Which was more important to the taxpayers of the United States? he asked.

Gross then made a strong appeal to the federal prosecutors: If anything ever came of Veliotis's allegations, the government would have egg on its face and it would look like a cover-up. "You ought to go find out what he has to say," Gross argued. "How can you just let him sit there?" If Veliotis could not deliver, the government could always indict him the day after prosecutors returned from Greece empty-handed. Gross believed the government had to be crazy to turn down a chance to talk to a witness like Veliotis, whose credentials as a key executive in the nation's largest defense contracting firm offered the Justice Department the opportunity to get at the truth in the cost-overrun case in a way it never had during four years of investigations. And he was offering it for free—no immunity from Frigitemp, no strings.

No deal, the prosecutors repeated. The indictment was handed up by the federal grand jury sitting in Manhattan on September 6, 1983.

Within days of Veliotis's indictment, David Lewis directed the company lawyers to seize all of Veliotis's assets in the United States and Canada. He was going by the book. He had to protect the stockholders' assets, but to Veliotis, it looked like a vicious overreaction. Veliotis went into a rage when the company attached his homes in Massachusetts and Florida, as well as his stock account, which was held by a broker in Canada and contained about $6 million in General Dynamics stock he had purchased during his eight years with the company. At most, Veliotis was accused of receiving $1.35 million personally in the kickback scheme. General Dynamics had engaged in overkill, Veliotis believed, and he was mad enough for violence if he could have gotten his hands on Lewis.

Veliotis sent a message to General Dynamics that the company was welcome to maintain its grip on enough assets to cover the maximum amount he might be liable for in the kickback case, but he wanted the rest and he wanted it now. A reporter for *Forbes* magazine was trying to locate Veliotis. Veliotis sent word that he just might grant an interview—and who could tell what he would say. But for General Dynamics, it was a public relations problem. Company officials couldn't release any of Veliotis's assets in full view of the stockholders, the press, and the Frigitemp bankruptcy lawyers, who were holding the corporation legally liable for Veliotis's actions.

In late 1983, Veliotis revealed to the Justice Department that he had tape recordings and other documents that implicated the highest officials in General Dynamics in fraud against the government and against the stockholders of the company. Still, there was no reaction from the government.

At the end of 1983, Rickover and Veliotis, two of the three men who had made the greatest impact on America's nuclear submarine fleet during the decade of the 1970s and the threshold years of the 1980s, had been toppled—Rickover due to his irascibility and old age; Veliotis due to his greed. Only David Lewis remained, the gentleman actor, the survivor, and both Rickover and Veliotis, in their own ways and for their own reasons, were committed to bringing him down.

In January 1984, when I was asked by the national editor of *The Washington Post* to follow up on an article in *Forbes* about Takis Veliotis entitled "The One That Got Away," I knew nothing of this history. The article seemed to indicate that Veliotis had dropped off the face of the earth. I telephoned John Gross to find out whether it would be possible to interview him.

"He's in Greece, he's not hiding," Gross said. Then he added that he had been locked in negotiations for months trying to convince the government to meet with Veliotis and hear his allegations that Electric Boat had submitted fraudulent claims against the navy for cost overruns on *688*-class submarines. Veliotis said the government had missed the boat. Gross said he first had used Veliotis's offer in an attempt to block the indictment, but now he was offering what Veliotis knew "for free."

I asked whether Veliotis would talk about it with me.

"I don't know. He's sitting over in Greece, he may be willing. I'll ask him. Why don't you call me back?"

I hung up and dialed the overseas operator. There were two P. Takis Veliotis listings in Athens. I dialed the first one and a woman answered. She said she was a cousin of the Veliotis who had worked for General Dynamics, but she had not seen him in five years. I asked if I could leave my name and telephone number.

"But we have not seen him. It would not do any good," she protested.

"Could I please just leave it? You might hear from him," I said.

Thirty minutes later, Veliotis called me at my desk in the newsroom at *The Washington Post*. The connection was poor, so Veliotis said he would call back. But when he did so, the clerk who took the call cut him off accidentally.

The following Monday, I telephoned Gross, and he said Veliotis had issued a statement. He was negotiating with the Justice Department to offer testimony that "General Dynamics should not have gotten one penny" for its cost-overrun claims because they were false. Gross said Veliotis was not bargaining for immunity in the Frigitemp case in return for his testimony and had asked only for immunity against any incriminating statements he made in giving new information about the claim. Gross, the former prosecutor, said it was in the public interest for the facts to come out.

The next day, January 17, I reported for the *Post* that Veliotis had "offered to tell the Justice Department how the nation's largest defense contractor allegedly reaped hundreds of millions of dollars by submitting fraudulent contract claims on nuclear attack submarines it was building for the navy." The article said Veliotis was close to an agreement to meet prosecutors outside the country.

Heavy trading in General Dynamics stock followed immediately, and within a few days, the stock had lost more than $200 million in value. The corporate public relations man, Fred Bettinger, who had tangled so viciously with Veliotis three years earlier, telephoned me to complain: "Your story has done tremendous damage to this company." He said the stock had dropped three points in the first day and at that very moment was down another one and seven eighths. "We have received literally scores of calls from analysts."

Bettinger argued that since other newspapers and wire services were reporting conflicting accounts of whether the Justice Department intended to meet with Veliotis, the *Post* ought to issue a clarification. That would help the company on Wall Street. I said I would not clarify the story because it had been accurate and I had no information to the contrary. Bettinger then called Benjamin C. Bradlee, the

Post's executive editor, and lodged the same complaint, but Bradlee replied the story would stand.

Rickover was also working the telephone in the wake of the article. He telephoned me at my desk and introduced himself. "This is Rickover." He said the claims case was one of the worst scandals in history and would take a lot of time to uncover, but anyone who did "could make a name for himself because this is bigger than Teapot Dome." He remembered Teapot Dome, he said; he read about it in *The Washington Post* when he was a boy at the Naval Academy in the 1920s.

Initially I was not inclined to resurrect the shipbuilding claims. But two months later a staff investigator for Representative John D. Dingell, chairman of the House Energy and Commerce Committee, telephoned me to say that Veliotis had taken documents and tape recordings with him when he left General Dynamics and was prepared to make a very detailed presentation of what he knew to the Justice Department. That was when I left for Athens, thinking that Veliotis's information could provide the initial basis for a history that had never been told.

Veliotis's relationship with the Justice Department turned out to be stormy and contentious from the outset. During the first week in May, an attorney from the fraud section in Washington traveled to Athens accompanied by two FBI agents, and Veliotis spent three days haranguing the federal officials for missing the boat in their earlier investigation of General Dynamics, the one he had sweated out as general manager of Electric Boat. He refused to turn over any tapes or documents to them because, he said later, "They looked at me like I was vermin and would not shake my hand."

Veliotis still had his pride, and he wanted the Justice Department to deal with him on his own terms. He wanted to become the central witness against General Dynamics. He wanted the prosecutors to call him every day and consult with him about where to look for other documents buried in the company's files. He wanted to direct them to the information they had missed. And he was always skeptical that the Justice Department would really go after the case having once closed a four-year investigation into the very same issues.

Veliotis knew that if he did become the central witness in a new case against General Dynamics, the Justice Department could not bring him back to the United States without disposing of the Frigitemp indictment by offering an acceptable plea bargain. The prosecutors demanded that Veliotis turn over everything he had. Period. They left Athens empty-handed and Stephen Trott, head of the criminal division at Justice, began telling reporters and congressional investigators interested in the case that he did not believe there were any tapes. Veliotis was just a big con-artist.

Within a few months, after Veliotis had turned over to me the first of his tapes, and reports about them began appearing in newspapers, magazines, and on network television, Justice Department officials returned to Greece. This time, the federal prosecutor leading the team shook Veliotis's hand and told him the department's goal was to make him a witness against General Dynamics. Between October and December 1984, Veliotis turned over the bulk of his tape recordings and documents. By December, the Justice Department began calling witnesses before a federal grand jury impaneled in New Haven, Connecticut.

The release of Veliotis's tapes had a devastating impact on David Lewis. On September 24, I wrote about the tape recording which captured Lewis's strategy to cover up the overruns on the *688* during 1981, when it appeared James Ashton was bent on disclosing them. The article appeared while Lewis was out of the country on a business trip, but I had read it in its entirety to the company's general counsel and public relations man beforehand. Both had said it was fair to General Dynamics and to Lewis. The day after publication, several officials representing General Dynamics telephoned the *Post* to say that while the article—based on the tape—posed difficult problems for General Dynamics and personally for David Lewis, the newspaper had been extremely fair in reporting it.

This consensus view was not shared by Lewis.

October 5, my telephone at home rang at 6:30 p.m. It was a Friday evening and I recognized the voice of Flo Stark: "I have David Lewis on the line," she said. Lewis came on and said that he had just returned from overseas and had read all of the newspapers and watched videotapes of the television pick-up of the story. He said he wanted to call to tell me, "you have just about wiped out my reputation" with the story, and to state his complaint—if I was interested in hearing it.

I told him I was, and then listened to his long and emotional presentation. It was just like Lewis. He started at the beginning. The headline, he said, and the first paragraph concluded that he had wanted to withhold information about a $100 million overrun. He said that was "a goddamned lie." He said the article did not give General Dynamics' side of the story until forty or more inches into the article. He had measured it—with a ruler.

"You remember when you played that tape, I visibly relaxed," Lewis said, referring to the August day Bob Woodward and I had spent asking him questions and playing the tapes for him. His entire purpose, he said, in trying to head off Ashton was to protect the settlement with the navy, not to cover up the overrun. "But the conclusion from your article is that I'm a crooked CEO."

I told him that I was distressed to hear his reaction, especially since I had gone to the trouble of reading the article to his general counsel before it ran, and had given the company the opportunity to make a statement that would run along with the article. I told him that his aides had said the article was so fair that they did not avail themselves of the offered space for a statement.

"Is that true?" Lewis said on his end of the line. At that point I discovered that two other people were monitoring Lewis's conversation with me. He had me on the speakerphone. Present in the room were his general counsel and his public relations man, who now acknowledged that the company, in Lewis's absence, had turned down the chance to make an additional statement to run with the article.

Lewis said he knew that he would have to live with his statements on the Veliotis tapes. He felt horrible about having said that deceiving Ashton would not be the honest thing to do. "I have to live with my own mistakes, but I hate to live with the fact that you have interpreted my actions in every instance in the most callous way."

I was trying to figure out what Lewis hoped to accomplish with this conversation. I did not think by any standard that he could say the article was unfair to him. His side of the story was not buried. I believe I was talking to David Lewis the actor. He was selling, knowing that even his contest with Veliotis was in part a performance between two men, each of whom claimed that he had brought the greater amount of honesty, loyalty, and integrity to the relationship, and had experienced the greater betrayal by the other.

"Obviously, I'm hypersensitive," Lewis said near the end of the conversation. He said he knew there were going to be more stories in the future, and that I was dedicated to making an in-depth look at what happened between General Dynamics and the navy. "I guess we're still friends," he said. I asked him if he would feel better if he repeated his complaint to one of the editors at the *Post*, but he said it didn't matter.

"I'm just kind of heartsick and I really don't want to go through it all again."

One of the things I had not considered Veliotis was trying to do with his tape recordings during the fall of 1984 was to lay a final trap for Lewis and for General Dynamics. He had given the key tape recordings and documents to the Justice Department, but he had also sent an indirect message to General Dynamics that they were for sale.

The message was carried from one Greek lawyer to another Greek lawyer, and then to an employee of General Dynamics' international sales office in Athens.

Robert H. Duesenberg, Lewis's general counsel, was drafting the telexes for General Dynamics and then sending them through a scrambler to the office in Greece. The company believed the U.S. National Security Agency or the Greek intelligence service monitored their telex traffic, and they wanted a secure channel to deal with Veliotis. Duesenberg cleared every new message with David Lewis and brought Lewis every reply.

Veliotis's message—as relayed through an intermediary—was this: He wanted to meet. He had a lot of evidence. He was willing to turn over the originals of all the tapes if General Dynamics was willing to settle the $140 million lawsuit Veliotis had filed against the company in Athens after the company froze his assets. After this initial message was passed from Veliotis's Greek lawyer to a General Dynamics' employee in Athens, there followed intense posturing in new telexes that went back and forth between the parties. Both sides accused the other of trying to obstruct justice by linking the tapes and the criminal investigation with the settlement of a civil lawsuit in Athens for money damages.

The meeting was once called off because the mistrust and posturing were too intense. Then suddenly, in November, there was another flurry of telexes. The rhetoric cooled off and the final terms of the meeting were this: Veliotis agreed to play all the tapes for General Dynamics. After the tapes were played, General Dynamics would be happy to discuss any settlement proposal Veliotis might wish to discuss, since a court date was coming up on the suit Veliotis had filed in Athens.

The General Dynamics team for the secret trip consisted of Duesenberg and Nick Chabraja, a partner in the Chicago law firm of Jenner & Block, which represented General Dynamics and the Crown family. What the lawyers did not know as they prepared to leave for Greece was that Veliotis was turning over all of the evidence he proposed to sell them to a Justice Department prosecutor, James J. Graham, a quiet lawyer from the fraud section. Graham had traveled to Athens to collect the evidence, and while there, Veliotis told him that he had arranged a secret meeting through his Greek lawyer with two lawyers representing General Dynamics. They were on their way to Greece at that moment. "I'm sure they are going to try to buy me off," Veliotis asserted. "Can you wire me up?" he asked the prosecutor.

Graham said he would have to make a formal request through the American Embassy to the Greek government to bug a meeting in

Athens, but Veliotis did not want that. He was sure someone in the embassy or in the Greek interior ministry would tip off General Dynamics. The company was politically connected to the Socialist government. Greece was considering the purchase of forty F-16 Falcons from General Dynamics. Graham suggested that Veliotis undertake to carry a tape recorder into the meeting himself, but Veliotis protested that he was too much of an amateur to be bugging hotel rooms by himself.

Near the time for the meeting on Saturday, December 1, Veliotis telephoned me in Washington to tell me about the impending meeting and about his discussions with federal prosecutors. He sounded very frustrated and said it made him suspicious that the Justice Department was so slow to seize an opportunity to tape the extraordinary secret meeting between Veliotis and private emissaries from David Lewis.

"Can you people wire me up?" Veliotis asked me.

For a moment I wanted to say yes. I wanted to rush to Athens and listen through the keyhole, and I was puzzled why Graham had not found a way to capitalize on what appeared to be an opportunity to see what was motivating David Lewis. But there was no way for me to do it and remain a reporter. "We are not in that business," I replied. "The Justice Department should do that."

There was a long silence on the line. "I hope the Russians are worse than we are," Veliotis sighed. It was one of his favorite expressions.

Veliotis rented an elegant suite on the fifth floor of the Hotel Grande Bretagne on Constitution Square in the heart of Athens. At ten o'clock the two lawyers from General Dynamics arrived, accompanied by their Greek lawyer. Veliotis was accompanied by his Greek lawyer and his son, Teddy, who wore Rayban sunglasses, said nothing, and acted as if he were his father's bodyguard.

The six men faced each other across a coffee table in Suite 520, where the balcony overlooked the Acropolis. The first discussion was whether anyone was bugging the room. All gave assurances there were no hidden microphones. The second discussion was about the agreement to keep the meeting absolutely secret. No press, no cameras. All agreed.

Veliotis's Greek lawyer started. He said he hoped the meeting would lead to a settlement of all outstanding civil litigation. He wished the General Dynamics lawyers could have come a week earlier because Mr. Graham of the Justice Department had been in Athens and had pressed for a session with Veliotis and Veliotis had not had been able to hold him off.

At that point, Nick Chabraja, the Jenner & Block lawyer, spoke up, saying it made no difference to him whether Veliotis met with the Justice Department. His interest, he said, was to hear what Veliotis had to say and to listen to the tapes that Veliotis had been playing for reporters and for prosecutors.

Veliotis spoke next. He said he had met with the prosecutors, but he had only covered old ground. He had not turned over any more tapes, he said. He was saving the rest of them. His choice was very simple, he said. He could make a deal with the Justice Department or he could make a deal with General Dynamics. He needed money. He had all of the tapes and could steer the Justice Department to incriminating records in the company's files. He said he really did not want to do what he had been doing, but he had the goods and he was going to make the best deal for himself.

"I want big money," Veliotis said, and thumped his chest. He reminded the lawyers that he had been willing to settle in the fall of 1983 for the release of about $1.3 million from his accounts in Canada, but the company had turned him down. His price was much higher now. "Big money," he said again. Veliotis denigrated the lawyers, saying they were merely agents and he should be dealing with the principals. "You should tell Lewis, MacDonald, or Lester Crown to come over and lock themselves up for twenty hours to listen to the tapes, and then they will pay me because there is enough evidence that Dave Lewis and his St. Louis Mafia will be growing long beards in jail! "

Veliotis paused and looked at the lawyers.

Then, "Let me speak plainly," he continued. "We are all here to obstruct justice. That is the purpose of this meeting. I have to make the best deal for myself and you want to buy my silence." The words were blunt, provocative.

Veliotis looked like he was getting mad and his lawyer tried to calm him down. The General Dynamics lawyers were shaking their heads, saying, "No . . . no . . . no . . ." to Veliotis's remarks. Chabraja protested they were not there to buy his silence, but were prepared to take any settlement proposal he had back to the "appropriate officials" of the company.

"Do you think me naive?" Veliotis asked.

"Certainly not," Chabraja said, but the lawyers added that Veliotis had spent enough time in General Dynamics to know that neither Duesenberg nor Chabraja could make a decision. They were there to evaluate and make recommendations to the company. Chabraja and Duesenberg then said they needed to caucus alone and they excused themselves to the next room. When they were alone, Chabraja said he wanted to get the hell out of there after what Veliotis said about obstruction of justice. For all he knew, the room was bugged. He thought Veliotis was evil and the two of them were taking a big risk by staying a minute longer. But the General Dynamics lawyers remembered the tapes. They still wanted to hear them. Bert Jenner had told Chabraja to go to Greece because "You're going to hear the tapes." They decided to give it another try, even though Veliotis was mad that they did not have the authority to make him a settlement proposal.

When they returned to the room, Veliotis's lawyer said Veliotis would not play tapes, but if they returned to the hotel later in the day, he would play them a single composite, snippets from a number of tapes.

During the break, Veliotis telephoned the United States and got the prosecutor, James Graham, out of bed at five o'clock in the morning to give him a detailed account of the meeting, including his own inflammatory remarks. The prosecutor was surprised that General Dynamics would set up a secret meeting in Greece without having discussed the matter with the Justice Department. Upon his return to Washington, Graham had found a telephone message on his desk from one of the General Dynamics lawyers, but he was suspicious about the message because when it was left, company officials knew Graham was on an airplane returning from Greece. The prosecutor had to consider that the company could have made a verbal deal with Veliotis in Athens. General Dynamics could have settled the civil litigation for millions of dollars and Veliotis could have become suddenly uncooperative. In that case the Justice Department would never be able to find out the truth.

When Graham heard what Veliotis had said in the meeting, he realized that Veliotis had been too heavy-handed. If he was trying to draw out an obstruction of justice offer, he was doing it all wrong. Veliotis was overtly inducing the company to try to buy his silence. Graham was suspicious of Veliotis's motives, even though Veliotis had said he was cooperating with the Justice Department.

"You should have wired me, you people," Veliotis said in frustration to Graham, after giving an account of his performance.

"Well, the more explicit they get," Graham replied, "the better it is for us to understand what's going on . . . they're going to want to write something down, there's going to be an exchange of money as they get more explicit as to how this is going to be done. . . . I think the only thing we can do at this point is string them along and see what they, see how they propose to do it, and it's going to require a written agreement, and it will require some discussion about how much money."

"Okay," Veliotis said, "I will go back, and if there is something that comes up, I will give you another call."

Veliotis was disturbed that the Justice Department expected him to get an offer of obstruction of justice in writing. Who were they kidding? He felt he had demonstrated good faith by turning over all of his tapes to Graham and by promising full cooperation, but Justice was unwilling to wire him or give him miniaturized equipment to tape the discussions with the General Dynamics lawyers. Veliotis next placed an overseas telephone call to me. He explained everything that had happened that morning, including his conversation with the prosecutor, which he had taped. He asked me if Graham's assertion was true, that the Justice Department could not secretly bug a meeting in Greece without the Greek government's permission. I said that I had talked with two federal prosecutors about the issue, and based on what they had explained to me about the constraints on prosecutors in foreign countries, I believed Graham was telling the truth.

"You are my insurance policy," Veliotis said to me. "If General Dynamics calls a press conference and says, 'Veliotis wants to be bought off,' you will know, you can ask Graham, and I will make sure you get the tape [of his call to the prosecutor]."

I asked Veliotis what he would do if the General Dynamics men offered him $10 million to buy his silence.

"Ten million!" Veliotis repeated. "No, they won't be buying me for $10 million. Maybe $100 million." He laughed.

"But you have already given Graham the tapes and you've given me the tapes," I said.

"That's right," he said. "Too much has happened for them to be buying me off now."

I was puzzled at Veliotis's behavior. He appeared to be running a high-stakes sting operation. He had all sorts of options and possibilities before him. He could let General Dynamics make him a big settlement offer on the $140 million suit, and the company would never be the wiser that the Justice Department already had the tapes that he had pledged he was holding back. He could double-cross them as his coup de grâce against Lewis.

Or, he could take money, big money, and cut off all cooperation with Justice. He could stand up and say he faked the tapes and refuse to authenticate them as part of some verbal agreement to obstruct justice in return for the settlement. In playing out the con, he hoped to lure Lewis or one of the principals to Athens for a final secret meeting. He would bug the meeting himself and perhaps obtain incriminating statements that would help him deliver the final blow to Lewis. He was fishing for the kind of incriminating information which the Justice Department would be grateful to receive. Then, possibly, the prosecutors would come to terms with whether they were more interested in prosecuting Veliotis for accepting a million dollars in kickbacks, or prosecuting the men at the top of the largest defense contracting firm in the United States for filing hundreds of millions of dollars in fraudulent claims against the Pentagon, and for obstruction of justice.

Veliotis said he was lightheaded after the first performance. He prepared for his second meeting with the General Dynamics men on December 1 by making a potpourri recording, so the company lawyers could hear Nate Cummings talking about sending his Sarah Lee cakes to Mrs. Rickover; so they could hear Gorden MacDonald being told by Veliotis that the changes and drawing revisions that were the underpinning of the company's claims were "small" and "negligible"; so they could hear David Lewis talking about the deal he had cut with the Secretary of the Navy to trade the insurance claim for higher profits on new submarine contracts.

Before Veliotis returned to the hotel suite late that afternoon, he received a telephone call from the prosecutor with some last-minute instructions about strategy and how he should comport himself in the meeting.

"General Dynamics will say, if we ask them what they're just doing there, they will say, 'Just getting evidence like everybody else, just like *The Washington Post*, just like the Justice Department.' They're going to characterize this meeting with you as an attempt merely to find out what you have to say, as opposed to any attempt to obstruct justice, all right?"

"Yes," Veliotis said.

"But I think you have to be sure that it develops so that it's actually clear what's happening, and it's not just that they're over there to find out what you have to say. Get them to use their own words, not even your characterization, in their words what they want you to do with your documents and evidence, what they want you to do with respect to further talking to the Justice Department, and what they're going to do for you. But I think it's important that it be in their words as opposed to yours. You understand that?"

The prosecutor said it was obvious that the General Dynamics lawyers were trying to put a "nice gloss" on the meeting, and, "My sense is they're interested in protecting Lewis and that's why it's reasonable for you to press them" for a meeting with the principals in Athens or outside the country.

"Well, I cannot offer another country," Veliotis interjected, "because I cannot get out of Greece, you know, I have my problems with your department and if I go out under your protection, they will know that something's fishy there. They are not stupid."

Graham agreed and sent Veliotis back to the next meeting at the hotel suite.

Veliotis played the portions of tapes and the lawyers scribbled notes as fast as they could. When he was done, Veliotis walked around the conference table to where they had set up the machine and sat down and spoke to them philosophically. "You see, I am not bluffing about the tapes. I have documents, I have tapes. . . . I really do not want to [do this]. I am not bluffing. If we can settle things"—he paused—"you know I am being pressed by Graham." Veliotis rambled on about how reporters for American television networks were "kissing my rear end" to get an on-camera interview. Then he talked about Electric Boat and the claims.

"We mismanaged the job, Dave knows it. MacDonald was there only as a cover, to conjure up the claims. The assets in Canada, I have lost them. I do not care. . . . I have nothing more to lose." He talked about how nice his life was in Athens, about the new home he had bought north of the city. He said he was in no hurry to return to the United States and was not sure that he liked the idea of becoming a Justice Department witness and living in a hotel in New Haven for months on end while he tutored the grand jury.

At the end of the meeting, Veliotis conferred with his lawyer in Greek, then told the General Dynamics men that a settlement of the lawsuit he had filed in Athens might be worked out if they got back to him quickly. He said nothing more about the tapes.

The General Dynamics lawyers said they would get back to Veliotis within forty-eight hours. But there was nothing but silence from the General Dynamics side. No settlement offer, no suggestion that there be a meeting of the principals. A few days after the General Dynamics lawyers returned to the United States, Philip Tone, a Jenner & Block partner, met with Graham at the Justice Department and gave him an account of the meeting. He said the company's reason for meeting with Veliotis was to gather information—just like the newspapers and the Justice Department.

The episode was closed by the Justice Department. Unresolvable.

Lewis believed that his reputation had been crushed by the impact of the first round of Veliotis's revelations. But a second, more devastating round was coming, this time in Congress. The congressional investigation into Veliotis's allegations had built slowly. Representative John Dingell had turned loose a host of auditors on General Dynamics' overhead accounts in St. Louis, Groton, and Washington. Through these accounts, the corporation charged the government for the legitimate costs of doing business. The auditors found that General Dynamics had been billing the government for country club memberships, for parties, for entertainment of military officials, personal trips on the company's corporate jets, even for the boarding of an executive's dog.

Representative Dingell's oversight subcommittee investigated the circumstances surrounding Lester Crown's bribery case and how the younger Crown had received a top-secret security clearance after he admitted secretly paying off Illinois legislators in the early 1970s and embezzling General Dynamics funds to reimburse himself for the bribe money. The subcommittee also probed the Rickover gifts and followed up on the tape recordings that Veliotis had released to *The Washington Post* and to the Justice Department.

Months of investigation had built to the first of two hearings early in 1985, and Dingell's hearing room became the scene of an emotional attack on David Lewis's personal integrity. The first hearing was called for February 28. Lewis, MacDonald, and the corporate legal team spent the entire day prior to the hearing in rehearsal. They set up a mock hearing room at the St. Louis club, complete with hot lights and hostile questions because Lewis had never testified before Congress. He was the chairman of the largest defense contracting firm, yet he had never been called to account for his performance before the body that oversaw his industry on behalf of the taxpayers.

The next day, Lewis and MacDonald arrived at the real hearing room. They had been coached: Don't be defensive, don't explode, and above all, show respect to the public's representatives. Behind them was a solid phalanx of counselors: Duesenberg, the general counsel; Tone, the Jenner & Block partner; Stan Brand, a young lawyer who had been chief counsel to the House of Representatives before he set up in private practice; and Ted LeFevre, the company lobbyist.

Dingell asked Lewis and MacDonald to stand and take the oath. After they were sworn, public relations men distributed to the press tables Lewis's forty-page defense of the company. Lewis read the forty-page defense into the record.

Then the hearing really began. It was one of those events on Capitol Hill where the room is absolutely packed under hot television lights. There was electricity in the air from the moment Dingell read his opening statement quoting President Eisenhower about the need to guard against the domination of the military-industrial complex. A dozen television cameras lined the wall. The table for print reporters overflowed into the gallery and there was a line out in the corridor where three dozen spectators waited to fill any vacancy in the audience of two hundred and fifty people.

Dingell had been mild in his opening, but Lewis knew it was going to be a personal attack when the five young Democratic congressmen on Dingell's right started in. The five had scarcely heard of General Dynamics until a few weeks earlier, when the staff had started briefing them, preparing their opening statements, and scripting their questions. The congressman from Minnesota talked about the small contracting firms in his state and how they would never have gotten away with what General Dynamics had gotten away with. "Who else can buy in on major defense contracts, do a miserable job of managing the construction of the weapons system, overrun fixed price contracts by $1 billion . . . and later receive close to $1 billion in taxpayers' money?" he demanded. "What small contractor could knowingly provide illegal gratuities to a top navy admiral . . . ? What top official of a small contractor . . . has access to an extensive fleet of corporate jets to get away to his family plantation . . . ? How many other chief executives would nominate for a position on the board of directors a fellow who was under criminal investigation by a grand jury for admittedly having bribed a bunch of state legislators . . . ?"

The next congressman was from Oregon. He accused Lewis of putting General Dynamics above the law and of fleecing the American taxpayer. Then all of them got to the Lester Crown affair. Lewis had not been expecting the attack over the decision to put the younger Crown on the board in 1974, and he stumbled in his answers.

Q: Now, apparently, Mr. Jenner did not inform you of the bribery scheme or the falsification of records until August 17, 1973. During this time, Mr. Jenner apparently was arranging an immunity agreement with the U.S. attorney without your knowledge. My first question to you: Wasn't your corporation a victim of Mr. Crown's embezzlement of funds to get his money back from the bribes?

A: I do not believe that we are the victim of embezzlement. No, Mr. Crown paid that from his personal funds and the corporate funds were paid back by him to the company.

Q: But he falsified the documents of the company to get paid back.

A: He was not reimbursed in the final analysis. No.

Q: Because he paid it back after he got caught!

When they asked Lewis whether he thought bribery was a crime involving moral turpitude, he stumbled saying he could not comment on legal definitions. Then they asked him whether he had nominated Lester Crown to the board of directors knowing Crown was under criminal investigation.

"Well, first of all, I did not nominate him to the board of directors."

But when the congressman challenged Lewis's assertion, Lewis said, "I personally supported his nomination to the board" and "I did recommend him and I voted for him."

"Why would you nominate someone with Mr. Crown's problem," the one from Oregon fired back, "someone who is under grand jury investigation, someone who is an admitted felon, an embezzler of corporate funds? Why in the world would you nominate him to the board of directors?"

Each of the words seemed to fly like bricks across the hearing room, landing as body blows against Lewis, who sometimes glared at his questioner and other times looked like he was on the verge of tears.

"I discussed it at length with counsel, Mr. Jenner," Lewis answered, "who had known Lester Crown all his life, who told me that this is a complete aberration; that Mr. Crown is deeply regretful of this action, which is the only blot on his career."

The members called Lewis's behavior a "disgrace." They said he had personally violated the public trust and that he lacked integrity. Those were the worst things you could say to a man like David Lewis, who had spent two decades at the top of the defense establishment and whose self-image was one of great honesty and integrity.

The hearing room got real quiet, and then Dingell gave a nod. The sound of Veliotis's voice and the static of the telephone line filled the room as the subcommittee played the tape-recorded exchanges from the 1977 argument over what to put in the General Dynamics press release about the delivery date of the Trident. ". . .*Only to stop the stock from sliding*" was the phrase that turned heads in the hearing room as MacDonald explained his and Lewis's concern over telling the truth about Trident's delay.

When they turned off the machine, the congressman from Minnesota hammered Lewis. What he and MacDonald had done was a classic violation of the anti-fraud provisions of the securities laws, the congressman charged.

"You didn't tell the truth," another member said.

"That is absolutely not so . . ." Lewis said loudly and indignantly.

"YOU LIED—" the congressman shouted.

"We were told by people who were more expert than Mr. Veliotis, who had only four weeks on the scene . . ." but the rest of the explanation was lost in the noise and the residue of "YOU LIED" as it washed across the room.

The hearing did not break for lunch. During the long, hot afternoon, Lewis was visibly fading, his voice losing its energy. When he was asked whether there were any other members of the board of directors who had committed crimes, he seemed disoriented.

"Well, I must say, that's a surprise question." He turned and glanced up and down the row of his lawyers behind him, then supplemented his response by adding, "I certainly would doubt it."

Right before the brutal finale, Dingell brought laughter to the room when he asked MacDonald who Fursten was.

"I don't understand what you mean." MacDonald said.

Dingell said he had a voucher that MacDonald had signed billing the government for a boarding charge at Maple Leaf Farms for Fursten. "Is Fursten a dog?" Dingell asked. "Are the taxpayers paying for dog boarding?" he said mockingly.

The hearing room erupted, but the moment of levity was brief.

The slaughter came at the end. The young congressmen appeared to be competing as to which one could articulate the most sensational attack on Lewis's character over the Lester Crown affair. It started when one of them asked what Lewis was going to do from that day forward to clean up "the stink" in the corporation. Lewis tried to give an answer, but his blood sugar was low and he was at a loss for a coherent statement.

Q: Are you going to keep Mr. Crown on the board?
A: I would think so, yes.

Q: We have admitted bribery. We have someone who was involved with state legislators. I mean the record of his moral turpitude is very clear, and you are still going to keep him on the board? Is that going to satisfy the taxpayers of this country that you are really trying to clean up the stink?
A: I think that is a subject for the shareholders of General Dynamics to decide. . . .

But the answer was not good enough and the congressman from Dallas started hurling words at Lewis, and you could feel their energy leap across the room to smack David Lewis:

Q: You have got a crook on your board of directors, and you are telling us today he ought to stay there. He is a crook! He bribed people! He falsified documents! You have admitted that he sees sensitive classified documents. You are telling us today that you are going to keep him on the board and he is going to continue as a member of the board of directors of your company? YOU are the problem with your corporation. If you can stand here and tell a congressional committee that you are going to let him stay there and continue to see these classified documents, the stink in the corporation and the problem we have got with General Dynamics is sitting at this table right here.

The congressman pointed accusingly at Lewis.

Q: You ought to be hanging your head in shame. I am absolutely disgusted that you can stand here and make an admission like that with a straight face.

A: Sir, I am very sorry you feel that way, and I know your statement is fully accurate, [however,] in our judgment. . . .

But the congressman was not finished, and Lewis's face was full of dread when he saw it coming again, because he knew that within three hours those words were going to be broadcast to fifty million people in the United States on the seven o'clock news with Dan Rather, and Tom Brokaw, and Peter Jennings, and what was left of David Lewis's reputation he was going to have to scrape off the bottom of this little shitass's shoe.

Q: I am in a position of responsibility to taxpayers back in Dallas, Texas. You, unfortunately, are in the position of being able to look at all the sensitive classified documents that pertain to the U.S. military equipment that you manufacture. Now what has been inaccurate about what I just said? Do you not have a crook on your board of directors? Do you or do you not?

A: To my knowledge, he has never been tried.

Q: Did he commit the crime of bribery or not?

A: I do not know.

Q: You don't know and you have never bothered to ask him, since you are chairman of the board? Have you ever asked him?

A: I have understood that he volunteered. . . .

Q: Have you ever asked him? It is about time you say yes or no to our inquiries. Have you ever asked this guy if he committed bribery?

A: I did not ask him if he committed bribery, no.

Q: Have you ever discussed the matter with him?

A: Yes.

Q: Do you have some reason to believe that he did not commit bribery?

A: No, I do not.

Q: You do not?

A: No, I said of no reason. You asked the question, do I have any evidence that he did not, and I said I do not have that evidence.

Q: You are aware, are you not, of the documents that make it very clear that he committed bribery; are you not aware of those?

A: Yes. That is what I said.

Q: And you are going to keep him on your board of directors?

A: [Lewis nodded his head affirmatively in response.]

The problem with General Dynamics is you! The problem with General Dynamics are the people that you hire and cater and cowtow to . . . and [who] follow your moral leadership. Anybody who comes before this committee and says he has doubts about whether moral turpitude is involved in bribery should be disqualified from any further connection with contracting with the U.S. government. I don't care if it is submarines or paper clips.

The words that cut David Lewis so deeply were indeed broadcast on all of the networks and quoted on the front page of dozens of newspapers across the country. The chief spokesman for the Pentagon said the next day that he found Lewis's admissions "nauseating." The hearing, and another one that followed in March, were the limit for Lewis. He told Henry Crown and the other members of the executive committee in April that he had had enough.

Negotiations for the succession were accelerated. Lewis's retirement announcement was held up past the annual meeting in May only because one of the Crown directors on the executive committee leaked to *Business Week* that Lewis was finished. At the annual shareholders' meeting, Lewis asserted that he would stay in the chairman's job until he had cleared his name, but by the end of May, the corporation issued a press release announcing that Lewis would retire no later than the last day of 1985.

Veliotis heard the news about the demise of Lewis over the telephone.

"Good," he said.

The same week, Admiral Hyman Rickover was formally censured by the Secretary of the Navy for having accepted gifts from General Dynamics. After a sixty-year career, the last entry in Rickover's file would be a censure. His reaction: "My conscience is clear."

EPILOGUE

What remained were the submarines—and the system.

For thirty years the submarines would be on silent patrols in the silent war, gathering intelligence and making torpedo- and mine-laying runs along the Kola Peninsula and out beyond the great northern rim of the Soviet land mass. They were fine machines; perfect as far as their technology took them, but also imperfect in that they were not what they could have been. The consequences of the political trade-offs and the ad hocism that had sown the weak seam into their diving armor radiated out across the decades. The existential moment awaited them like a distant coordinate somewhere in the future where the latitudes of war and the limitations of machinery would intersect for the final test.

The *November*-class Soviet submarine that had chased U.S.S. *Enterprise* from San Francisco to Hawaii two decades earlier was no match for the stealth and lethal weaponry of the *688*s. But the Soviets had not stood still. If the dreaded discipline of war should send the superpower navies to general quarters once again in this century, the *688* class will find itself facing a formidable array of killing machines in the red-bannered fleets of the Soviet navy. And in the lonely black reaches of the deep ocean basins, the American sub drivers will be forced to push their machines to the limit to protect the American armada—the aircraft carrier battle groups—on the surface. Only then will they confront the brutal physics of survival in combat.

To some, the interim oceanic routine begged the peacetime question: did it really matter? Had the trade-offs been so significant in the absence of war? After all, a 950-foot diving range versus 1,300 feet were just numbers on the spec sheets of rival navies.

To say "yes, it did not matter," was the worst evasion, however. It was a logic that destroyed any procurement strategy. Of course it mattered. The Falklands War had shown how quickly a nation can be desperately dependent on its navy to execute national policy. The Cuban missile crisis had shown that sea control was the key to denial of any adversary's hostile adventure in the nuclear age. And the military test of the future in a world trying to find its way toward arms reduction required a parity of wartime instruments between the superpowers.

The shame of the long history of the nuclear attack submarine fleet is the shame of those who helped create the system and those who accepted it, opting for expediency and short-term success at the expense of long-term sanity.

In early 1986, a blue-ribbon commission on defense procurement reported to President Reagan on the shortcomings of the system. In one of the drafts of its report, the commission compared defense procurement to the alchemy of the Sorcerer's apprentice, who had unleashed the magic of technology only to lose control of it, lacking the master's wisdom to make it perform. The commission's final report discarded this metaphor in favor of more neutral language, but still the indictment was clear: There is no rational system in America for planning and procuring the instruments of our common defense in a world where other industrial nations—some of them our adversaries—have conquered the industrial process to a much greater extent.

President Reagan and his Defense Secretary enthusiastically embraced this report, pledging to study or implement those reforms that were not already under way. But coming on the heels of several years' worth of procurement scandals laid out in Congress and in the press, Reagan's embrace of the Packard Commission recommendations appeared to be more of a political imperative than any intellectual recognition that defense procurement and weapons planning ought to be restructured and managed by a well-organized, long-tenured, and forward-thinking defense bureaucracy.

In the American system, short-term gains, short-term success, remain the dominant incentives for the military men who pass through the Pentagon's chain of command, for the political administrations seeking global military realignments in the instant of a decade, and for corporations seeking shareholder gratification on a quarterly basis. Until these incentives are modified, there is little prospect that the Packard Commission recommendations will take hold.

This story of three men is a story of towering potential and achievement, and a tragedy of lost American resources. In the end, each man conspired to deny the country the best that he could offer.

Hyman Rickover's contribution to nuclear propulsion had so magnified his personality and his legend that his power became the magic unleashed. There was no countervailing power, no wisdom to moderate Rickover's fissioning dynamo running critical through the defense establishment, making and breaking deals to get his ships—and only his ships—to sea. His power crushed some of the best and brightest submarine designers in whom the navy had invested greatly. The loss of men like Captain Don Kern of the submarine desk and Jack Van Leonard from the engineering department at Electric Boat—both of whom fled before the Rickover onslaught—is a loss of human potential that no military establishment should tolerate.

Rickover is virtually gone now, after giving the U.S. Navy sixty years of service. And although he has seeded a generation with his standards of excellence, there are no Rickovers on the horizon, no naval thinkers who were there at the creation; no one to whom an untutored Congress can turn for the long view of history. Rickover, the outcast of the Reagan Pentagon, was fading from view while Admiral Gorshkov, the father of the modern Soviet navy, was still tutoring the new generation of Soviet leaders who sit at the Politburo table.

David Lewis, whose contribution to military aviation is the supersonic fighter squadrons that will be flying into the next century, has also made his exit, lost in the maze of legal preparation for the battles that may lie ahead as the federal investigations of his long-tenured autocracy come to their conclusion. In his mind swirls the intuitive knowledge of advanced fighter concepts, but he is no longer applying them, trapped by the misjudgments of his other histories. A new broom has swept through General Dynamics: the company has assured the Pentagon that the mistakes of the past will not be repeated. There is a new code of ethics in the corporation and promises of improved performance.

In Takis Veliotis, the fugitive, rests a lifelong storehouse of shipbuilding and marine engineering experience, yet he lives in exile half a world away from where it is needed. The Greek industrial establishment has approached him to help with the still-desperate problems of underdevelopment in that country, and he has toyed with the idea of designing a new attack submarine for the European and Mediterranean powers; but much of his mental time is still devoted to the old ghosts on the waterfront and in the boardroom of General Dynamics.

Their legacy is the system—the corporate system, the defense procurement system, and the political system—of which each man was a product. It is a system which, on the long scale of history, is capable of learning, though the waste is often immense and the corruption long lived.

In the last decade of the twentieth century, the system will lurch forward in pursuit of a new attack submarine that the navy hopes will fulfill the dream begun with *Albacore* and *Nautilus: SSN-21*, an attack boat for the twenty-first century. Her planning is in the hands of men who may have been too busy to study in depth the history they need to understand: Rickover, General Dynamics, and the *SSN 688* class. The new navy leaders are men who want their new weapon by yesterday. After all, the tours in the Pentagon last only three or four years, and the Reagan administration arms buildup offers the opportunity to seize the moment and get a new ship to sea to meet the still-increasing Soviet threat.

She is not going to be a perfect boat. She will not dive to two thousand feet and her hull will be steel, not titanium, but she will probably break thirty-five knots and, yes, she is going to cost $1 billion per copy because she will carry a monster power plant—less efficient than the Soviets'—to push her ten thousand tons through the dead weight of ocean.

At General Dynamics and at Newport News, a fresh cadre of young managers is hoping to seize this latest business, knowing that the navy is going to spend billions and that there are only two shipyards where the navy can spend it. Some executive is going to make a name for himself by pulling down that kind of business. After all, Wall Street pays attention to the magic that huge government contracts confer on a contractor.

The temptation to bid lean in order to get those contracts is going to be strong, and the pressure from the navy is going to be intense because Congress will be sweating over that psychological barrier of $1 billion for a single attack submarine.

Perhaps, in the midst of the debate, the system—Congress and the Pentagon—will manage to tap the deep well of knowledge that exists in each institution and apply the learning curve of history toward a more reasoned policy for the nation's defense.

ACKNOWLEDGMENTS

This book could not have been written without the support of Benjamin C. Bradlee, the executive editor of *The Washington Post*. His wisdom, guidance, and friendship have sustained me during my seven years at the newspaper and the strength of the institution reflects his genius as America's foremost editor.

For their patience, I am indebted to Donald Graham, the *Post*'s publisher, who also has steadfastly stood behind my reporting enterprises; Leonard Downie, Jr., the *Post*'s managing editor; and Robert G. Kaiser, my immediate boss and friend on the national desk. For his overall guidance, support, and friendship, I am grateful to Bob Woodward, who as much as anyone has been my benefactor and counselor at the *Post*.

During many months of reporting, I had the privilege of sharing my workload, discovery, and deadline terror with Kevin Spear, a graduate of the University of South Dakota, and now a reporter for the *Winston-Salem* (N.C.) *Journal*. Kevin's contributions were many, but his work was particularly distinguished by the way in which he penetrated the industrial process at Electric Boat through long and patient interviews with shipyard welders. This reporting was indispensable for the shipyard scenes throughout the book.

Kevin was preceded by Catherine Eisele, a 1986 graduate of Brown University, who heroically tackled the enormous volume of transcriptions from my initial round of interviewing, and who set up a system of chronologies that was essential in constructing the story later on.

I am indebted to those friends and colleagues who read various drafts of the manuscript and provided invaluable assistance in focusing the narrative. These included: Al Kamen, Jonathan Z. Larsen, Christian Williams, John Ward Anderson, Milton Benjamin, Bob Woodward, and Taylor Branch. There were other readers who cannot be named here due to their former affiliations with the government, but I am grateful to them for their attention to the technical details in the manuscript.

At Harper & Row, Brooks Thomas, Norman Pomerance, and Ed Burlingame showed enormous flexibility when I notified the house in early 1984 that I was switching the subject of my book, though I already was under contract to write a history of Mobil Oil Corporation. I am very grateful for their support at each critical juncture in the preparation of the manuscript. Most of all, Harper & Row gave me the essential creative ingredient in the person of Harriet Rubin. This being my first book, I cannot speak with the greatest authority on book editors, but I cannot imagine discovering a more tireless and imaginative one. Over many months, she drew from this newspaperman a narrative voice that had never been exercised. Whatever credit accrues from the work must be shared with her.

SOURCE NOTES

Part I: The Silent War

confidential sources. CIA intelligence summary on Soviet submarine program provided by confidential sources.

52–61   Captain [Ret.] Kern's perspective from interviews with author. Details about the "concept formulation," or Conform, submarine provided by confidential sources. Impact of U.S.S. *Thresher* loss on Rickover and submarine design provided by confidential navy sources. J. Kneel Nunan perspective from interview with author. History of U.S. nuclear submarine prototypes provided by confidential sources. Account of Captain [Ret.] Kern, Nunan meeting with John S. Forster based on interviews with Captain [Ret.] Kern, Vice Admiral [Ret.] Philip A. Beshany, who also was present, Nunan, and summary included in documents placed in congressional hearing record cited above.

61–64   Information on classified "fish oil" project provided by confidential sources. Hearing excerpts taken from record of Preparedness Investigating Subcommittee of the Senate Armed Services Committee, March 13, 15, 19, 27, 1968.

64–67   Deliberations of ad hoc committee on *SSN 688* design taken from confidential sources and from interviews with Admiral [Ret.] Rickover, Vice Admiral [Ret.] Joe Williams, Jr., Rear Admiral [Ret.] Donald P. Hall, William Wegner, deputy director, Naval Reactors Branch, Vice Admiral [Ret.] Phillip A. Beshany, and Admiral [Ret.] Thomas H. Moorer.

67–69   From June 21, 1968, hearing record of Joint Committee on Atomic Energy and from confidential sources.

69–72   From interviews with Captain [Ret.] Kern, Nitze, Admiral [Ret.] Elmo R. Zumwalt, Jr., and from contemporaneous memoranda of meetings provided by a confidential source. The destruction of the Conform records was confirmed by two confidential sources.

Part II: Cover-Up

PAGES

75–76   Interviews with Hilliard W. Paige.

76–82   History of struggle to control General Dynamics based on interviews with Paige, David S. Lewis, and from contemporaneous accounts that appeared in *Forbes*, March 1, 1969; *Business Week*, October 4, 1969, March 21, 1970, and July 11, 1970; and *Fortune*, June 1970.

82–87   Interview with Paige, Lewis, and Admiral [Ret.] Rickover.

87–95   Interviews with shipyard workers, welders, supervisors, managers, and navy officials.

96–98   Lewis reaction to Rickover from interview with Lewis. Information on ARPA study provided by confidential sources and interviews with Lewis, Kern, and Jack Van Leonard, senior engineer at Electric Boat.

98   "Rickover Problem Meeting" based on interview with Lewis and notes from Lewis's file dated May 3, 1971.

98–99   Lewis encounter with Rickover at USS *Lipscomb* keel laying from interview with lewis.

100   Quotations from David Lewis's notes of telephone conversation with Rickover October 29, 1971, and from interview with Rickover aide present in Rickover's office during call.

100   David Lewis "personal and confidential" letter to Rickover, October 29, 1971.

101–102   Summary information on gifts to Rickover provided by Oversight and Investigations Subcommittee [Rep. John D. Dingell, Chairman] of the House Energy and Commerce Committee inquiry, 1984–85, and from investigation of U.S. Navy Ad Hoc Gratuities Board report of May 3, 1985.

103–104   Information on "black" electromagnetic detection research program provided by confidential sources.

105   October 30, 1972, Pierce telephone call to Lewis based on Lewis's notes. Lewis perspective from interview with author.

105–106   From November 1, 1972, minutes of General Dynamics executive committee of the board of directors. Detailed discussion of Rickover "deal" to provide General Dynamics with set quota of submarines summarized in November 13, 1972, memorandum No. 149 from H. W. Paige to D. S. Lewis.

106–112   Paige perspective from interviews with author. Portions also from interviews with P. Takis Veliotis.

113–114   From report entitled "Notes from E. B. Visit," including a report on "RADCON problem," dated March 5, 1973, by Fred H. Hallett, General Dynamics official who reported on his February 27–March 3 shipyard visit to David S. Lewis and Max Golden, vice president for contracts. Also from interviews with Electric Boat and navy officials.

114–128   This section on the radiation-control crisis at Electric Boat was reconstructed from General Dynamic files, particularly from David Lewis's Rad-con file, which included a large set of notes of key conversations and meetings. The section is also baded on interviews with William Wegner, Murray Miles, William Bass, Hilliard Paige, and David Lewis.

116   Study referred to is "Private Eyes Only" memorandum from Algie A. Hendrix, chief of industrial relations at General Dynamics, to David Lewis.

117   Lewis memo on cleaning up Rad-con situation from Lewis's file and dated November 22, 1972.

117   Pierce-Lewis discussion on employment contract from Lewis notes dated October 26, 1972.

118   January 23, 1973, Rickover call from Lewis's notes.

118–119   Discussion of management changes at Electric Boat from Lewis's notes dated January 26, 1973.

122   Miles-Paige conversation from Paige's typed "Summary of Paige/Miles telecon 26 February 1973."

123   From Lewis's notes dated February 27, 1973.

124   Rickover's attack on Lewis from Lewis's notes dated March 5, 1973.

124–125   Pierce letter to Rickover dated March 14, 1973.

125   Rickover's reaction to Paige comment that Rickover was out to get
       Pierce from Lewis's notes dated March 8, 1973.
125–128 Radiation drill and test results from various sets of notes in
       Lewis's Rad-con file and from interviews with Miles.
129   Lewis's statement on bidding strategy from *Forbes*, October 15,
       1971.
128–135 Section on "flight two" bid based on interviews with Lewis,
       Barton, and confidential navy sources, as well as documentation
       and notes from Barton's files at Electric Boat and Lewis's files in
       St. Louis.
130–131 Meeting account from Barton's "Notes from the St. Louis Review
       of SSN 688 Bid" dated April 6, 1973.
132   Pierce report on Newport New's bid strategy from Lewis's notes
       dated June 13, 1973.
132   "Act of God" clause noted in U.S. Navy "Business Clearance
       Memorandum" dated November 19, 1973.
132   "Going after all the business in sight . . . " from corporate office
       memorandum dated February 1973 by Fred H. Hallett, who
       attributed remark to John W. Rannenberg, Electric Boat's
       contracting officer.
132–133 Lewis's final bid reduction from notes of his August meeting and
       from interview with Lewis.
133   Discussion between Rickover and Zumwalt from interview with
       Zumwalt and from Zumwalt notes cited in Elmo R. Zumwalt, Jr.,
       On Watch (New York: New York Times Book Co., 1976), p. 119.
134–135 Lewis-Rickover discussion based on Lewis's notes dated December
       10, 12, 1973, and interview with Lewis.
137–138 Construction difficulties on *688*-class reactor compartment based
       on interviews with shipyard welders and navy officials.
138   Procurement outlook from February 12, 1974, memorandum by
       Electric Boat's Procurement Engineering Department entitled
       "Overview of Procurement Price and Delivery Trends."
138–139 Reporting scarcity of structural welders from "SSN 688 Class
       Critical Items Letter No. 79," dated December 21, 1973, and
       attached handwritten note to J. D. Pierce from Z. Henry Hyman,
       688 program manager.
139–148 Section on cover-up at Electric Boat based on contemporaneous
       documents as well as on interviews with Lewis, Barton, Veliotis,
       John R. Wakefield, the navy's deputy project manager for the *688*,
       and confidential navy sources.
139   Barton's loss estimate from August 5, 1974, memorandum from
       Barton to J. D. Pierce, entitled "Division Profit and Cash Flow
       Outlook," and from August 9, 1974, memorandum from Barton to
       Pierce, entitled "Division Performance Forecast—Special Study."
140   Barton private note to Norman Victor, E. B. director of planning,
       dated June 12, 1975.
140   Curtis's statements to Barton recounted by Barton to Bruce M.
       Prouty of Arthur Andersen & Co., Electric Boat's outside
       accounting firm. Prouty recorded Barton's remarks in
       "Confidential" memorandum for the files on July 1, 1976. Curtis's

"We'll make it up" attitude based on interviews with shipyard officials.

140   1974 Plan reference from January 14, 1974, memorandum from Z. Henry Hyman to M. C. Curtis and Pierce, entitled "SSN 688 Class Construction Program . . . Projected Costs at Completion."

140–141   Memorandum on cost-saving measures from Barton to Pierce and Curtis entitled "Quarterly Review Presentation" and dated July 19, 1974. Lewis remarks cited therein.

141   November 19, 1974, cost review with Lewis from interview with Barton, Veliotis, and Lewis. Detailed breakdown of man-hour estimates presented to Lewis during this review are summarized in November 23, 1977, memorandum from T. S. Wadlow, Barton's deputy, to Veliotis, entitled "Summary of Cost Engineering Forecasts."

142–143   December 2, 1974, meeting between Pierce and Wakefield, the deputy project manager, was reported to Lewis by Pierce. Lewis's notes of this conversation are dated December 3, 1974. Confidential navy source also contributed to reconstruction of this episode.

143   Corporate team's cost projections summarized in January 6, 1975, report entitled "SSN 688 Class Construction Program Overview."

144   Cash drain of $90 million from December 6, 1974, letter from Wayne Wells, General Dynamics vice president and treasurer, to J. D. Pierce.

145   Preparation of the claim based on interview with David J. Rylander, former senior claims analyst at Electric Boat, and with Barton. Also based on Rylander's letter to Barton dated January 27, 1975.

145–146   The minutes of the June 1975 board meeting were not available, but an account of the meeting appears in the files of a Chase Manhattan Bank vice president, H. E. Colwell, one of General Dynamics's bankers. Colwell drafted a detailed memorandum of a meeting with Gorden MacDonald in which MacDonald described the "heated" June board meeting and the "recriminations" over the sudden jump in cost projections.

146   $940 million loss projection from July 3, 1975, memorandum from T. S. Wadlow to Barton regarding "688-I and II Costs."

146–148   MacDonald actions in taking over supervision of Electric Boat based on interviews with Barton, Veliotis, and several confidential sources, and on Arthur Andersen memorandum dated July 1, 1976.

148–149   Lewis conversation with Rickover based on Lewis's notes dated April 9, 1976. Lewis's offer to settle on all eighteen *688s* for $150 million is based on interviews with Rear Admiral [Ret.] Leroy E. Hopkins, former chief contracting officer for the navy shipbuilding command, and with an aide to Admiral Rickover. Hopkins and the Rickover aide were present for a speaker-phone conversation with Lewis's vice president for contracts, Golden, when Golden made the offer. The offer is also reflected in an option paper prepared by Barton for Lewis on February 5, 1976. Item No. 3 in the option paper is: "Settle 688-I & 688-II for $150 million."

149–150   Rickover's reaction to Jimmy Carter's candidacy based on interviews with Rickover aides. Lewis's dinner with Harold Brown and Charles Duncan based on interviews with Lewis, Brown, and Duncan.

152–156   The section on *Alpha-2* and Soviet submarine advances is based on confidential sources in the navy and the U.S. intelligence community.

156–158   Holloway perspective on Rickover and *688* program based on interview with the author. Rickover's discovery of Zumwalt's "black" research program based on interviews with confidential sources.

158–159   Rickover-Carter trip aboard U.S.S. *Los Angeles* based on interviews with Williams and Rickover aides. Rickover's statement to Carter about nuclear power was repeated by Carter in an interview with CBS News *60 Minutes.*

159   Rickover quotes from Lewis's notes of telephone conversations dated April 9, 12, 1976. Authur Andersen statement from General Dynamics annual report to shareholders, 1976.

160   Draft memorandum dated January 27, 1977.

160–161   Meeting between Rickover, Lewis, and MacDonald based on three pages of Lewis's notes dated May 18, 1977.

161–162   Account of Rickover's interrogation of MacDonald was typed and cosigned by Rickover and MacDonald on July 30, 1977.

162–163   These gifts were reported by the author in the *Washington Post* on July 18, 1984, based on interviews with Veliotis and Rickover and on documentation provided by Veliotis.

Part III: The Takeover, the Bailout

PAGES

167–182   Section based on interviews with Veliotis, Spencer Reitz, L. Emmett [Bim] Holt, William Gorvine, Vice Admiral [Ret.] Joe Williams, Jr., Hilliard Paige, David Lewis, and Hal Foley.

182–184   Dialogue taken from contemporaneous tape recording made by Veliotis.

184–187   Section based on interviews with Veliotis. Barton's cost estimates referred to on page 185 were preserved by Veliotis and provided to the author. Barton, in an interview, confirmed their authenticity.

187–194   Section based on internal General Dynamics documents, minutes, and memoranda, and on interviews with Lewis, Veliotis, Edward Hidalgo, W. Graham Claytor, Jr., Charles W. Duncan, Jr., Vice Admiral [Ret.] Francis F. Manganaro, Vice Admiral [Ret.] C. R. Bryan.

188   "Lewis operative" from Max Golden, vice president for contracts, who gave his intelligence report to Lewis in a memorandum dated August 10, 1977.

189   Telephone conversations between Lewis and Claytor recorded in Lewis's notes dated September 29, 1977, and October 4, 1977.

194–196   Section based on interviews with Veliotis and from contemporaneous tape recording made by Veliotis.

196–198   Section based on various accounts in the local and regional press, from interviews with Veliotis and Senator Christopher Dodd of Connecticut. Rickover quote on page 198 taken from contemporaneous tape recording.

198–200   Dialogue taken from tape recording.

200–202   Section based on interviews with Veliotis. Dialogue taken from tape recording.

202–205   Section based on interviews with Veliotis, confidential navy sources, and local press reports. Dialogue taken from tape recording.

205–206   Section based on interviews with Veliotis and Barton. Documents on page 206 were preserved by Veliotis and provided to the author.

207–209   Section based on interviews with Veliotis and on tape recording of Rickover conversations made by Veliotis.

209–214   This section is expanded from an article the author wrote for the *Washington Post*, October 18, 1984. It is based on a series of tape recordings made by Veliotis and on interviews with Lewis, Veliotis, MacDonald, Rear Admiral [Ret.] Donald P. Hall, and Vice Admiral [Ret.] C. R. Bryan.

214   Veliotis perspective on legal advice from interview with author.

214–221   Section based on interviews with Hidalgo, Lewis, Rickover, various Rickover aides, Max Golden, Veliotis, and Charles Duncan; also, numerous source documents from General Dynamics internal files, including contemporaneous memoranda of meetings quoted in the text.

214–215   Hidalgo's order was transmitted through Chief of Naval Material, Admiral [Ret] F. H. Michaelis. The December 1, 1977, order is addressed to Manganaro: "You are hereby directed to terminate the NCSB effort on the subject claims and furnish all data developed to date to . . ." the assistant secretary of the navy's office. Rickover's letter of protest is dated December 2, 1977, and Hidalgo's reply, December 5, 1977.

215–216   Rickover's report on alleged fraud in the General Dynamics claim is dated December 10, 1977, and stamped "Sensitive, Official Use Only."

216   Hidalgo testimony excerpt from Hearings before the Subcommittee on Priorities and Economy in Government of the Joint Economic Committee, December 29, 1977, page 166.

217   December 8, 1977, meeting account reconstructed with: Lewis's notes, dated December 8, 1977, of Max Golden's telephone report following the meeting with Hidalgo; MacDonald's typed notes dated December 9, 1977; interviews with Golden, Lewis, and Hidalgo.

218   Dialogue between Golden and Veliotis taken from tape recording made by Veliotis.

218–220   Most comprehensive account of this meeting was made by Max Golden as a six-page memorandum to file dated December 22, 1977.

221–223   Dialogue between Rickover and Veliotis taken from tape recording.

223–224   The investigation of Pedace's activities on behalf of MacDonald was documented by Veliotis in memoranda signed by various participants, including Pedace. Veliotis's summary memorandum, dated February 15, 1978, was made available to the author.

224–227   Briefing of President Carter based on interviews with Duncan, Claytor, Hidalgo, and Vice Admiral [Ret.] C. R. Bryan. In addition, the author obtained Duncan's outline notes for his presentation, as well as the detailed briefing outline used by Hidalgo during the Oval Office session.

227–232   Section based on interviews with Veliotis and Lewis. Reference to Frigitemp on page 227 based on information from indictment returned in U.S. District Court, New York, Southern District of Manhattan, September 6, 1983. Lewis's trip to Groton for the February 9, 1978, review was confirmed by his business calendar, which Lewis checked during an interview with the author. Veliotis's typed presentation to Lewis was also obtained from General Dynamics files and was helpful in the reconstruction. The Veliotis memorandum to Lewis on page 232 is dated February 15, 1978.

232–235   Section based on interviews with Lewis, Hidalgo, and Veliotis, and on contemporaneous notes made by Lewis of key telephone conversations and other General Dynamics documents. Veliotis's report to Rickover on shutdown taken from tape recording.

235–239   Rickover statements can be found at page 463 and page 484 of the Hearings before House Defense Appropriations Subcommittee, March 16, 1978. Rickover-Veliotis dialogue taken from tape recording.

239–241   Section taken from hearing record of the Subcommittee on Priorities and Economy in Government of the Joint Economic Committee, May 19, 1978. Rickover-Veliotis dialogue from tape recording.

241–244   Section based on interviews with Lewis, Senator Christopher Dodd of Connecticut, and Hidalgo, and from internal General Dynamics memoranda.

245–248   Section based on interviews with Hidalgo, Lewis, Veliotis, and Senator Dodd, and on internal General Dynamics notes and memoranda.

Part IV: The Final Assault

PAGES
251–258   Section based on interviews with Lewis, Veliotis, Rickover, Rickover aids, Hidalgo, Vice Admiral [Ret.] C. R. Bryan, Claytor, Spencer Reitz, and Vice Admiral [Ret.] Joe Williams, Jr. Rickover-Veliotis dialogue taken from tape recording. Hidalgo-Veliotis dialogue also from tape recording.

258–265   Section based on interviews with Veliotis, Vice Admiral [Ret.] Williams, Reitz, Holt, confidential navy sources, and Vice Admiral [Ret.] Bryan. Veliotis-Rickover dialogue taken from tape recording.

265–269   Section Based on interviews with Veliotis, Lewis, and confidential navy sources. Veliotis statements in Frigitemp deposition taken from the document. Veliotis-Rickover dialogue and Veliotis-Boileau-LeFevre dialogue taken from tape recording.

269–276 Section based on interviews with Veliotis, Lewis, and confidential navy sources, Veliotis-Lewis dialogue and Veliotis-Rickover dialogue taken from tape recordings.

276–280 Section based on interviews with Lewis and Veliotis. Veliotis-Lewis dialogue and Veliotis-Boileau dialogue taken from tape recordings.

280–283 Section based on interviews with Veliotis, Lewis, and a confidential source who provided information regarding the status of the Frigitemp investigation at this time. Veliotis-Boileau dialogue and Veliotis-Lewis dialogue taken from tape recordings.

283–285 Section based on interviews with Veliotis, Lewis and confidential navy sources. Fowler's testimony from Hearings of the Seapower Subcommittee of the House Armed Services Committee beginning at page 188.

285–291 Section based on interviews with Veliotis, confidential navy sources, and press reports of Veliotis's sendoff. Veliotis's testimony contained in same hearing volume as cited above of the Seapower Subcommittee beginning at page 355. Veliotis-Gorvine-Holt dialogue taken from tape recording.

291–295 Section based on interviews with James Aston, Veliotis, Lewis, Reitz, Holt, and Vice Admiral [Ret.] Williams.

295–300 Section based on interviews with Veliotis, Lewis, Holt, and confidential navy sources.

300–309 Section based on interviews with Lewis, Veliotis, and confidential navy sources. Press statements by Veliotis and Hidalgo taken from *Norwich* (Conn.) *Bulletin*, July 16, 1981, and July 3, 1981. Lewis-Veliotis-LeFevre dialogue taken from tape recording.

309–319 Section based on interviews with Lewis, Veliotis, James Ashton, Reitz, Holt, Dan Stets, Fred J. Bettinger, and confidential navy sources. Veliotis-Lewis dialogue taken from tape recording.

319–323 Section based on interviews with Lewis, Veliotis, Ashton, David Rubenstein, confidential navy sources, and Rickover aides.

323–324 Soviet submarine and antisubmarine advances from open and confidential navy sources.

325–330 Section based on interviews with Veliotis, on indictment returned against Veliotis in U.S. District Court, New York, Southern District of Manhattan, September 6, 1983, and on interviews with confidential sources.

330–334 Section based on author's reporting notes.

334–341 Section based on author's notes, various documents, telexes, and memoranda of conversation relating to the Grande Bretagne meeting as provided by both General Dynamics representatives and Veliotis. Dialogue between Veliotis and James Graham on pages 338–341 based on tape recording.

341–347 Section based on author's notes of the hearing, interviews with Lewis, and hearing record of the Subcommittee on Oversight and Investigations of the House Energy and Commerce Committee, February 28, 1985.

INDEX